The Cruising Guide to

CENTRAL AND SOUTHERN CALIFORNIA

GOLDEN GATE TO
ENSENADA, MEXICO,
INCLUDING THE OFFSHORE ISLANDS

BRIAN M. FAGAN

INTERNATIONAL MARINE / McGRAW-HILL
Camden, Maine • New York • Chicago • San Francisco
• Lisbon • London • Madrid • Mexico City
• Milan • New Delhi • San Juan • Seoul
• Singapore • Sydney • Toronto

The McGraw-Hill Companies

8 0 FGR/FGR 0 9

Library of Congress Cataloging-in-Publication Data
Fagan, Brian M.
The cruising guide to central and Southern California : Golden Gate to Ensenada, Mexico, including the offshore islands / Brian M. Fagan.
p. cm.
Includes index.
ISBN 0-07-137464-7
1. Boats and boating—California—Pacific Coast—Guidebooks. 2. Boats and boating—Mexico—Pacific Coast—Guidebooks. 3. Pacific Coast (Calif.)—Guidebooks. 4. Pacific Coast (Mexico)—Guidebooks. I. Title.

GV776.C2 F36 2002
797.1′09794′9—dc21 2001002881

Questions regarding the content of this book should be addressed to
International Marine
P.O. Box 220
Camden, ME 04843
www.internationalmarine.com

Questions regarding the ordering of this book should be addressed to
The McGraw-Hill Companies
Customer Service Department
P.O. Box 547
Blacklick, OH 43004
Retail customers: 1-800-262-4729
Bookstores: 1-800-722-4726

This book is printed on 60# Finch by Quebecor World/Fairfield, PA
Design and Production by Dede Cummings Designs
Maps by Steven Brown
Project Coordination by Dan Kirchoff
Edited by Alex Barnett and Constance G. Burt

NOTICE: The information, charts, and illustrations contained in this book are not for navigational purposes. Any references herein to certain courses, GPS waypoints, anchorages, or navigational information are intended merely as illustrations. None of the material in this book is intended to replace any government-issued navigational charts or other government publications. Refer to those publications, including *Notices to Mariners*, for current information regarding changes, additions, and deletions to existing navigational materials. All mariners should have up-to-date navigational charts on board.

Similarly, inclusion in this book of such features as marine facilities and services, restaurants, places of interest, attractions, or sporting events (including information provided by advertisers) is for informational purposes only, and no guarantee is provided as to their accuracy or current status, nor are they in any way recommended.

All material in this book is subject to change at any time. The author and publisher do not guarantee or warrant that the information in this book is complete, correct, or current. The author and publisher shall not be liable to any user of the book for any loss or injury allegedly caused, in whole or in part, by relying on information contained in this book.

*To Commander James Alden, USN; George Davidson;
and the many other government surveyors of the
U.S. Coast Survey, 1848–1859, who first charted
the California coast.*

CONTENTS

PREFACE

And now let me say that should you spy my vessel on the water, do not expect her to be handled by a faultless seaman. I've misjudged every situation in this book at least twice and probably will again.

Roger Taylor, *The Elements of Seamanship*

THIS BOOK HAS EVOLVED from two earlier cruising guides and a third that was never published. In 1979, the late Graham Pomeroy and I published *Cruising Guide to the Channel Islands*, which remained in print through three editions. This was followed in 1983 by *California Coastal Passages*, which covered longer passagemaking between San Francisco and Southern California, and its sequel, *Cruising Guide: San Francisco to Ensenada, Mexico*. A third volume covering the much-traveled waters between the Santa Barbara Channel and the Mexican border was also planned but never published. The book you are holding is an amalgam of these three books in a single volume.

The new format reflects both economic realities and the changing small-boat cruising scene. When the first of the three volumes appeared, almost no yachts ventured down-coast from San Francisco to the Channel Islands or from Southern California to the Golden Gate. The specters of an inhospitable coast, strong headwinds on the passage north, and the perceived horrors of Point Conception made most people think of Northern and Southern California as separate cruising grounds, with the dangerous and rugged Big Sur coast in between.

Today, an explosion in the number of larger cruising yachts, the rising popularity of cruises to Mexico, more long-distance races between the Bay area and the south, and GPS technology have brought the two areas much closer together. Whereas a generation ago, a passage from Marina del Rey to San Francisco was a real adventure, it is now a routine passage for hundreds of small craft every year. *The Cruising Guide to Central and Southern California* is for both Northern and Southern California skippers. It is also for those who travel the coast in smaller craft—power or sail—as well as those in larger cruising boats. For those who assume I am a diehard sailor, unqualified to write about powerboating, please be aware that I also own a 20-foot outboard Alaskan fishing skiff, which I regularly take offshore!

This book is divided into an introductory section followed by three sections with sailing directions, arranged by region. The Background offers general background information in four chapters: everything from a spot of history to a briefing on weather and passagemaking strategies, anchoring, and safety issues. The final chapter in this section, Exploring Southern California Waters in Small Craft, is unique in cruising guides like this and is included for small-powerboat skippers.

Region 1, Golden Gate to Point Conception, is a passagemaking guide to Central California and its ports, starting in the north at the entrance of the Golden Gate and ending at Point Conception. Region 2 carries us through the Santa Barbara Channel and the northern Channel Islands, a favorite cruising ground for many California sailors. In region 3, we move south of Point Mugu into Southern California, covering both the mainland coast and Santa Catalina Island. Our sailing directions end south of the border at Ensenada, Mexico.

This book is the result of my own research and cruising in the waters of Central and Southern California for more than thirty years. It also incorporates the experiences of dozens of readers who have taken the time to share their impressions, comments, and criticisms with me. In addition, the manuscript was reviewed by a number of expert cruising people and commercial fishermen, who generously gave me the benefit of their knowledge. I am deeply grateful for their cooperation. A book like this is inevitably impressionistic in places, so the cumulative sum of our experience is better than that of just one person.

Because it has worked well, I have kept the format of my earlier guides largely intact. However, this book has involved major revisions, a complete redesign, and much reillustration. I have also taken note of some long-term trends; for example, there appears to be a tendency toward shallowing in many anchorages, both at the islands and on the mainland. Therefore, you should use depths given as approximations and be guided by your depth-sounder or lead and line when coming to anchor.

You will find frequent references to kelp beds in the sailing directions. In recent years, kelp growth has thinned—even vanished—in many areas, and is only now beginning to recover from the effects of El Niño visitations. But I decided to leave the references to kelp in place, on the—I hope reasonable—assumption that it will return in the future.

The Cruising Guide to Central and Southern California is an attempt to provide a definitive account of the anchorages and harbors of the Central and Southern California coast and their offshore islands. It was compiled from official and unofficial sources, and is not designed as a substitute for charts. Use it in conjunction with the appropriate National Oceanic and Atmospheric Administration (NOAA) charts for the region, which are listed at intervals in the text.

I have used the following sources in writing this book:

- *U.S. Coast Pilot* for 1998 and earlier editions, as far back as 1858
- NOAA charts for the area and charts dating back to 1853
- Army Corps of Engineers, *Small Craft Ports and Anchorages* (1949)
- Leland R. Lewis, charts by Peter E. Ebeling, *Sea Guide*, volume 1, *Southern California* (Sea Publications, Newport Beach, 3rd ed., 1973)
- articles in *Sea* magazine and other periodicals
- and, most important, my own experience of the coastal waters of Central and Southern California, accumulated during more than thirty years and supplemented by the experience of many others

Readers should be aware that I am based in Santa Barbara, so the sailing directions occasionally may reflect a slight bias. My coverage of Santa Barbara must be particularly detailed not because I'm based in Santa Barbara, but rather because the entrance of this popular harbor can be tricky, especially in the winter. I have also given special attention to the western portions of the Santa Barbara Channel, which are less well known to pleasure craft.

Although I am satisfied that this book is accurate at the time of publication, I am well aware that conditions are changing constantly. I encourage interested skippers

to send me their comments, criticisms, and updates in care of the Department of Anthropology, University of California, Santa Barbara, CA 93106; or by e-mail at brian@brianfagan.com.

IMPORTANT WARNING

This book expresses numerous opinions about anchorages and ports in Central and Southern California, and about general cruising conditions in the area. If anything, my opinions are on the conservative side. Bear in mind, however, that these are the opinions of the author, and that your own judgment on any course of action—whether to use an anchorage or attempt a passage—may differ according to the current conditions. In the end, safe cruising comes down to sound judgments on the spot—and I cannot make them for you. Rest assured that the cautions in this book are based on hard-won experience. The weather off California may be perfect day after day, but the ocean never lets us relax and you should be on your guard.

CONVENTIONS

While writing this book, I made certain arbitrary choices that are carried through the entire text.

- Points of the compass and directions are not always written out in full—that is, "north," "northwest," and so on are often given by letter designation: N, NW, and so on—except when I am referring to a landmark (e.g., Northwest

Anchorage) or a weather phenomenon (e.g., southeaster).

- Bearings are given in degrees magnetic (as of 2000). Although normal convention is to use true bearings, I felt that a magnetic bearing would be less trouble for small craft fitted with magnetic compasses. Check the variation for the year in which you are using this book, and remember to convert true bearings from other sources, such as publications and weather forecasts.

- All distances are given in nautical miles (1 nautical mile = 2,000 yards) or yards and feet, including distances on land.

- I provide depths in feet and usually as a range; for example, 25 to 30 feet. All soundings are given to mean lower low water. In other words, calculate your tidal depths from our baseline soundings. Note that NOAA charts sometimes give depths in fathoms (1 fathom = 6 feet). Government charts will convert to metric soundings in the near future; please be alert to the pending change.

- Light characteristics are given as they existed in November 2000. Check later editions of charts and U.S. Coast Guard notices for corrections. Light characteristics provided are those used on NOAA charts, as explained in *HO Chart Number 1, Chart Symbols*. For example, "Gp. Fl. W.R. 5 sec., 200 ft., 10 miles" signifies "group flashing white and red every 5 seconds, light exhibited 200 feet above high tide, visible (theoretically) for 10 miles."

- Anchorage and landmark names do not always conform to those on the charts in

those cases in which I know the official source is in error. These discrepancies are identified in the text, along with some name changes in the last century.

- Finally, some of the anchorages described in this book may be unsuitable for larger vessels or deep-draft yachts. A given anchorage might be safe for a small powerboat but unsafe for a 25-foot sailboat. I have been conservative in my descriptions and deliberately omitted some small anchorages in difficult areas such as inside Talcott Shoals or the northwestern coast of San Miguel Island.

FACILITIES, GPS, AND OTHER POINTS

I have chosen not to list shoreside facilities in detail in these pages. All harbors along the Central and Southern California coast provide basic services, including self-service laundry, showers, and most repairs. Provisions are invariably available within a short taxi ride. Facilities ashore change frequently, and a guide that details them is soon out of date. Wherever possible, I list useful Web sites where you can obtain the latest information before or during a cruise. Likewise, I provide contact information for major harbors. Again, be aware that this information goes out of date constantly, especially changes in telephone area codes.

Few small craft now go cruising without a GPS aboard, so I have included GPS coordinates for major anchorages, harbors, and landmarks. However, I did not go overboard with this, as the volume of detail could confuse the user. GPS coordinates refer to the center of the entrance of an anchorage or port, unless otherwise indicated. GPS coordinates for lights are usually for the structure itself, on land. Please plot all coordinates before using them and do not rely blindly on the readings. A good old-fashioned dead-reckoning (DR) plot is a wise precaution, especially at night or in thick weather.

REFUGE ANCHORAGES

Where do you take refuge in storms? There are some surprisingly good refuge anchorages, especially in the Santa Barbara Channel. Specific information on refuge anchorages relative to the strength of the wind is provided in sidebars. I did not designate refuge anchorages for the Central California coast to Point Conception or for the mainland south of Santa Barbara because the best refuge ports are artificial harbors, which are usually within easy range. If you are caught out off the Big Sur coast, it is best to head for open water and heave-to until the weather eases. The few anchorages are death traps in gale-force winds, even if they offer some shelter from northeasters.

ACKNOWLEDGMENTS

This book updates earlier sailing directions and incorporates suggestions from literally hundreds of people—users of this book, casual visitors, and sailors met by chance at the islands or at various yacht clubs and lectures in Southern California. I am deeply

grateful to all for their praise of the book and, more importantly, for their criticisms. In general, the instructions have stood up well to intense use and scrutiny; it is rumored that they are even consulted by the U.S. Coast Guard!

So many people have contributed to this book that it is difficult to thank all of them individually. I owe a particular debt of gratitude to the late Carey Stanton for checking over the Santa Cruz Island sections and descriptions, and to Peter Howorth for allowing me to use his valuable weather and refuge-anchorage data. Bob Kieding has been a constant source of advice and local knowledge.

Steve Brown drew the plans and maps for the book with his customary skill. Jonathan Eaton, Alex Barnett, and the entire staff at International Marine were a constant encouragement.

Although individual credits are given with each photograph, I want to acknowledge the following people for permission to use their photographs in this book: Jim Aeby, Gene's Photo and Rock Store (Avalon), Bob Greiser, F. G. Hochberg, Peter Howorth, Lesley Newhart, Patrick Short, and the late Graham Pomeroy.

Uncredited photographs were taken by the author.

BACKGROUND

All this time there was not a cloud to be seen in the sky, day or night; no, not as large as a man's hand. Every morning the sun rose cloudless from the sea, and set again at night in the sea, in a flood of light. The stars, too, came out of the blue one after another, night after night, unobscured, and twinkled as clear as on a still frosty night at home, until the day came upon them. All this time the sea was rolling in immense surges white with foam, as far as the eye could reach on either side.

RICHARD HENRY DANA
Two Years before the Mast;
on a NW gale off the Central
California coast

THE FOG HANGS ON

E by NE about fifty leagues; then ENE in the general direction of the Ladrones; through Los Volcanes or the higher Ladrones NE by E to thirty-one degrees latitude and longitude twenty-eight and a half east of Manila; ENE to thirty-six or seven degrees in longitude forty; thence to the region of Cape Mendocino, SE to thirty-five degrees latitude without sighting land; SE to the landfall at the island of Cenizas in thirty degrees . . .

Sailing directions for Spanish galleons traversing the Pacific from the
Philippines to California and New Spain by pilot Cabrera Bueno

WHEN I FIRST SAILED to Southern California's Channel Islands more than thirty-five years ago, I foolishly left in the early afternoon, arriving at Santa Cruz Island after dark. Fortunately, there was a full moon, I had someone on board who had been to the island before, and we could feel our way into the anchorage at Prisoner's Harbor. But I was astounded to learn that there were no sailing directions for the islands, and little more than government charts and the *U.S. Pilot* even for larger ships. Had there been a cruising guide, I might not have been so foolish as to arrive at my destination in darkness, for the northern coast of Santa Cruz Island is unlit.

Two years later, we were sailing south from San Francisco to Morro Bay in Central California on the wings of a boisterous July northwesterly. The anemometer showed a steady 30 knots over the deck. A low overcast hung over the yellow-brown cliffs, casting a distinct chill on deck. We tacked downwind to keep the rugged cliffs in view, ticking off the few conspicuous landmarks in the hazy afternoon sun. This was years before GPS and the Web. My cruising companion, John, kept a dead reckoning (DR) plot on the chart as Susan, the third member of our trusty crew, kept peering into the gloom for white lighthouse buildings ashore. Porpoises played around the bow casting streams of bioluminescence in the opaque sea. We hurried past Pfeiffer Point, the ship light on the helm. We sailed into the foggy night with a dying wind, which faded completely in the small hours.

As dawn turned night into murky gray, a slight morning breeze came from astern. We stopped the diesel, drifting under main and genoa. Our foghorn sounded forlornly into the dense fog. I alternated between hatchway and the chart table, checking our log for boat speed. John updated the DR plot, estimating our position since the fix on Point Sur. He calculated that we were close to Morro Bay, nearing a rapidly shelving coast frequented by occasional tankers and numerous fishermen. There was nothing to do but plot depth-sounder readings, look for the 10-fathom line, and hope we could anchor in relatively shallow water to wait out the fog. First 18 fathoms, then 16, then 12: the bottom slowly shallowed. I stared into the gloom, looking for the white flash of imminent breakers. Then, like a miracle, the fog lifted just as we reached the 10-fathom line. Morro Rock, bathed in a momentary bright ray of sunshine, stood out like a signpost 0.75 mile

ahead. In a surge of relief, we motored into the harbor entrance as the fog settled in again. Once more, I felt an acute need for a cruising guide where none existed. I realized that had I timed the passage better, we would have arrived in the afternoon when the fog had burned off.

Some years later, I felt my way northward from Marina del Rey to Channel Islands Harbor close inshore on a day when the fog hovered near the water far longer than usual. We could hear automobiles on Highway 1 behind the beach. Momentary gusts revealed snatches of cliff, beach, and a conspicuous yellow sand dune. Fortunately, I remembered seeing the

Morro Rock on a hazy day. Power-plant smokestacks to the left.

dune on a clear day from Point Mugu 2 miles north, and quickly fixed our position before the gloom returned. A few days later, I stopped at the dune while driving south to Los Angeles and realized what a wonderful sailor's landmark it was—yet no one seemed to think of it that way.

As I sat atop the dune, I realized that I had a lot of miles under my keel. I remembered other memorable times off the California coast: ghosting slowly southward on a foggy night south of Dana Point 0.5 mile from the breakers, hearing cars just behind the beach; sheltering in San Simeon Bay as a gale blew overhead, bored out of my mind; anchored in Fry's Harbor on Santa Cruz Island with the full moon as solitary company; crossing San Pedro Bay at 25 knots in a fast runabout on a flat calm fall day; lying at anchor on a warm night in Catalina Harbor, wineglass in hand, listening to someone play the guitar on a nearby yacht; fighting a bonito a few miles off Newport Beach on a May afternoon. This book was conceived at that moment.

Like all sailors, I have a wealth of vivid memories. As a sailor based on the California coast, I probably have more than most, because I am fortunate enough to live in the heart of one of the finest boating environments on earth. The weather is almost always predictable—temperatures rarely fall below 55 degrees—and we can go boating every day of the year. We take malicious delight in telling callers from New York in February that we're going fishing or sailing that afternoon. We have everything at our doorstep: great racing water, magnificent fisheries, world-class

diving, and superb kayaking. You can dine in some of the finest waterfront restaurants on the West Coast one night and anchor in a quiet offshore island cove the next. This book is a result of those and other experiences.

ABOUT THIS BOOK

The mix of sailing directions, pilotage, and general reading in these pages is a deliberate one, the result of many quiet hours off watch when one has nothing to read yet needs to escape that slight sense of apprehension that gnaws at even the most experienced sailor. Perhaps the wind will pipe up or fog will descend at dusk. You are short of water or fuel, and the engine is proving erratic. That's when it's comforting to realize that others have had the same uncertainties and lived to write about them. William Buckley, the well-known conservative commentator, wrote brilliantly about cruising under sail: "The ocean and the sky and the night are suddenly alive, your friends and enemies, but not any longer just workaday abstractions. It is most surely another world and a world worth knowing."

But this book is not really designed for the long-distance sailor, rather for us more common folk, who are content to make occasional coastal or offshore island passages, then spend the rest of our time exploring remote anchorages and marinas or simply lying quietly at anchor somewhere.

As I said in the preface, this book is based, above all, on my own first-hand

At anchor: Santa Cruz Island.

experience during more than thirty years of passagemaking and gunkholing along our coasts. It is also based on the experiences and observations of dozens of fellow cruisers and on classic and lesser known writings about the California coast. The book draws on the experiences of the Spanish explorers, George Vancouver, Richard Henry Dana, and George Davidson. I have been to every port and anchorage described in this book (most of them many times) and in all sorts of weather. This guide is as accurate as I can make it.

The ancient Greeks had a good word for a book such as this: a *periplus*, a "sailing about." Perhaps the most famous such book in the scholarly world is *The Periplus of the Erythraean Sea*—sailing directions for the Indian Ocean and its coasts compiled by an anonymous Greek sea captain who lived in Egypt in the second century. That book is a cross between a trade directory and a piloting guide to the East African Coast—the reader is treated to a little navigation and then, perhaps, a description of the native boats. My book might well be called *The Periplus of the West Coast* because it is designed as a "sailing about" for cruising Central and Southern California.

Most of us spend our entire cruising lives within the narrow confines of our home waters, rarely venturing farther afield. More's the pity because, apart from the delights of San Francisco Bay and the Sacramento Delta immediately to the north, Central and Southern California offer some extraordinary cruising grounds. There are rugged coasts and completely sheltered anchorages, state-of-the-art marinas, and some of the finest fishing around—in short, any kind of cruising you want. I have sailed many miles in Europe and the Caribbean, but I have enjoyed more perfect sailing days off the California coast than anywhere else in the world. Day after day dawns calm and foggy. By noon, the sun burns off the gloom and a fine westerly fills in. The wind and sea drop down at sunset, leaving just the endless Pacific ground swell, which never completely lies down. Quite simply, we sail in paradise on earth—and year-round in the bargain. Nonetheless, there is more to California cruising than just heading out to sea and turning left at the lights. At some point, inevitably, your guard goes down. With so many perfect days, it's easy to be lulled into a false sense of security. In the summer, the morning fogs and afternoon winds come and go with monotonous regularity. You settle into a comfortable routine: the wineglasses appear in the cockpit as the sun dips to the west, and you forget that Neptune may have one up his sleeve.

On one occasion, I anchored at Secate anchorage near Point Conception. It was a perfect summer evening at high tide, with the moon high overhead. Happy to be snugged down for the night, I never bothered to check the depth or weather forecast. The next morning, as often happens, a dawn breeze came in from the southeast. It was a little stronger than usual, so the boat swung inshore to the edge of the breaker line. I awoke to find it rolling wildly in steep waves moving in toward the breaker line less than 200 feet away, the anchor line jerking at the bow. We quickly broke out the anchor from the bottom with the engine and made for deep water. Re-anchoring for breakfast at Cojo Anchorage to the west, I resolved to be more careful in the future.

Even in our benign waters, we must never forget that the sea is unforgiving to those who ignore its warnings. I once tried to sail northward past Point Conception against a 30-knot summer wind. The day began well enough: we rounded the point after a leisurely breakfast, beating easily into a fine 10-knot breeze, which was blowing earlier than usual—a warning of worse to come, which I ignored. Half an hour later, the boat was pounding into a rapidly rising headwind, with two reefs in the main and the storm jib. A steep vicious sea pushed us to leeward, ever closer to land. Our stomachs rebelling, we soon ran back to the welcome shelter of Cojo Anchorage in the lee of Point Conception. That night after dark, we upped anchor and motored north in a flat calm—as common sense should have told us to do in the first place.

It is no wonder that we are frightened when we sit becalmed in a fog so dense that the bow is invisible, worrying about unseen steel juggernauts lurking in the gloom. Small wonder we feel apprehensive when heading offshore for unknown coasts and anchorages. Any sailor who does not admit to feelings of anxiety—not occasionally, but on a regular basis—is not being completely honest. We can alleviate our fears by prudent seamanship, thorough preparation, and adequate safety precautions— the three basic principles of safe cruising and enjoyable passagemaking.

Most California cruising is straightforward. The complications begin when you head offshore to the northern Channel Islands or along the coast north of Point Conception. North of the point, the prevailing northwesterly winds blow harder, the waters are cooler, and the ironbound coast is exposed to the fetch of thousands of miles of open Pacific. A passage up or down the Central California coast is a different proposition from battling 30-knot winds in the relatively sheltered waters of San Francisco Bay or crossing the Santa Barbara Channel. To the novice, a passage around Point Conception can seem as daunting as an ocean voyage. Stories abound in every yacht club between Vancouver and San Diego about this historic promontory, the notorious "Cape Horn of the Pacific." The fact that Transpac racers sail to Point Conception's windy vicinity to practice heavy-weather sailing—sometimes returning with their sails in tatters— has not helped its reputation.

Yes, these waters are more challenging than those of Southern California. They do sometimes see powerful winds and big seas. The weather can be unpredictable, especially when it blows off the land. Come fall, when the famous Santa Ana winds blow into Southern California from high deserts far inland, the wise skipper stays in port. And, of course it's foolish to go past Point Conception or sail off the Big Sur coast during a winter gale. But remember that we have many advantages over our hardy predecessors, who tacked laboriously northward—often halfway to Hawai'i—on their way to San Francisco. We have powerful diesel engines and efficient masthead rigs that enable our boats to point as close as 30 degrees to the wind. We use sophisticated electronic navigational instruments and proven, efficient anchors. The government maintains lights, buoys, and navigational satellites, and provides continuous and readily accessible weather forecasts. There are often calm days when flat conditions at night and during the morning hours allow us to power to windward in comfort. We will never take three days to beat from Ventura to Santa Barbara, as our nineteenth-century forebears did. Careful skippers with a well-prepared ship have nothing to fear if they judge the weather and take their time to reach their destination.

I wrote *The Cruising Guide to Central and Southern California* for the family that wants to make passages to windward as comfortably as possible and not go thrashing about in pursuit of a racing trophy. It's for people who use calm gray days and fog cycles to slip north past Point Conception under power, easing their way along the cloud-shrouded Big Sur coast while the northwesterly sleeps. It's for skippers planning a trip to the Channel Islands, or a quiet cruise to Catalina, or along the fine marinas of the Southern California coast.

Point Conception from the air.

This book will help you get there and back, navigating from headland to headland, with a stop now and then to enjoy a comfortable port or a spectacular anchorage along the way.

EARLY NAVIGATORS

We live in historic waters. People have lived and worked along the California coast in quiet anonymity for at least ten thousand years, leaving nothing but the more durable of their artifacts behind. We know about the Native American coastal dwellers from scattered historical accounts, translations of ancient languages, anthropological studies, and dozens of archaeological excavations from Point Reyes to San Diego. In particular, we have *shell middens*: enormous, gray-colored heaps of discarded shells from centuries of shellfish-foraging along the coast. Middens stand out from the surrounding terrain and are easily spotted from the ocean because of their light gray soil. A close look at the exposed layers of a prehistoric shell midden reveals thin layers of charcoal, shell, and occasional artifacts. Such unspectacular evidence comprises the priceless scientific records an archaeologist uses to reconstruct the history of the first seafarers and fisherfolk to live in our waters. Please leave the shell middens undisturbed; they can be destroyed easily by eager souvenir-hunters.

NATIVE AMERICANS

The first Native Americans entered Alaska from Siberia across the Bering Strait at least fifteen thousand years ago. Within four thousand years, their descendants had settled in Central and Southern California, along a Pacific Ocean that was hundreds of feet lower than it is today. San Francisco Bay was a deep estuary. Low-lying continental shelves extended out from modern shorelines, making the Santa Barbara and San Pedro Channels much narrower than they are today. Tantalizing signs of this early occupation, such as grinding stones, sometimes come to the surface in fishing nets.

Between about 6,000 and 1,000 B.C., when the ancient Egyptians built the pyramids by the Nile River and Stonehenge in southern England was a revered Bronze Age temple, the people of the California coast settled in greater numbers closer to the shoreline. They collected all types of plant foods and became increasingly expert fishermen. By 4,000 B.C., as sea levels stabilized near modern levels, the people turned to fishing and fall acorn harvests for most of their diet. Coastal populations increased steadily. About 3,000 B.C., the California climate dried up considerably, resulting in rainfall patterns similar to those today. Unpredictable rains and long droughts challenged the ingenuity of coastal groups, with starvation a constant threat. The people responded by exchanging foodstuffs and other commodities with their neighbors.

By about 2,000 B.C., people from the interior had settled in the rich and diverse environment of the San Francisco Bay region. Here they lived off the fish, shellfish, and waterfowl around and in the Bay, in the Monterey region, and along the central coast. Many settlements lay close to freshwater streams and marshlands, where the people could take ocean fish and harvest nuts, hunt game, and exploit other land foods. Smaller hamlets eventually surrounded the larger communities, and each territory had its own leaders.

After A.D. 1400, coastal villages proliferated dramatically. Local leaders participated in ceremonies and gift exchanges, as well as warfare, with their neighbors. Trade among villages occurred over a large area of the coast using clamshells as a form of currency. The Santa Barbara Channel was home to one of North America's most elaborate hunting and foraging societies, the Chumash. By the time Europeans arrived in California, an estimated fifteen thousand Chumash lived along the mainland coast and on the Channel Islands. Well-built, dome-shaped grass and reed dwellings housed as many as a thousand people in large communities. The largest Chumash villages served as political "capitals" over several lesser settlements, and warfare among villages was common as neighbors quarreled over food supplies and territory.

The Chumash had a wide-ranging diet. They harvested acorns in the autumn, ate dried fish and seaweed in the winter, and moved inland for fresh plant foods in the spring. Hunting went on year-round, while fishing was concentrated in the warmer months. Peaking in late summer and early fall, huge schools of tuna and other fish swarmed in open waters. Chumash fishermen ventured offshore for tuna and other deep-water species. But most of the time, in season, they could harvest thousands of anchovy feeding on phytoplankton upwelling from the deep cold waters of the Pacific. One Spanish missionary wrote of the Chumash: "It may be said for them, the entire day is one continuous meal." But, with its highly variable rainfall, the Santa Barbara Channel was no paradise. Periodic El Niños brought violent storms, caused fish to move away from the coast, and uprooted inshore kelp beds. Much of the time, the Chumash lived on the edge of starvation. Their skeletons show clear signs of malnutrition and dietary stress. Likewise, the marks of clubs and arrows seen on Chumash bones should contradict any notion of Eden.

The Chumash were superb seamen. They used plank canoes (called *tomols*) about 25 feet long. Master canoe-builders constructed each tomol from driftwood planks, painstakingly adzed and fitted together to form light, carefully ballasted canoes with distinctive "ears" at bow and stern. When loaded, the stable tomol could move swiftly on the water, easily propelled by a crew of four or more using double-ended wooden paddles. These remarkable sea craft were used for fishing, trading with people on the islands, and carrying passengers along the shore. A skilled crew kept up a steady pace all day, paddling to a canoe song repeated over and over again. Boat speed depended on the wind direction. With a following wind and swell, a modern replica canoe can make 6 to 8 knots; if it blows 8 knots from ahead, the tomol makes no headway against wind and waves. Almost certainly, the Chumash seafarers made their island journeys and fished offshore during calm weather and morning hours. Average passage speeds of 7 knots to and from the offshore islands were probably not uncommon in smooth conditions. Because tomols leaked constantly, one of the crew would bail constantly using an abalone shell. Tomols required almost daily caulking and repair.

Farther south, the Gabrileño occupied the coastal areas now under the urban sprawl of Los Angeles and Orange County. This group controlled valuable soapstone deposits on Catalina Island. The soft soapstone is ideal for making stone griddles and pots. The Gabrileño traded these implements along the coast and into the interior.

Reconstruction of a Chumash tomol.

Santa Barbara Museum of Natural History

Even farther south, the Luiseño and nomadic bands of Dieguieño peoples moved seasonally between the coast and the interior, harvesting acorns and seeds as well as shellfish and marine mammals. They also fished in estuaries and close to shore.

THE SPANIARDS

On June 27, 1542, two poorly outfitted ships under the command of Juan Rodríguez Cabrillo sailed northward along the Baja coast to explore the unknown shoreline beyond Cabo San Lucas. After three weary months of battling headwinds, Cabrillo reached landlocked San Diego Bay on September 28. After obtaining firewood and water, he coasted northward in pleasant weather, anchoring on October 10 off what is now the Rincon near Carpinteria in the heart of the Santa Barbara Channel. (A large Chumash settlement named Skuku lay close to shore, which is today partially buried under the U.S. 101 freeway.) Cabrillo's two ships were blown offshore by a strong headwind off Point Conception to Cuyler Harbor on San Miguel Island.

There he waited for favorable winds. Then he scudded northward past the Big Sur coast before the November gales and made landfall on the rocky shoreline near Fort Ross, 75 miles northwest of the Golden Gate. His battered ships turned southward and entered the Gulf of the Farallones, but they failed to see the narrow Golden Gate entrance. The ships coasted south to winter at Cuyler Harbor, where Cabrillo died as a result of injuries suffered in an accident. Pilot Bartolomé Farrelo then took charge. He also forced his way northward to the vicinity of Fort Ross but, at the last minute, had to retreat—this time to Baja—in the face of the prevailing north-westerlies. He never returned.

The windswept California coast offered few attractions to gold-hungry conquistadors. After the discovery of a return trans-Pacific route to the New World from the Philippines in 1565, Spanish ships regularly sailed south along the California coastline after making landfall on Point Mendocino. Serious exploration began with the Spanish explorer Sebastián Vizcaíno in 1602. Vizcaíno sailed through the Santa Barbara Channel, where he admired Chumash tomols. He wrote: "A canoe came out to us with two Indian fishermen, who had a great quantity of fish, rowing so swiftly that they seemed to fly. . . . After they had gone, five Indians came out in another canoe, so well constructed and built that since Noah's Ark a finer and lighter vessel with timbers better made has not been seen. Four men rowed, with an old man in the center singing . . . and the others responding to him." At the time, thousands of Chumash lived on the offshore islands of the Santa Barbara Channel.

Vizcaíno's small squadron battled its way north past Point Sur and into Monterey Bay, where they anchored in "the harbor that is called Punta de Piños." The port was named Puerto de Monte-Rey in honor of Don Antonio de Mendoza, Count of Monte-Rey, then Governor of New Spain. Vizcaíno reported: "There is a great extent of pine forest from which to obtain masts and yards . . . oaks for shipbuilding and this close to the seaside in great number." Viz-

caíno was the first to map the Gulf of the Farallones, but he too missed the Golden Gate because of strong headwinds and the dangerous waters around the Farallones themselves. For years, Spanish ships, with their poor sailing qualities, stayed outside the Farallones, lest there be too little water between them and the mainland.

For many years, Vizcaíno's reports and simple maps comprised the only information about the coast. Sailing directions were guarded jealously by navigators, a professional fraternity that received special pay and privileges for their expertise. The Spaniards kept their navigational information under lock and key because local knowledge had vital strategic importance. By the mid-eighteenth century, the California coast was relatively well known to them, even if there were no permanent settlements or ports of refuge. The situation changed after the land-based Gaspar Portola expedition explored the coastline between San Diego and San Francisco in 1769 and 1770.

The Portola expedition set out from San Diego to assess the potential of the coast. Portola and his entourage spent several weeks in the Santa Barbara Channel, where Father Juan Crespi, a priest in the party, observed the Chumash carefully. He visited a large village known as Syuhtun, a settlement of sixty houses with a good stream and fertile soils nearby. Crespi decided this was a good location for a mission. Seventeen years later, the Santa Barbara Mission was founded on the higher ground above a Royal Presidio erected near Syuhtun in 1782.

Portola traveled north into Central California, inland from the Big Sur coast. Crespi wrote: "We encountered the Sierra Santa Lucia, which is a very high range, white, rough, and very precipitous toward the sea." Governor Portola mapped Monterey with its lagoon and stream, which ran close to the Spanish camp. From there, he marched northward along the coast. Exhausted and running short of food, he discovered an *estero*, "a great arm of the sea, which extends inland at least eight leagues; its narrowest part is three leagues wide, and in its widest stretch it will not fall far short of four. In a word, it is an extremely large and most famous port, which could not only contain all the navies of His Catholic Majesty, but those of all Europe as well." This was the "port of San Francisco," with a narrow entrance that, Portola felt, would be deep enough for large ships to enter.

On a second expedition, Portola founded the Presidio and Mission of Monterey on June 3, 1770. In 1774, Captain Don Fernando de Rivera y Moncada, the commander of Monterey, climbed to the summit of Point Lobos at the mouth of the Golden Gate. He and his party erected a standard of the Holy Cross on the outer rocky summit of the headland. A year later, the supply ship *San Carlos*, under Lieutenant Juan Bautista de Ayala, was ordered to take soundings in the Golden Gate. She arrived off the Gate on August 5, 1775, and a small launch was sent in on the afternoon flood tide and wind. Evening set in and the boat did not return, so the *San Carlos* felt her way in using the failing light. Ayala found safe anchorage off the southern shore by moonlight, somewhere near the current site of the Presidio. The next day, he moved across to a secure berth off what is now Sausalito, where he found abundant water and fuel. For forty days, he explored every corner of the great estero, a piece of sheltered water so large that some navigators called it a Mediterranean Sea. A year later, Lieutenant Colonel Juan Bautista de Anza explored the Bay during an eighteen-day foray from Monterey to determine locations for a fort, presidio, and mission; the latter was dedicated on October 8, 1776.

The Golden Gate itself was originally named La Boacana de la Ensenada de los Farallones (the large entrance from the Gulf of the Farallones) by Pedro Fages in 1772; that name did not stick. In June 1846, J. Charles Fremont presented to the U.S. Senate a formal "Geographical Memoir" in which he referred to the "Golden Gate" for the first time. The narrow strait has been called Golden Gate ever since, appearing in the *U.S. Coast Pilot* of 1857 and on all subsequent coastal charts. Fremont took the name from the harbor entrance of Classical Byzantium, which was called *Chrysopylae*, or the Golden Horn. He said: "The form of the harbor, and its advantages for commerce . . . suggested the name the Greek founders of Byzantium used." Using the same principle, Fremont named the San Francisco Bay entrance—"The Golden Gate."

THE SURVEYORS

Mexico ceded California to the United States on May 30, 1848. At the time, ships operating along the West Coast relied on school atlases, informal word of mouth, and rough sketch maps, many of them compiled from Spanish sailing directions. The Federal Superintendent of the Coast Survey stepped in during the fall of that year, assembling the first survey parties with experienced mapmakers to work on a systematic survey of the Pacific Coast. For nine years, Commander James Alden, USN, worked up and down the coast in small ships, refining early reconnaissances and making recommendations for light-house sites. His survey parties worked from small schooners in every weather condition imaginable. Alden started work at the height of the Gold Rush, which made it almost impossible to retain a crew. His col-leagues included a young man named George Davidson, an unsung hero to Cali-fornia seamen, who devoted the rest of his life to mapping and geographical work on the West Coast. He later became an emi-nent professor of geography at the Univer-sity of California, Berkeley.

Davidson fixed the precise latitude and longitude of Point Conception in 1848. Working from small rowboats and sailing craft—often windbound for days on end—Davidson and his colleagues recorded tidal data and magnetic variation, and then tri-angulated prominent landmarks from Puget Sound to San Diego. Davidson him-self traveled more than 50,000 miles in small boats, giving him a close-up view of the smallest indentations along the coast-line. Few people have ever acquired such a thorough knowledge of our waters. He spent days on end with the lead and line, once remarking, "When seeking for an anchorage, drifting with currents, or on

boat duty, I have invariably kept it going from my own hand."

George Davidson's *Directory for the Pacific Coast of the United States* first appeared in 1858. A true labor of love, as well as an official publication, it became an instant best-seller in the marine world. Davidson's short work forms the basis of the *U.S. Coast Pilot* of today. In some respects, the *Directory* is more useful than its modern descendants because it caters to the small-boat sailor. For instance, we read that the outer edge of the kelp along the western shore of Point Loma, San Diego, "marks the line where the depth of water suddenly changes from 20 to 10 fathoms." I checked this observation myself some years ago and found it is a useful pointer in thick fog for anyone in a small boat. Only someone working close to the water would record such a detail. Another exam-ple is the directions for entering San Diego Bay itself, a model of clarity for a small sailing vessel: "Round up gradually until Ballast Point is brought in range with the easternmost house of La Playa (distant one mile from Ballast Point and on the same side of the bay), and be careful not to open more of the village, as the shoal called Barros de Zuniga stretches south from the east side of the entrance."

Imagine a sunburned Davidson and a handful of sailors slipping into the bay on a warm summer day, with no diesel engine to speed them along. His book is also full of minor tidbits; for example: at Monterey, "Landing on the beach is generally dis-agreeable"; and along the shores of the Santa Barbara Channel, "Crayfish of a very large size are found in great numbers."

View of Cuyler's Harbor, San Miguel. *A sketch of one of the Channel Islands' most famous anchorages by the* U.S. Coast Survey *of 1853.*

Many of the passagemaking strategies and navigational ideas presented in this book have been gleaned from the talented, hardworking nineteenth-century surveyors who persevered under harsh conditions and in all weather to chart our coasts for the first time. Some of those men have been commemorated in small anchorages and near rocky headlands and hills overlooking the waters where they labored. When they packed away their theodolites and compasses, a string of powerful lighthouses marked a thoroughly mapped coastline. So much of the lore in this book goes back more than a century, to the days when everyone navigated the coast under oars and sail.

PLEASURE BOATING

Pleasure boating has been part of the California scene for more than a century. The early years of the twentieth century saw luxury steam and sailing yachts in San Francisco Bay and comparable vessels in the south, crossing to Catalina and exploring Mexican waters. Sailboat racing was early on the scene and cruising powerboats were popular long before the Great Depression. Wooden boat building has a proud tradition in the Bay area. Talented California designers produced magnificent custom power and sailing yachts that were built in Wilmington and elsewhere before World War II. However, the real explosion in pleasure boating came with the advent of mass-produced fiberglass powerboats and sailboats in the 1960s. When British sailors like Peter Pye and Eric and Susan Hiscock explored Southern California in the late 1950s and early 1960s, there was nothing like the number of yachts there today, although places like Newport Beach were already crowded with moorings.

The 1960s and 1970s saw a surge of marina construction between Ventura and San Diego, which—combined with the expansion of commercial shipping—turned much of the mainland coast of Southern California into a humanly constructed marine environment. Today, in the high season of the summer months, Catalina is jammed with visitors from the mainland

and moorings command astronomical prices. Dozens of yachts anchor in once-deserted offshore island coves. Yachts are now commonplace off Point Conception. But move a little distance away from the crowd and you can still find the unhurried California of Richard Henry Dana's time, where the only sounds are soft waves lapping on sandy beaches and the gentle sloughing of the afternoon wind.

WEATHER AND WIND

Don't worry too much about predicting the weather; people have been at it for years with little success. Rather, be ready for all kinds of weather—the sure prediction is that they're all coming your way sooner or later—and be prepared to keep her going through their endless variety.

Roger Taylor, *The Elements of Seamanship*

A GUIDE TO THE CALIFORNIA coast must begin with the weather, for the vagaries of the coastal climate govern all our cruising and passagemaking. Richard Henry Dana hated the passage up the California coast—the inexorable northwesterlies that blew day after day in summer and the interminable, oily calms of the night watches. Even in our modern diesel-powered sailboats and sleek motor yachts, we dread passagemaking to windward along the California shore. Sailing downwind before the strong prevailing winds north of Point Conception can be a nerve-racking experience too—tacking inshore and offshore to avoid a dead run, striving to keep in touch with the foggy coast to port and prevent an accidental jibe, all the while beset by the endless corkscrew motion from seas on the quarter. Yet, with careful planning, you can avoid these ordeals and take advantage of the pre-dictable (and not-so-predictable) weather cycles of the California coast.

The key to successful passage-planning in California is in understanding the weather: the many factors that produce 35-knot headwinds or infuriating calms.

WEATHER INFORMATION

Compared with sailors in many parts of the world, we live in an information-rich environment that brings us weather data at every turn. Radio, television, newspapers, recorded telephone messages, Weatherfax, and the Internet—there is a wealth of forecasts, warnings, and recommendations at your fingertips—not to mention the advice and lore of fishermen, experienced cruising people, and competitive sailors.

WEATHER FORECASTS

Weather forecasting is still an art as well as a science, despite the awesome predictive power of modern computers and the nearly instantaneous data provided by satellites, radar stations, weather buoys, and a host of observers on land and sea. Our ability to track the development of long-term phenomena (such as El Niños) has improved dramatically. Local forecasts are also getting better all the time, to well over 75 percent accuracy. In general, forecasting weather is much more difficult at sea than on land because observation points are few and far between. The situation is improving in California with the placement of permanent weather buoys along the coast. Each observation station is, of course, a reflection of existing local conditions. The best forecasts assimilate information drawn from many sources, such as weather satellites high in space and data on jet streams.

Marine weather reports are prepared by the National Weather Service (NWS), a NOAA agency. Marine forecasts generally predict weather conditions on the high seas and in coastal waters 24 to 36 hours in advance; longer-term forecasts predict weather 72 hours or more in advance. When listening to forecasts, remember that they are somewhat generalized: because they must be short and to the point for transmission, they cannot reflect your precise local conditions. For example, you can be certain that a 20-knot northwesterly off the coast will funnel much more strongly through the narrow Golden Gate, and local conditions off Point Conception can bring much stronger gusts and considerably higher seas than those in the marine forecast (see the section entitled The Point Conception Phenomenon, pages 114–15). *Always assume that marine forecasts are for open waters, away from distorting land features.*

Using weather forecasts well is a matter of monitoring trends: combining the conditions you are experiencing, say, 10 miles off Morro Bay, with broadcast information. I was once anchored in Cuyler Harbor on San Miguel Island at the western end of the Santa Barbara Channel. The morning forecast spoke of an approaching, fast-moving front that would bring strong SE winds to the offshore islands by midafternoon. I was skeptical at first because the skies were clear and a moderate westerly was blowing, with no signs of clouds streaming across the sky—signs of an impending frontal passage. I soon changed my mind. A short lumpy sea soon set in from the southeast and high gray clouds masked the sun. The wind was still in the west, but the cloud cover thickened inexorably through the morning. By noon, the distant San Ynez Mountains on the mainland had hard gray-black edges, a sure sign of impending rain and wind. All the local indicators now pointed to an imminent southeaster. Cuyler Harbor is dangerous in a southeaster, so we made a fast downwind passage to the northern shore of Santa Cruz Island and anchored in Fry's Harbor—a fine all-weather anchorage—just as a wild, cloudy sunset and backing winds gave further warning of the approaching storm. By monitoring changing weather signs, local conditions, and future trends, we had made sensible, strategic decisions.

We spent a comfortable night despite the wind howling high above as torrential rain pelted the decks.

Marine weather forecasts come in three major categories. *High-seas forecasts* cover areas more than 250 nautical miles from shore; offshore forecasts cover waters between 250 and 60 miles out. *Coastal forecasts* cover a strip from 60 miles offshore to the coast. *Inland forecasts* cover San Francisco Bay and other sheltered waters.

What kinds of information can you expect from a broadcasted forecast? On the largest scale, high-seas forecasts always give the positions of high- and low-pressure centers. Coastal forecasts focus mainly on wind speeds and sea state. Sometimes information on approaching fronts and expected rainfalls indicates a trend. Track such predictions for several days before your planned passage; this way, you have a picture of the next 24 hours. These longer-term trends will affect your passage-planning more than anything else.

The most important element in any forecast is how to use the information. For example, a 50-foot diesel trawler with an experienced skipper can easily handle a summer windward passage along the Big

Rough seas in Windy Lane off the northern coast of Santa Cruz Island in the Santa Barbara Channel; more than 40 knots on deck.

Peter Howorth

Sur coast against 30 knots of northwesterly and the accompanying swell. A forecast of 20- to 25-knot winds in Windy Lane (the notorious patch of rougher water off the northern coast of Santa Cruz Island) should give pause even to an experienced owner of a 25-foot inboard/outboard fishing boat. The forecast is an educated guess at local conditions; only you can decide whether the intended passage will be hazardous to your boat and your crew. As the skipper, you are limited, first, by your experience; second, by the design and capabilities of your vessel; and last by the wind and sea conditions.

FORECAST SOURCES

The official NWS forecasts are available 24 hours a day on NOAA Weather Radio (VHF-FM). They are updated every 6 hours at 0200, 0800, 1400, and 2000 Pacific Standard Time, sometimes more often. They can be picked up on most FM receivers and on all modern VHF marine radios. The frequencies are as follows:

Weather 1 (WX1): 162.550 MHz

Weather 2 (WX2): 162.400 MHz

Weather 3 (WX3): 162.475 MHz

Weather 4 (WX4): 161.650 MHz

Forecasts broadcasted on television and commercial radio are, for the most part, targeted for people living on land. Television weather maps provide a general impression of highs, lows, and weather fronts; keep them in mind when you listen to NOAA broadcasts. Most commercial radio stations use canned forecasts (like the classic, "Point Conception to the Mexican border, winds light to variable night and morning hours, westerly 10 to 15 knots in the afternoons"). Some radio stations do make a point of broadcasting marine forecasts, especially on the weekends; however, readily available NOAA forecasts make them superfluous.

Many newspapers publish satellite maps, synoptic charts, and weather forecasts categorized by many local areas. The *Los Angeles Times* has a particularly useful weather page.

All harbormasters' offices display weather forecasts and, even more useful, reports of prevailing conditions at key coastal stations in the region. You can usually learn local weather conditions by calling your harbormaster or a port near your destination. This is the best way to learn about prevailing swell conditions at Ventura and elsewhere.

The Internet is now the major source of weather information at both the local and national levels. The Internet makes weather forecasts available whenever you want them, day and night, provided you have access. Wireless technology will soon make it possible for even small yachts to access the Internet in coastal waters. However, traditional sources are still important and readily available. Following are a few of the numerous sources:

- The NWS home page is at www.nws.noaa.gov/.
- For coastal marine forecasts, go to CoastWeather.com (http://clipper.coast

NOAA Weather Buoys:
The Ultimate Forecasters

Log on to NOAA's National Data Buoy Center (www.ndbc.noaa.gov/station_page.phtml) to obtain real-time data on current conditions, as well as forecasts. Select the Southwestern region and click on the buoy nearest your location. You can also obtain valuable data on wind and wave changes over the previous hours, as well as limited historical data. Most weather buoys along the Central and Southern California coast are of 3-meter disc design and are painted yellow.

Golden Gate to Point Conception
46026–San Francisco
    Lat. 37°45.32′ N, Long. 122°50.0′ W
46012–Half Moon Bay
    Lat. 37°23.12′ N, Long. 122°43.4′ W
46042–Monterey
    Lat. 36°45.1′ N, Long. 122°25.2′ W
46028–Cape San Martin
    Lat. 35°44.08′ N, Long. 121°53.11′ W

46062–Point San Luis
    Lat. 35°06.3′ N, Long. 121°0.4′ W
46011–Santa Maria
    Lat. 34°52.5′ N, Long. 120°52.1′ W
46023–Point Arguello
    Lat. 34°42.5′ N, Long. 120°58.0′ W
PTGC1–Point Arguello (Land Station)
    Lat. 34°58.0′ N, Long. 120°65.0′ W
46063–Point Conception
    Lat. 34°15.0′ N, Long. 120°39.5′ W

Santa Barbara Channel to San Diego
46054–Santa Barbara Channel West
    Lat. 34°16.8′ N, Long. 120°26.5′ W
46053–Santa Barbara Channel East
    Lat. 34°14.10′ N, Long. 119°50.5′ W
46025–Catalina Island (RDG)
    Lat. 33°44.4′ N, Long. 119°05.0′ W
46047–Tanner Banks
    Lat. 32°26.0′ N, Long. 119°32.0′ W

weather.com/CWHome3.html). Here you can request a seven-day forecast for any location along the coast and out for 200 miles or more.

- Another good source is Marineweather.com (www.marineweather.com/FrameWestCoast.html).

- The best raw data come from weather buoys along the coast, which give you a reliable picture of conditions offshore, especially of sea states (www.ndbc.noaa.gov/index.html). You

can also call Dial-A-Buoy (223-668-1948), but you need the station number of the buoy to do so (see sidebar).

WEATHER WARNINGS

We cruise along a coast where powerful gales and very strong winds are not unknown. The NWS issues wind and storm warnings under three categories.

Small Craft Advisories (SCA). These are winds of 21 to 33 knots, either with or without 10-foot or greater swells. SCAs are common occurrences throughout California waters, especially in the Monterey Bay and Big Sur regions, off Point Conception, and in the offshore island waters of Southern California.

Gale Warnings. These are winds of 34 to 47 knots and severe sea conditions. Avoid passagemaking in these conditions if you possibly can. If caught out, stay well clear of the coast and heave-to if necessary.

Storm Warnings. These are winds of 48 knots and greater. Sailors, take up golf! If caught out, you will have to heave-to under bare poles or run before the storm.

Fortunately, such conditions are rare south of the Bay area, although Santa Ana winds and other local phenomena can achieve storm-force velocities.

WEATHER LORE

An official forecast can never be a substitute for your own experienced eye and careful observation of local weather conditions. Make yourself an expert on clouds and troughs of low pressure, on ridges and pressure gradients. Your assessment of weather will gradually become sounder through experience. Confidence in passagemaking strategy comes with this practice.

The best way to make educated assessments is to become familiar with long-term weather patterns, listen to experienced local mariners, and compile your own data by direct observations. Many years ago, I anchored in a sheltered cove on the northern coast of Santa Cruz Island. Only one other boat was in the anchorage—a battered fishing boat. With the warm weather, perfect visibility, and not a breath of wind,

we enjoyed a glass of wine before dinner. A gentle popple set into the anchorage, making us rock slightly. A few minutes later, the fishing boat got under way. We rejoiced at having the cove to ourselves for the night. As the fishermen passed close by, the skipper yelled, "Best get out now! The Santa Ana's coming in. It's already blowing on the mainland." Over the protestations of my hungry crew, I followed his lead. We ate dinner in open water, then beat and motored our way to the mainland. Back in port, we learned a fierce Santa Ana had come in soon after dark, turning all the anchorages along the northern coast into vicious lee shores. A few days later, I met the fisherman by chance and thanked him for his timely warning.

"How did you know the Santa Ana was coming?" I asked.

"Simple," he said. "They had wind warnings on the radio for campers and trailers on Interstate 5 and then small wind waves came in from the northeast."

Although official weather forecasts had talked about "strong winds below canyons and passes," we hadn't listened to the radio, talked to experts, or paid attention to subtle weather signals. If it weren't for the battered old fishing boat and her skipper, we would have been in big trouble.

Weather lore and "local knowledge" are largely a matter of common sense and experience on the water. It can be intimidating to ask the experts. They smile sagely and study the distant horizon with wizened faces, as they contemplate the vital signs—a veil cloud, a pearly line of haze, a line of foam in the breakers. They utter mellifluous predictions as if by magic—frequently correct and sometimes completely different from official forecasts. I always feel intimidated by such people. We shouldn't be. They are merely using their powers of observation, honed by years on the water—in the case of fishermen, by making their living in conditions in which pleasure sailors would not leave the harbor. Such knowledge is easy to acquire by making daily observations of the weather, even when not afloat; by learning the basics of interpreting weather maps (which I do not cover); and by understanding the fundamental forces that shape local weather.

Many mariners around the world still make passages on the basis of their long-term experience with the weather and their knowledge of winds, clouds, and swells. They often do as well as we do with all the information that is so readily available at our fingertips. The secret is not so much acquiring information as it is using it effectively.

GENERAL FACTORS AFFECTING CALIFORNIA WEATHER

The California coast has an enviable climate: plenty of sunshine, near-perfect temperatures, and markedly seasonal rainfall. It shares this distinction with parts of the Mediterranean, the Cape of Good Hope in South Africa, portions of Chile, southern Australia, and New Zealand. Our wonderful sailing waters experience weather shaped by global weather factors and local phenomena.

THE PACIFIC HIGH

The Pacific High usually sits about 400 to 600 miles off the California coast, a huge dome of air that exercises a profound influence on sailing conditions inshore and offshore. The movements of this vast high-pressure zone vary from season to season. When the high is in its usual position, low-pressure systems are deflected from the California coast. When it is weak or displaced farther south or west, high pressure weakens along the shore and lows approach and pass over coastal California.

High pressure varies seasonally. In December and January, the Pacific High is at its weakest, located about 30°N and 137°W. Storms now move into the Pacific Northwest, their fronts sweeping through California, bringing rain to the parched coast. By March, the high begins to strengthen, to shift northward along the coast. High pressure blocks storms as the landmasses of Mexico and the extreme southwestern United States warm up. Onshore winds increase as cool, moist air moves inland to replace hot, rising air from inland valleys.

Between June and September, the Pacific High sits offshore, blocking storms from our cruising ground. Strong winds blow clockwise around the high, bringing strong northwesterlies to the coast. Weather expert Kenneth Lilly has likened the summer high to "a giant balloon," whose shape and orientation causes the wind and weather to vary through the summer months. For example, when the Pacific High moves farther offshore and extends a ridge of high pressure into the regions north of San Francisco, the high temperatures found east of the coastal mountains flow over the coast, bringing hundred-degree temperatures and unaccustomed heat waves.

Come October, the Pacific High weakens gradually and weather patterns become more irregular. The first storms edge into California, ushering in the wet season and the winter months. The fall is a transitional season, during which much depends on the intensity of the Pacific High. In drought years, for example, the high can stay far north, blocking storm after storm far to the north, to the point that several years can pass with well-below-average rainfall.

Keeping track of the vagaries of the Pacific High is vital for planning long passages along our coast.

AIR MASSES

Both continental and maritime air masses pass through our cruising grounds and exercise a strong influence on our weather. Maritime air masses originate far out in the Pacific. Most of those reaching the California coast come from cool, moist air from more northerly latitudes offshore, which accounts for our generally cool and equable coastal climate. Warm maritime air masses regularly reach Southern California from the tropics or subtropics during the summer, occasionally affecting areas as far north as San Francisco Bay and Northern California. In this case, winds tend to be light, the air is extremely muggy and humid, and large swells from distant tropical disturbances can pound south-facing beaches.

Continental air masses are usually dry because they originate over the interior of North and Central America. The hot desert areas of the Great Basin, the Southwest, and Mexico bring intense heat to the coast during late summer and fall; the cold and dry air in the winter comes from Canada and the subarctic regions. When higher pressure is N and NE of San Francisco Bay, continental air enters Central California. An enormous dome of chill arctic air forms in the lower atmosphere in the north. Then N to NE winds bring the cold through gaps in the Rocky Mountains, causing temperatures to plummet in California ports.

JET STREAMS

Jet streams are like rivers, but high in the atmosphere. Several hundred miles wide, they separate cool and warm air masses and lie at altitudes between 18,000 and 40,000 feet. The Northern Hemisphere jet stream flows in a generally west to east direction, but it varies in speed and direction over days and weeks. In particular, it contorts into *ridges* and *troughs*, configurations that bring about major changes in the weather we experience near sea level. In general, a ridge occurs when a mass of warm air pushes north; a trough occurs when a mass of cool air pushes south, toward the equator. High-pressure systems tend to form on the surface under the influence of high-altitude ridges; surface lows form in the area of troughs. The jet stream is strongest during the winter months, from September through early June. During those months, the movements and configurations of the jet stream determine the development of storm systems approaching the California coast.

Really intense low-pressure systems—those with readings below 960 millibars—are unknown along our coast. Low-pressure systems tend to mature off the Oregon and Washington coasts, having originated far away in the tropics. They move northeastward up the coast, with the fronts ahead and south of them sweeping through California. The volatile mixing of tropical and polar air when subtropical and polar jet streams meet radiates outward from the center of the low and can batter coastlines hundreds of miles away.

Low-pressure systems and their associated fronts approach the California coast from SW to NW. The weather they bring greatly depends on the course and strength of the jet stream. The stronger the jet stream and the closer it is to the coast, the worse the storm.

FOG AND THE MARINE LAYER

Fog is endemic in California waters. Although the reasons are complex, a major factor is water temperature. We cruise in waters that are hardly tropical; even Southern California waters warm up no higher than the lower to mid-70s. California is also home to an important phenomenon known as *upwelling*, in which cold, deep ocean water rises to the surface near the coast. Water temperatures play a major role in coastal weather along a shoreline where upwelling occurs.

As discussed previously, the Pacific High exercises an enormous influence over our weather. Through the summer months, this long-lived area of high pressure sits off the California coast while a low-pressure area lies over southern Nevada and the California deserts. These conditions produce a pressure difference and a steady flow of air in from the Pacific and across our cruising grounds—the constant summer northwesterlies. As this air passes over the relatively cool waters of our coast, it cools and sinks. If the air is moist enough, dense sea fogs can develop that blow inland through gaps in the coast like the Golden Gate. At the same time, this cooling effect produces a *temperature inversion*—a situation in which a layer of cooler air near the sea surface (the *marine layer*) contrasts sharply with the mass of warmer air that lies at higher altitudes over the coast. The transition zone between the cooler marine layer and the warmer air above it (the *inversion layer*) acts like a lid, suppressing vertical air movement. Cooler air tends to stay inside the layer because it is too dense to rise into warmer zones. The intensity of this effect depends on the temperature difference between the cold and warm air. The dense fog and low stratus clouds so familiar to California sailors tend to form under these marine-layer conditions. Fog is intensified when it is trapped between the ocean surface and the base of the inversion, especially when the warmer air is less than 1,300 feet above water.

Our coastline sees a couple of distinct types of fog. *Advection fog* develops when warm, moist sea air blows inshore and strikes cold water near the coast. The air condenses, forming a thick fog bank. The cold water near the coast is the result of

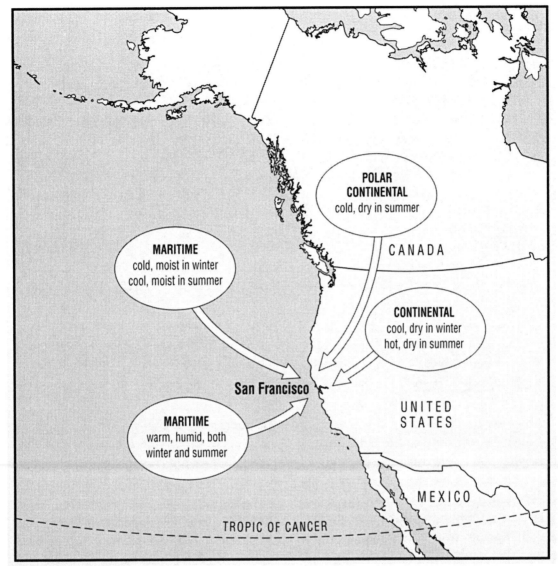

Air masses affecting the California coast.

upwelling: cold, deep ocean water is drawn to the surface to replace warmer surface water that has been dispersed seaward by persistent northwesterly winds and the Pacific High far offshore. Such winds are frequent between Gaviota and Point Arguello, at the northern boundary of the Santa Barbara Channel; the combination of upwelling cold water and warm Pacific winds produces fog banks that can lie close offshore for weeks. When the wind subsides, the fog drifts inshore over the coast. Sea fog like this is prevalent between May and July.

Upwelling

Our old friend the Pacific High causes complex changes in water temperatures near the coast. By late summer, the persistent high offshore and the regular northwesterly winds along the coast cause warm surface water to move offshore. Much colder water from the depths of the Pacific rises to the surface to replace it. Such massive but irregular upwelling, especially off steep coasts and south of major headlands like Point Conception, enriches the fertility of the marine environment.

Upwelling constantly replenishes the surface layers of the ocean with nutrients. In turn, the nutrients foster plant growth and cause unicellular algae—photoplankton—to flourish. A submerged peninsula running SE from Point Conception, of which Santa Rosa and San Nicolas Islands form a part, intensifies the upwelling process near the Santa Barbara Channel. Before the days of modern commercial fishing, billions of spawning sardines fed on the nutrients and zooplankton lying near the surface close offshore. The sardines moved inshore in summer, where pelicans and larger fish fed on them, as did Native Americans. This regular food supply encouraged many ancient coastal groups to live in permanent settlements.

This kind of upwelling of very deep water to the ocean surface occurs in only four other locations in the world: off the coasts of Mauritania, Namibia, and Somalia in Africa, and close inshore along the coastal plain of Peru. California and these four areas, a mere 0.1 percent of the ocean's surface, account for about half of the world's commercial fish catch.

Radiation fog, sometimes called *ground fog*, forms as the land radiates heat after sundown. The warm air rises, drawing in colder air just above the ground. The air cools, condenses, and rapidly forms a fog bank that usually burns off by midmorning. Radiation fogs are most common between September and January.

Fog and low clouds are commonplace along the California coast and tend to be thickest during the night and morning hours. As the land heats up during the day, lower air layers reach a temperature similar to the air above the inversion, and the fog dissipates into hazy afternoon sunshine. As cooling proceeds toward sunset, the layer of clouds thickens toward the surface.

According to the NWS, if the layer of clouds is less than 800 feet above sea level, the chance of fog (rather than low clouds) is much higher. If the dense haze associated with the low clouds persists near the coast, then the inversion layer is intense, and dense fog may be possible in the evening. Sometimes fog banks linger offshore and then are swept inshore by the sea breeze. These fog belts can be very dense and should be avoided, if possible, even though sailing from dense fog into bright sunlight and into fog again is dramatic and unusual. Very often, the wind is strongest along the fog line—a useful racing tip.

Meteorological expert Kenneth Lilly quotes studies by Dale Leipper of the Naval

Postgraduate School in Monterey, which found that coastal fogs often form in ten-day cycles. The inversion layer gradually descends, reaching its lowest point on the fourth and fifth days and giving prolonged periods of visibility of less than 0.5 mile. Then the inversion layer gradually lifts, eventually rising above 1,400 feet, when the fog disperses. I am intrigued by Leipper's research because he corroborates what I have noticed—that the fog thickens and then gradually disperses over ten days or so in Southern California. The fog brings relatively calm conditions and often lighter northwesterly winds, an important factor to bear in mind when planning a passage northward from Southern California to the Bay area.

Coastal topography determines the routes by which fog moves inland. The only sea level defile is the narrow Golden Gate. Here the fog may hang around for weeks at a time, keeping summer temperatures low. Now and then, gray stratus clouds blow farther inland to Alcatraz Island. The warmer water of the Bay causes the surface gloom to lift and form a high fog. The temperature inversion aloft keeps the trapped fog from dispersing completely into the warmer atmosphere.

Monterey Bay, famous for its prolonged summer fogs, sucks the grayness inland as far as the Salinas Valley and mantles Carmel in a foggy gloom. Farther south, along the Big Sur coast all the way to Point Piedras Blancas, where the Santa Lucia Mountains rise steeply from the ocean, the fog tends to stay on the seaward side. Between Piedras Blancas and Point Con-

ception, where most of the coastline is low-lying, the fog spreads inland to San Luis Obispo and, more persistently, to Santa Maria, which also tends to stay foggy in the summer.

Persistent fog exists in the summer southward of Point Conception, along the shores of the Santa Barbara Channel and Channel Islands. It covers the low-lying coastal plain of the Los Angeles Basin. The Santa Ynez Mountains act as a barricade, keeping the fog close to the coast in the Santa Barbara–Ventura area, while the southern shores of the Channel Islands can be sunnier than the northern island coasts. Summer temperature differences between the coast and the interior can be as much as 30 to 35 degrees. The marine air flowing inland heats rapidly as it passes through gaps in the coastal mountains. For example, the gaps in the Berkeley hills or at Avila Bay in Central California rarely bring cooler temperatures inland.

Peter Howorth

Gray, cloudy days like this are commonplace in California waters, sometimes with a visibility of only a few hundred yards.

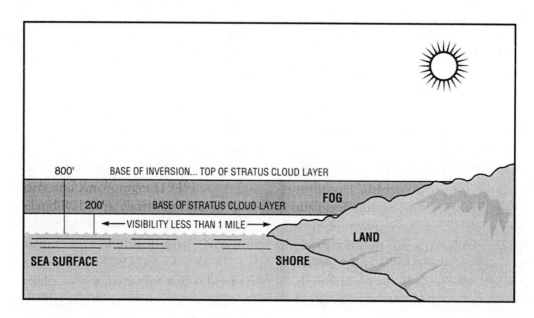

When the inversion is lower than 800 feet, the chance of dense fog over coastal waters increases.

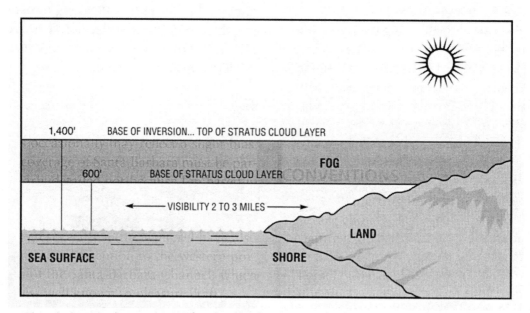

When the inversion is around 1,400 feet, low clouds rather than fog form over coastal waters.

Because fog conditions change constantly, they are difficult to predict accurately. You must always rely on your own judgment to decide whether a particular passage is safe under prevailing conditions.

SOUTHERN CALIFORNIA'S CATALINA EDDY

As discussed previously, the pressure gradient between the Pacific High and low-pressure zones of the southwestern United States dominates the weather patterns over the coast in the summer and ensures a prevailing NW air stream along most of the coastline. This wind blows almost parallel to the coast until it reaches Point Arguello, where the shoreline turns east. A wind of 25 to 35 knots inshore at Point Arguello now fans out both offshore toward San Nicolas Island 60 miles off Port Hueneme, and inshore along the east–west mainland coastline. This counterclockwise swirl of air is known as the Catalina Eddy.

If the Eddy is blowing, winds at Point Arguello will come from the N or NW at 20 to 30 knots, and at slightly less velocity from the same direction off San Nicolas Island. Winds in the Santa Barbara Channel will blow more south than usual: SE in the night and early morning, and SSW to SW in the afternoon. The increased south component of the winds is a good sign that Eddy conditions are in effect. The Eddy often brings more fog and low clouds.

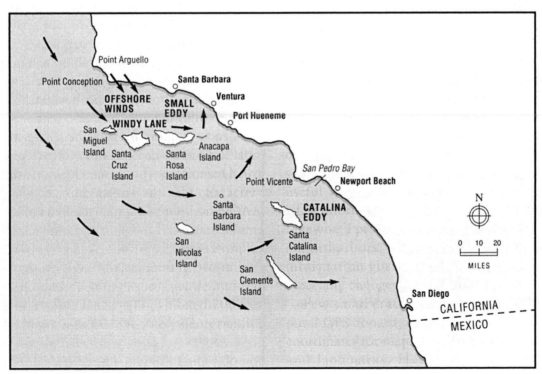

Catalina Eddy conditions in Southern California.

The Eddy can be modified by sea- and land-breeze conditions. Sometimes a persistent land breeze deflects air currents from the Eddy to the north, forcing a S or SW breeze; however, the sea breeze increases the tendency for the morning SE winds to veer W. Forecasters normally predict the Eddy by using small variations in pressure not normally available to small-craft skippers. However, as a general rule, they say that when San Nicolas Island has a NW wind of less than 10 knots, Eddy conditions are absent. The Catalina Eddy is most common in the spring, summer, and early fall, when the Pacific High is well established.

LAND AND SEA BREEZES

When high- and low-pressure systems lie some distance off the Southern California coast or are of weak intensity, they have only a minor effect on cloud cover or winds near the mainland. At times like these, the land- and sea-breeze cycle becomes a dominant factor in our weather pattern.

After sunset, the land cools and air over land cools and sinks to lower levels. This air first moves down north- and east-facing slopes, which lose the sun earliest, then down the south- and west-facing slopes. As this breeze moves downslope and reaches the coast, it gains momentum. The downslope wind blows in a direction determined by the slope of the land and by the headlands and bays that indent the shoreline. Once it fans out over the water, the land breeze loses velocity rapidly and rarely extends more than 5 or 10 miles offshore.

Nighttime cooling is most pronounced on long winter nights with clear skies.

Land breezes, therefore, tend to be more prevalent in the winter and can persist all night, but often blow strongest around sunrise. As the land begins to warm up, they die rapidly.

The sea breeze is a reverse process of the land breeze. Air over the warming land tends to move upslope because it also warms on hilly coastlines. Air over the ocean, however, remains cooler, and tends to move inshore to replace the rising warm air over the land. As this sea breeze approaches the coast, it changes direction toward the easiest shoreward path. It bends around hills, cliffs, and headlands, leaving a zone of confused winds in the lee of the land. Sea breezes are strongest in the summer months when the Southern California deserts and inland valleys warm up rapidly. Their greatest influence is felt within 5 or 10 miles of the coast; however, winds farther offshore can be affected by a strong sea breeze, the former changing flow in the same general direction. Sea breezes blow most strongly between June and September, are nearly equal in force in the spring and fall, and are weakest from late November to March. They should not be confused, however, with the strong and persistent NW winds of mid-March to mid-May.

SANTA ANA WINDS

We coastal sailors usually enjoy moderate temperatures, despite great temperature variations between the coast and the interior. Temperatures climb to extreme levels only when the Pacific High moves over to cover part of Oregon and Northern California. Then pressure builds inland, caus-

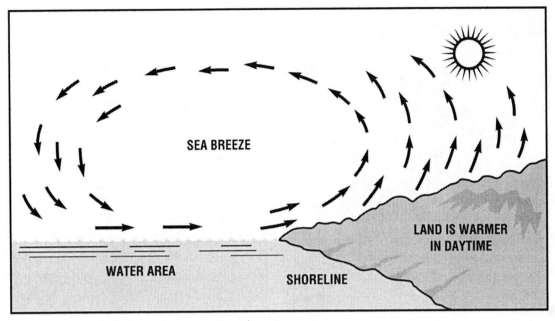

SEA BREEZE

LAND IS WARMER
IN DAYTIME

WATER AREA

SHORELINE

The circulation of air during sea-breeze conditions near the coast.

ing NE winds to blow over the California coast and sweeping extremely hot interior air out over the Pacific. The glassy calm conditions can leave you panting for air in an open cockpit or stuffy deckhouse. When a heat wave hits San Francisco and Monterey, edging temperatures into the 90s or even higher, a sailor can be caught becalmed for hours. Once when I was on a downwind passage from the Bay area in September, I was expecting a wonderful, boisterous spinnaker run. Instead, I found myself motoring in a flat calm. We sailed for a total of 4 hours the entire way, and the wind never rose above 8 knots. Air temperatures at sea were in the 80s.

In the fall and winter, a buildup of high pressure in Utah and Nevada often follows the passage of a front inland through Northern California. The pressure difference between the coast and the interior can be as much as 2.5 millibars, bringing strong northeasterly winds to Southern California. As the winds move into the region, they sweep over the coastal mountains via the passes, being heated at a rate of about 5.5°F per 1,000 feet by compression. These are the notorious Santa Ana winds, which can gust for hours at speeds exceeding 40 to 60 knots, turning anchorages and ports on exposed coasts like the northern shores of Catalina and Santa Cruz Islands into death traps. Santa Anas are most common between September and January, although similar conditions can develop at any time of the year when high pressure in the interior brings dry NE winds and high temperatures to the coast.

Santa Ana conditions usually last from four to six days. As the high weakens

The awesome destructive power of a Santa Ana wind unleashed in Avalon Harbor on Catalina Island, on a brilliantly clear day.

inland, the marine layer reforms. Coastal clouds and fog return to the coast. If the descending winds are warmer than the marine air, as is usually the case, then the "warm" Santa Anas stay confined to passes and to areas below coastal canyons. "Cold" Santa Anas are far more intense and dangerous; under these conditions, the descending, heated air is cooler than the air overlying the coastal plain. A cold Santa Ana pushes inshore marine air out to sea and sweeps over the coastal plain with tremendous velocity, often causing property damage and leaving small craft battered and strewn ashore.

Major segments of Southern California affected by Santa Anas are shown in the accompanying illustrations: Point Mugu, Anacapa, eastern Santa Cruz Island, and the eastern shores of Catalina and Santa Barbara Islands are affected; all should be avoided during Santa Ana conditions. Ironically, some of the most beautiful Califor-

nia days are among the potentially most dangerous.

Santa Anas and other offshore winds are difficult to forecast, except in the most general terms. Because they often occur following frontal passages along the seacoast, vigorous Santa Anas and down-canyon winds are often associated with strong northerly jet streams. Unlike low pressures and many passing fronts, Santa Anas and their equivalents give little advance warning, especially at the Channel Islands. The wise mariner avoids passagemaking when pressure is high inland. The weather will be hot, dry, and crystal clear, with signs of impending downslope winds in the form of slight wave movement from the NE.

In Southern California, stay in port when radio broadcasts warn of restrictions on trucks and high-sided vehicles on Interstate 5! Santa Ana conditions are blowing or are imminent. If berthed in an exposed anchorage, be prepared to leave on very short notice. You may find yourself anchored on a lee shore in gale-force winds, as dozens of yachts did at Santa Cruz Island over Thanksgiving 1977. Many boats were driven ashore and became total losses.

You can experience highly localized downslope winds in many places at any time of the year, especially off prominent headlands like Point Reyes or Point Conception. I was knocked on my beam ends by a sudden squall off the latter headland in late summer. Luckily, we were well reefed down against such a contingency, but that did not prevent dinner from flying off the stove into the navigator's berth.

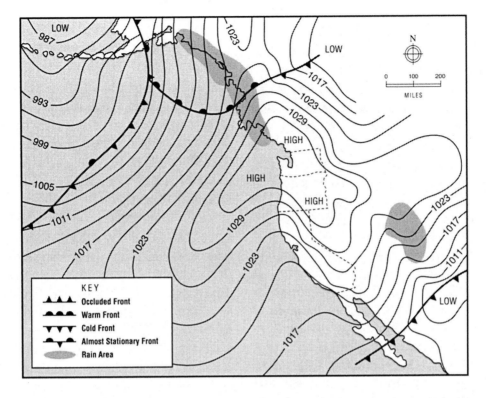

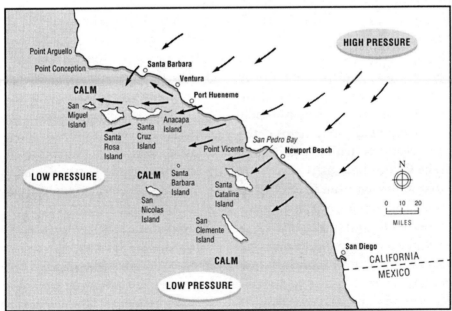

Top: *Santa Ana conditions over the California coast, November 19, 1956.* Bottom: *Wind patterns in severe Santa Ana conditions in Southern California.*

Winter months bring more unsettled weather to Southern California. As previously discussed, the Pacific High wards off constant low-pressure systems that cross the Pacific from California during the summer. But when the high weakens, Pacific lows and associated weather fronts reach the Southern California coast at least ten to fifteen times a year. Weather forecasters carefully track these low-pressure systems as they move toward the coast. The circulation of air around the low center is such that leading edges, or *fronts*, between warm and cold air masses are formed. Clouds, shifting winds, and rain develop along these fronts, caused by mixing and turbulence. "Warm" fronts are the leading edge of a warm air mass; "cold" fronts are the opposite. Clouds form most densely to the east of a weather front, which is why our winter storms are often preceded by 24 to 36 hours of cloudy weather.

Most low-pressure systems move inland north of Southern California. Our storms are caused by the trailing portion of the front as it crosses the coast. The position of the Pacific High pressure area helps determine the directions from which lows approach the California coast.

Lows that approach from the SW bring some of our heaviest rainstorms that can last from 36 to 48 hours. Massive cloud layers herald the approach of rain from the SW. SE winds between 10 and 20 knots veer to the SW, 15 to 25 knots as the low approaches the islands and coast. Clouds and rain clear more slowly and temperatures remain relatively constant.

Lows from the NW are cooler than those from the SW, and move SE from the Gulf of Alaska toward the California coast. They bring unstable cold air with them, their rain is often short-lived, and gusty winds are associated with their fronts. Skies clear rapidly as the front passes—the S or SE winds in advance of the front veer to the W and blow from 15 to 35 knots out of a clear blue sky.

Lows that approach from the W are often associated with a broad area of low pressure extending over the middle latitudes of the east Pacific. This area can direct a wide series of lows toward Northern California, and we enjoy several days of rain as a result.

Winter storms and the cold fronts associated with them typically yield the following sequence of phenomena:

- About 24 to 36 hours ahead of the front, a low cloud layer forms, often a thickening of coastal fog.
- The wind fills in from the SE, initially at 10 to 20 knots, increasing to 20 to 30 knots about 6 hours before the frontal passage.
- As the front passes overhead, the winds become more gusty, with heavy rain, and a sudden wind shift to the SW may be experienced.
- Some 6 hours after the frontal passage, the wind may continue to veer west to the NW and blow from a clearing sky at speeds of 20 to 40 knots, with locally stronger gusts. The roughest coastal sea conditions are likely to occur from 12 to 36 hours after the frontal passage.

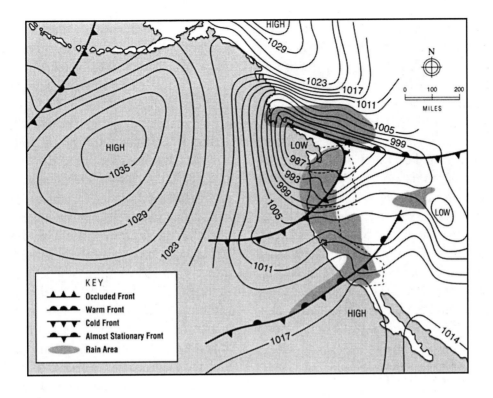

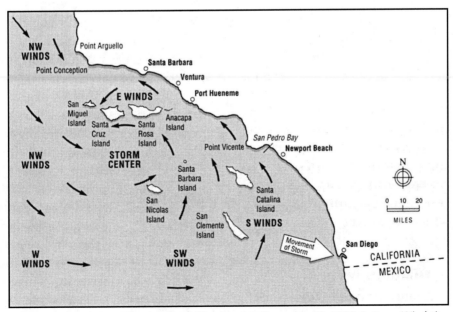

Top: *Frontal systems passing over the California coast, December 29, 1966.* Bottom: *Wind circulation patterns off the Channel Islands and adjacent mainland during severe storm conditions.*

Sometimes a vigorous front leaves behind it a period of blustery weather with squalls. Unstable cold air may extend up to 20,000 feet, with the turbulent air causing squalls and heavy rain showers. Gusts up to 35 or 40 knots are not uncommon. The movements of these squalls can sometimes be detected by watching the direction in which cumulus clouds lean or the curtains of rain associated with them.

Occasionally, waterspouts form in unstable conditions over the ocean. Every year, several are spotted in the Santa Barbara Channel and off Southern California. Because severe circulating winds gust to 60 knots around the visible vortex of a waterspout, do everything you can to avoid them.

WEATHER CONDITIONS THROUGHOUT THE YEAR

California's cruising grounds have hundreds of different, highly local climates, where rainfall and wind velocity may vary dramatically in areas only 10 miles apart in the course of a single day. However, the various weather conditions discussed previously and local observations over more than a century from meteorological stations along the coast and offshore form enough of a consistent pattern that a broad outline of seasonal conditions is possible, keeping in mind that the "average year" does not exist.

JANUARY THROUGH MARCH

During the winter, the Pacific High tends to weaken and migrates to the south. Fog and low clouds are still common during periods of dry stable weather. Weakening and southern movements of the anticyclone allow large Pacific storms to approach the coast. Many more low-pressure systems pass through Northern and Central California than through Southern California.

The air circulates around the low center in such a manner that the fronts, caused by mixing warm and cold air masses, create the turbulence of clouds, shifting winds, and rain to develop into southeasters. These fronts seldom strike without warning, and are tracked by satellites far offshore. As a storm approaches, prevailing westerlies die out and dark cumulus clouds gather. The water close inshore, usually turbid, begins to clear. The clouds appear to settle, and then squalls occur, followed by steady rain. After several hours, the SE wind decreases. As the storm passes, skies begin to clear and the wind shifts to the NW or W, depending on your location. If you intend a passage during a period of stormy weather, watch the direction from which the lows arrive.

The first three months of the year are often the wettest. Active weather fronts pass through California with varying frequency during these months, giving us four to six rainy periods a month in an average year. These periods of rain can last as long as a week if a close succession of fronts passes overhead. SE winds are associated with these fronts, with the wind veering to the W or NW as the front passes over, frequently blowing between 25 and 35 knots out of a clear sky. Downslope winds and Santa Ana conditions may develop once or twice a month after a frontal passage, with occasional strong winds and often NW breezes. Fog is relatively infrequent, but 4- to 6-foot swells and high surf generated by intense Pacific storms from far offshore are not uncommon.

Lows from the NW come from the Gulf of Alaska and bring unstable cool air with them. The SE winds associated with the system gradually veer to the W as the rain and gusty winds pass through. As the skies clear, the winds can blow up to 50 knots. Avoid passagemaking under these conditions.

Lows from the W are often associated with a broad area of low pressure extending over the latitudes of the eastern Pacific. Such conditions can bring a whole string of rain-filled storm systems to Northern California. The entire state enjoys a relatively prolonged period of wet and stormy weather. Your chances of having some longer periods of SE wind are somewhat improved under these circumstances, but do not be tempted to take on a lengthy passage.

Lows from the SW often bring the heaviest rainfall. Massive cloud banks precede the storm, with the winds shifting to the SE and then to the WNW as the bad weather clears relatively slowly compared with NW lows. Temperatures remain more constant. You may have more warning both of approaching SE conditions and of postfrontal winds with SW lows.

The greatest danger with low-pressure systems lies in the unstable, blustery conditions that can develop after the system has moved on. Violent squalls, heavy rain showers, even waterspouts are not uncommon. I have been caught offshore on days like these, when the winds are so strong that the kelp dances in the wind. It is best to stay in port and enjoy a good book when the postfrontal northwesters howl.

Southeasters become less common by April. Gusty NW gales now pose a dangerous hazard, especially in Northern and Central California. An onshore flow of moist air displaces rising warmer air over the land. Then night falls and the land cools to nearly the same temperature as the ocean. The wind drops close inshore. Moist air condenses on coastal mountain ranges where the air is coldest, especially near the low passes. Once the air temperature is cooler than the water, winds begin to blow offshore, usually until early morning. By noon the next day, the onshore wind fills in again, repeating the same cycle.

Veil clouds, or cloud caps, are valuable indicators of NW conditions. They are easily recognized as white, solid-looking clouds that cling to mountain passes and ridges and to the W end of the offshore islands. At dawn or dusk, veil clouds may resemble an enormous wave breaking over the mountains. As the wind picks up and the land warms, the huge cloud breaks up into spinning cotton balls, sometimes called "puff clouds." The clouds usually disappear by late morning and reappear after sundown. Following are some pointers on northwesters and veil clouds:

- The extent of the clouds is determined by the amount of wind that initially formed them.
- The more clouds present in the early morning, the stronger the wind will be.

- If other clouds are present as well, the northwester will last only a few hours.
- If the other clouds disappear and the veil clouds remain, plan on a three- to five-day gale. The longer blows are most common in the spring months.
- Severe northwesters often strike the northern coastline before the southern.

Study weather reports from Point Piños and Piedras Blancas on the Big Sur coast. The Point Arguello, Western Channel Buoy, and San Nicolas Island reporting stations in Central and Southern California also lie in the direct path of the strongest northwesterlies, thereby providing a valuable check on cloud indicators.

APRIL THROUGH SEPTEMBER

Coastal fog and low clouds are more frequent in the spring as frontal activity dies down. The usual frontal weather pattern occurs once or twice, normally in April, when strong W to NW winds blow along the coast. Santa Anas are rare and 3- to 5-foot swells from far offshore are not uncommon. Frequent, strong NW winds are experienced west of Gaviota and Santa Cruz Island and north of Point Conception.

After April, the Pacific High dominates the weather map off the California coast. This creates a common situation in which a long-lived high-pressure system lies off the coast while low pressure sits in the interior. These conditions create a pressure differential that maintains an air flow from the Pacific over the coast. As this air passes over the cool waters of the coast, the relatively cool marine layer is formed. The pressure gradient between the high and low zones dominates weather patterns over the coast and creates a prevailing NW airstream par-

Veil clouds over the Santa Ynez Mountains.

Peter Howorth

allel to most of the California coast. This wind blows almost parallel to the coast until it reaches Point Arguello, where the shoreline turns E. A wind of between 25 and 35 knots now fans out, both offshore toward San Nicolas Island and inshore along the east–west mainland coast.

When the wind blows from the NW at 15 knots or more along the outer Channel Islands, it slows as it fans toward shore, sometimes changing direction. The NW wind backs to the W past San Nicolas Island, then to the SW as it approaches Catalina Island. The Catalina Eddy forms when the breeze approaches the shore, loses strength, and then comes out of the S and SE. By this time, it has reversed its original direction, forming the characteristic eddy. The Catalina Eddy is often accompanied by fog and low clouds at the coast. If San Nicolas reports clear skies and NW winds over 15 knots, the Eddy is probably in effect.

During the summer months, the North Pacific High strengthens and migrates northward, with its eastern edge off the coast of Oregon and California. Cold water that flows southward along the coast maintains cooler temperatures and assists in chilling the overlying air and causing the inversion, resulting in stable weather conditions along the coast. Low-pressure systems passing across the Pacific are diverted to the north, far away from California.

May, June, and July are usually the foggiest months from Ventura northward. Thick, gray, overcast conditions can persist for days, even weeks. Such conditions reduce visibility at sea but are often the best weather for making passages to windward.

In other words, a yacht wanting to cruise to San Francisco from the south may have excellent conditions for the passage between May and June—but not every year. There is no such thing as totally predictable weather conditions!

If a thermally induced low-pressure center is created in southwestern Arizona, then the sea breeze tends to strengthen along the coast during the afternoon, increasing the strength of the prevailing NW winds. This can cause strong headwinds N of Point Conception with less favorable passage conditions.

Strong onshore NW winds can sometimes bring cool sea air into land basins near the coast. When the NW breeze drops, the trapped air heated by the land sweeps out of the basins down the coastal canyons. Such winds are sometimes called "sundowners" because they are most common at dusk.

Occasionally, maritime tropical air invades Baja and Southern California during the summer, bringing hot, humid weather and thunderstorms to the coast. The winds are light and sailing tends to be unpleasant.

Extremely rare tropical storms have been recorded in Southern California, in which case you should be snug in port. Even distant Mexican storms can generate 6- to 8-foot swells that radiate from storm centers hundreds of miles away. Without warning, these can arrive in south-facing anchorages in sets of half a dozen or more swells that could throw you up on the beach. Your best guard against these "sneakers" is to monitor the VHF weather channels and Web sites that track the course of tropical storms off Baja. Heavy, sudsy foam close inshore can be a sign of heavy surge; watch south-facing beaches carefully for this condition when tropical storms are reported—usually between June and early October.

Frontal weather is rare in summer—except occasionally in mid to late September—but few of these systems bring heavy rainfall. Fog and coastal low clouds are frequent as the coastal inversion becomes stronger, most commonly from mid-May to July. Drizzle is not uncommon and low cloud conditions can persist all day. The afternoon sea breeze can reach 15 to 20 knots, especially near the Channel Islands, where it can reach 30 knots when the Catalina Eddy is present. These winds are so predictable that Richard Henry Dana called them the "California trades." Generally, weather conditions are very settled during the summer, although tropical air can move into Southern California from the SE, bringing warm, humid conditions and possible rain or thunderstorms. Sometimes four to six days of very high temperatures and low humidity in the late summer provide magnificent visibility and very high fire danger. Santa Anas and downslope wind conditions also begin in September. Seas are generally calm, causing few problems for small craft.

OCTOBER THROUGH DECEMBER

Our old friend the weather front appears more frequently from October onward, bringing several days of rain and strong winds. In October and November, down-slope winds often develop after weather fronts have passed through, generating periods of very strong offshore winds (30 to 40 knots) below coastal canyons. Short periods of very warm, brilliantly clear "Indian summer"–type weather are not uncommon in October and November. By December, weather fronts are often more frequent, with some form of downslope or Santa Ana conditions on four to six days of the month. Coastal fog and low clouds are of shorter duration, but can occur on six to eight days during December along much of the coast.

Weather patterns between San Francisco and San Diego follow a fairly regular annual cycle, despite major variations in the amount of rainfall and its concentration; in 1969, Santa Barbara had 16 inches of rain in four days. It is perfectly possible to enjoy a week or more of glorious almost fall-like warmth in January—days when the air feels like crisp champagne and cruising in small boats seems the only possible lifestyle!

WEATHER SIGNS

Intelligent tracking of weather is a skill you can develop on land, even by looking out an office window! You will soon develop your own telltale signs of different weather conditions on land and at sea. Following are some passagemaking points that I have found useful over the years. Perhaps they will provide a foundation for your own arsenal of weather signs and help you amplify forecasts and weather maps.

- Fog and low clouds with hazy sunshine in the afternoon are typically signs of settled conditions, especially in the summer. You will usually experience afternoon westerlies. To make sure, keep a check on the position of the North Pacific High.

- Dew in the morning tends to indicate settled weather. In Central California waters and in the western parts of the Santa Barbara Channel, dew may indicate NW winds.
- Good visibility associated with hard gray profiles of distant land formations and offshore islands, as well as constantly changing gray cloud banks, may indicate an approaching frontal system and rain. A SE swell can indicate the approach of a rainstorm. Postpone your departure until things settle down.
- Stratus or layer clouds on the summits of coastal mountain ranges indicate that strong NW winds are imminent.
- Clear skies, brilliantly crystal visibility, and billowing white veil clouds streaming from mountaintops and island summits offshore are probably signs of strong winds. Veil clouds are reliable indicators of strong NW winds. The clouds usually disappear by late morning and reappear after sundown.
- Clear, cool weather with snow on the mountains can mean cold unstable conditions offshore.

- Cumulonimbus clouds over the mountains or turbulent clouds in the same area indicate that summer showers and squalls from the SW are likely.
- Southern California: A low layer of white, sea-level haze at the offshore islands with the mountain peaks clearly visible above is sometimes a sign of strong winds close to their northern shores and in interisland passages.
- Southern California: When at the Channel Islands or Catalina, dry decks, clear visibility, and swells from the NE when the wind is calm can warn of impending strong offshore winds from the mainland. If in doubt, leave your anchorage—fast. Stay offshore or make for home. Smog near coastal canyons spreading seaward indicates NE (Santa Ana or downslope wind) conditions.

For the most part, our weather patterns are settled and relatively predictable, with passagemaking a matter of careful planning and common sense. You soon learn to use the changing rhythms of our coastal climate to your advantage, just as the Chumash and the conquistadors did centuries ago. Passagemaking strategies follow in the next section.

Area coverage, region by region.

PASSAGEMAKING STRATEGIES

It took us three days to cover a distance of only one hundred and twenty miles. The mist hung on, and for a day and a night we navigated by the sound of the traffic along the coast road, coming about, for the wind was ahead, when the roar of the traffic grew too loud, and again when it had almost ceased.

Peter Pye, *The Sea Is for Sailing*

T IME AND AGAIN, I run across sailors who have suffered on passage when they needn't have! "We fought a 30-knot headwind off Conception for hours," one skipper told me in Morro Bay. He had left northbound in midmorning instead of after dark, when the winds often quiet down. We had departed 12 hours later and had motored comfortably the entire way. Recently, I talked to another crew who had tried to beat northward close inshore from Point Dume to Point Mugu on a windy summer afternoon—they had not enjoyed the experience. The golden rule of going to sea is to enjoy yourself. For me, that means smooth seas and a minimum of headwinds. Unless you are one of those special people who enjoy tough windward races, there is no point in beating your brains out against prevailing winds when some careful planning makes it unneces-

sary. Of course, we all get caught out occasionally because the weather gods are rarely consistent, but forethought and common sense can help you avoid many uncomfortable days at sea.

Passages along the California coast fall into two broad categories: nonstop voyages with the intention of covering as much mileage as possible in the shortest possible time, and more leisurely cruises from port to port. Most people traversing the coast prefer to take their time, to explore different harbors along the way. Whatever your plans, the most successful passagemaking in California depends on careful planning beforehand. This chapter discusses some of the strategies you can adopt to reach your destination in safety and comfort without battling headwinds and steep seas or running ashore on Point Conception in zero visibility.

46   PILOTING

We live in changing times, where a GPS receiver and radar can tell us where we are within a few feet and a depth-sounder can give us contour maps of the surrounding bottom under the vessel, even ahead of it. Nineteenth-century devices such as protractors and parallel rulers seemingly have become extinct. Actually, they have not, for even the coastal sailor faces the prospect of total electronic failure in the middle of a fog or on a dark night. Even in these days of $100 GPS units and easy backups, electronics do not always work. Besides, there is satisfaction in making your way across fogbound Monterey or Santa Monica Bay or offshore to Catalina or San Miguel Islands with a compass, a dead reckoning (DR) plot, and simple bearings. This brief discussion on navigating our waters assumes you have a GPS on board and know how to use it, but applies whether or not you go the electronic route.

Central and Southern California have no major currents or tidal streams such as those that complicate navigation in the San Francisco Bay area or the Pacific Northwest, which makes pilotage immeasurably easier. Most of the time, we can rely on simple line-of-sight navigation to make passage from one port to the next—say, from Santa Cruz to Moss Landing with its conspicuous power plant—or to cross from Santa Barbara to Pelican Bay on Santa Cruz Island simply by setting course for a conspicuous landmark like the low-lying saddle of land at Prisoner's Harbor. However, there are days when fog and haze restrict visibility and make your landfall,

even over shorter distances, somewhat more difficult. As a rule of thumb, it's a good idea to lay off a course to your destination in hazy or foggy weather, even if you are following the coastline; offshore, it's essential. Be sure to set your course to a point somewhat to windward of your destination so that you don't have to fight your way to windward if your course slips below it. You can always correct your heading once you have made landfall and know exactly where you are. Under such conditions, also maintain a DR plot on your chart. Then, if you acquire a fix or sight your landfall, you can calculate whether any lateral drift has occurred. More importantly, in the event that fog develops suddenly or night falls when you are out of sight of land, you have at least a rough estimate of your position. (GPS technology makes this irrelevant, of course, but what happens if your batteries go flat?)

Line-of-sight navigation is straightforward once you have a mindset to look for convenient landmarks onshore. Become familiar with conspicuous headlands, high-rise buildings, and oil-storage tanks, as well as the color of buildings, scarred cliffs, and other seemingly trivial markers that can serve as valuable signposts to your destination in thick weather. This was the way nineteenth-century mariners found their way around and it is as useful today as it was in their time. Call it local knowledge, if you will, but it is as powerful a navigational tool as any GPS. For instance, the massive Diablo Canyon nuclear plant provides an excellent fix in foggy weather, and airliners taking off from Los Angeles International Airport are a priceless indicator for Marina del Rey, which lies just W of the takeoff pattern. The artificially flattened top of Point Dume is a distinctive landmark on a full-moon night, and Redondo Beach Harbor is backed by power-station smoke-stacks visible in clear weather from miles away. Catalina Island's skyline profile, if carefully memorized, can bring you right into the Isthmus, Avalon, or points between.

As a general rule, you should try to know where you are inshore within 0.5 mile and offshore within a couple of miles, just for peace of mind; do this as a matter of course, without switching on the GPS.

A good depth-sounder is essential, especially when navigating along a fogbound coastline. The 10-fathom (60-foot) mark is relatively close inshore along the entire coast and can be used to estimate an approximate distance off when combined with the charts for harbors like Morro Bay and Santa Barbara.

If you do not rely entirely on GPS, most pilotage and navigation south of Point Dume—and often farther north—is common sense. If you want to see how simple and entertaining it is, ship out with a copy of *The Practical Pilot* by Leonard Eyges (International Marine, Camden, Maine, 1989), which speaks of the very kind of basic pilotage we commonly use in Southern California. Quite apart from anything else, Eyges's methods are entertaining, simple to use, and sometimes challenging. Above all, they represent the kind of mind-set that leads to navigational peace of mind in any weather.

RESOURCES

Planning your voyage requires the appropriate charts and sailing directions for the task. You need not carry a vast library of navigational publications in our waters as you would need in, say, Maine or Scandinavia with their many islands and intricate channels. But you need the basics.

CHARTS

The figure on page 48 shows the main NOAA chart coverage for passages through Central and Southern California. You either can buy the charts individually, which will cost you a bundle, or purchase bound sets of reduced copies of NOAA charts published by Bay and Delta Yachtsman (Northern California) and *Chart-Kit* (Southern California). Many people use them for harbor and close-in pilotage, but I recommend using a full-size chart for all long-distance passagemaking and DR, as well as in situations in which you are plotting bearings.

Whether you choose a portfolio or buy charts for your specific needs, keep them updated either by having them corrected or by consulting *Local Notices to Mariners*, issued by the U.S. Coast Guard and found on the Web at www.navcen.uscg.mil/lnm/default.htm. Many *Notices* concern changes in regulations, temporary oil-drilling activity, and other esoterica of relevance to big ships; however, it is worth wading through the detail for the occasional priceless nugget of information.

Some people photocopy NOAA charts at full size; indeed, some stores offer this service. Whatever you do, make sure you

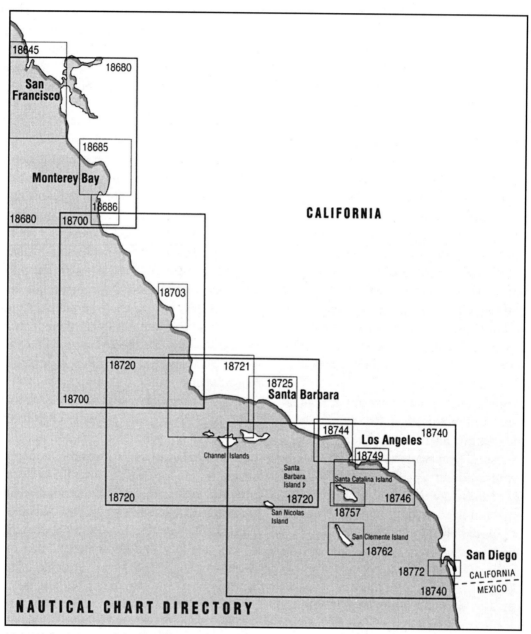

18645
18680
San Francisco
18685
Monterey Bay
18686
18680
18700
18680
18700
18703
18720
18721
18725
Santa Barbara
18744
Los Angeles 18740
18749
Channel Islands
Santa Barbara Island ▷
Santa Catalina Island
18720
18720
San Nicolas Island
18757
18746
San Clemente Island
18762
San Diego
18772
CALIFORNIA
18740
MEXICO

CALIFORNIA

N A U T I C A L   C H A R T   D I R E C T O R Y

Major chart coverage of the area discussed in this book.

have comprehensive coverage not only for your line of passage, but also for alternative ports. I will never forget the experience of making landfall on the British Virgin Islands after a transatlantic crossing in a 40-footer using a sketch map from a charter-company advertisement in a sailing magazine! We were bound for the Bahamas and ran low on diesel fuel, necessitating an unplanned change of course off the margins of our passage charts.

SAILING DIRECTIONS

This book covers the basics for the entire area and I hope, of course, that you carry it aboard!

Charlie's Charts, U.S. Pacific Coast (Seattle, Washington, to San Diego, California) by Charles and Margo Wood (Charlie's Charts, Surrey, BC, Canada, 1995, with 1999 addenda) is designed primarily for boats taking passage along the entire coast from Seattle to San Diego. The focus is on major ports and anchorages, and there are excellent maps and plans, with plenty of commonsense information.

U. S. Coast Pilot 7 (Pacific Coast: California, Oregon, Washington, and Hawaii) (NOAA) is a veritable bible of navigational information and bureaucratic regulations for the West Coast. Buy a copy for reference and for leisurely browsing, but don't try to use it while on passage. The information is too dense and requires careful matching with the relevant charts. The language is clear enough, but does not have the immediacy of small-boat guides.

All sailing directions must be used in conjunction with charts; they are useless without them.

OTHER PUBLICATIONS

If you have up-to-date charts, you have no need of light or radio-beacon lists when sailing our waters. The government produces annual tide tables, as well as current charts and the annual *Nautical Almanac*, which is essential for celestial navigators. A current chart is essential, especially for the Golden Gate, but many marine stores offer pocket-sized tide tables that save you the expense of buying the government computations. Alternatively, you can purchase a tidal calendar for our waters, readily available at outlets like West Marine. All this material can also be found on the NOAA Web sites, referred to previously.

That's it, unless you want a videotape of the Channel Islands or the San Francisco Bay area, or feel you want to ship out with Richard Henry Dana's *Two Years before the Mast*, some wildlife books, and shore-side guides that inventory attractions onshore. The selection of land guides is so enormous and growing so rapidly that my recommendations would be out of date before they appeared in print. Any good local bookstore can satisfy your needs.

GENERAL PASSAGEMAKING STRATEGIES

Unless you are bound from the mainland to the Channel Islands or Catalina, almost all longer passages in our waters are to windward or to leeward. Whatever your desti-

Sea otters are a common sight in central California waters.

Peter Howorth

nation, your advance planning, based on the following set of fundamental principles, ensures a comfortable passage:

- Lay off courses to carry you clear of all navigational hazards. For example, there's a nasty rock 220 yards off Point Conception that has claimed many a victim trying to take a shortcut. To carry you past the point, stay at least 0.75 mile off the land, even more in rough weather.
- Take advantage of the prevailing weather conditions for the season of the year, using the various hours of day and night with proportional care between calm and windy hours.
- A good cruise plan reflects the objectives of your passage in addition to the realities of weather conditions and time available. For example, a harbor-hopping passage from Monterey to San Simeon Bay in the summer needs careful timing to take advantage of afternoon winds, the reality of an unlighted anchorage at your destination, and off-lying rocks at Piedras Blancas 5 miles to

windward. The solution: time your passage so that you arrive at San Simeon Bay in late afternoon, in good visibility.
- Whatever your plans, be flexible enough to allow for sudden changes in the case of bad weather, an emergency, or simply a desire to do something different. Plan to have charts of all alternative ports and anchorages on board.
- Wise plans reflect the age and expertise of your crew. Young, prehensile sailors can undertake a nonstop, offshore passage from San Pedro to San Francisco in a 35-footer with impunity. An older couple or a family with small children will probably have quite different plans.

These principles, although obvious, are often overlooked. I'm always surprised when I meet exhausted crews who have taken on too much and tired themselves out in the early days of a cruise. People who venture unprepared out of San Francisco Bay or north of Point Conception in entirely unsuitable weather conditions overtax their endurance levels.

The decision of whether to depart is a matter of individual judgment. Britain's Royal Ocean Racing Club starts every ocean race on schedule, whatever the weather conditions. It's up to individual boatowners to make the call. You can be sure those skippers have thought out their race strategies and alternatives very carefully if they do decide to start in the face of a 40-knot gale. Every cruising sailor, whether in a trailer yacht or a plush mega-yacht, faces the same decision-making process every time he or she puts to sea.

With careful passage-planning, decisions become easier, more logical. I reiterate: *If in doubt, stay in port until you are absolutely comfortable about leaving. And, if you do set out and find conditions unbearably uncomfortable or deteriorating after 10 or even 20 miles, please turn back without hesitation.* Better to be safe than sorry.

Remember, only the foolish go to sea to prove they are tough. The best sailors are quiet, low-key cowards who will do anything they can to avoid bad weather or strong headwinds. They know the inevitability of meeting both one day, and so never leave port unless well prepared for unexpected weather conditions.

NORTHBOUND PASSAGES

Whether we like it or not, we spend an inordinate amount of time voyaging to windward in California. The prevailing N to NW winds follow the shoreline and often blow with considerable violence. Without careful timing, a windward passage from Southern California to the San Francisco Bay area or points beyond can turn into a brain-numbing nightmare of headwinds and pounding waves.

NONSTOP PASSAGES TO WINDWARD

Relatively few people elect to sail nonstop from a southern port to the San Francisco Bay area unless they are in a medium- to larger-size powerboat or are on a delivery trip. Even then, it may pay to stop at strategic points such as Morro Bay, San Simeon, or Santa Cruz Harbor to await favorable conditions.

Sailing nonstop is a rarity in this day and age of efficient, lightweight diesels. The skippers I know who have made this demanding passage have headed resolutely far offshore on the starboard tack, taking the fluctuations in prevailing winds as they come. By the time they are 50 miles or more offshore, they will encounter the sometimes more dependable NW winds that blow away from the coast. There is a risk, however, that you will run out of wind far offshore, and you may encounter large swells that will inhibit rapid progress. A passage from Marina del Rey, Santa Barbara, or Channel Islands Harbor, for example, takes you offshore hard on the wind and well clear of Point Conception. You can plan on at least four or five days on this windward course before tacking inshore. The timing of the inshore tack requires good judgment and depends on the course you make good to windward under prevailing conditions. This is where GPS is invaluable because you can track your progress to the mile, then predict with reasonable confidence where your landfall will be. Make progressively shorter tacks as you near the San Francisco Bay area. This passage option is only for larger, well-founded yachts with experienced crews. Do not attempt this passage in midwinter—nor is it recommended for single-handed sailors.

I have met only one skipper who enjoyed this passage. He was in a well-founded 40-footer and had a tough, young crew that thrived on hard thrashes to windward and steady winds of 15 to 20 knots most of the way. "The moonlight nights were magnificent 50 miles offshore, once

Patrick Short

Commercial shipping is a constant presence off the California coast. There is only one strategy for the small-boat skipper: Stay clear.

we cleared the main shipping lanes," he told me. Even so, they encountered hours of calm, bumpy conditions when heading inshore. It took thirteen days before they sailed triumphantly through the Golden Gate. Richard Henry Dana made the passage several times; his fastest voyage was twenty days from Santa Barbara to San Francisco. His ship, the *Alert,* was under reefed topsails for a week and was blown a good way toward Hawai'i.

Unless you are a true fanatic and just like windward passages, or you are racing, I strongly recommend that you break up the passage and make progress northward close to the coast.

According to late eighteenth-century navigator George Vancouver, a skipper can sail long distances close inshore at night along the Central California coast, using the light NE land breeze to move you gently to windward. Such winds are erratic in their occurrence and they cannot be relied upon as part of a passage plan. However, you may encounter them when motoring at night—in which case, turn off the engine and enjoy!

A few bold souls wait for winter southeasters, then ride the favorable wind far north of Point Conception. I have made the passage from Santa Barbara to the Golden Gate in a fast 40-footer in 34 hours with a strong southeaster at our tail—but it was a gamble because we were well aware that the wind would switch onto our nose directly once the system passed through. And so it did, just hours after we reached port. We made the passage because we had to. I do not recommend the strategy for most people, especially because southeasters turn the coast into a dangerous lee shore.

Powering nonstop is a viable option, especially for those able to maintain cruising speeds of 10 knots or more, at which the miles seem to melt away. Northbound, the best course is the rhumb line, passing well clear of Point Conception and other headlands. If fuel economy is your goal, then consider taking four or five days and harbor-hopping to minimize headwinds and seas.

Nonstop windward passages in Southern California are frustrating and often boring, especially if you are under sail.

Under typical summer conditions, you will be lucky if you have 6 to 8 hours of sailing breeze a day, from late morning to sunset. The rest of the time, you will be under power. Unless you prefer long hours becalmed in lumpy seas or you have a specific destination about 8 hours ahead, I recommend harbor-hopping and motoring to windward in the calm hours. Once again, nighttime land breezes can help you along, especially in late summer. Some bold souls ride northeasterly Santa Ana winds up the coast in the fall and winter, but if you do so, equip your boat with strong gear, prepare yourself for sudden gusts, and tuck in one or two reefs—especially when sailing near the mouths of canyons. The bonus is smooth water, especially inshore, but only experienced crews use these conditions—and even they hesitate. One of my most memorable passages off Southern California was when we were caught on a lee shore at Santa Barbara Island. A Santa Ana came in unexpectedly. We clawed up the anchor, set a double-reefed main and storm jib, and enjoyed a magnificent sail northwestward past Anacapa Island and on into Santa Barbara. The Santa Ana dropped when we were 4 miles from port, just as the rising sun clothed the mountains in orange light. A memorable sail because we had a stout ship; however, it was rough and we were exhausted at dawn.

HARBOR-HOPPING NORTH

When harbor-hopping, the identical strategy applies both north and south of Point Conception: Make progress to windward under power during the calm night and early morning hours. Stay in port and go for a walk onshore while the afternoon northerlies blow. If you are a purist who turns puce at the word *engine*, be my guest and sail from port to port—it will take you two to three times longer to reach your destination, and you will acquire a well-earned reputation as a glutton for punishment. Personally, I thank the powers that be for a reliable diesel and scurry to windward whenever calm conditions permit. Then I can enjoy all the fast sailing I want on the leeward leg. You can be sure that Richard Henry Dana and his contemporaries would have embraced diesels with enthusiasm.

The same strategy works best for a powerboat, especially a trawler yacht—even if she has stabilizers—and if you're in no hurry with only comfort in mind. I always plan my windward legs in short realistic bites to try and time my arrival for midmorning—leaving either after sunset or as early as 0400 if necessary—so I don't have to fight headwinds. In terms of an overall cruising plan, this means that I harbor-hop to windward, then sail longer passages downwind. Such a strategy works like a charm, especially if inexperienced sailors are on board.

The best conditions for passages to windward are during calmer periods, especially those when fog and low clouds mantle the coast. As discussed in the Weather and Wind section (see pages 28–29), such cycles tend to last about ten days, especially in early summer and sometimes in the fall. Very often, the afternoon winds and sea conditions are so light that you can keep going day and night—a boon when making the long passage along the Big Sur coast, where about the only shelter is Pfeiffer Point anchorage.

People often ask me which months are best for heading north to the San Francisco Bay area. I always tell them to look at June or September, but there are no guarantees. Periods of calm conditions at night and foggy conditions in early morning can occur any time in the summer and winter. The chances of headwinds at night are somewhat higher in calm weather.

Slogging your way north in Southern California waters calls for long hours of

hugging the mainland, motoring from port to port. Until you reach King Harbor or Marina del Rey, your task is simple, for there are always harbors within a short distance. On the next leg, plot a northbound course outside Anacapa Island during the night, arriving there in early morning. Just as you reach the Anacapa Passage by Santa Cruz Island, the afternoon westerly should fill in. Then take a long inshore tack under sail alone to Santa Barbara Harbor. From there, it's a 40-mile passage from the city marina to Cojo Anchorage near Point Conception. This 8-hour journey is best tackled

Peter Howorth

Migrating whales sometimes accompany you on longer passages.

by leaving at about 0400 and then picking up the afternoon winds off Gaviota, because they sometimes allow you to lay a course for Cojo Anchorage. If you are bound for San Francisco Bay, resist the temptation to visit the Channel Islands until your return passage. The slog to windward up Windy Lane can be very uncomfortable. After all, why motor if you can sail?

Farther northbound, the timing of your passage revolves around two key legs: the rounding of Point Conception and the long haul from Morro Bay or San Simeon to Monterey or Santa Cruz. The section beginning on page 114 fully describes Point Conception waters and stresses that Cojo Anchorage in the lee of the point is the ideal jumping-off spot for rounding. Under prevailing summer conditions or in foggy weather, enjoy dinner, then up-anchor and motor northward. By dawn, you will be well clear of Point Conception and Point Arguello, rejoicing at your brilliant timing.

I recommend much the same strategy when heading north along the Big Sur coast. You can shorten the journey considerably by spending a day at San Simeon Bay. A trip to the Hearst Castle and its ocean views will give you a foretaste of conditions farther up the coast. When the wind drops, motor north all night, laying a course to keep you clear of all dangers. With a boat speed of 5 to 6 knots, you'll be well up to Point Sur or even in Monterey Bay before the next day's afternoon winds set in. And if you cannot make it that far, you can dodge into Pfeiffer Point anchorage south of Point Sur for a few hours,

where there is reasonable shelter. A few bold skippers simply head inshore and find a temporary anchoring spot behind off-lying rocks or small headlands with some shelter until the wind moderates. This may be a viable strategy in moderate weather, but it is suicidal when any swell is running. I have done it in an outboard fishing skiff on very calm days, but I had the speed to get out of trouble. It is best to leave such strategies to fishermen, who are used to operating close inshore.

You can comfortably make northbound passages in the fall, winter, and spring, but you must monitor weather forecasts carefully. The calmest conditions sometimes occur in late fall, when pressure is high in the interior and the Santa Anas are blowing in Southern California. If you encounter such weather, motor flat-out for your destination. The landmarks will be clear, the sea negligible, and the wind almost nonexistent. I have only made the passage once under these conditions. We were in shorts and T-shirts much of the time. Do not attempt a northbound passage in unsettled weather. You are asking for all hell to break loose, and it will—on your very nose.

A typical itinerary northbound from the Santa Barbara Channel has several potential stopping places: Cojo Anchorage to Avila, Morro Bay, or San Simeon Bay, then to Monterey or Santa Cruz, on to Half Moon Bay, and finally the Golden Gate. With favorable conditions, the typical windward passage under power takes about four or five days from Point Conception.

If you are from Southern California and bound for the Golden Gate, time your arrival for the late morning or early afternoon. You can then enjoy one of California's great cruising experiences: entering San Francisco Bay under the Golden Gate Bridge on the wings of the westerly.

SOUTHBOUND PASSAGES

Theoretically, at any rate, the wind is astern, so you just sit back and let her rip. If the northwesterlies are in form, the passage south from the Bay is definitely one of those times when the sailor has it over a powerboat skipper. I have vivid memories of surfing downwind past Point Sur with the coastal mountains off to port mantled in barreling clouds. The low rocks of Piedras Blancas came into sight at dusk. Our ship's main and jib were set wing and wing, so we had sailed downwind with the sea dead astern all afternoon. But the passage is more complicated than just laying off a course and heading along the coast nonstop—unless you are prepared to countenance long hours of motoring.

Just as when you head north, you must take advantage of the diurnal wind patterns when heading south. Unless you are racing nonstop from the Bay to Santa Barbara or Catalina Island—as people do—I recommend making the trip in three or four relatively long legs. On the first day, leave the Bay at slack water, timing your departure to use the ebb and the midday wind to speed you rapidly on your way. Then spend the first night at Half Moon Bay, rising early the next morning for a full-day's passage to Monterey Bay. Again, time your passage for maximum exposure

to the afternoon winds. This time, use the winds rather than avoiding them. (Some people prefer to go all the way from the Golden Gate to Santa Cruz in one day; it doesn't matter either way.) The leg from Monterey Bay down the Big Sur coast will involve a night at sea: time your passage to take advantage of the winds and make mileage down the Big Sur coast in daylight. This scheduling should have you off Morro Bay at dawn, a good choice in clear weather. In foggy conditions, leave Monterey Bay at night to be able to enter port at your destination in the clear late afternoon hours. The fog can be very thick off Morro Bay.

Apart from being an attractive port, Morro Bay is the ideal jumping-off harbor for your passage around Point Conception. Again, a successful passage is a matter of timing. Leave harbor comfortably after breakfast. As you clear the land, the wind fills in astern, sucking you southward past Point Arguello and into the turmoil of Point Conception. If the wind shows signs of piping up, it is best to put in a reef early in the game because gusts can come in suddenly and lay you on your beam ends. With a stout breeze, you will have ample daylight in summer to tuck yourself into Cojo well in time for dinner. However, if night falls, do not attempt to find Cojo Anchorage after dark; it is unlighted. It is best to stay in open water and reconcile yourself to a night at sea.

Unless conditions are quiet, resist the temptation to come inshore north of Point Conception. Nasty swells can take the wind out of your sails and the terrain is brutal. I was once close inshore off Point Arguello on a calm winter day in a fast powerboat, close to the unforgiving rocks. Suddenly, the skipper opened up to full throttle and spun the boat offshore. We climbed a huge, vertical-faced swell that had swept inshore without warning. Had he not been watching offshore, we would have capsized on the rocks. You can never relax in this vicinity. Recently, the NOAA vessel *Ballena* capsized under these circumstances in the same general location; fortunately, there was no loss of life.

Whatever the conditions, stay sufficiently offshore when sailing downwind to stay well clear of outlying dangers—especially Point Arguello and its missile gantries—but well inside the commercial shipping lanes that pass about 10 to 20 miles offshore. The entire coast is lit by well-spaced major lights, so navigation should not be a problem. Watch carefully for the oil rigs that flourish in these waters; they generate considerable small-boat traffic.

Once south of Point Conception, the weather conditions moderate dramatically, to the point that sometimes—almost without warning—you may find yourself becalmed, sails aback. If you sail past Point Conception in the middle of the day, you should have sufficient westerly to carry you a considerable distance toward your next destination. Options include Cuyler Harbor on San Miguel Island, the anchorages along the northern coast of Santa Cruz Island, and even Santa Barbara Harbor, although it lies 40 miles to leeward.

A word of warning: Under no circumstances should you try to make a landfall on the extreme western end of San Miguel Island, especially in reduced visibility. The area is a morass of unlit rocks, uncharted currents, and submerged reefs and outcrops. Stay inshore of the island, identify Harris Point midway along the northern coast, and then steer inshore.

As you sail eastward in the Santa Barbara Channel, winds lighten and seas moderate, but the same strategy for passagemaking to leeward applies. Make good use of the afternoon winds. Currents are effectively negligible, but swells can be a consideration.

If you do plan to sail nonstop from the Golden Gate to the Santa Barbara Channel or ports beyond, which course should you take? Usually, when bound for Catalina or San Diego, you are faced with several decisions: Should you pass outside the Channel Islands or sail through the Santa Barbara Channel? If bound for Santa Barbara or Ventura, should you stay well offshore at Point Conception or shape an inshore course, planning to spend the night at Secate, Refugio, or some other leeward anchorage? As always, skippers contradict one another, but following are some points worth considering:

- As far as Point Conception, the rhumb-line course appears to be most commonly used, aiming to pass between 2 and 5 miles off the point.
- Nearly everyone I have talked to has complained of progressively lighter winds outside the Channel Islands, with a high probability of nighttime calms in the entrance to the San Pedro Channel,

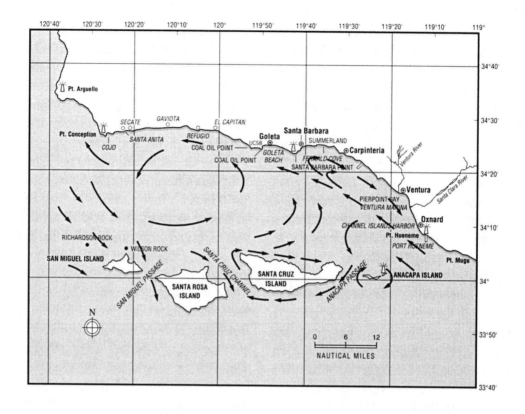

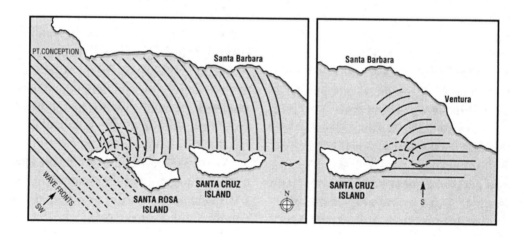

Top: *A rough map of currents in the Santa Barbara Channel. Effectively, they are not of much benefit to small-boat sailors, except locally.* Bottom: *Swell patterns in the Santa Barbara Channel, in normal westerly conditions* (left) *and during Mexican storms in summer* (right).

especially in the summer. In my experience, most skippers elect to ride Windy Lane down the inshore coasts of the Channel Islands, then head outside Anacapa Island, and from there stay some distance offshore into San Pedro Bay or head for Catalina Island. If you go outside the islands, you risk encountering patchy wind conditions.

- Those who hug the mainland south of Anacapa Island will most likely, but not invariably, enjoy the sailor's kiss of death: flat calm at night.
- If you decide to head into Santa Barbara from Point Conception in late morning, stay well offshore on the edges of Windy Lane, then shape a course toward the mainland once Santa Cruz Island is well abeam. You will then reach fast toward the coast. If the wind drops in the evening, you may be lucky enough to pick up the light SE breeze that sometimes wafts in at about sunset. Never head inshore and follow the coastline east of Point Conception unless you want to enjoy the coastline. The scenery is spectacular, but the wind drops early in the evening, and you will just sit there. However, there are several anchorages along the way (see page 131).
- Once in the Los Angeles area, plan rhumb-line courses to your destination. If you are bound for San Diego, stay offshore and clear of the commercial shipping vessels bound for San Pedro and Long Beach. Again, keep your stops to a minimum and plan to get south as fast as possible.

A pleasant way to reach Ensenada, Mexico, in early May is to stop at Newport Beach and join hundreds of other crews on the annual Newport to Ensenada Race. All you need is a PHRF (Pacific Handicap Racing Fleet) handicap, provided that you enter in advance. The race is not only fun, but also a magnificent spectacle. Entrants run the full gamut from ultra-dedicated racing crews to club racers and the dozens of yachts that go along for the spectacle and the partying in Ensenada. It is an unforgettable experience to drift southward surrounded by hundreds of red and green lights. The Ensenada Race is the ultimate cruise in company, especially with gourmet cuisine, even for the diehard cruising family. Again, opinions vary about whether you stay out or work your way inshore. A course that takes the middle ground, some distance offshore but not out of touch of land, seems the most conservative and reliable strategy.

The problem with the Ensenada Race is that you have to slog your way home. Unless you are lucky enough to encounter a rare southeaster, you are faced with a long beat or a prolonged motor sail back to San Diego.

We southern sailors enjoy one advantage: at least we get our windward work over at the beginning of the cruise so, as we reach our destination, we can sit back, relax, and know the worst is over. (Perhaps I should mention that I have classic sailor's luck: the wind invariably dies or blows in the opposite direction of my destination. Of course, every time I want to sail south past Point Conception, it's flat calm . . . and blowing from the NW at 40 knots when I am northbound.)

PASSAGES TO THE OFFSHORE ISLANDS

Sooner or later, most California sailors visit the offshore islands of Southern California. Unless bound direct from north of Point Conception, they reach them after an open-water passage from the mainland or the Santa Barbara Channel or the Los Angeles area. A passage from Newport Beach to Santa Catalina Island, for example, or from Santa Barbara to Santa Cruz Island will bring you hard on the wind for the first few hours, then allow you to ease your sails onto a close reach for the last few miles. If you enjoy motoring, plan to leave early in the morning so you are anchored at the islands before the afternoon winds fill in. Those who prefer to sail usually leave about 1100, pick up the strengthening westerlies, and arrive in the late afternoon after 3 to 6 hours of sailing. The return passage is typically a comfortable reach. If you depart about noon, the prevailing winds should carry you home in comfortable style.

Lesley Newhart

The major complication of a passage to the northern Channel Islands is the famous Windy Lane, the zone of strong winds that blow down the islands' inshore side. It may be blowing 30 knots close to Santa Cruz Island when it is calm at Channel Islands Harbor or Ventura. If you are even slightly doubtful about the island winds, try calling a yacht anchored there or check NOAA Weather Buoy 46054 (Santa Barbara Channel West). A sure sign of windy conditions offshore: tumbling clouds on the peaks of the Channel Islands—especially at the W end of Santa Cruz Island—or a layer of thick, almost pearly haze at water level on clear days (see the photograph on page 203). Be particularly careful on foggy days: the winds can be strong even when visibility is restricted. (For more on Windy Lane, see page 198.)

Santa Barbara Island, San Nicolas, and the western offshore islands of Santa Rosa and San Miguel require careful passage-planning. The best way to reach Santa Barbara Island is from Catalina Harbor or Santa Cruz Island, a 40-mile passage over open water. Check the Pacific Missile Range first, and choose settled conditions (see page 258). Santa Rosa and San Miguel are notorious for strong winds. The best way to reach them is by motoring to windward from Santa Barbara along the mainland, then crossing from Goleta, Refugio, or Cojo. Be sure to set an accurate course because a strong westerly set can sometimes be encountered in midchannel, taking you far off course (see page 175).

Bound from San Diego to Avalon on Santa Catalina Island, you are best advised to make an overnight passage from Point Loma to the island under power. You will arrive at Avalon for breakfast. The alternative is to hug the coast and call in at Oceanside and Newport first. This seems to be a waste of time when you can enjoy these marinas on a downwind cruise home.

With careful planning of your longer passages, you can enjoy California's gorgeous coastline to the full. Throw tightly drawn cruising schedules out of the cockpit, stock up with food and good wine, and enjoy the sensuous experience of making landfall in the bosom of a fair wind.

EXPLORING SOUTHERN CALIFORNIA WATERS IN SMALL CRAFT

Think out all the possibilities of the proposed passage, not only what one proposes to do under favorable conditions, but also what one would do in the event of bad weather, fog, or rain sufficiently heavy to prevent one seeing buoys or marks.

Claud Worth, *Yacht Navigation and Voyaging*

SOUTHERN CALIFORNIA IS unique among West Coast cruising areas in that you can cruise and fish safely offshore in much smaller craft than would be appropriate off the Golden Gate or Point Conception. By "offshore," I mean making regular passages to Catalina, or even to Santa Barbara Island, in search of new fishing grounds or simply to explore. In recent years, there's been an explosion of interest in trailer-sailboating, both along the coast and at Catalina, bringing a whole new population of boaters to open water.

Our benign weather provides unusual opportunities to make long passages across to the islands that would be unthinkable elsewhere—provided that you monitor weather forecasts and have the right boat and equipment for the job. During the predictable summer months, the worst you will probably encounter are some steep wind waves or large ocean swells from Mexican tropical storms. If you time your passages carefully, you will be able to cross the twenty-odd miles that separate Catalina from the mainland in comfort and, with the right outboard boat and flat calm conditions, in less than two hours. Taking a small runabout to the northern islands is a risky proposition unless it is longer than 20 feet overall, although I have seen them there. This section is for small-boat skippers in Southern California, although many of the principles mentioned apply anywhere.

The advantages of small craft are obvious—lower cost, trailerability, and the ability to make fast passages. Provided you choose your weather and time your island passages, you should manage to keep warm and dry—two of the obvious disadvantages of smaller, open boats. This section is written from the perspective of outboard-boat skippers, but most of it also applies to trail-

erable sailboats, which spend much time under power.

OUTBOARD BOATS

Small outboard boats come in many configurations, everything from insubstantial pontoon-like craft to highly sophisticated rigid inflatables with powerful outboards favored by divers. For offshore outboard use, a planing hull is essential if you want to cover the ground fast and safely. The so-called modified-V-hull configuration is best for ocean use. The deep V in the bow gives way to a smaller V aft, which provides better handling and the ability to handle different wave conditions. Quick response and quick acceleration are vital attributes for any offshore outboard boat, with ample power in reserve for sudden emergencies. When you choose your boat, consider how it will perform at displacement speed in crowded harbors or in rough seas. Be sure to test any boat you plan to buy under different sea conditions so that you

purchase exactly what suits your specific needs. Much of what I have said about outboard boats applies equally well to smaller stern drives.

Any outboard boat, whether decked with a small cuddy or in an open configuration, should meet the following criteria:

- handle precisely and predictably at displacement speed in close quarters (remember the 5 mph speed limits in all harbors)
- accelerate smoothly to a solid stance at high speed, jumping up onto the plane without any traces of sluggishness
- turn safely and predictably at a moderate speed, with no signs of engine cavitation (racing)
- show no signs of porpoising (oscillating up and down uncontrollably) at high speed with even weight distribution
- offer excellent visibility, convenient grab handles in rough seas, and comfortable seating at the helm and for passengers
- float when swamped

- be of adequate size for the job; about 20 feet overall is the smallest size I would take offshore (16-foot open runabouts may be fine at Catalina on calm days, but they reduce your safety margins to dangerously low levels)
- have enough outboard power to cruise at about 15 to 20 knots, with ample power in reserve

In the wrong hands, a fast outboard boat can become a lethal weapon in smooth water and even more dangerous offshore. Sure, it's fun to race along at full speed, but, in reality, a comfortable cruising speed is far more important, especially in rough water or a head sea. Outboards tend to be fast and enormous sums can be spent in the quest for ever more horsepower. The days when you can run at full speed on the open Pacific are few and far between, although Southern California sees more than many places. So choose a boat that is comfortable cruising at half throttle or slightly more for hours on end at 15 knots. You'll find that the urge to go faster is, at best, a transitory emotion! Above all, have ample power in reserve for emergencies. At half throttle, you'll save a lot of gas and get there almost as fast.

Your choice of designs is open-ended. A lot of people settle for a center-console fishing boat like the well-known Boston Whalers, Makos, and Radons, which are rugged, seaworthy, and easily trailerable. Equipped with a 50 to 90 hp motor or an inboard/outboard and a small backup low-horsepower unit, they make a fine fishing package for two or three people, although space to move around becomes

cramped. Some people camp aboard open center-console boats, inserting a filler floor between the console and the raised platform forward for their sleeping bags. A canvas dodger helps keep passengers dry in lively head seas. Many people who buy center-console boats are serious fishermen, but such designs also make fun cruising boats, especially for day-cruising or beach-camping. They are light, seaworthy, and fun to handle. Small wonder you may have trouble finding a nice one on the second-hand market. Many skippers keep their center-consoles for years.

Runabouts are another popular breed. Typically, they have a large well astern, fore and aft seats on either side of a walk-through aisle, and a bow well with seating. A steering console lies to starboard amidships. Most runabouts are best in smooth water or coastal conditions, but their forward driving position and low freeboard tend to make them wet and uncomfortable. A semi-dory or skiff makes more sense; that is, a boat with a widened flat or shallow V-bottom and a long, flat run aft. In their workboat configurations, these craft can carry a lot of weight, yet they are fine sea boats with light displacement. The downside is that they tend to pound in head seas—but they are never difficult to control and are safe in rough weather.

Skiffs are the outboard boat of choice among many Alaskan and Californian inshore fishermen. There are relatively few pleasure-boat skiff designs on the market; if you can find a working skiff, you may be short on glamour but you will have a tough boat when the conditions get tough offshore. A skiff is also easy for an amateur to build in plywood covered with epoxy-saturated fiberglass cloth, resulting in a boat at a fraction of the cost of a fiberglass design. A skiff is my outboard boat of choice in Southern California.

EQUIPPING YOUR OUTBOARD

When equipping your boat, your primary concern must be safety, especially in open water, where complete engine failure on an empty ocean could mean a long and perhaps fatal drift into the open sea. The list that follows may seem like overkill; however, if ever there was a form of boating where "it's never happened to me" rings hollow, it is this one. Be well equipped and well prepared. The following are essentials, beginning with U.S. Coast Guard–mandated equipment:

- U.S. Coast Guard–approved personal flotation devices (PFDs) for everyone on board
- Class IV (throwable) cushion or life ring.
- Sound-signaling device, such as a foghorn or whistle.
- At least one fire extinguisher (not required on smaller boats without enclosed machinery spaces, but essential nonetheless).
- Visual distress signals, such as flares.
- Running lights (for boats operating at night).
- A plastic bailer and a bucket; both are invaluable if you ship a lot of water, and they have many other uses (a cut-out plastic bleach bottle makes an ideal bailer).
- A first-aid kit.

- An anchor—preferably a C.Q.R., Danforth, or Delta—attached to a short length of galvanized chain and 150 feet of line.
- A tool kit in a waterproof box that contains a hammer, pliers, screwdrivers, and wrenches, including a fuel filter wrench (keep the tools oiled). Also pack electrical and duct tape; galvanized wire; stainless steel nuts, bolts, and washers; screws; a small hacksaw; and some twine.
- Engine spares: fuel filters, propeller, spark plugs, and shear pin; don't forget the manual. (For ambitious trips, carry a spare engine or a kicker.)
- A spare (full) fuel tank, separate from your main tank and compatible with your kicker.
- A compass, charts, and—of course—this book.
- A handheld GPS and spare batteries (a handheld set may be best because you can keep it dry).
- A VHF radio. (All electronics are vulnerable to the marine environment and an elaborate inventory is unnecessary in a small boat where the water flies. A VHF is useful insurance. I also carry a waterproof portable set in a special bag for emergencies.)
- Fenders and mooring lines; the orange balloon-type for fishing are the best.
- A sharp knife and a flashlight.
- Drinking water—an often-forgotten essential—and emergency food supplies.

PERSONAL GEAR

"Keep it simple" is a good motto, but bear in mind the basics for a day trip:

- PFDs. (Anyone boating regularly should own a PFD. Now that the U.S. Coast Guard has approved inflatables, there is no excuse for not wearing one all the time when on the water. If you are traveling after dark, attach a light and whistle.)
- A spare change of clothing (although you may not need this on a larger vessel, you may well get wet on an outboard boat, where the spray flies all the time, even in a light chop).
- Good footwear (if you know you are going to get wet, a pair of light sea boots is ideal for use under way).
- Sunglasses, a good sun hat, and sunscreen; also a towel for drying off (some people take another small towel to keep spray from going down their neck).
- Lightweight foul-weather gear. (This is essential if you are going any serious distance, and especially when it is cooler or the wind is blowing. There are numerous brands on the market, but it is best to purchase a top-quality outfit from an established manufacturer. It will last longer and be more waterproof. A two-piece suit is ideal for small boats.)
- A waterproof bag or bags to store your personal gear (invest in a specially manufactured bag—domestic plastic bags tear easily).

PASSAGEMAKING

Contrary to popular belief, there is a great deal more to handling an outboard boat than merely starting the engine and driving away. Good seamanship is as important in a small boat as it is on a large yacht—especially the ability to foresee problems (such as a blocked fuel filter) and to solve them calmly and efficiently. Good seamanship is being prepared and assuming responsibility for your actions in a boat that is faster—and can react faster—than almost anything else out on the water. This preparedness and responsibility assumes particular importance when you are crossing to Catalina or making another longer passage some distance offshore. Advance preparation is everything, especially in a small boat where you are potentially more vulnerable to unexpected mishaps.

Passage-planning is all-important. Begin by monitoring the weather forecasts over a period of several days to be sure that nothing unexpected is on the way. This is especially important during the more unpredictable winter months, when fast-moving fronts can bring strong postfrontal northwesterlies or Santa Ana winds in their train. If the weather is settled, then schedule your passage offshore for the calm morning hours, when chances are there is little or no wind and the sea is an oily calm. Overcast days with light fog are ideal for fast passages because you will typically have good visibility and absolutely calm conditions. It is best, for example, to leave the mainland soon after dawn to ensure the calmest conditions possible. With such a departure time, you are normally over at Catalina for a late breakfast and well before the 1100 witching hour when the prevailing westerlies begin to fill in. If you are making a longer passage—from Marina del Rey to the Channel Islands or Newport Beach to

Bob Greiser

San Diego, for example—you might want to contemplate a night passage, leaving after sunset as the wind dies down and conditions glass out. That way, you will have the maximum calm time. If you still have some distance to go by midmorning the next day, plan a stop at an intermediate port or anchorage to sit out the windy hours.

Returning from Catalina in midafternoon also can mean bumpy conditions. If these are bothersome, you should probably plan departure either in the morning or, if you want to make the most of the last day, close to sunset as the wind drops. Typically, the return trip to the mainland is somewhat smoother than the outbound journey due to the lie of the prevailing swells. I have often made it in midafter-

noon, even in a light to moderate westerly. It's a matter of personal preference and judgment.

Night passages can be delightful, especially if there is a full moon to light your way. Don't take chances with your speed because you will not be able to see semisubmerged objects, unlit mooring buoys, and similar hazards as easily as you might in daytime. Set a moderate cruising speed and keep a sharp lookout for ships. You will also require the correct navigation lights and a chart to see your way into harbor.

Once you have the mileage in your head and your waypoints entered on the GPS, calculate your average speed and fuel consumption. It seems obvious that you should plan on carrying enough fuel, but it is surprising how many people run out far offshore and have to be towed in. Carry enough fuel for the outward and return trip and a sufficient supply for local running at your destination, plus 20 percent for contingencies. Also carry a separate, full emergency tank. You can carry less if there is fuel at your destination, which there is at Avalon and Two Harbors. Top off whenever the opportunity arises, just for peace of mind. Another good strategy is to divide your fuel supplies among at least two tanks and an emergency can so that you can keep running if you purchase contaminated fuel.

Your planning should also allow for a safe average speed. Obviously, this depends on prevailing sea and swell conditions, as well as the capabilities of your boat; however, always plan conservatively. For example, for a 20-foot outboard fishing skiff that cruises easily at 25 knots in calm water, plan on a realistic cruising speed of 12 to 15 knots to allow for rough water.

PASSAGEMAKING IN TRAILERABLE SAILBOATS

Time was when trailerable sailboats sailed poorly and were little more than slow motorboats with badly fitting sails. Today, these vessels sail much better and can be used for serious beach- and island-cruising, provided you realize their limitations. They sail well with the wind abeam or from astern, but make slow progress to windward, especially against the typical wind waves encountered on so many summer afternoons. This makes passage-planning very important. When planning an island cruise, take a reach or downwind sail to and from Catalina by the simple expedient of trailering the boat to Marina del Rey, for example, and then arranging for someone to meet you at Newport Beach on your return. By using your trailer, you'll overcome the most serious limitation of your sailboat.

As an overall strategy at Catalina, try and make windward miles during the calm hours under engine, then sail downwind to coves below your destination. You can, of course, do this windward work on the mainland with your car!

Whatever your plans, make sure that you have a first-rate outboard with ample power to drive your boat against a head sea at about 5 knots. Many people under-power their trailer boats, which is a mistake.

Typically, you may have to reef somewhat earlier than you would in a large sailboat. Before taking off for Catalina, be sure you know how to operate your reefing gear and ensure that your sails set well when reefed. Otherwise, most of the rules for outboard craft apply.

HANDLING WAVES

Sailboat skippers and kayakers approach the water and waves in a much more intimate fashion than powerboaters. They soon develop a sense of subtle changes in wind and wave height that affects their boat-handling. Their progress through the water depends on their skill at judging wave conditions and adjusting their course accordingly. This kind of sea sense eludes many larger power-yacht skippers, but it is vital for outboard vessels. In Southern California, we have to contend with ocean swells generated hundreds, even thousands, of miles out in the Pacific, as well as wind waves that rise rapidly when the afternoon breeze fills in. The wind waves are of the greatest importance to small-boat skippers because they are often steeper with a shorter distance between crests. Although you may be able to drive over even quite a large swell without too much pounding, wind waves can make life uncomfortable in a few minutes as you fall off the crests into the troughs. Such pounding can be psychologically devastating, especially to people who are conditioned to believe that powerboats go in a straight line from departure point to destination. Therefore, they tend to not go out when, in fact, conditions are quite favorable—if you develop a sea sense through practice in bumpy conditions.

HEADING INTO WAVES

Every boat has a range of wave conditions that it does not like—usually those that are between the largest and the smallest—which cause it to heave and plunge wildly. This happens frequently, even on summer afternoons. Your first and correct reaction is to slow down. Chances are that this may work for a while, but as the wind continues to build, you start pounding again. At this point, you need to change your thinking and head off by about 45 degrees in either direction, which has the effect of almost doubling the length between wave crests. This either reduces or eliminates pounding because you progress toward your destination by "tacking," just as you would in a

sailboat. If the pounding persists with the highest crests, temporarily turn your boat 30 degrees farther off and go over the wave almost sideways. By exposing a profile almost as long as your length, you should roll smoothly over the crest. Do not turn abeam because you could roll over.

All of this assumes that you have reduced speed in the rougher water. Then, with the steepest waves, cut the throttle to idle and let the buoyant boat carry you over, accelerating again once the wave is astern. Remember that a properly trimmed and handled small boat will survive very rough seas indeed.

FOLLOWING SEAS

The previous discussion also applies to following seas, except that you must reduce speed to prevent your stern from burrowing into the back of the next wave instead of lifting to it. Trim is important, too. If you place the maximum weight just aft of amidships in high following seas, you will prevent the boat from taking a bow plunge into deep wave troughs. This is especially important for undecked boats, but proper trim works miracles with any outboard craft.

Never stop suddenly in a following sea because a steep wave behind you may wash over the stern. Insurance companies' files are full of sinking incidents that resulted from this happening.

MORE ON WAVES

Southern California winds are generally so predictable that you can almost guarantee they will drop partially or completely toward sundown. You can live more comfortably by timing your passages for the calm hours.

Avoid breaking surf if you possibly can, although it's a reality that fish are found in the surf zone. Remember that potential danger is both ahead and behind you. Keep a sharp lookout all around you, wear PFDs, and keep your engine running at all times. When you need it, you will have mere seconds to react. Watch for sets of higher waves and think about them not as single phenomena, but rather as a group. You can then get out of the way beforehand. If you are caught with an approaching breaker and you have time, accelerate fast to try steering right or left to avoid the worst—banking into the breaking water before it comes aboard. Alternatively, turn head into the wave, accelerate to get the boat moving and acquire steerageway, then let the momentum of the hull carry you through. Above all, back off speed to avoid going airborne as the wave passes. And tell the crew to hang on!

Be aware when going past breakwaters or steep cliffs that you may encounter confused water from waves bouncing back to sea from the shore. Under these circumstances, either head offshore to avoid the phenomenon or slow down. Out at sea, you can sometimes encounter cross-seas, which produce much the same effect, especially when wind waves from the southeast drive across a prevailing westerly swell. Nasty conditions like this require extreme care and reduced speed.

Afternoon conditions in Southern California often bring occasional steeper wind waves and whitecaps. Approaching white-caps are a sure sign of a larger wave than usual. Once you have reduced speed or angled off to ease yourself over the wave, you will almost invariably encounter a patch of smoother water. Accelerate and make progress in the correct direction before you have to bear off again for the next large wave.

There is only one way to find out how your boat behaves in rough water: go out in varied conditions and try her out. It is not enough to merely speed across a passing wake—you need to try different speeds and angles so that you can reduce that awful bone-breaking pounding to a tolerable thumping. Some boats are wet; others, like a skiff with flared bow, are drier. Learn your boat's hidden secrets and trim her right, and she will look after you in surprisingly rough conditions. Above all, develop your own sea sense so you can act confidently when the spray begins to fly.

ANCHORING

Everything begins with good ground tackle. For Catalina, a C.Q.R. or Delta anchor gives good all-around performance for small boats. Many people use Danforths, but you need quite a weight for them to work well—a short length of chain and at least 100 to 150 feet of line. Because small boats tend to sail around quite a lot at anchor, weight is all-important, so allow at least 15 to 20 pounds for boats up to 24 feet—and even more if you want to sleep well at night. For serious anchor work at Catalina or elsewhere, you should carry the following:

- two plow-style anchors, 15 to 20 pounds; two short lengths of chain in the 6- to 12-foot range, one for each anchor; and two anchor rodes, each at least 100 feet long and of sufficient diameter for easy handling with bare hands when under load. The 15- to 20-pound Delta anchor works especially well in small boats.
- shackles and wire to join anchor, chain, and line and secure them against accidentally working loose
- two large plastic paint buckets, in which the anchor lines and chain are flaked in loose coils so they run free

ANCHORING PROCEDURE

Good anchoring depends on the weight and design of the anchor, proper scope, and a good set—just as with big boats. Plan on at least a 6:1 scope for overnight anchoring (that is, six times the distance from the bottom to the bow cleat at high tide). If you have a reasonably heavy anchor, a 3:1 scope is adequate for a lunch hook, but I recommend laying out more as a precaution, especially if you are going ashore or swimming from the boat.

Whenever you anchor, clear away the anchor and bucket ahead of time—and make sure that the inboard end of the line is attached to the boat! Then choose your anchoring spot, stop the boat head to wind, and lower the anchor over the side until it hits the bottom. Let the boat fall off with the wind, easing her astern with the engine if necessary until the anchor catches hard. Give it a hard pull, then let out the scope. Before doing anything else, watch the boat

for a couple of minutes relative to two points on the coastline to check that she is not dragging.

SELECTING AN ANCHORING SPOT

Anchoring at a destination like Catalina can be tricky: most prime spots are crowded with moorings. But take heart—compared with larger boats, the outboard skipper has a wealth of anchoring choices, especially in shallow water. Be sure to carry tide tables with you to save grounding or in case you want to ground your boat deliberately at low tide. When selecting an anchor spot, bear in mind the following considerations:

- Is there sufficient shelter from wind and swell?
- Is there enough water at low water?
- Are you clear of other vessels? Do you have to lay one anchor or two?
- Do you have space to get out if the wind changes suddenly or weather conditions deteriorate?
- Is there good landing?

Choosing the right spot is a matter of experience and constant judgment. In the settled conditions of a Southern California summer, you can anchor almost anywhere off Catalina where there is some shelter from wind and especially swell, which is nice because you can avoid congestion. If you anchor in a moorings-infested cove, be prepared to lie in deeper water because anchoring is often forbidden close inshore—even better, go elsewhere.

For picking up a mooring at Catalina Island, see pages 315–16.

Swinging Free and Windbound. Most Catalina anchoring involves smooth water and the prevailing wind. Head the boat into the wind and use it to drop the vessel back on her anchor. If there is enough space, you can swing freely to a single hook, which is fine in smooth water but not so nice when a swell is running. This procedure is satisfactory if you plan to anchor in deeper water with enough room to swing free of the shore and have no neighbors.

Two Anchors. Anchoring bow and stern is a common procedure at Catalina, both to avoid neighboring boats and to keep you head-on to swell. Enter the anchorage and choose a spot, then approach again, dropping the stern anchor and paying out the line to double the length needed after setting it. Then drop the bow anchor, set

it, and equalize the lines. Try and lay the bow anchor into the swell or prevailing wind for maximum comfort. To recover the anchors, reverse the procedure, remembering that you will probably have to stand right over the anchor to lift it from the bottom.

Anchoring with a Stern Anchor Close to Land. Some skippers make use of a stern anchor to moor close to the beach, an ideal setup if you are beach-camping and seas are smooth. Drop a stern anchor as you approach shore and let out the line as you move inshore after it is set. Jump off the boat onto the beach, taking the forward anchor line attached to the bow with you. Unload your gear, then walk along the beach with the bow line, letting it out until the boat is well clear of the breakers. Then make fast the bow line with the anchor or

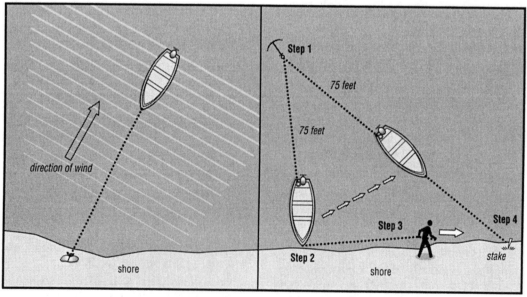

Anchoring off the beach.

to a rock or tree. Take the bow line upwind if possible.

Hauling-Off. Hauling-off is an ideal procedure for beach-camping at Catalina; however, surprisingly it is rarely used. Set your anchor hard in deep water with at least 7:1 scope. Tie the anchor line to a float with a ringbolt attached to it. Run a long line through the ring and take both ends to shore, forming a continuous loop. (This is why you should carry lots of spare line to allow for extra distance. Be sure the knots do not run through the ring because they will jam.) Tie a short line from the boat to the haul-out line and haul her out to the float, where she will sit nicely until you need her again. Experts recommend a cruciform float to prevent the line from tangling.

Many skippers are apprehensive about anchoring, but it is straightforward if you obey two simple rules: Dig your anchor in properly and lay plenty of scope.

EMERGENCIES

A well-prepared skipper is ready for sudden emergencies, but inevitably something unexpected happens. Following is a description of common mishaps that *befall* even the best-prepared small boat, with emphasis on prevention.

CREW OVERBOARD

You can do a lot to avoid this by taking simple precautions. For starters, insist that everyone wear a PFD whenever you go out

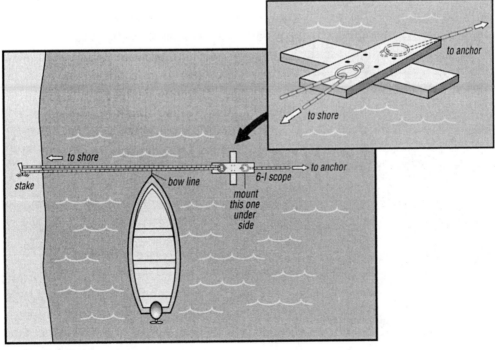

Haul-out anchoring.

of the harbor. This considerably increases the margin of safety from the beginning. Second, insist that every member of the crew sits inside the boat, not perched on the rail or at the bow with their feet over the side. If you hit a sudden wave, the unwary sitter can be pitch-poled into the water. Third, make sure that everyone knows where the safety gear is and how to use it. Last, practice the crew-overboard drill again and again so that everyone knows what to do. Make sure that every member of the crew knows that in any safety situation, one person—the skipper— is in charge and gives the orders. This eliminates confusion from the start. A wise skipper also makes sure that at least one other crew member knows how to stop and start the engine and how to handle the boat, just in case he or she goes overboard.

Overboard incidents happen without warning, usually when someone trips or a sudden wave causes them to lose their balance. For this reason, it's a good idea to wear safety harnesses on passage, and certainly at night, when every lifejacket should have an emergency light.

If someone goes overboard, follow these procedures.

- Cut power immediately, consistent with boat safety.
- Designate one crew member to keep the person overboard in sight at all times.
- Throw your life ring or Lifesling overboard immediately.
- Circle around and aim toward the victim, approaching from downwind and coming up alongside. Put your engine(s)

in neutral and turn it off if possible as soon as the person is alongside or close to the props. If necessary and conditions allow it, let the victim drift down to you to avoid any danger of prop injury. If possible, recover the victim over the stern or use a rope sling to bring him or her over the side. Take immediate steps to change the victim's clothing and get him or her warm.

SWAMPING

Swamping usually occurs over the stern or in very rough conditions, when a rogue wave comes aboard. If you are swamped, try to keep the boat moving to avoid engine damage. Turn on your electric pumps and bail out as much water as possible from the boat using buckets and other receptacles. If you are lying too low in the water to get water out of the boat, you will have to radio or use flares to obtain outside help. Whatever you do, stay with the boat if at all possible.

If you are swamped in the breakers, turn off your engines to avoid getting sand in the intake. You will probably have to bail her on the beach and then confront the problem of refloating her.

The danger of swamping can be minimized by careful driving and monitoring of weather forecasts.

COMPLETE ENGINE FAILURE

Short of swamping, the most common cause of a complete outboard shutdown is fuel-filter blockage. If this happens, try connecting one of your spare fuel tanks to the engine, bypassing the main filter. If it starts, then you have located your problem. Always ship out with a spare filter and the wrench for changing it so you can make quick repairs. Directly upon reaching port, or in open water if you must, change the filter and your engine should start again. You may have to fill the element to prevent the engine from sucking in air.

Another suggestion: attach your kicker to the alternative fuel tank and start it to keep the boat moving while you fix the filter. You'll certainly be more comfortable.

If you change your plugs regularly and carry out the manufacturer's recommended servicing, you should rarely encounter serious engine problems.

Most passages are pleasure-filled and uneventful; however, you must be mentally and physically prepared for the nautical equivalent of a bad-hair day. Believe me, they happen, and very often just when you are least expecting them.

See you on the bay!

Region 1

GOLDEN GATE TO POINT CONCEPTION

After doubling Point Piños we bore up,
set studding sails alow and aloft, and
were sailing off at the rate of eight or
nine knots, promising to traverse in
twenty-four hours the distance which
we were nearly three weeks in
traversing on the passage up.

RICHARD HENRY DANA
Two Years before the Mast

GOLDEN GATE
TO SAN SIMEON BAY

GOLDEN GATE

The Golden Gate is the northern limit of the area covered by this book, so the discussion is confined to basic information about the approach and the transit of the Gate. Inside is a sailor's paradise. You can spend weeks exploring its well-charted and sheltered waters, or enjoy the myriad channels of the San Joaquin and Sacramento Rivers of the Delta. For information on San Francisco Bay marinas and anchorages, see *San Francisco Bay: Boating Guide* by Brian M. Fagan (Caractacus Corporation, Santa Barbara, 1998), and *Cruising Guide to San Francisco Bay* by Bob and Carolyn Mehaffy (Paradise Cay Publications, Arcata, 1996).

Sea Breeze and Fog in the Bay. San Francisco Bay is a meteorological world unto its own, where conditions change rapidly and are often unlike those outside the Golden Gate. The novelist Mark Twain

Golden Gate Bridge.

was not taken with Bay weather: "Even the kindly climate is sometimes pleasanter when read about than personally experienced, for a lovely cloudless day wears out its welcome by and by." Unlike sailors, he complained of the summer winds, and thought of falling on his knees and begging for rain, calling the winters something between spring and summer. Twain was right on one point: San Francisco Bay weather is unique. But anyone sailing regularly in these fascinating waters soon develops their own weather portents and local lore.

You will find an excellent narrative account of San Francisco weather at www.ggweather.com/sf/narrative.html. Detailed forecasts are available at www.nws.mbay.net/marine.html.

For days on end, the onshore wind blows through the Golden Gate and through gaps in the coastal mountains. The Pacific High pushes air toward the coast. Meanwhile, the interior heats up, causing lower pressure over the land. The sea breeze persists over the Bay between March and October, and especially during the summer months, when it is as regular as a trade wind. These conditions cause a strong and weak sea breeze. Intense heating of the land causes the natural inland flow of the winds to increase through the day. The onshore winds decrease when the land cools in the evening and overnight. A layer of gray stratus clouds persists all day, keeping the sea breeze low. The extent that the sea breeze penetrates inland depends on the thickness of the marine layer, where fog and stratus clouds may form. The marine layer is usually about 1,300 feet thick and will persist unless the land heats up to destroy the inversion (see the Weather and Wind section, pages 26–31). Thus, the thicker the marine layer, the farther inland the sea breeze will travel. When the marine layer is only about 800 feet thick or less, fog and stratus clouds will not extend into

the Bay much farther than the Golden Gate. A thick layer causes fog and stratus clouds to mantle the entire Bay, and sometimes covers the skies as far inland as Sacramento.

The summer sea breeze can achieve considerable velocities, especially through the Golden Gate—where 30-knot winds are common—flowing inland as far as the San Mateo Bridge and into San Pablo Bay as the day wears on. Typically, more sheltered locales like Sausalito enjoy less wind. Mornings are quiet, often flat calm. The sea breeze fills in about 1000, rising steadily to a peak around 1700, then decreasing gradually toward sunset. The sea breeze seems to blow in cycles of about a week to ten days, blowing more than 30 knots for several days, then lessening for some time before the cycle begins again. The prevailing sea breeze tends to die down toward sunset, but sometimes persists through much of the night—in some places averaging 3 to 10 knots or more.

Local experts predict the strength of the afternoon sea breeze with some assurance by observing pressure gradients, the position of the high, and the strength of the winds blowing offshore at Point Bonita and Pillar Point at the entrance to the Golden Gate. Light winds at those locations indicate the sea breeze will fill in later than usual because the onshore flow will take time to overcome the gentle downslope winds of the night hours.

Sea, or advection, fog forms at sea, then flows into the Bay through convenient gaps. If it were not for the coastal ranges, San Francisco would be much foggier. According to the experts, advection fog hangs over the Golden Gate about 16 percent of the time during the summer and fall.

The coastal fogbank off the California coast approaches or retreats from the shore as the Pacific High shifts position and the strength of the coastal current waxes and wanes. Warm Pacific winds are cooled by the cold water upwelling to the surface. They cool rapidly and rush through the convenient gap of the Golden Gate like a giant air conditioner, flowing fog over the Bay and sometimes far inland. The variations in this natural air conditioner determine fog and wind conditions inside the Gate. Strong wind and an intense Pacific High cool the land so much over a period of days that the inversion collapses. The fog retreats, the wind drops, and the westerlies are light on the Bay. However, as the central valley heats, pressure falls inland so the inversion slowly reforms. The fog reappears and another cycle of strengthening winds begins. For days on end, too, the Pacific High weakens and wind circulations are slow offshore. Grayness covers San Francisco day after day because the wind and fog are never sufficient to cool the valley and cause marked cycles in the weather pattern.

By closely watching fog and wind patterns relative to local geography, you can soon learn to predict weather trends with some accuracy. For example, a flood tide brings cool water from offshore into the Bay. Sometimes the flood brings a dense blanket of white fog hugging the surface and reducing local visibility near the Golden Gate to almost zero. Foghorns blowing in the approaches give the only warning of a potential whiteout.

Radiation fogs occur in the Bay area from late fall through early spring. They occur when the surface of the land cools rapidly during clear, cold nights—especially during periods when high pressure settles over the Bay region and Central California. Then skies are clear, winds are light. When cool air flows lightly over the waters of the Bay, radiation fog may form, soon dispersing in the morning.

The sea breeze moderates as the Pacific High weakens in October and November. San Francisco sometimes broils under intense heat waves resulting from high pressure building over the interior. Then comes winter with gentler breezes, except when storm systems pass between December and March. Winter winds in San Francisco Bay usually average about 8 knots, a far cry from the boisterous winds of summer. Spring and summer are the seasons to cruise the Bay, when you can fully enjoy its reliable winds and expect 20- to 30-knot breezes every day.

Tides and Currents. The currents and tidal streams through the Golden Gate require careful attention in any weather. Start with the NOAA tide tables and current charts, which are tidal predictions compiled from data from past observations, as well as multidimensional calculations based on changes in the position of the sun and moon. They are remarkably accurate along the open coast, within 30 to 45 minutes or so, which is remarkable given the many variables that operate on local tidal streams. The predictions are based on experience of local factors in the Bay area, with its complicated pressure and wind changes and water discharging from at least sixteen rivers.

When using the tide tables, you will find two high and two low water times and level readings for each day. San Francisco Bay has semidiurnal tides, with a mean tidal range of 4 feet at the Golden Gate. The equinoctial spring tide range is about 9 feet. The falling (ebb) tide flows out of the Gate, the rising (flood) tide into the Bay. The young flood flows through the narrows, overcoming the weakening resistance of the ebb.

The tidal streams through the Golden Gate are of paramount importance to the visitor. The mean rise of the tide is about 5 feet at the entrance to San Francisco Bay. High and low tides occur about 1½ hours later at the S end of the Bay, with a mean rise about 2.5 feet higher than in the Golden Gate. It takes about 8 hours for high water to pass from the Gate up the Delta to Sacramento on the Sacramento River, the mean rise being about 2.6 feet.

Entering the Golden Gate, the young flood tide crosses the San Francisco Bar and converges toward the entrance. You will encounter it earlier off Points Bonita and Lobos than in the middle of the main shipping channel. You also may be set slightly N and W by a coastal eddy current off the entrance, but this varies in intensity with the time of year. The ebb sets WSW along the S edge of the Potatopatch, through the main shipping channel. Interestingly, it flows weakly through the Bonita Channel, the main small-craft access route to the Gate from the north. You may experience a flood

tide here while the ebb still flows strongly through the main shipping channel.

The Golden Gate is 2 miles wide between Points Bonita and Lobos—a narrow, deep-water defile with strong tidal streams that sluice in and out of the entrance. The strongest currents run on either side of the Golden Gate, close to Mile Rocks off Lime and Fort Points, the two termini of the bridge. Violent overfalls may be encountered in these areas, especially when a strong wind is blowing against the tide. Tidal streams change hourly and can attain a strength of 6.5 knots under the bridge. The times of maximum ebb and flow are listed in the *Tidal Current Atlas*. This excellent publication provides a conversion table, as well as hour-by-hour flowcharts that enable you to predict the direction and strength of the tides for any hour of the day. You can obtain daily and hourly predictions from the Web at www. nws.mbay.net/sunset.html.

The flood tide sets straight into the Golden Gate, but you must guard against lateral sets and strong overfalls. The ebb sets out of the entrance at velocities of up to 6.5 knots, flowing from inside the N side of the Bay toward Fort Point. On both ebb and flood, you will experience an eddy in the bight between Fort Point and Point Lobos. Stay clear of Mile Rocks and at least 0.5 mile off Point Bonita, where heavy overfalls can be experienced on the ebb. You also will find strong eddies near the bridge foundations.

The amount of snowmelt runoff can affect the velocity of streams at the Gate. Information can be obtained from the Web site mentioned previously.

Vessel Traffic Service. More than nine thousand large ships pass through the Golden Gate each year, navigating through narrow tidal waters. The San Francisco Vessel Traffic Service (VTS), the maritime equivalent of an airport traffic-control organization, is designed to prevent collisions and keep inbound and outbound ships well separated from one another. VTS controllers monitor all large-ship movements in the Golden Gate area with VHF and radar. Each vessel over 300 tons checks in before arrival and departure, and enters and leaves port under VTS control with a pilot aboard. Small craft are exempt from VTS, but you can monitor traffic on VHF channels 13 and 16.

Three traffic-separation schemes, from north, south, and west, converge on Buoy SF (Fl. W. 6 sec., 14 miles), 14 miles SW of the Golden Gate Bridge, bringing ships into a 6-mile-radius precautionary area surrounding the buoy. Here, vessels pick up pilots and alter course preparatory to entering or leaving the main shipping channel or one of the three separation schemes.

Passage through the Gate. Use the *Tidal Current Atlas* to coincide your passage with a favorable tide or with slack water, which normally occurs for a short period 3 hours after maximum flood and ebb. *Do not attempt passage when a strong wind is blowing against a full contrary tide—the resulting steep seas and overfalls can be very dangerous.*

Any approach to the Golden Gate involves crossing the San Francisco Bar, which extends in a broad arc some 5 miles offshore from the Golden Gate Bridge, from 3 miles S of Point Lobos, to about 0.5 mile off Point Bonita. The most dangerous part of the bar is Four Fathom Bank, a notorious area of vicious overfalls and shallows, known generically as the Potatopatch, where water depths are little more than 23 feet. Avoid this nasty place at all costs. The safest route across the bar is the main shipping channel, but even it can be hazardous to small craft in rough weather, especially when the wind blows against the ebb tide. Do not attempt to enter the Golden Gate in strong winds and high seas unless you have long experience of local conditions; it is better to wait for the weather to moderate.

Approach Landmarks from Seaward (Charts 18680 and 18649). The Golden Gate is readily identified from both north and south in clear weather by a series of useful approach landmarks, including the following.

The *Farallon Islands*, 23 miles W of the Golden Gate, is a group of rocky islets that extend NW for 7 miles. Southeast Farallon, the highest landmass, is 350 feet high.

Farallon light (Fl. W. 15 sec., 25 miles) is located here and is an invaluable guide at night. You can anchor in about 50 feet in Fisherman Bay just N of the light; however, this is decidedly a fair-weather berth. Stay well clear of Fanny Shoal 9.8 miles NW of the light. Noonday Rock, the shallowest part of the shoal, has only 13 feet. A red and black whistle buoy "N" (Qk. Fl.) lies 0.6 mile W of this danger.

Mount Tamalpais, 7 miles N of Point Bonita, the northern extremity of the entrance, can be seen from as far as 60 miles

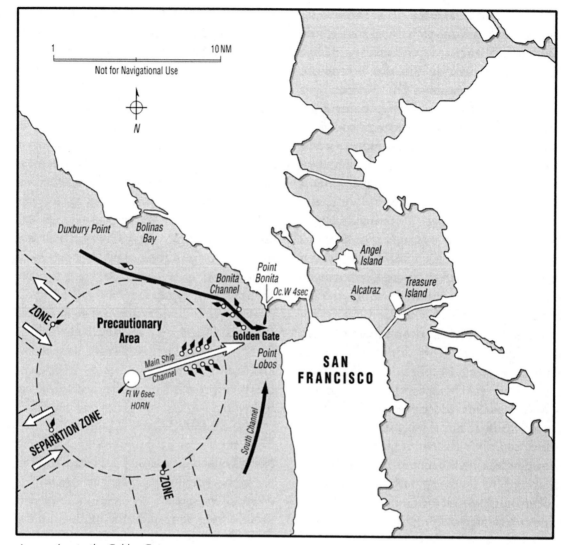

Approaches to the Golden Gate.

away. The three summits, the easternmost of which bears a lookout tower, are conspicuous. This densely vegetated mountain contrasts sharply with the surrounding countryside.

Point Bonita, a 100-foot-high black cliff, is surrounded by high slopes—the northern promontory of the Golden Gate. The white lighthouse (Oc. W. 4 sec., 18

miles) can be seen from a considerable distance in clear weather. A 100-foot-high black and white rock lies about a third of a mile to seaward.

Point Lobos, the southern promontory at the Golden Gate, is a rocky point with a water tank on its summit. The houses of San Francisco and Pacifica cover the shoreline S from Point Lobos. The white hospital buildings high above the Golden Gate are also conspicuous E of the point.

Point San Pedro, 11 miles S of the Golden Gate, is easily recognizable either northbound or southbound. San Pedro is the termination of the Montara Mountains inland.

The *russet-red piers of the Golden Gate Bridge* can be discerned above the city as you approach from S, but the entire bridge is only visible if you approach from W.

San Francisco Approach Lighted Horn Buoy (SF) lies 9 miles WSW of the Golden Gate entrance. This huge red buoy is 42 feet high and is lit (Fl. W. 6 sec., 14 miles).

The suburbs of San Francisco spill over the low hills and coastline between Point San Pedro and Point Lobos to the S of the Golden Gate and are a convenient landmark from some distance offshore, especially in clear weather.

Approach from W: The Main Shipping Channel.

Most coasting yachts approach the Golden Gate from the N or S, using either the Bonita or South Channel. However, the directions for a westerly approach follow:

Identify San Francisco Approach Lighted Horn Buoy (SF) (Lat. 37°45′ N, Long. 122°41.5′ W) 14 miles SW of the Golden Gate Bridge. A 6-mile-radius precautionary area surrounds Buoy SF, where three traffic-separation schemes converge. Stay outside the precautionary area and pass well inshore before picking up the buoyed main shipping channel.

You can use the main shipping channel (070 degrees toward Alcatraz light) if you follow the traffic flow. Stay to the right of the channel, just outside the four pairs of marker buoys. This way, you'll be clear of large ships, yet in deep water. You must always give way to such vessels in the main shipping channel.

Once inside the four pairs of marker buoys, shape your course through the Golden Gate Bridge, staying well clear of large vessels and of the strong eddies that swirl around the bridge foundations.

Approach from N: Drake's Bay and the Bonita Channel (Charts 18647 and 18649).

When bound for the Bay from the N, time your transit through the Bonita Channel and into the Golden Gate for the flood, which begins in the channel while the ebb is still flowing strongly in the narrows. With clever timing, you can carry the flood through the Bonita Channel, then into the Golden Gate. Close the rocky coast about 3 miles N of Point Bonita, the northern promontory of the Golden Gate. Identify the red channel buoys, which mark the offshore side of the Bonita Channel, and the green buoy "3" (Fl. G. 4 sec.), which marks Sears Rock, Centissima Reef, and the inshore edge of the Bonita Channel. Exercise caution: at its narrowest point, Bonita Channel is only 0.2 mile wide.

Point Bonita is a sharp black cliff, 300 feet high on its seaward face. Point Bonita light (Oc. 4 sec., 18 miles) lies 124 feet above the water on the S head of the point, with the tower and radar antenna of the San Francisco VTS conspicuous on the N head. Stay at least 0.5 mile off the point, altering course to enter the Golden Gate when the Golden Gate Bridge opens up ahead. A bell buoy with red and green bands (Fl. 2+1 R. 6 sec.) marks the southern end of the Bonita Channel and the edge of the Potatopatch Shoal.

Once inside the entrance, proceed under the Golden Gate Bridge, staying clear of the main shipping lanes. If you want to anchor in the entrance area, try Bonita Cove, close under Point Bonita, in about 36 feet. Here you are out of the strong currents that run in this vicinity, but watch for unpredictable eddies.

Caution. Use care when departing the Golden Gate and using the Bonita Channel on the ebb. Strong tidal sets can push you toward the rocks off Point Bonita. Sets toward the Potatopatch are also reported.

Approach from S: South Channel (Chart 18649). Most yachts approach the Golden Gate from the S, coasting past the shore of South San Francisco inside the traffic-separation zone, but well clear of off-lying coastal rocks. This approach is fine in calm and moderate weather, but it should not be attempted in rough conditions or when high swells are running.

Your approach begins N of Pillar Point, when you identify Point Montara with its light 70 feet above the water (Fl. W. 5 sec., 15 miles) (Lat. 37°32.2′ N, Long. 122°31.2′ W). Point San Pedro lies 2.5 miles N, a rocky promontory that is the seaward end of Montara Mountain, and is remarkable for a large, triple-sided rock with a white southern face projecting about a third of a mile from the point.

Stay at least a mile offshore past Point San Pedro, a rocky area with breaking swells that extends a mile N of the point.

Your next landmark is a conspicuous municipal fishing pier about 2.5 miles NE of Point San Pedro. Follow the coast northward toward Point Lobos and the Golden Gate, staying about 0.7 mile offshore. Be alert to day-fishing boats that operate close inshore in this area. This course brings you into South Channel, an unmarked passage with a least depth of 15 feet, which runs parallel to the peninsula shore with a width of 0.7 mile. South Channel is dangerous if any sea is running; under those circumstances, it is best to stay offshore 1.5 miles until you reach the main shipping channel.

Maintain a course through the middle of South Channel until Point Lobos is close ahead. A large water tank lies on its rocky summit. The Cliff House on the S side of the point and Seal Rocks close offshore are conspicuous. Give Seal Rocks a wide berth. Mile Rocks, 700 yards NW of the northern extremity of Point Lobos, are two 20-foot-high black rocks about 100 feet apart, and are marked by an orange and white horizontally banded tower on the outermost rock (Fl. 5 sec., 15 miles). Do not attempt to pass between Mile Rocks and the shore, where there is foul ground. Pass well outside Mile Rocks light and shape a course for Golden Gate Bridge ahead, staying clear of the main shipping lanes.

The Golden Gate Bridge has a 4,028-foot channel span between the two 740-foot-high supporting towers. A fixed green light with three fixed white lights in a vertical line above it marks the center of the span.

Entering the Golden Gate under sail ranks among the finest of California cruising experiences. The high rugged cliffs, the strong winds and fast-flowing currents, eddies of white and gray fog rolling in and out of the entrance—all combine to give this short passage a unique atmosphere. As you sail under the Golden Gate Bridge, you burst into another world of tall skyscrapers and wooded hills, of rollicking winds and ever-changing tides. Find yourself a comfortable home base, grab the *Tidal Current Tables*, and enjoy sailing the Bay—it's an addiction. San Francisco Bay is the place where you can enjoy boats large and small, cruise at 30 knots in a fast motor yacht, plane frantically in a Laser dinghy, or man the windward rail in a high-tech ocean racer. Enjoy the Bay in wind fair and foul, heavily reefed down, dodging rocks on a foggy day, rowing softly in a mahogany dinghy on a quiet morning. Journalist Kimball Livingston's *Sailing the Bay* is one of the immortal books of Western sailing.

POINT LOBOS TO PILLAR POINT

Chart 18680

The first stage of a passage from the San Francisco Bay area to Southern California takes you out of the Golden Gate through the South Channel, close under Point Lobos, then along the rocky and often-windy coast to Monterey Bay.

The coastal passage between the Golden Gate and Monterey Bay can be broken at Pillar Point Harbor (Half Moon Bay), which requires careful approach due to the reefs near the entrance. Otherwise, few outlying dangers present a hazard on passage. At an average speed of 5 knots, you need about 4 hours to sail from Point Lobos to Pillar Point Harbor at Half Moon Bay. It's about 9½ hours from there to Santa Cruz Harbor at the same average speed.

This stretch of coast is well lighted and easily navigated, even on the darkest night,

using the major lights on Point Lobos, Pillar Point, and Año Nuevo as signposts. Watch for fishing boats and coastal shipping vessels.

The South Channel passes close inshore of the San Francisco Bay Bar. Thereafter, stay about 0.75 mile off the low-lying coast with its long sandy beach, with the suburbs of South San Francisco and Pacifica to port. Identify 640-foot-high Point San Pedro and its conspicuous off-lying rocks, and shape a course to pass 1.5 miles offshore. Beyond Point San Pedro, the coast rises steeply and rocky as far as 60-foot-high Point Montara (Lat. 37°32.2′ N, Long. 122°31.2′ W), which exhibits a light (Fl. 5 sec., 15 miles). Identify red buoy 10A, which lies 1.5 miles off the point, and pass outside, avoiding the reefs and other obstructions off the promontory. With its bare trees, Montara Mountain makes a conspicuous landmark 2.5 miles inland. From the N, the summit looks like a flat-topped mountain with four hillocks. The same hillocks look less prominent from the S, where the mountain appears to be a long ridge. I have often used Montara Mountain as an offshore landmark for the Golden Gate.

Pillar Point, 18 miles S of the Golden Gate and 4 miles S of Montara Mountain, forms the southern end of a low ridge that extends S from Point Montara. The two white radardish antennas and a white building near the summit of the point can be identified from a long distance. They offer an excellent landmark, both north- and south-bound, and make a convenient point of reference for the approach to Pillar Point Harbor. At night, you can see the bright lights of the facility from miles away. Off-lying rocks extend

Pillar Point Harbor entrance, distant ½ mile.

over 30 yards S of the point. Half Moon Bay lies between Pillar and Miramontes Points.

Pillar Point Harbor
Chart 18682
Approach Buoy "Y": Lat. 37°28.9′ N,
  Long. 122°19.0′ W
Pillar Point Harbor, formed by two long stone breakwaters, is lit with two lights. You can see the light on the southern breakwater from 14 miles (Fl. W. 5 sec.).

Approach. From N. The approach from the N means a wide detour to avoid the ledges and rocks lying off Pillar Point. Pass outside buoy "1" (Fl. G. 2.5 sec.) SW of Pillar Point. Then shape your course for the approach bell buoy "Y" (Fl. G. 4 sec.). For extra safety, plan to turn inshore when this buoy is broad on the port bow. Once inshore of the buoy, steer for the entrance, which lies just W of N.

From S. Northbound, identify Pillar Point and its two radar antennas, then look for the two buoys that mark Southeast Reef. Southeast Reef extends over 2 miles SE of Pillar Point, has a least depth of 4 to 20 feet,

and a pinnacle rock awash at the extreme SE end at low-water springs. A gong buoy (Fl. G. 6 sec.) marks the S end of the reef; leave this to port, pass outside buoy "3," then steer for the entrance breakwaters.

The approach to Pillar Point Harbor can be tricky in thick weather and at night, when the buoys are sometimes difficult to identify. The area can be hazardous in strong SE winds. Even in calm weather, the reef-disturbed swells off the entrance can be bumpy.

The outer breakwaters angle out from Pillar Point and the mainland, the entrance trending NW between the two lighted ends. The outer harbor is congested with moorings, and the marina lies behind three breakwaters at the NE corner.

Berths. A marina protected by three breakwaters offers transient slips for yachts. The outer breakwater is marked by three lights with about 12 feet at the slips. Apply to the harbormaster's office near the pier for a space on an end tie or a mooring, if one is available. You can anchor in the outer harbor (12 to 20 feet, mud and

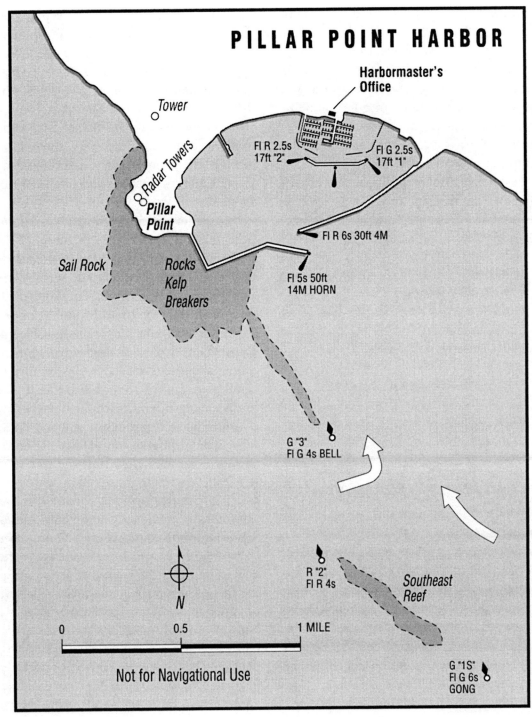

PILLAR POINT HARBOR

Harbormaster's
Office

Tower

Radar Towers

Pillar
Point

Fl R 2.5s
17ft "2"

Fl G 2.5s
17ft "1"

Fl R 6s 30ft 4M

Sail Rock

Rocks
Kelp
Breakers

Fl 5s 50ft
14M HORN

G "3"
Fl G 4s BELL

N

R "2"
Fl R 4s

Southeast
Reef

0   0.5   1 MILE

G "1S"
Fl G 6s
GONG

Not for Navigational Use

Pillar Point Harbor plan.

sand), but it can be congested because of moorings. The anchorage offers complete shelter, even in NW winds up to 45 knots. However, be careful to anchor clear of the permanent moorings that take up much of the space. A launching ramp lies immediately S of the marina, where the facilities are excellent—except that surge on the ramp can be a nuisance.

Facilities. Water and fuel can be obtained in the marina, and all other provisions are available within a short distance. There are limited repair facilities.

Contacts.
Pillar Point Marina,
No. 1 Johnson Pier: 650-726-5727

Harbormaster: 650-726-4723

Harbor Fuel Dock: 650-726-4419

www.smharbor.com/pillarpoint/
index.htm

PILLAR POINT TO SANTA CRUZ HARBOR

Chart 18680

The 46-mile passage between Half Moon Bay and Santa Cruz takes a full day. The coastline consists of high, often yellow bluffs; a short coastal plain; and low, tree-covered mountains. The scenery can be particularly attractive in the spring and early summer, when the coastal hills are heavy with green vegetation.

Immediately S of Half Moon Bay, the shoreline consists of low and flat tableland

for about 9 miles, marked by deep gullies. This tableland culminates in a prominent, whitish cliff more than 10 feet high. A pale yellow building with numerous antennas is a conspicuous landmark to the S. The cliffs now become more rugged as you approach Pescadero Point, the next headland along the coast. S of Pescadero, the reddish coastal cliffs form a near-straight line. Stay about 1.5 miles offshore here, well clear of the many off-lying rocks.

By this time, 115-foot-high Pigeon Point lighthouse (Lat. 37°10.9′ N, Long. 122° 23.6′ W) (Fl. 10 sec., 24 miles) will be clearly in sight, associated with white buildings with red roofs. The light is 20 miles S of Pillar Point and cannot be seen E of a line that joins the two points. Pigeon Point, named after a nineteenth-century clipper ship that wrecked in this vicinity, is a low promontory about 50 feet high that forms a ridge inland, with off-lying rocks.

Both Pigeon Point lighthouse and Point Año Nuevo make unmistakable landmarks. Año Nuevo, with its conspicuous sand dunes and famous elephant-seal rookeries, is 5 miles to the S. The distinctive skeletal tower and associated white houses leave no doubt about where you are. Pass at least 1.5 miles offshore, well outside the lighted buoy (Fl. R. 6 sec.), which lies S of the tower. Temporary anchorage may be obtained immediately S of Año Nuevo in a bight protected by the rocks and kelp extending SE from the point. Anchor in the smoothest water inshore, with the light bearing about 260 deg. M. You will find about 5 to 6 fathoms (sand). Año Nuevo anchorage is frequently used by fishing boats and provides a welcome respite when you are northbound against strong winds. However, a strong smell of bird droppings emanating from the rocks to windward can spoil your berth. (There are restrictions on landing due to the wildlife refuge here. The elephant-seal breeding season is from December through April; visit www.parks. ca.gov/DISTRICTS/bayarea/ansr228.htm for more information).

If you are southbound, the final moment of decision is Año Nuevo. A visit to Santa Cruz or Monterey takes you a considerable distance off the rhumb-line course to points farther S. If you decide to continue S, lay off a course of 142 degrees M, which takes you to a position about 3 miles W and offshore of Point Sur on the far side of Monterey Bay.

The 18-mile coastal passage to Santa Cruz Point is extremely pleasant with a commanding wind. Sail well inside the 20-fathom line, following the shoreline. However, there is often heavy kelp off the coast, so stay well off to avoid it. As the shore trends toward the SE, there are no significant off-lying dangers. The rock formations and colorful cliffs show up well in the afternoon sun. The steel tower and buildings of the Davenport cement works, which lies 9 miles S of Año Nuevo, can be seen from a considerable distance.

Santa Cruz Point light (Fl. W. 5 sec., 17 miles) is displayed from a 39-foot-high white lantern house on a square brick tower and brick building near the S extremity of the point. Shape your course to pass outside the lighted black and white whistle buoy "SC" [Mo(A) W] 1.1 miles SE of the light. Santa Cruz Harbor lies in the bight between Santa Cruz Point and its light and Soquel Point 2.5 miles E.

Monterey Bay forms a large bight, extending from Santa Cruz Point around to Point Piños. Much of this large bight is backed by long sandy beaches and sand dunes, and swept by strong summer NW winds. The so-called Monterey Wind Gap sucks onshore breezes and fog into the low terrain between the mountain barriers to the N and S of the bay. Monterey Bay can be a very windy place, where fogs persist for days. At the same time, the prevailing NW–WNW swells off the coast change direction to the W as they enter the bay. The long curved beaches at the back of the bay make for a very nasty lee shore indeed, even in typical summer conditions. Most sailing yachts stay well offshore and sail directly between Santa Cruz and Monterey. Moss Landing does offer shelter, but the entrance is dead to leeward and should not be attempted in strong winds or at night without prior experience.

The 528-foot smokestack at Moss Landing is visible from a long distance, providing a useful barometer for wind conditions. On summer mornings, the smoke plume blows offshore nearer the surface but onshore at higher elevations. By late morning, the smoke streams vertically, flowing inland as the afternoon wind strengthens.

Santa Cruz Harbor
Chart 18685
Approach Buoy: Lat. 36°56.3′ N, Long. 122°0.6′ W
Santa Cruz Harbor is a crowded but delightful haven with a narrow, artificial en-

trance that can be dangerous in SE conditions. The weather is pleasant here in summer, and the harbor has a very active sailing community.

Approach. From N: Identify Santa Cruz Point and buoy "SC." Santa Cruz municipal pier will come into view, extending 0.4 mile into the ocean with 26 feet at its outer end. The harbor lies 0.8 mile E of the pier. Once the pier is abeam, look for the harbor breakwaters and the roller coaster and casino, which are famous landmarks E of the town.

From S. Identify Santa Cruz Point light and Soquel Point, then steer for the roller coaster, visible from some distance offshore.

Two breakwaters protect the harbor, the longer lying to the W, where a light is displayed (Oc. G. 4 sec., 6 miles). The narrow harbor entrance has about 20 feet in the seaward end of the channel. Constant dredging has made the channel safe in the summer, but you must exercise caution in the winter.

Do not attempt entrance in strong SE winds or when high ground swells are running because extensive shoaling can develop between the breakwaters. If in doubt, contact the harbormaster's office on VHF channel 9, 12, or 16. The harbor authorities will guide you through the entrance on request.

Be careful about entering Santa Cruz Harbor at night without prior daytime experience, especially in foggy conditions.

A fixed bridge with an 18-foot clearance separates the upper and lower harbor basins.

Anchorage and Berths. Anchorage may be obtained on either side of the municipal pier in 30 feet (sand) with good shelter in

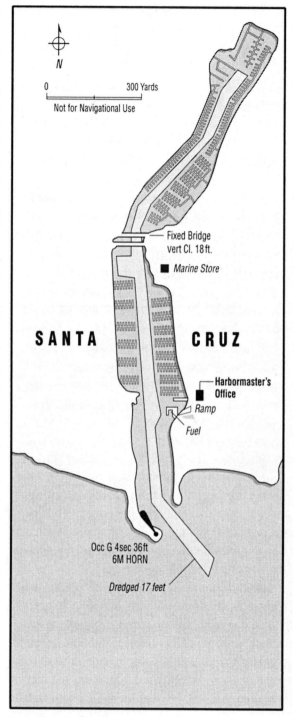

Santa Cruz Harbor plan.

Santa Cruz Harbor entrance, distant ½ mile.

northerly conditions, especially closer inshore. However, a heavy ground swell can sweep into the anchorage with strong NW winds. This berth is completely exposed to the S. Note that there are restrictions on approaching the pier. Small buoys mark the swimming areas.

Guest slips are available in Santa Cruz Harbor by applying to the harbormaster's office in the SE corner of the harbor or by calling on channel 16. The harbor is a very busy place, especially in high summer and during regattas. Berths are assigned on a first-come, first-served basis and you may be rafted up against other yachts. There is a launching ramp on the E side of the harbor near the entrance.

Facilities. Fuel, water, and marine supplies are available at the harbor, and full provisioning is within a short distance.

Contacts.
Port Director, 135 5th Ave.:
831-475-6161

An excellent Web site, including a virtual tour, is at
www.santacruzharbor.org/

SANTA CRUZ HARBOR TO MOSS LANDING

Chart 18685

You will have deep water close inshore all the way from Point Soquel to Moss Landing, with 60 feet at 0.75 mile offshore. Nevertheless, exercise caution along this coast. Fog can be very thick in the summer months, especially in the early morning hours. Heavy swells can be experienced along the shoreline, making it difficult to claw to windward. A Naval Operating Area lies NW of Moss Landing. Regulations are listed in the *U.S. Coast Pilot*.

Moss Landing
Chart 18685
Approach Buoy: Lat. 36°47.9′ N, Long. 121°48.1′ W

Moss Landing is a small fishing harbor overshadowed by a vast generating plant. Elkhorn Slough behind the harbor is a nature reserve and a paradise for birdwatchers.

Approach. From both N and S: Moss Landing is easy to identify from the 528-foot-high twin smokestacks of the power plant that operates behind the harbor. For working purposes, the smokestacks can be used to identify the general position of the harbor entrance until you are close enough inshore to identify the stone breakwaters and approach buoy. Two conspicuous radio masts mark Palm Beach, 4 miles N of Moss Landing.

Under strong NW conditions, approach the entrance from upwind to counteract any leeward set below the harbor entrance.

A mooring and fueling facility for deep-draft vessels is located 0.8 mile NW of the harbor entrance, with its limits marked by white buoys. A buoy in the center of the demarcated area marks the fuel pipeline; stay well clear of this vicinity.

Entrance by day or night is straightforward except in strong onshore winds. Seas can be very confused in the approach, especially in SE conditions or after a local wind shift. Exercise caution under these circumstances. Identify the red and white

approach buoy (Fl. W. 5 sec.) and stay seaward of it until the northern stone breakwater (Fl. G. 4 sec., 3 miles) is clearly in sight. The S side of the entrance has a shorter breakwater (Oc. R. 4 sec., 8 miles). A private buoy 250 yards SW of the south jetty light marks an area of violent water discharge from the power plant; stay clear of this danger.

The entrance channel carries about 15 feet, with the centerline marked by leading marks on a line of 052 deg. T at the back of the turning basin. These marks are lighted and visible from about 8 miles out. The concrete bridge carrying Highway 1 across Elkhorn Slough behind the harbor is conspicuous from seaward. Overfalls on an ebbing spring tide can make the entrance or exit bumpy.

When traversing the entrance channel, keep to the N side in strong NW winds (if traffic permits) to avoid any possible leeward set.

Once in the turning basin, visitors should turn to starboard and follow the inner channel into the marina area. A shallower channel to port with about 8.5 feet and marked with private buoys leads to the Elkhorn Yacht Club and a small-boat-launching ramp. Do not attempt this by night without local knowledge and sound carefully by day. There is a 5 mph speed limit in the harbor.

Berths. Visitors' berths are assigned by the harbormaster's office at the head of the inner channel, on the port side. You can visit in person or call on VHF channel 16. Berths must be vacated by 0900 on the day of departure and all visitors are warned

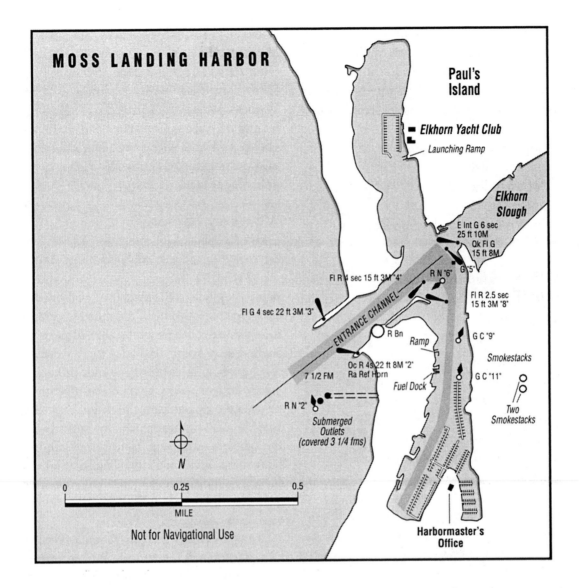

MOSS LANDING HARBOR

Paul's Island

Elkhorn Yacht Club

Launching Ramp

Elkhorn Slough

E Int G 6 sec 25 ft 10M
Qk Fl G 15 ft 8M

Fl R 4 sec 15 ft 3M "4"

R N "6"

G "5"

Fl R 2.5 sec 15 ft 3M "8"

Fl G 4 sec 22 ft 3M "3"

ENTRANCE CHANNEL

R Bn

Ramp

G C "9"

Smokestacks

7 1/2 FM

Oc R 4s 22 ft 8M "2"
Ra Ref Horn

Fuel Dock

G C "11"

Two Smokestacks

R N "2"

Submerged Outlets (covered 3 1/4 fms)

N

0   0.25   0.5

MILE

Not for Navigational Use

Harbormaster's Office

that they may have to relocate on a day-by-day basis.

Elkhorn Yacht Club is very friendly and welcomes visitors to its two guest slips at the end of the docks. Sea otters often play around the boats, while pelicans and sea lions sun themselves on the nearby sand spit. The launching ramp is immediately S,

with excellent facilities. A second ramp without facilities is in the main harbor.

Facilities. Moss Landing has an excellent fuel dock, where water can be obtained. Provisions can be purchased near the harbor, showers are available, and you can pump out your holding tank at a facility in front of the harbormaster's office. Marine mechanics that service the many fishing boats in the harbor are also available.

A dinghy excursion into Elkhorn Slough Ecological Reserve is recommended, but first check local restrictions and regulations.

Contacts.
Harbormaster's Office
7881 Sandholt Rd.
831-633-2461
www.mosslandingharbor.dst.ca.us

MOSS LANDING TO POINT PIÑOS

Chart 18685

Sand dunes and yellow beaches mark the featureless, low-lying coast between Moss Landing and Monterey Harbor. Stay outside the 10-fathom line when making passage close inshore. The 18-foot line is about 150 yards offshore, so you have little warning of shallow water when sailing here at night.

The coastline rises and becomes more rugged at Monterey and NW to Point Piños. George Davidson described it as "rugged, composed of granite, and covered with a heavy growth of fir"—to which one now adds urban sprawl because the coastline is heavily developed. Monterey is a bustling tourist resort, fishing harbor, and foreign-language center. Davidson recorded how small Portuguese whaling boats operated in Monterey Bay from May to November; more than 16,000 gallons of whale oil came from those hunting operations in one year alone.

Point Piños, which marks the S end of Monterey Bay, is low and rocky with off-lying rocks about 0.3 mile offshore. Point Piños light (Lat. 36°38′ N, Long. 121°56′ W) (Oc. W. 4 sec., 17 miles) is exhibited from a 43-foot white tower and is 89 feet above sea level. When rounding the point, pass outside the bell buoy (Fl. R. 6 sec.) 0.7 mile off the land.

Monterey Harbor
Chart 18865
Entrance Buoy: Lat. 36°36.50′ N, Long. 121°53.34′ W

Monterey was a favorite port of call for early Spanish ships and for nineteenth-century steamers, which anchored off the town sheltered by Point Piños. In foggy weather, an approaching mail ship would fire a gun when off the point, listen carefully for an answering report from the town, and then fumble her way to anchor by monitoring the gunfire—a far cry from today's sophisticated navigational aids. Today, the busy fishing harbor offers shelter in any weather and can be approached in all but the strongest winds.

Approach. *From N:* When offshore, identify Point Piños and the higher ground with buildings immediately W of Monterey. The harbor lies 3.0 miles SE of Point Piños. Nearing shore, identify the two radio towers close inshore at the marina, 6.5 miles NE of the harbor. Approaching land, you will see high-rise hotel buildings and the smokestack and buildings of the Monterey Aquarium just SW of the harbor entrance.

Next, pick up lighted bell buoy "4"

0.5 mile off Point Cabrillo. The long rock breakwater of Monterey Harbor (sometimes called Coast Guard Pier) lies 1.0 mile farther SE. A light (Oc. R. 4 sec., 7 miles) is exhibited at the piling at the end of the breakwater, where a horn sounds in foggy conditions.

From S: Round Point Piños, passing outside the off-lying bell buoy; then shape a course SE along the shore, staying 0.75 mile off the land until buoy "4" is identified. The Monterey Aquarium with its smokestack just W of the harbor will be conspicuous to starboard. Stay well clear of the kelp and off-lying rocks.

The harbor entrance lies between the

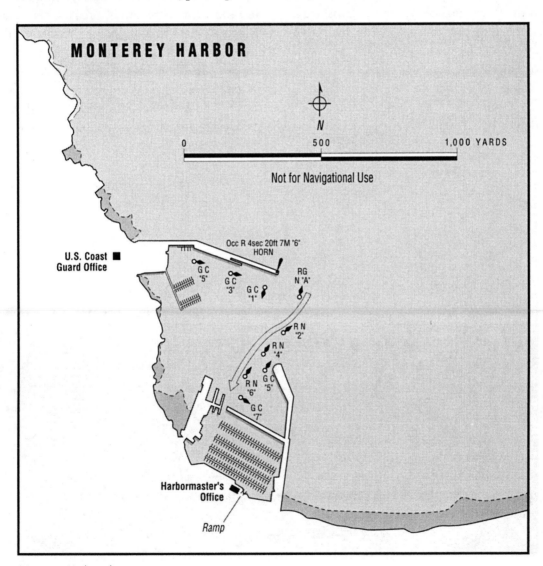

MONTEREY HARBOR

N

0   500   1,000 YARDS

Not for Navigational Use

U.S. Coast Guard Office

Occ R 4sec 20ft 7M '6' HORN

G C "5"

G C "3"

G C "1"

RG N "A"

R N "2"

R N "4"

R N "6"

G C "5"

G C "7"

Harbormaster's Office

Ramp

Monterey Harbor plan.

main breakwater and Municipal Wharf 2, which forms the eastern boundary of the harbor. Enter midway between the pier and breakwater, staying alert to fishing boats and other local traffic.

A narrow entrance between Municipal Pier 1 (Fisherman's Wharf) and a seawall extending out from Municipal Pier 2 leads to the inner harbor where the slips are located. Exercise caution when using this narrow defile, sound your horn, and watch for exiting boats.

Anchorage and Berths. Anchorage may be obtained S of the breakwater off Del Monte Beach in 30 feet or so (sand and clay), but this is an uncomfortable berth.

You can also anchor E of Municipal Pier 2 in similar holding ground, but watch your depth-meter for shelving.

Visitors' slips are located at Pier H, inside the seawall. Call the harbormaster on VHF channel 16 before entering the harbor. The Monterey Municipal Marina is the usual visitor berth. Some people prefer to take a transient slip in Breakwater Cove Marina closer to Fisherman's Wharf, but a reservation is recommended. There are three boat-launching ramps.

Facilities. A self-service laundry, fuel, water, and provisions are readily available, as are marine supplies and mechanical or yacht service. A small trolley is available

Monterey Harbor approach, distant ½ mile.

for transportation to town, which is a short walk from the harbor.

Contacts.
Harbormaster: 408-646-3950 or www.monterey.org/harbor/

Breakwater Cove Marina, 32 Cannery Row: 408-383-7857

BIG SUR COAST

Charts 18686, 18700

Point Piños to Point Sur
Chart 18686

The low-lying coastline between Point Piños and Pinnacle Point is densely populated, with patches of dense woods. Pacific Grove, Pebble Beach Golf Course, and Carmel extend more or less continuously along the shore. The gray buildings of the state-run Asilomar Conference Center are conspicuous. On a clear night, the lights of Carmel and Pacific Grove can be seen from a long distance offshore. To avoid off-lying rocks, stay at least 1 mile offshore along this stretch of coast.

Carmel Bay lies between steep, low-lying Cypress Point and Pinnacle Point 2.8 miles S. It forms an open bight, where heavy swells can roll in, especially in the winter. Water depths are extreme here due to Carmel Canyon in the SE corner of the bay, with 50 fathoms near the beach in places. Stay well clear of Carmel Beach to avoid swell and off-lying rocks.

Anchorage. Anchorage may be obtained in northerly conditions in Pebble Beach Cove to the W and Stillwater Cove to the E, both on the N shore of Carmel Bay. Anchor in 9 to 30 feet (rock and gravel), avoiding kelp beds wherever possible. Both bays offer quiet berths in moderate summer conditions, but do not enter them at night on a first visit because caution is required in the approaches. According to several recent visitors, Stillwater Cove is now so choked with kelp that holding is affected. Also, moorings in the anchorage area off the Pebble Beach pier leave little space for visitors to anchor.

Whaler's Cove, in the SE corner of Carmel Bay, offers shelter in S conditions, but it is in the Point Lobos State Ecological Reserve. Do not anchor there.

Pinnacle Point is the outer point of Point Lobos, a jagged headland about 100 feet high. Sea otters and sea lions are often seen in this vicinity. Give the rocks a berth of at least a mile. Forming a convenient landmark for finding Whaler's Cove, 200-foot Whaler's Knoll is conspicuous 0.5 mile ESE of the point.

From Pinnacle Point, the coastline becomes bold and rocky, and increasingly steep as you approach Point Sur. Several headlands project from the shoreline, but pass at least a mile offshore and shape your course to pass clear of Point Sur. Ventura Rocks are two prominent outcrops about 0.6 mile offshore, 2.2 miles N of Point Sur. The conical and northernmost rock makes an excellent landmark when sailing S because it stands out against the sand bluff N of Point Sur. When traversing this stretch of coast, Highway 1 will be your companion. At night, the headlights of passing cars flash continually as they speed along the last length of relatively straight highway before Big Sur.

Point Sur stands out from the coast at a great distance, making intermediate landmarks unimportant except when close inshore. The *U.S. Coast Pilot* describes it admirably: "A black rocky butte 361 feet high with low sand dunes extending E from it for over 0.5 mile. From N or S, it looks like an island and in clear weather is visible about 25 miles." Point Sur, 121 miles NW of Point Arguello and 96 miles SSE of the Golden Gate, is a major landmark by any standard, with a lighthouse 250 feet above the water (Lat. 36°18.4′ N, Long. 121°54.0′ W) (Fl. W. 15 sec., 25 miles). Give the point a wide berth because winds can be strong and seas confused in this vicinity. Most yachts on passage pass about 2 miles offshore, sometimes farther, shaping their course to pass within sighting distance of Point Piedras Blancas, 49 miles S, when bound for Morro Bay or San Simeon Bay.

Northbound, try to time your passage around Point Sur for the night or early morning hours, when winds are calm or of lower velocity. If necessary, take shelter in Pfeiffer Point Anchorage, 6.9 miles S, until the wind drops down.

As you pass Point Sur, remember the Navy dirigible USS *Macon*, the largest humanly made object ever to fly. The 785-foot-long airship was held aloft by 6.5 million cubic feet of helium. On February 12, 1935, she was gliding north 3 miles off Point Sur when a sudden gust shattered her upper fin. The *Macon* suffered structural failure, lost lift, and settled tail-first into the Pacific. In 1990, a Navy submersible lo-

Point Sur on a hazy day; typical summer afternoon conditions for this coast.

cated the wreck of the *Macon* in 1,450 feet of water. The corroded girders of the bow and forward deck lie on the bottom, as well as the control car, where chairs and chart tables can still be seen. Four "hook-on" Sparrowhawk F9C2 fighter planes went down with the *Macon*. Their silt-covered remains are in surprisingly good condition, although they would probably fall apart if an attempt were made to lift them.

Big Sur Coast Passage. A passage along this stretch of coast ranks among the most spectacular for scenery anywhere in the world. The shoreline is often swept by gale-force winds and high ocean swells, especially in the winter, which makes for dangerous off-lying waters. Do not linger along the Big Sur coast except on the calmest of days, when a small boat with a powerful engine can explore myriad small coves and deep-water nooks.

Northbound vessels tend to keep close to the land, making landfall on major headlands along the way. This strategy allows you to take advantage of nearby refuge anchorages if the wind pipes up on the nose.

Maintain an accurate DR plot and GPS watch at night to monitor progress and to allow estimates of when Point Sur light will be sighted. I try to leave San Simeon Bay as the afternoon wind dies down so that I am close to if not beyond Point Sur by morning. If you meet headwinds up the coast, you can duck into a refuge anchorage like Pfeiffer Point or Carmel, and then slip on around to Monterey or across Monterey Bay in the evening. A nonstop passage from the Piedras Blancas area to Santa Cruz and points beyond is entirely possible when a ten-day fog cycle hangs over the coast (I have timed my last three northbound passages for such conditions and had flat calm most of the way.) For planning purposes, however, I recommend breaking up the trip into shorter segments in your mind, so you have alternatives available if you need them.

Southbound sailing yachts usually find themselves with a dead run, often before a considerable swell. Many skippers stay well offshore and set a clear course; others tack downwind, to minimize the danger of jibing and to stay in touch with the land. A course about 5 miles offshore often leaves you with the tops of the mountains clear while lower elevations remain in fog. Southbound, I always try to be well past Point Sur as the midday wind fills in from astern. You then enjoy a fast passage with spectacular scenery, reaching San Simeon Bay by sunset. If bound farther afield, I stay well offshore to avoid the thick fogbanks that sometimes form off Piedras Blancas and Morro Bay. A typical summer afternoon brings a healthy NW wind and surprisingly steep wind waves, so you enjoy a boisterous roller-coaster ride, often under reefed main and jib. Even if the wind is blowing, you can encounter areas of restricted visibility, so watch for the fishing boats that operate in all weather within the 5-mile zone.

Point Sur to Pfeiffer Point Anchorage
Chart 18700

Immediately S of Point Sur, stay at least 2 miles offshore to avoid off-lying rocks along much of the 6 miles of coastline between the headland and Pfeiffer Point, the next major landmark. Pfeiffer Point, a bold cape at the seaward end of a 2,000-foot-high ridge 1.5 miles NE of Point Sur, is light colored when viewed from the S. From N, the pointed summit stands out from a considerable distance. A conspicuous, 172-foot-high pinnacle rock marks Cooper Point, 1.5 miles NW of Pfeiffer Point. The first time I came south, this rock was a useful landmark for identifying Pfeiffer Point.

Anchorage. Many fishing boats use an anchorage 0.9 mile ESE of Pfeiffer Point (Lat. 36°14.0′ N, Long. 121°48.7′ W). This convenient bight offers considerable shelter in summer N and NW conditions, making it an ideal stopping point when seeking respite from strong headwinds. The approach is straightforward. Identify Pfeiffer Point, then shape a course to head inshore into the shelter of the land. Select an anchoring place in about 40 to 50 feet (sand), setting your anchor clear of the kelp beds. This temporary anchorage offers some shelter in NW conditions, but the motion can be severe if the swell is up. Shore access is limited and there are no facilities.

102 *Pfeiffer Point to Lopez Point Refuge Anchorage*

You now pass the most spectacular section of the Big Sur coast, where high mountains rise precipitously from the shore. The coastline forms a series of shallow bights, offering no shelter to small craft. Only fishing boats move inshore along these 17.5 miles. The cuttings and bridges of Highway 1 are visible from seaward, as are the headlights of occasional cars at night.

Several mountain peaks form good landmarks, notably Junipero Serra Peak, which is 10 miles NE of Lopez Point and can be identified by the pine trees growing on and near its summit.

Point Lopez is a 100-foot-high tableland feature marked by 51-foot-high Lopez Rock, which has a prominent cleft in the middle, lying 0.3 mile off. To avoid an off-lying shoal SW of the promontory, give Lopez Point a berth of at least 0.75 mile.

Anchorage. Anchorage may be obtained in an open roadstead in the lee of Point Lopez. The best berths lie about a mile SE of the point inside the kelp bed in about 60 feet (sand). (Depths are substantial all along the Big Sur coast; lay plenty of scope.) Watch for a rock (5 feet) in the kelp 0.5 mile SE of the point. This refuge anchorage offers some shelter in NW conditions, but the motion can be severe if there is any strength in the wind or the swell is up.

Point Lopez to San Simeon Bay

From Point Lopez 9.5 miles to Cape San Martin, the coast continues to be rugged, forming an open bight. While most small craft stay well offshore, a distance of 1.0 mile will keep you clear of all dangers. Particularly beware of Tide Rock, 4 miles N of Cape San Martin. People who have passed close to it in calm weather say it leaves little disturbance on the surface in these conditions.

The three San Martin Rocks, which extend 0.5 mile offshore, readily identify Cape San Martin, a precipitous headland. The innermost rock is white, 144 feet high, and stands out from S; a cone rock and a triangular-shaped rock comprise the other two. Willow Creek bridge, 0.3 mile N of the Cape, makes a prominent sight from offshore.

Cape San Martin and Piedras Blancas are separated by 16 miles, with the topography changing dramatically at Ragged Point, the 10-mile mark. The rugged cliffs fall away, as the coastline becomes low bluffs and rolling, treeless hills. Few notable landmarks appear before Ragged Point; easily recognized, it is the first point S of the deep San Carpoforo Valley. I always stay some distance off the coast here; numerous kelp-fringed rocks extend offshore.

You can anchor SE of La Cruz Rock, 3 miles NNW of Piedras Blancas, a berth that is said to be safe in strong NW winds; however, I have no first-hand experience of this spot.

Piedras Blancas is a low, rocky point that projects out about 0.5 mile from the general coastline. Two large rocks lie about 500 yards offshore and about 0.8 mile E of the promontory. George Davidson said: "Nothing else like them is found on this part of the coast." He's right! Piedras Blancas light, with its 74-foot white conical

Piedras Blancas lighthouse from the S, distant 1½ miles.

tower, is 142 feet above sea level (Lat. 35°39.9′ N, Long. 121°17.1′ W) (Fl. 10 sec., 25 miles). It is visible from a long distance both day and night.

Anchorage. Most passagemaking yachts pass at least a mile offshore, then head for either San Simeon Bay or Morro Bay Harbor. However, you can anchor under the lee of Piedras Blancas in about 25 feet (sand) with the lighthouse bearing about due W, distant about 0.2 mile. The berth offers moderate shelter in NW winds.

A 5-mile low-lying coast leads to tree-covered San Simeon Point, which projects SE. The dark trees, visible from a considerable distance, offer an excellent landmark for the anchorage tucked behind the point. At night, the lights of Hearst Castle can be seen 2.7 miles NE from far offshore.

San Simeon Bay
Chart 18700
Bell Buoy: Lat. 35°37.8′ N, Long. 121°11.4′ W

This pleasant cove makes an excellent stopping point both when waiting for suitable conditions to traverse the Big Sur coast and for visiting Hearst Castle. San Simeon Point offers good shelter in NW conditions, although swells can sometimes come around into the anchorage. The cove becomes a suicidal lee shore in strong SE winds.

Approach. *From N:* Identify the dark patch of trees on San Simeon Point, then the bell buoy (Fl. W. 6 sec.) 0.4 mile SE of the point. Pass outside the buoy and shape a course for the middle of the cove, well clear of kelp and any moorings.

From S: The red-roofed buildings and pier may be more obvious than the dark trees of Point San Simeon. You will also see Hearst Castle high on the hill and the visitor's center near sea level inshore. Steer for the middle of the cove, leaving the bell buoy well to port.

Due to extensive kelp and the lack of approach lights, arriving at night is not recommended without local knowledge.

Anchorage. There is anchorage in the center of the bay, in 30 feet (hard sand). Take careful account of the surge when settling on a berth. Extensive kelp grows outside and sometimes inside the anchorage, so set your anchor accordingly.

Landing and Facilities. Land at one of the ladders on the pier, but watch for surge on windy days. Do not leave your dinghy at the pier—beach it. This is a wet landing in any swell, so tend to land toward the W at the head of the Bay, although this does not guarantee a dry arrival.

San Simeon Bay is a state park, with restrooms and a small concession ashore. The main attraction is Hearst Castle. The

San Simeon Bay from the SE, distant 1 mile.

Jason Hailey

modern visitor's center is a short walk on the other side of Highway 1. Throughout the year, you can take conducted tours of parts of the 168-room castle. Call the visitor's center (800-444-4445) for information on tours, hours, and shuttle buses. Hearst Castle is a unique experience and should not be missed, even by the most ardent socialist.

From San Simeon Bay, you can enjoy an easy day's sail to Morro Bay or embark on a more ambitious passage to Point Conception and Southern California.

MORRO BAY TO POINT CONCEPTION AND COJO ANCHORAGE

Point Conception is the most prominent and interesting feature between San Francisco and the peninsula of Lower California. It has very justly and appropriately been termed the "Cape Horn" and the "Hatteras" of the Pacific, on account of the heavy northwesterlies that are met here.

George Davidson, *Directory for the Pacific Coast*

GEORGE DAVIDSON SURVEYED Point Conception in 1853. He spent endless days on the windswept headland, remarking with some feeling that "once seen it will never be forgotten." By the same token, a rough-weather passage around this headland is a memorable experience. The sailing directions in this section describe the coastline between San Simeon Bay and this most famous of Pacific capes. Included are strategies for rounding Point Conception.

SAN SIMEON BAY TO MORRO BAY

Charts 18700 and 18703
San Simeon Bay is a popular jumping-off point for a passage past Point Conception. However, a visit to Morro Bay is strongly recommended, especially for those in need of fuel and provisions.

From San Simeon, the coast runs nearly straight in a SE direction 14 miles to Point Estero, where the mountains recede from the coast, leaving rolling topography at a low elevation. Now good cattle country, Davidson observed "wild oats growing here over six feet high—not one or two stalks, but in acres." Today, Highway 1 and the San Simeon motel sprawl run behind the cliff, where thick groves of pine trees are scattered on higher ground. Cambria Village lies about a mile inland 6.5 miles S of San Simeon, with some of the houses visible from offshore. You cannot anchor or land at Cambria, beyond which the cliffs become higher. Maintain a course to pass at least a mile offshore, watching for water breaking over submerged Von Helm Rock (8 feet), 7.2 miles NW of Point Estero and nearly a mile offshore.

Point Estero marks the N extremity of Estero Bay (Chart 18703), which curves E for 5 miles, then S for 11 miles to Point Buchan. The northern shores of Estero Bay are often heavily infested with kelp, with some off-lying rocks. The Estero area is notorious for its fogs, which persist for days in the summer. Low bluffs, cliffs, and sandy beaches extend from Point Estero to Morro Rock, which lies 6 miles N of Point Buchan.

Cayucos Pier lies in the NE part of Estero Bay, 4.5 miles N of Morro Rock, with 12 feet at the outer end. An approach buoy lies 0.5 mile off the pier. Anchorage may be obtained over a sandy bottom in 50 to 60 feet, with the white concrete tank on a hill W of Cayucos bearing about 010 degrees M; however, the shelter in prevailing conditions is not exceptional.

Morro Rock not only marks the entrance to Morro Bay Harbor, but also is the most prominent natural landmark in Estero Bay. Named by the Spaniards "El Moro," the cone-shaped rock stands out from the low-lying coastline and can be seen from miles away.

Stay clear of the tanker-mooring area marked by white buoys and extending for 3 miles N of Morro Rock. You will sometimes see quite large tankers loading crude close inshore from these moorings.

Morro Bay Harbor
Chart 18703
Approach Buoy: Lat. 35°21.7′ N, Long. 120°52.5′ W

Morro Bay is one of my favorite places, perhaps because I have used it so many times. This busy fishing port has escaped much of the ruthless gentrification that has descended on so many of California's har-

bors, although the town has the usual quota of tourist stores.

Approach and Entrance. From N: Morro Rock and the three 450-foot power-plant smokestacks 0.5 mile E of the rock are clearly visible from a long distance. They provide all the landmarks needed to find the harbor on a clear day. In foggy conditions, Estero Point, Morro Rock, and Point Buchan make excellent radar targets. As you approach the Rock, stay well offshore until you sight the approach buoy (Fl. G. 4 sec., 3 miles) and the stone breakwater extending 600 yards S of the rock. This breakwater is lit (Fl. 5 sec., 36 feet, 13 miles) and has a foghorn. You can then shape a course for the entrance, which lies between this breakwater and another built out 600 yards from the sand dunes to protect Morro Bay.

From S. Again, Morro Rock and the power plant offer excellent landmarks. Stay well offshore and sight the two breakwaters, which are inconspicuous against the land, especially on foggy days. When visibility is poor, give the beach S of the entrance a wide berth because the ground swell can sweep you too close to shore and literally into the breakers.

The Morro Bay Harbor entrance—notorious for rogue waves, strong currents, and shoaling—can be dangerous, especially in rough weather. The harbor bar also can be hazardous, with breaking waves at low water, especially during periods of strong W and SW winds or when the entrance has not been dredged in a while. If you have the slightest doubt about the entrance, call the local coast guard office or the harbormas-

Approach to Morro Bay, showing Morro Rock, power-plant chimneys, and breakwaters; distant 1 mile.

ter on VHF channel 16. It's a good idea to approach the entrance from the SW, watching for strong currents, especially during the flood. Stay to the W side of the entrance because the worst shoaling is on the E side. The buoyed channel shifts according to shoaling conditions, and you must keep within its boundaries.

Once inside the breakwaters, follow the buoyed channel around into the harbor area protected by the sand dunes and mud flats that form Morro Bay itself. Watch for strong flood streams that may set you toward the city dock.

Anchorage and Berths. Most visitors who are yacht-club members avail themselves of the Morro Bay Yacht Club's hospitality. The club maintains a dock and a row of moorings opposite the clubhouse, which lies about 0.5 mile up-harbor from the U.S. Coast Guard pier. The club harbormaster monitors channel 16 from 1630 to 1800 most days, especially in the summer. I have always found this to be a very friendly club.

You can tie up to a floating dock near channel buoy 12 for a maximum of thirty days or anchor outside the harbor channel opposite the same marker. The tide runs strongly in the anchorage, so use ample scope or consider a Bahamian moor, with anchors set in the direction of ebb and flood.

Morro Bay State Park at White Point maintains a small marina, but there are no visitors' facilities. There is an excellent boat-launching ramp S of the Morro Bay Yacht Club, but beware of the lateral tidal streams.

Facilities. Morro Bay is a tourist town with excellent seafood restaurants. All provisions are available in town; fuel and water are obtainable at waterside. Diesel maintenance and other marine services are available at the harbor.

Contacts.
U.S. Coast Guard cutter: 805-722-1293

Harbormaster (at the foot of the city pier): 805-722-6254

www.morro-bay.ca.us/harbor.html

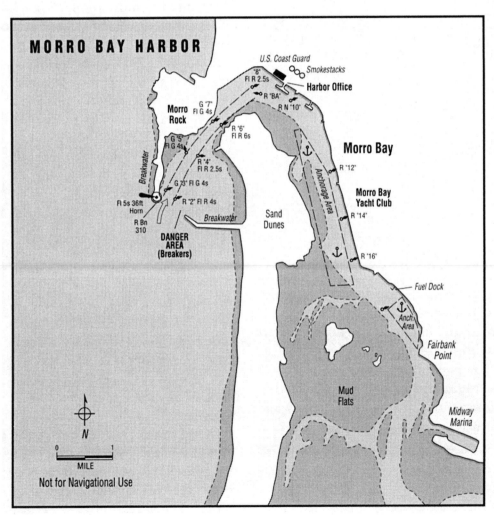

Morro Bay Harbor plan.

MORRO BAY HARBOR TO PORT SAN LUIS

Chart 18704

Point Buchan forms a distinctive headland 6 miles S of Morro Bay. The cliff rises 40 feet with a low tableland behind it. A whistle buoy (Fl. R. 6 sec.) lies 1 mile WSW of the point. Pass outside the buoy, even in calm weather.

The coast now trends SE for 9 miles, much of it cliffs between 40 and 60 feet high, with submerged rocks and ledges extending more than a mile offshore in places. Mount Buchan's rugged mass dominates this stretch of coast and can be seen from many miles away. On a clear day, Saddle Peak, 4.1 miles NNW of San Luis Obispo light, is visible for more than 40 miles. The two concrete domes and other large buildings of the Diablo Canyon nuclear power plant, 5.8 miles NW of Port San Luis light, are visible from well offshore. The 136-foot-high Lion Rock, with a leonine profile, lies 0.9 mile NW of the power plant. You may encounter fishing boats working the artificial reef 3 miles WNW of Port San Luis light.

Point San Luis marks the W side of Port San Luis. San Luis Obispo light (Lat. 35°09.6′ N, Long. 120°45.6′ W) (Fl. W. 5 sec., 116 feet, 24 miles) on the point has a foghorn. Both this bold promontory and Point Buchan make good radar targets in bad weather.

Port San Luis

Chart 18704

Breakwater Whistle Buoy: Lat. 35°09.3′ N, Long. 124°44.9′ W

Port San Luis serves as the harbor for the town of San Luis Obispo, 10 miles inland. Predominantly a commercial oil and fishing port, San Luis has little appeal for passage-making yachts with Morro Bay so close at hand; however, it can be warmer and less foggy, and has more room for anchoring off. It offers good shelter in NW conditions, but can be very rough in SE gales.

Approach. From N and W: Pass a mile offshore until the breakwater running SE from Whalers Island off Point San Luis is identified. You can pass inside Westdahl Rock buoy (Lat. 35°08.7′ N, Long. 120°47.1′ W) (Fl. G. 6 sec.), 1.3 miles SW of San Luis Obispo light, laying a course to go outside the whistle buoy "Y" (Fl. G. 4 sec.) at the end of the 2,400-foot-long breakwater.

From S. Identify Point San Luis and the Whalers Island breakwater. The tank farm at the NE corner of the anchorage stands out against the land. Lay off a course to pass between Westdahl Rock and Souza Rock buoys, the latter lying 1.5 miles SE of the breakwater (Lat. 35°07.8′ N, Long. 120°44.4′ W) [Fl. (2+1) R. 6 sec.]. This heading brings you to a safe point E of the breakwater.

The bay is clear of dangers, except for Atlas and Lansing Rocks inside the breakwater. Steer between the two buoyed rocks toward the Port San Luis pier.

The commercial-oil port is on the N shore of the bay, its head surrounded by

Approach to Port San Luis, distant 1 mile.

mooring buoys. Sometimes a tanker will be loading there. Stay clear of this pier and of the County Wharf special anchorage area below the village of Avila Beach and the tank farm at the NE corner of the bay.

Anchorage. Fishermen make heavy use of Port San Luis wharf. You can use the busy boat hoist that lies N of the pier, which only operates on either side of high water until about midtide.

Anchorage may be obtained in an area inside a line between Fossil Point below the tank farm, and the outer end of the main breakwater. However, you must avoid the two special anchorage areas below Avila Beach and in the western part of the bay, shown on the chart. The recommended area is between Avila Pier (County Wharf) and the Unocal Pier. In practice, the harbormaster may tell you where you can anchor, but if not, stay clear of the moorings and tuck in as much as you can to avoid the surge that often rolls into the bay. (The mooring area is marked with orange buoys.) The maximum tidal range is about 9 feet at equinoctial springs, so lay anchor accordingly.

Alternatively, apply to the harbormaster for a visitor's mooring, which costs a modest sum. Every time I have tried to get one on a summer weekend, they have been booked up, so try reserving one in advance. Contact the harbor patrol on channel 12 or 16 for an assignment.

Facilities. Fuel, water, and limited repairs and marine supplies are available near the wharf, where there is a 60-ton mo-

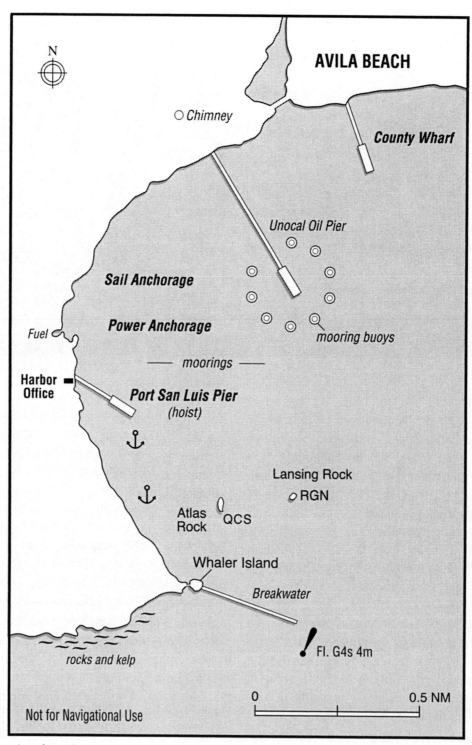

Plan of Port San Luis.

bile hoist. Provisions are available within walking distance.

Contacts.
Port San Luis Harbormaster's Office
P.O. Box 249
Avila Beach CA 93424
805-595-5400
www.portsanluis.com/

PORT SAN LUIS TO POINT ARGUELLO

Charts 18700 and 18721
The low-lying eastern shore of San Luis Obispo Bay, of which Port Luis is a part, is a mixture of sand dunes and long sandy beaches, ending in Point Sal. The houses and hotels of Pismo Beach and Shell Beach, communities that are famous for their clamming, string along the shoreline near Port Luis. Pismo Beach pier is 1,200 feet long, but should not be approached because of submerged pilings and the ocean swell, which can reach considerable heights close inshore. I always keep well offshore along the 14 miles of coastline down to Point Sal. There is nothing to attract the sailor. In any case, most people are on passage around Points Arguello and Conception, which keeps you offshore.

Point Sal is a bold headland, remarkable for its patches of yellow sandstone that are visible from some distance, especially in the oblique light of morning and evening. From the NW, Point Sal looks like a conical hill, with two conical hills behind it rising gradually to a ridge 3 miles E. From the S, Point Sal tends to merge into the surrounding coast, but it can be identified by 54-foot-high Lion Rock, 200 feet off its southern face. Stay at least a mile off Point Sal because reefs and breakers extend 0.6 mile S and W.

Anchorage. Anchorage may be obtained under the lee of Point Sal in 30 to 50 feet (sand), but the berth can be uncomfortable with relatively little protection from the swell the odd times I have put an anchor down there. The best anchorage is about 500 yards SE of Lion Rock, but watch for the shoal water in the SE corner of the area. Fishing boats are common users of the Point Sal anchorage. Coasters used to load hides and tallow here during the nineteenth century.

From Point Sal, the coast trends S for 19.5 miles in two shallow bights separated by Purisima Point, 10.6 miles N of Point Arguello. Although there is deep water inshore, there is little of interest along this low-lying coastline except for the missile gantries of Vandenberg Air Force Base, which seem out of place in such a remote landscape. The Southern Pacific Railroad runs close inshore. The yellow station house and a white water tower about 7 miles N of Point Arguello are prominent.

Caution. Vandenberg Air Force Base is a major launching point for the Pacific Missile Range. Firings occur throughout the year, at which time passage through the Point Arguello–Point Conception area is restricted. For information on launches, call 805-606-1857 or visit www.vafb.af.mil.

POINT ARGUELLO AND POINT CONCEPTION

We come now to the area known since the nineteenth century as the "Cape Horn of the Pacific." Points Arguello and Conception form a pair of formidable headlands that are fog-ridden, extremely windy, and famous for their winter storms. Many small-boat sailors spend their entire cruising lives south of Point Conception, never venturing farther north. They are missing something because this stormy and desolate corner of California has a great fascination. But heed these words of warning: This area of the Santa Barbara Channel is not for the inexperienced. Stay clear until you know your boat intimately! Although caution and prudent seamanship are the order of the day, there is no reason why a well-founded vessel cannot navigate these stormy waters in complete safety. The secret lies in advance preparation.

The golden rule of rounding Point Conception is to schedule your passage for the right time of day and the most favorable weather.

A description follows of the special conditions that make Points Arguello and Conception so formidable.

The Point Conception Phenomenon

The western end of the Santa Barbara Channel is notorious for its gusty winds and confused seas. The north–south coastline turns E at Points Arguello and Conception. A new weather pattern develops east of these two points, which enjoy local weather of their own. As long ago as 1858,

surveyor George Davidson described how he had seen "vessels coming from the eastward with all sail set, and light airs from the north in a very short time reduced to short canvas upon approaching the cape."

Point Conception is not the only prominent cape on the Pacific Coast with a notorious reputation; Cape Flattery in Washington and Cabo San Lucas in Baja are other windy spots. Each of these points is the bold edging of a landmass, a promontory backed by mountains that act as a barrier to prevailing winds. Each projects into an area of relatively constant onshore winds; in the case of Point Conception, the N–NW breeze that blows down the California coast most of the year. Point Conception is an abrupt interruption of the steady onshore winds that have suffered minimal friction loss over the ocean and of the long regular swells that have traveled over open water for thousands of miles.

Daylight calms are unusual between Points Arguello and Conception. When offshore winds are relatively stable and cool, the point causes the air to lift some seven to nine times the height of the Cape to windward, leaving a fluky area immediately windward of the promontory. Both wind and sea conditions quiet down and conditions off Point Conception are peaceful. This stable weather condition usually occurs at night during periods of cooler, settled weather, when fog is present. Sometimes the calm conditions persist into the daylight hours and you can enjoy an idyllic passage around the Cape. Once I sailed close offshore on a calm evening when the wind was barely 10 knots and the entire landscape was bathed in pink sunset light. I felt uneasy, for it was as if Point Conception was holding its breath, gaining strength for another day.

Point Conception rarely enjoys such stable conditions because there are many factors that act together to make air flows more complex. Frontal systems or pressure changes far offshore can alter conditions without warning. As a general rule, winds around Point Conception tend to increase during the afternoons. But the stronger winds can last for longer periods if onshore wind conditions are inconsistent or stronger than usual.

An unstable onshore wind results in no lifting; the air mass hits the cape in full flow. It compresses and squeezes past the point in a "venturi" effect that funnels it through a small area at the land and causes wind velocity to rise sharply. As the sun begins to heat the land, warm air rises in a thermal effect, and a sea-breeze effect results. The sea-breeze circulation causes lower pressure at the cape, and the onshore wind further accelerates to fill the low-pressure area. Offshore, the downflow of the sea breeze brings gustier upper-level air down to the surface. This mixture of sea breeze and upper-level, higher-speed air is then drawn into the air flow, funneling around Point Conception. The winds at the cape can be 50 to 130 percent higher than the strong breeze well offshore. In other words, an 18-knot breeze offshore may have a local velocity of 27 to 42 knots close to the point. The onshore wind increases all day as the sea-breeze effect gains strength and land-heating persists. A wind shadow extends to leeward beyond the cape and can extend a distance of twenty to thirty times the height of the point away from the land, or about a mile off Point Conception. You may be taken aback for a few seconds as you sail into the shadow, which can be felt as far as a mile off the point.

Swell conditions off Point Conception are rougher than offshore. Swells are refracted around the headlands and heightened by the increased wind speed. Although turbulent eddies and currents may further confuse swells off Points Arguello and Conception, the roughest conditions are typically found where the winds are strongest or immediately to leeward of the windiest area.

Fog is a major problem at Point Conception. You can count on from twelve to twenty foggy days a month at Point Arguello between June and October—days with visibility of less than 0.5 mile. The worst months are September and October. Foggy conditions are highly localized so that Point Conception can be clear while Point Arguello is fogbound. Although wind conditions tend to be quieter on these days, it is not an invariable rule.

Southbound Conception Passage

Rounding Point Conception in either direction is always risky to a degree. Much depends on local weather conditions and the unpredictable behavior of the northwesterlies, which are capable of blowing all night in the face of all predictions to the contrary. On the other hand, the last eight times I have been up at the point, it has been flat calm—yet I know others who have waited for days in Cojo Anchorage for that quiet night when they can motor north in comfort. Point Conception is always a gamble, but one in which intelligent planning reduces the odds of a rough baptism.

Southbound is the easiest way under sail, for chances are that you'll have a strong northwesterly to speed you on your way. Most people set out from San Simeon Bay or Morro Bay. The most economical passage is from San Simeon because you avoid the extra miles into Morro Bay. Timing is of the essence if you are bound for Cojo Anchorage in the lee of Point Conception because the approaches to the cove are unlit and there are no lights on shore to help you find your way toward land. Plan the entire passage so that you arrive off Point Conception in full daylight. This timing takes advantage of the afternoon northwesterly as you approach the Arguello–Conception area with time left to anchor safely. As you come abeam of Purisima Point far to port, the wind will increase dramatically, sucking you downwind toward your destination. Reef down, watch for gusts, and enjoy the ride!

If you are bound nonstop for Santa Barbara, Channel Islands Harbor, or destinations beyond the Santa Barbara Channel, then timing considerations are of lesser importance. However, you will enjoy the passage more if you carry the full strength of the afternoon wind past Point Conception.

In a powerboat, the smoothest conditions for your passage are during the calm nighttime hours. Unless you have radar and GPS, plan to stay at sea and not attempt the unlit Cojo Anchorage. Whether under sail or power, be sure to keep well off Point Conception to avoid the outlying rock off the point.

When bound nonstop from Northern California past Point Conception, your best course lies about 5 to 7 miles offshore, where you will miss the worst of the confused seas off the point. This course takes you into the Santa Barbara Channel, while allowing you the benefit of the stronger winds that blow along the N shores of the Channel Islands. As you approach the mouth of the channel, you will encounter shipping vessels entering the traffic-separation lanes in these waters.

Northbound Conception Passage

None other than the great British circumnavigator Eric Hiscock waited for days at Cojo Anchorage to round Point Conception. He retreated in despair, remarking to a friend of mine that the California coast was a demanding cruising ground.

Like a southward passage, a northbound voyage uses the same set of general weather conditions: be sure to round the point during the calm nighttime hours. Although there is no guarantee, the best months for rounding Point Conception are in early summer or September and October, when fogs are common and fog cycles can last ten days or more. Under these conditions, you *may* be able to motor north past the point in the middle of the day, with a reasonable guarantee that the afternoon northwesterly will not be unduly strong.

Predicting weather conditions at the cape is not easy; area forecasts refer to areas north of Point Conception or a broad corridor of the Pacific labeled "from Point Conception to San Nicolas Island and outer coastal waters." While strong winds in this forecast may well mean heavy air at Point Conception, conditions are so localized that you may find a quite different situation when you finally reach Cojo Anchorage. The Santa Barbara Channel West Weather Buoy (46054) provides information on current conditions close offshore. If you are bound from Santa Barbara to Point Conception, you can sometimes predict wind and swell conditions at "Cape Horn" by studying the wave sets on Leadbetter Beach, immediately W of the Santa Barbara Harbor breakwater. Steady, quite high waves despite locally calm conditions may be a sign of high afternoon winds at the point. It takes some days to get accustomed to the changing sets on the beach but, after a while, you can tell which sets mean wind at Point Conception. When foggy conditions have settled over the Santa Barbara Channel for a couple of days, you can be relatively confident that winds at Point Conception are calm, making these the best circumstances for motoring north.

Whatever wind strengths you expect at the cape, your best strategy northbound is to anchor in Cojo Anchorage and then wait for a period of calm winds, such as what often prevail at night. It's always a mistake to generalize about the weather anywhere, much more so at Point Conception, but even strong afternoon winds tend to drop at nightfall on many days of the year. With patience, you'll have the calm conditions you need.

While some brave (or rash) souls make nonstop passages from Southern California past Point Conception, a first-time voyager should pause at Cojo to enjoy the luxury of choosing the calmest hours for rounding the point. Many people adopt the strategy of leaving Santa Barbara in early morning, arriving at Cojo Anchorage after a passage of about 40 miles in the late afternoon. Once at Cojo, they enjoy a leisurely dinner and a short sleep; then they up-anchor at midnight and round Point Conception about 1.5 miles offshore. Even if conditions are calm, you may experience some bumpy swells, but close Morro Bay or San Simeon Bay by midmorning. Be prepared, however, for a wait—you might be forced to remain in Cojo for several days before conditions are suitable, even at midnight. Both fog and wind should shape your decision. Do not hesitate to return if you find open-water conditions unsuitable.

If circumstances dictate that you not stop at Cojo, then time your arrival off Point Conception for the late evening so you can motor northward during the calmest hours. To attempt the passage at midday is to invite discomfort and slow progress. If you are impatient or on a timetable and want to pound into strong headwinds, be my guest: Point Conception is best mastered by exercising patience; most of us go to sea for pleasure.

The nonstop passage from Point Conception to Morro Bay or San Simeon Bay takes you through the oilfields of Point Arguello, where you can expect small-boat traffic. The offshore oil rigs are brilliantly lit, but stay well clear and watch for unlit

Diablo Canyon nuclear power plant.

mooring buoys in their vicinity. You can fix your position electronically or by regular bearings on Points Arguello and Conception lights. On a foggy day, your first landfall near Morro Bay will be somewhere close to Point Buchan, perhaps near the large conspicuous domes of the Diablo Canyon nuclear power plant. Bound for San Simeon Bay, you may remain out of sight of land until somewhere around Cambria before the fog lifts. At that point, you should be able to see Hearst Castle high above and the white buildings of San Simeon Bay ahead.

Point Conception is no place for an inexperienced crew because the area can be unrelenting in its winds and swells. But with care and careful weather planning—using broadcasted forecasts and your own observations—you can round the "Cape Horn of the Pacific" in complete safety. While tales of 20-foot waves at Point Conception are not exaggerated (most of them are told by commercial seamen who have to work in such conditions), many of the bar stories that abound between San Diego and Seattle are just that. There is no reason why a well-founded yacht cannot cruise this fascinating area in comfort. The real problem for coastal passagemakers is getting there against the prevailing winds, which is largely a matter of time and careful planning.

Rounding Point Arguello and Point Conception
Chart 18721

Points Arguello and Conception lie in a magnificent natural setting. South of Purisima Point, the coast becomes rockier, and the railroad trestle over La Honda Canyon 2 miles N of Point Arguello is conspicuous. Give the shore a wide berth; onshore currents frequent this vicinity, and swells close inshore can be extremely dangerous. The seaward end of the Santa Ynez Mountains is near Point Arguello. The 2,170-foot Tranquillon Mountain can be seen behind the jagged, rocky promontory. Point Arguello is inconspicuous and rocky, projecting about 800 yards W of the coast. The small light structure exhibits a powerful flash (Lat. 34°34.6′ N, Long. 120°38.9′ W) (Fl. W. 15 sec., 24 miles) from a height of 120 feet above water level. The point is

unmistakable because of the huge missile gantries that rise up like silent monoliths at Vandenberg Air Force Base close inland. The railroad passes immediately inshore of the coastline.

Hondo, just north of Point Arguello, witnessed one of the worst disasters in U.S. naval history in 1924. A crack flotilla of destroyers southbound past Point Conception at full speed, and relying on DR plots in the days before radar, turned inshore too soon in a thick fog. Six of them ended up on the rocks—fortunately, with relatively minor loss of life.

I once sailed close inshore at Point Arguello on a quiet summer evening. The visibility was perfect, the wind a soft 10 knots. Even the swells were minimal, and birds fished from the weathered rocks close to the water's edge. The landscape resembled a moonscape of razor-sharp rocks,

Point Arguello, from the E, distant 1 mile.

desolate grass, and the ever-present sounds of the Pacific. The missile gantries towered high above us, silent and menacing in the soft light. Point Arguello was a surrealistic experience and an awesome place, even on a calm evening. This is no place to be caught on a lee shore; no sane sailor should approach this headland under anything but calm conditions.

S of Point Arguello, the coastline forms a 12-mile bight of cliffs and sandy beaches. Stay well outside this large bay, where currents are irregular. The shallow water swells on this coast must be seen to be believed. Temporary anchorage may be obtained inside the kelp off Jalama State Beach, but *only* in (rare) quiet conditions.

Point Conception is a bold headland with relatively low land behind it, so much so that you can confuse it for an island from offshore. The light (Lat. 34°26.9′ N, Long. 120°28.3′ W) (Fl. W. 30 sec., 26 miles) is displayed from a 52-foot-high tower behind a house at the W end of the point, and is 133 feet above sea level. From the S, the sloping geological strata and yel-

Point Conception from the air, taken from the SE.

Jim Aeby

low cliffs are very well marked. The land trends sharply E at the point, as you enter the Santa Barbara Channel. If you are passing close inshore, give Point Conception a berth of at least a mile. A low black rock lies 220 yards SW of the light, "upon which some of the California steamers have struck in very foggy weather," George Davidson tells us.

Chances are you'll sail past the point in fine style, perhaps well reefed down. As you admire the spectacular scenery and Point Conception comes on your quarter, the wind suddenly drops to less than 10 knots or dries up completely. This dramatic change is a testimony to the localized weather conditions in this area because you have now entered Southern California waters, where benign weather conditions are a relaxing norm.

Point Conception from the NW, distant ½ mile.

Lesley Newhart

Cojo Anchorage
Chart 18721
Lat. 34°27.1′ N, Long. 120°26.6′ W

Cojo Anchorage has been a popular resting spot ever since the days of the conquistadors, and it appeared on charts as early as 1793. Named after a long forgotten Chumash chief, Cojo was a major whaling cove in the early nineteenth century. Davidson considered this anchorage preferable to that off Santa Barbara, where the artificial harbor was built as recently as 1927: "The kelp is not so compact. There is a large rancho . . . and it is one of the very best tracts for grazing. The beef has a finer flavor and more delicacy than any we have met with on the coast."

He praised the large live oaks inland and willow logs used for fuel. The water, however, "is disagreeable to the taste." The large roadstead is well sheltered from prevailing N and NW winds. Cojo Anchorage is extremely uncomfortable even in moderate S and SE winds. NW gales can be bumpy here. Watch for swell running into the beach under such conditions.

Approach. From W: I cannot improve on Davidson, "Gradually round the bluff one mile distant from the cape, giving it a berth of half a mile run on a NNE course for three quarters of a mile, when the valley will open up with a sandy beach off it." A high railroad embankment traverses the back of the anchorage immediately above the beach, disappearing behind a high cliff to the S. A conspicuous railroad culvert offers a good landmark for entering the cove.

From E. Identify Point Conception and then the railroad tracks passing behind the anchorage along the conspicuous railroad embankment. Shape your course for the culvert in the embankment, which marks the center of the anchorage.

Anchorage. The anchorage lies under the lee of a low cliff 0.75 mile east of Government Point. The best spot is opposite a railway culvert in depths of 20 to 35 feet

Cojo Anchorage. The best anchorage is off the railroad culvert, well clear of the breakers and ground swell.

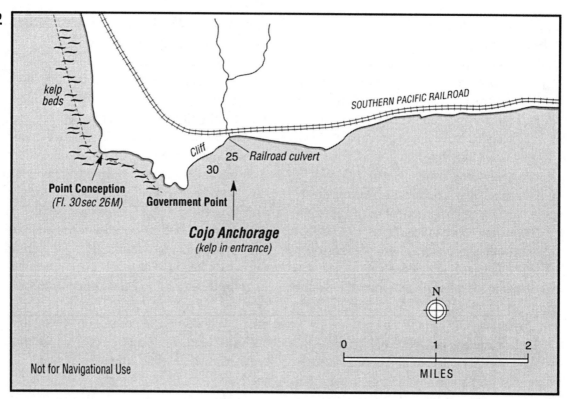

kelp
beds

SOUTHERN PACIFIC RAILROAD

Cliff   25   Railroad culvert
         30

Point Conception
(Fl. 30sec 26M)   **Government Point**

Cojo Anchorage
(kelp in entrance)

N

Not for Navigational Use

0   1   2

MILES

Plan of Cojo Anchorage.

(hard sand). It is preferable to lie between the shore and the kelp if the swell permits. I have seen from ten to fifteen small craft anchored here, fairly well sheltered by the cliffs from moderate N, NW, or W winds. You may have to navigate your way through the kelp to enter the anchorage, which should only be attempted in daylight. The unlit shore makes this a difficult spot to find at night, despite the presence of the Point Conception light and Gaviota aerobeacon 14 miles NE. Thick kelp beds can sometimes further complicate a night entry. The strongest summer NW winds blow between noon and sunset. This anchorage is unsafe in SE and SW

winds. Some people prefer to anchor immediately NW of Government Point, clear of breaking swells. However, do not attempt to anchor in Little Cojo 1.7 miles E of the main anchorage—it is foul with kelp and rocks.

Facilities. There are absolutely no facilities, not even Davidson's disagreeable water. However, Cojo Anchorage is an ideal place to wait for a propitious moment to round Point Conception.

This entire area is busy with oil traffic. The service companies have laid mooring buoys off Cojo Anchorage, which are often occupied by their working vessels. There is also occasional anchorage traffic at night.

Region 2

SANTA BARBARA CHANNEL AND THE CHANNEL ISLANDS

The surface of the sea, which was perfectly smooth and tranquil, was covered with a thick, slimy substance, which, when separated or disturbed by any little agitation, became very luminous, whilst the light breeze which came principally from the shore, brought with it a very strong smell of burning tar, or of some such resinous substance. The next morning . . . the sea had the appearance of dissolved tar floating upon its surface, which covered the ocean in all directions.

GEORGE VANCOUVER
on a natural oil seep near Goleta, California

Mainland: Cojo Anchorage to Santa Barbara

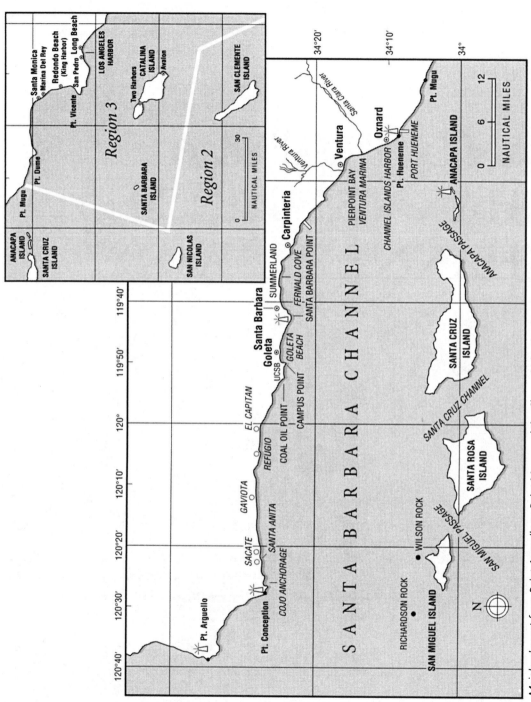

Mainland coast from Point Arguello to Point Mugu and the Channel Islands, showing major features and anchorages mentioned in the text. Inset: the southern islands.

MAINLAND:
COJO ANCHORAGE TO
SANTA BARBARA

THIS SECTION DESCRIBES the mainland coast between Cojo Anchorage and Santa Barbara Harbor, the western portion of the northern side of the south-facing Santa Barbara Channel.

BACKGROUND

The waters of the Santa Barbara Channel are one of the finest cruising grounds on earth. A bold statement, to be sure, but even the harshest judge would find it hard to disagree. Europeans navigated these waters for nearly five centuries; Juan Rodríguez Cabrillo was the first to record sailing into the Santa Barbara Channel. On October 10, 1542, his tiny squadron of two caravels anchored off what is now the Rincon near Carpinteria. A large Chumash village known as Skuku lay close to the shore, and consisted of circular thatched huts each housing as many as forty or fifty

people. Cabrillo marveled at the Chumash canoes that skimmed over the calm waters between the shore and his caravels in only a few minutes. His seamen named Skuku the Pueblo de las Canoas, which means *canoes* in Spanish. The village site itself lies partly under U.S. 101. Cabrillo explored north of Point Conception but returned to winter at the islands.

The Spanish expeditions that intermittently visited the channel after 1542 returned home with a patchwork of observations of Native American customs. After the discovery of a return route to the New World from the Philippines in 1565, Spanish ships regularly sailed south along the California coast after making landfall on the Northern California shore. Two centuries later, the Gaspar Portola Expedition explored the coastline between San Diego and San Francisco Bay in late summer 1769 and winter 1770. These Spaniards spent several weeks among the Chumash. Father Juan Crespi, a priest accompanying the expedition, was careful to set down his observations of the local people. He visited not only the Pueblo de las Canoas, which he called La Rinconada, but also another large village known as Syuhtun, at the site of modern Santa Barbara. Syuhtun contained sixty well-built houses. Seven canoes were fishing off the surf. "A good arroyo of running water" flowed into the Pacific near Syuhtun. The soil seemed fertile. Crespi and his superiors decided it would be an excellent place for a mission.

Five missions were founded in the Santa Barbara area in the next quarter-century. San Buenaventura Mission was built in 1782 and a Royal Presidio was established a short distance from Syuhtun the same year. Four years later, the Santa Barbara Mission was established close to this Presidio. A small Spanish settlement soon stood where Syuhtun had once flourished. Each mission was responsible for converting the surrounding Native Americans to Christianity, and civilizing them by teaching agriculture, Spanish, and new religious beliefs. The scattered population was to live in communities governed by Spanish social and political institutions. The celebrated British explorer, George Vancouver, anchored off Santa Barbara and Ventura in 1793 and witnessed this process of "reduction" in progress.

Crowded together at the missions and exposed to exotic European diseases, the Native American population was rapidly decimated. As Mexicanization of the Chu-mash accelerated, more of them intermarried with settlers and soldiers. Traditional Chumash lifeways and beliefs were gradually suppressed by an overwhelming Spanish–Mexican culture, although the missions experienced considerable difficulty in preventing the Chumash from reverting to their old ways. The mission fathers brought the last inhabitants of the islands to the mainland in the early nineteenth century, leaving their canoe ports for the seal, sea otter, and whale hunters who flocked to the offshore islands in subsequent years. Many Chumash became ranch hands or drifted into pueblos such as Los Angeles. The last traditional ceremonies were held in the 1870s. By the turn of the century, few of the Chumash could recall the rituals or their meaning.

Fortunately, a few local settlers took an interest in Chumash culture and interviewed the survivors about their culture. The Santa Barbara Museum of Natural History has thousands of pages of notes compiled by the anthropologist John Peabody Harrington, who studied the Chumash at intervals between 1912 and 1961. His records—in English, German, and Spanish, as well as Chumash—will take years to unravel. However, they are slowly revolutionizing our knowledge of the nearly extinct indigenous inhabitants of the shores of the Santa Barbara Channel.

In the early 1800s, Russian sealers ventured into the channel in search of sea otter, which were found by the thousands on the offshore islands. In a few years, their ruthless hunting methods almost eradicated the sea-otter population.

New Bedford whalers followed the sealers because the channel was an ideal place to hunt gray whales as they migrated along the California coast. The whalers were based in Cojo Anchorage under the lee of Point Conception, at Goleta, and on Santa Cruz Island. Harpooned whales were towed to shore and the carcasses rendered to whale oil in huge iron cauldrons that remained on the beaches long after the whalers finally left the area.

There were even pirates in the Santa Barbara Channel! In 1818, the French brigand Hypolyte Blanchard sacked the city of Monterey and then sailed into the channel to plunder the wealthy Ortega Ranch near Refugio. Fortunately, Ortega had been forewarned of the attack and moved his household and valuables inland to safety. Three of Blanchard's men were ambushed by a small party of soldiers from the Santa Barbara Presidio and thrown in prison. In retaliation, Blanchard burned the ranch buildings and killed all the livestock. Two days later, he anchored off Santa Barbara. His three hundred men vastly outnumbered the fifty defenders of the Presidio. However, the resourceful Spanish commander marched his small garrison around and around a thicket on the beach, who changed their clothes each time they came into view. Blanchard watched closely through his telescope, assumed he was outnumbered, and decided to negotiate. The three prisoners were quickly returned and Blanchard slipped away toward San Diego.

The nineteenth century saw the beginnings of a brisk coastal trade. Richard Henry Dana wrote an immortal account of his experience of the California sailing trade in the brig *Pilgrim*. In his book, *Two Years before the Mast*, he described the Spanish settlement at Santa Barbara, the long sandy beaches of Point Hueneme, and the SE storms that bring violent winds in their wake. He particularly complained about the long swells that rolled onto the beach every winter.

Southern California was a prime hide-producing region in those days. Dana described the backbreaking work of trading hides by boat, the Spanish grandees, and the occasional Americans who lived in this remote land.

In 1859, Dana returned to California, this time by steamer. He was strongly moved by the sight of the familiar landmarks of the Channel, Santa Cruz and Santa Rosa Islands, and Santa Barbara "on its plain, with its amphitheater of high hills and distant mountains. There is the old mission with its belfries, and there is the town, with its one-story adobe houses, with here and there a two-story wooden house of later build," he wrote nostalgically. "Yet little is it altered," Dana continued, "the same repose in the golden sunlight and glorious climate, sheltered by its hills; and then . . . there roars and tumbles upon the beach the same grand surf of the great Pacific." He called on the local worthies and *Pilgrim*'s former agent and remembered the harsh, monotonous routine of loading hides. Santa Barbarans were earning just enough from sheep, wine, and olives to keep the town going. Dana found one major difference, however: the weather seemed more predictable because ships were able to lie safely off the town inside the kelp all year-round.

The pace of American settlement accelerated dramatically after the Gold Rush of 1849 and the opening of the transcontinental railroad. Coastal trade gained momentum as numerous sailing vessels and, later, steamers plied between the various settlements carrying hides, tallow, lumber, hardware, and passengers. Santa Barbara gradually became a winter resort for wealthy Easterners. Stearn's Wharf was built out from the beach in 1872 and provided a convenient staging post for the coastal steamers. Even Chinese junks traded in the channel, hunting sea mammals and collecting abalone shells for far-off markets.

Despite the efforts of Sebastián Vizcaíno and other pioneers, the California coast was virtually uncharted until the 1850s. In 1782, Juan Pantoja's chart of the Santa Barbara Channel showed Cojo Anchorage and mapped soundings off the entrance to Goleta Slough. After the Gold Rush, the U.S. Coast Survey began a long-term mapping project on the West Coast and the federal government started lighting it. Surveyor George Davidson mapped much of the channel. Many well-known Channel Island anchorages, such as Cuyler's, Forney's, and Albert's, are named after the long-forgotten surveyors who labored long hours in open boats to complete the mapping of our cruising grounds. Much of their information is still valid today. Certainly the quality of the engraving on their charts will probably never be bettered (see the figure on page 16).

In 1887, the Southern Pacific Railroad reached Ventura and Santa Barbara. Slowly, the coastal trade declined as the railroad and, later, trucks took over load-carrying from steamers. The channel was still a relatively unspoiled and remote place, a favorite winter resort for the wealthy and famous. Santa Barbara boasted of its own film industry in the early years of silent movies. In 1929, Major Fleischmann paid for the erection of a rock breakwater to protect the anchorage west of Stearn's Wharf. The stone came from Fry's Harbor on the northern coast of Santa Cruz. Even so, there were only a few yachts in the channel, mostly large vessels. The great expansion of sailing in the channel has occurred since World War II, especially in the last three decades as mass-produced yachts have become widely available. So, the quiet coves of the offshore islands are now used by pleasure craft of all sizes rather than by the Chumash canoes, American whalers, Russian sealers, and Chinese junks of earlier centuries. And the once-deserted anchorages of Santa Barbara and Ventura now shelter hundreds of yachts and fishing boats of every shape and size behind protective breakwaters.

THE WEATHER OF SANTA BARBARA CHANNEL

Because weather conditions vary considerably throughout the channel area, the following information on forecasting (compiled by Peter Howorth) may be of use. Much of it also applies to other parts of Central and Southern California.

NW CONDITIONS

NW winds, usually strongest from mid-March to mid-May, are highly predictable through careful observation of natural weather indicators. Foremost are veil clouds, often called cloud caps, which cling tightly to coastal mountain passes and to the western ends of the offshore islands. These white cloud masses are usually seen in the morning and at dusk. As winds increase during the day, cloud caps often break into whirling round cotton balls, dubbed "puffers" or "puff clouds."

Puffers flying low to the land or islands indicate strong NW winds; high-fliers indicate moderate W to SW winds from Santa Cruz Island E, including the eastern offshore islands except San Nicolas.

When other clouds are also visible, NW winds will last only half a day or a day. If other clouds disappear and cloud caps and puffers remain, NW winds will usually persist for three or four days.

By observing the location and magnitude of cloud phenomena, surprisingly accurate estimates of wind velocities may be determined for each area, as follows.

- Early-morning cloud cap at Gaviota Pass and San Miguel Island and puff clouds over Santa Rosa indicate afternoon NW winds at 15 to 25 knots from Point Arguello to Gaviota and from the western half of Santa Rosa to San

Miguel. Winds for the eastern half of Santa Rosa will be W to NW at 5 to 15 knots, with stronger gusts likely at Becher's in the afternoon and evening. Winds at Santa Cruz will be W to SW at 5 to 15 knots, except for locally stronger westerlies at the Potato Patch. Anacapa winds will be SW to W at 5 to 10 knots. Winds will blow offshore along the mainland coast from Gaviota to Point Conception in the morning, slack off in the late morning, blow onshore in the afternoon, become calm about sundown, and then blow offshore again at night. Winds will blow from 5 to 15 knots in the morning, 10 to 20 knots in the afternoon, and 5 to 15 knots offshore until midnight.

- Early-morning cloud cap at Gaviota Pass, Refugio Pass, San Miguel, Santa Rosa, and occasional puff clouds at Santa Cruz indicate N to NE winds at 15 to 25 knots offshore in the morning from Cojo Anchorage to Point Arguello, switching in the afternoon to 15 to 30 knots N to NW. From Cojo to Gaviota, winds will be offshore 10 to 20 knots in the morning, changing to 15 to 20 knots NW in the afternoon. San Miguel will have winds at 15 to 30 knots NW, with stronger gusts in Cuyler and Tyler, particularly in the afternoon and evening. Santa Rosa winds will be at 15 to 25 knots NW, with locally stronger gusts at Becher's in the afternoon and evening. Santa Cruz will have winds 10 to 20 knots NW to SW from Coches Prietos to Gull Island and from Fry's Harbor to West Point. From West Point to Gull

Island, winds will be NW or W at 15 to 25 knots, with locally stronger gusts near Fraser Point. Wind from Fry's Harbor to San Pedro Point will be W to NW at 5 to 15 knots in the afternoon. From Albert's to San Pedro Point, winds will be calm or moderate in the morning, shifting to SW at 5 to 15 knots in the afternoon and W to NW at 10 to 20 knots in the evening. Anacapa will have winds at 5 to 15 knots SW.

- Early-morning cloud cap at Gaviota Pass, Refugio Pass, San Marcos Pass, San Miguel, Santa Rosa, and the western end of Santa Cruz indicate afternoon W to NW winds, 20 to 35 knots from Point Arguello to Goleta; generally offshore winds at 15 to 30 knots in the morning. San Miguel will have NW winds at 20 to 45 knots and Santa Rosa will have NW winds at 15 to 35 knots. From Gull Island to Fraser Point, winds will be at 15 to 35 knots, higher in the Potato Patch. From West Point to San Pedro Point, winds will be NW at 15 to 30 knots. From Gull Island to Coches Prietos, winds will be at 15 to 30 knots. From Albert's to Smuggler's Cove, offshore winds will be at 10 to 25 knots in the morning and at 15 to 30 knots in the afternoon.

NE CONDITIONS

NE winds also are quite predictable, although they often strike with less advance warning. Watch the sky and sea carefully. Northeasters generally hit in the evening and moderate by the following morning. They are most common September through November.

Natural indicators include warm, dry weather, particularly in the evenings. Smog, low on the horizon, frequently spreads offshore from the canyon at Point Mugu; the sky is otherwise clear or with high cirrus clouds. A spreading dark blue line on an otherwise glassy horizon often heralds a northeaster.

- A NE swell 2 to 4 feet at eastern end of Santa Cruz indicates that NE winds at 15 to 30 knots are imminent. A NE swell 4 to 6 feet at the same place indicates that a 30- to 45-knot NE wind is imminent. A NE swell 6 feet or more indicates a 50-knot or more NE wind is imminent. Note, however, that if the wind rises exceptionally rapidly, the preceding chop will give less warning. Often, the swell is relatively small until the wind has been blowing for a few hours.
- Wind blows offshore from coastal canyons and swings into Santa Barbara from the SE, with the same sky conditions. In Santa Barbara, a 2- to 3-foot swell means NE wind outside 25 to 35 knots; a 3- to 5-foot swell means 35 to 45 knots; and a 5-foot or more swell means 50+ knots. The weather in San Miguel will be excellent if the swell is 3 to 4 feet or more because NE winds are rare there.
- If puff clouds are visible over San Miguel and/or Santa Rosa, but a NE swell and smog are visible, expect localized SW to NW winds at 15 to 25 knots in Santa Rosa and San Miguel.

SE Conditions

Southeasters, which bring winter rain, usually begin during the day, start blowing at night and, by the next morning, are in full swing. They may occur October through April, although the peak months are December through March.

Natural indicators of southeasters are frequent wind changes, gathering dark clouds, and a stillness to the air. Often the sea has a strange leaden appearance and the water close to shore becomes quite clear, particularly early in the season before much runoff has occurred. Some people can even smell the rain coming. The cloud cover spreads and has peculiar, gently wavy, gray undersides. When a SE swell arrives, the normal W swell disappears or moderates.

- SE swells 2 to 4 feet indicate that a 15- to 25-knot southeaster is imminent; 4 to 5 feet indicates 25 to 35 knots; 5 to 7 feet indicates 35 to 50 knots. During a fast-moving front, it often takes a few hours more for the chop to build in proportion to the wind velocity.
- Watch for clearing in the W, followed by cloud caps developing at mountain passes and western ends of islands. These changes indicate that a shift to NW winds is imminent.

SW Conditions

The summer wind is usually relatively moderate. Natural indicators generally include high white cumulus clouds behind the coastal range and sometimes beyond the islands extending toward the coast of Point Arguello.

Refuge Anchorages of Western Santa Barbara Channel

Refuge anchorages are listed for the more remote western Channel region only because there are effectively no such anchorages E of Santa Barbara Harbor. In any case, a skipper would make use of harbors instead.

N to NW Winds 12 to 29 Knots
Western Channel Mainland: Cojo, Secate, and Gaviota, Refugio, El Capitan, or Goleta

N to NW Winds 30 to More Than 40 Knots
Western Channel Mainland: Secate; if possible, return to harbor

NE Winds 12 to More Than 60 Knots
Western Channel Mainland: Cojo, Secate, Gaviota (the latter to 30 knots only), Refugio (to 60 knots), El Capitan (to 45 knots), Goleta (to 30 knots)

SE Winds
Head to harbor; the mainland coast is a lee shore

COJO ANCHORAGE TO GAVIOTA

Chart 18720; Chart-Kit, p. 2
Small yachts frequent the rugged coastline between Point Conception and Coal Oil Point just west of Goleta less often than areas to the east. There are few secure anchorages and the weather can be unpredictable, but the area is well worth exploration. From Cojo Anchorage (see page 121)

Lesley Newhart

Santa Anita Anchorage from S, distant ¾ mile. The house on the hill (arrow) *is prominent.*

toward Gaviota, the coastline trends eastward for 12 miles. Low, yellow-brown cliffs lie behind the beach. Deep parallel gullies extend from the low coastal shelf up to the mountains behind. A silver-gray oil-storage shed and warehouse are located 1.7 miles E of Cojo Anchorage. Tanker buoys in this area are conspicuous from seaward. The coastline is almost deserted except for the Southern Pacific Railroad and a dirt road. The railroad passes over trestles and bridges that are clearly visible from offshore.

As you approach Gaviota, a series of hills with sloping rock strata between 600 and 800 feet high crowd in on the shoreline. Gaviota Canyon is a large gash in the Santa Ynez Mountains that can be clearly identified even at a considerable distance. A conspicuous railroad trestle lies on the coast north of the canyon. At this point, U.S. 101, the freeway between San Francisco and Los Angeles, brings traffic through Gaviota Pass and then east along the coast most of the way to Ventura. Gaviota Pier lies immediately east of the railroad trestle.

The coastline between Point Conception and Gaviota is protected by kelp beds that can extend in places more than a mile offshore. Most yachts pass Gaviota on passage direct to Cojo Anchorage and Santa Barbara, staying well offshore. This is a pity because the scenery inshore is gorgeous and there are two little-known but pleasant anchorages that offer good shelter from NW winds—anchorages that are frequently used by fishermen and surfers. Bound close inshore, it is recommended that you stay inside the kelp, where the water is smoother and you can spot anchorages and hazards more easily.

Santa Anita Anchorage

This is a useful bay enclosed by reefs and kelp. It forms a natural bight suitable for anchorage in calm or moderate NW weather.

Approach. Santa Anita lies 1.0 mile SW of Secate, which you should identify first. Two conspicuous houses are visible as you steer SW up the coast beyond Secate, just inside the kelp: one lies on a ridge about 1 mile inshore, the other is above the beach on the northern side of the cove. Staying clear of the reefs that extend 0.5 mile offshore on the eastern side of Santa Anita, head inshore after the houses are identified, keeping your bow between them. Two conspicuous cliff bluffs lie immediately W of Santa Anita.

Anchorage. Anchor in 25 to 35 feet (sand) about 300 yards offshore in a natural bight formed by the kelp and the eastern reefs, but well clear of them. If swells are moderate, this is a pleasant spot, but Secate offers more shelter.

Secate Anchorage

This spacious anchorage 4.5 miles west of Gaviota is frequently used by fishermen and surfers, and offers excellent NW protection, even in strong winds, and considerable shelter from the prevailing swell. Secate is recommended over Cojo Anchorage in rough weather, but it is bumpy in early-morning SE conditions in the summer.

Approach. As you approach from deep water or along the coast inside the kelp, look for two railroad embankments and Razorback Point, a prominent headland with sloping strata and a ledge of rocks extending 0.5 mile offshore from its base. The railroad embankments cross the mouth of Secate Canyon and the next arroyo W; both lie immediately SW of Razorback. Secate anchorage is an indentation in the coast, bounded by a steep light-brown cliff to the SW and by the embankments. Two railroad trestles can be seen on the coast between Secate and Gaviota. A conspicuous avocado grove lies on the hillside NW of Razorback Point and a wooden

Secate anchorage. Approach from S, distant 1 mile. Steer for the ridge between the two peaks.

Lesley Newhart

Lesley Newhart

Secate anchorage. Preferred anchorage spot is below the Southern Pacific signal standards (arrow) *in ample depth off the beach.*

ranch house is on a bluff SW of the bight. A long concrete seawall lies east of the point.

Anchorage. Anchor off the eastern embankment in 20 feet (sand and some rock), avoiding the kelp, or lie tucked behind the bluff W of the anchorage, protected by the kelp. One of the best berths lies opposite the railroad signal (see above). Watch for swells curling around the point and do not anchor too close to the beach because there is shallowing inshore, especially at low tide. This is one of the rare anchorages in Southern California where you have to take into account the tides.

Secate is a convenient anchorage for an overnight stay on the way to San Miguel Island or when on passage around Point Conception.

Watch for outlying ledges off Razorback Point and other headlands. You can anchor temporarily at many points along this coast at such well-known surfing points as Ranch House Beach, where swells and strong gusts can make the anchorage uncomfortable. Many surfers and fishermen frequent this area and have their own names for many localities.

Unpredictable gusts can sometimes sweep down through Gaviota Canyon and the coastal arroyos between Gaviota and Point Conception. Be prepared for a strengthening of W winds and for strong NW gusts even on days when conditions are almost calm nearer Santa Barbara. You can tell where the gusty winds begin by closely tracking your position relative to Gaviota Pier.

Gaviota (or Alcatraz) Landing

Gaviota Landing is part of the state-park system. A fine sandy beach lies at the mouth of Nojoqui Creek. Limited park facilities lie immediately inshore of the railroad trestle and can be reached by a road from U.S. 101. Gaviota Pier extends 434 feet seaward from the bluff immediately west of the railroad trestle. It is unlit, but has an electric hoist for launching small craft (1,500-pound capacity). This is a marvelous spot to launch for a quick trip to Point Conception, but it's a long haul along the pier, where vehicles are not allowed.

Approach. Gaviota Canyon is normally visible from a considerable distance in clear weather. Identify the Gaviota trestle and pier, which lie immediately west of the point where U.S. 101 turns inland. A series of large green oil-storage tanks and an oil refinery lie 1.5 miles east of the landing, providing useful markers with the trestle and pier when the cloud ceiling is low and obscures the mountains. Once the landing is identified, steer for the end of the pier, skirting kelp wherever possible. A night approach is not recommended, despite the flares from the refinery smokestacks and the red-flashing aerobeacon on Gaviota Peak 4 miles NE of the landing.

Anchorage. Good holding ground can be found immediately east of the pier in 25 to 30 feet (sand), but surge is a perennial problem. Gaviota Landing is a pleasant lunch or bathing spot, but is not recommended for an overnight stay. It can be

Lesley Newhart

Gaviota Landing from SE, distant ¾ mile. The railroad trestle is visible from a long distance.

very windy when strong gusts sweep down from Gaviota Canyon in the late afternoon and at night. The anchorage is untenable in SE winds. Two mooring buoys close offshore should be left alone if they are in position, which is not always the case.

Landing. There is a landing at the pier or on the sandy beach. Telephones, a snack bar, campsites, and toilets are available at the state park. Provisions are limited.

GAVIOTA TO REFUGIO

The coastline between Gaviota and Goleta, 20 miles east, is often lined with dense kelp beds. The Santa Ynez Mountains provide an imposing backdrop to the coast all the way to Ventura. Rolling foothills and steep canyons slope down to the low bluffs of the coast, typically between 50 and 100 feet high. Their yellow-white cliffs are conspicuous from offshore, with sandy beaches and breaking surf below them. Southern Pacific Railroad has built trestles along this stretch of coast, clearly visible from several miles offshore. U.S. 101 runs parallel to the railroad; the constant stream of cars and trucks provides a useful landmark. On busy days, the freeway traffic can be heard up to 10 miles out in the Pacific.

An offshore oil-loading terminal and refinery is conspicuous 1.5 miles east of Gaviota Landing. The green storage tanks are a useful landmark, as is a railroad trestle nearby. The terminal displays bright lights at night. Loading buoys and pipeline markers can be seen off this facility as far out as the 10-fathom line. Avoid this area if possible; the 6 miles of coastline between the terminal and Refugio Landing are of little interest. Numerous small arroyos drain into the ocean between low yellow cliffs. These coastal bluffs lead to Refugio Landing, which is formed by a small coastal indentation, where U.S. 101 and the railroad curve a short distance inland.

Refugio

In the nineteenth century, Refugio was a landing for the famous Ortega Ranch; today, it is a state park with a pleasant bathing beach. It provides a useful overnight anchorage in quiet weather, either as a weekend excursion from Santa Barbara or on passage to San Miguel or Point Conception.

Approach. The best way to identify Refugio is to watch for the spot where U.S. 101 makes a dogleg inland to cross Refugio Canyon. The concrete freeway bridge is conspicuous, as is a sizable russet-colored barn near a grove on the bluff immediately west of the anchorage. A warehouse lies a short distance west of Refugio and is visible from some miles offshore, as are the palm trees of the park area. The anchorage is sheltered by a low white bluff, which juts out to form the western side of the landing. Once the general area of the landing is identified, steer for the freeway bridge. Inshore, sound carefully and thread your way inside the kelp. A night approach is not recommended.

Anchorage. Anchor according to the draft in 15 to 25 feet off the beach (sand), making careful allowance for the depth at low tide. Tuck in behind the bluff as much as possible and lay a second anchor to

Refugio anchorage from SSE, distant 1 mile. The freeway trestle (arrow) is conspicuous from seaward.

counteract the swell that curves around the point. This is definitely a fair-weather anchorage and more comfortable in settled summer weather. The bluff offers limited shelter from W–NW winds. Clear out at the first sign of deteriorating weather. Be forewarned that swell conditions can vary considerably with high and low tide. Anchor far enough offshore so that you do not swing aground at low tide.

Landing. The landing is on the beach in calm weather. The best landing is at the W end, close to the point, on the sandy beach. Water, restrooms, and showers are available at the state park. Limited provisions and fuel are also available. There is a boat-launching ramp suitable for small outboard runabouts.

REFUGIO TO GOLETA

Between Refugio and Goleta, the coastline is generally low-lying with sandy brown-white cliffs. U.S. 101 runs just inshore along the coast, which indents east of El Capitan State Beach. It is possible to lie inside the kelp in 15 to 30 feet at the foot of a conspicuously sandy cliff. An old sycamore tree can be seen on shore W of the anchorage. El Capitan is exposed to prevailing westerly swells, although it can provide good protection from NW winds.

The coastline between El Capitan and Coal Oil Point 7.5 miles E is low-lying with white-brown cliffs, often with a conspicuous top layer. Six tanker-mooring buoys lie off oil-storage tanks 1.0 mile W of Coal Oil Point. Ellwood pier and its associated oil facilities are easily identified nearby, as the Spanish Mediterranean architecture of the Bacara resort behind the beach. You will occasionally encounter tankers coming inshore to this area. At 3.7 miles W of Coal Oil Point, a kelp-surrounded rock lies 0.9 mile offshore at a depth 15 feet—another reason to maintain some distance off the coast here. Bumpy water may be encountered even on calm days because shallow water extends some distance offshore.

Coal Oil Point marks the western extent of the Goleta–Santa Barbara urban sprawl. The point is surrounded by dunes and a sandy cliff, with a low red-roofed building on its summit. Oil platform *Holly* lies 1.5 miles SW of Coal Oil Point and is conspicuous from a long distance in clear weather. Extensive kelp beds front Coal Oil Point and the coastline that bounds Isla Vista and the University of California campus immediately to the east. Coal Oil Point acquired its name from a natural oil seep that surfaces nearby. You can smell petroleum in the air several miles to leeward. The seep has been known for centuries and does not necessarily have any connection with modern oil-drilling activities in the region. George Davidson recorded how the "bitumen, floating on the water, works against the summer or northwest winds even beyond Point Conception."

The university is recognized from a long distance offshore by its high-rise buildings and bell tower that stand out on the summit of the low cliffs leading E to Goleta Point. Goleta Point is a low-lying, sandy, 30-foot cliff that ends in semisubmerged rocks. A bed of kelp protects Isla Vista beach and the university shoreline. The oceanfront apartment buildings of Isla Vista are situated on the cliff at the back of the sandy beach. It is possible to pick up messy tar from the Coal Oil Point seep on your topsides off Isla Vista, and I recommend staying farther offshore if convenient. At Goleta Point, the land turns momentarily NE in a shallow indentation that provides some shelter for small vessels. Santa Barbara Municipal Airport lies behind Goleta Beach. Jet airliners landing at the airport can be spotted offshore and provide a useful, mobile landmark on occasion. The airport beacon is 1.5 miles inland and is easily visible at night.

Goleta Anchorage
Lat. 34°24.8′ N, Long. 119°50.2′ W
Goleta Beach lies immediately east of the university and offers sheltered anchorage in offshore winds and in calm conditions. The roadstead is completely open from E through SW.

Approach. Goleta Beach can be identified from a considerable distance in clear weather by the conspicuous buildings of the university campus to the west. Principal among these is Storke Tower, which stands up like a slim pencil on the low-lying coastline. As you close with the land, identify the western end of the anchorage, bounded by

Lesley Newhart

Goleta Pier and anchorage from SSE, distant ⅓ mile. The best anchorage is W of the pier and closer to the western cliffs.

Goleta Point, a low rocky shelf below the campus. The anchorage then curves east and is backed by a sandy beach. Past the low cliffs that bound the campus, the land dips down almost to sea level as you pass the end of the Santa Barbara Airport north–south runway. The cliffs rise again at the eastern end of the anchorage beyond Goleta Pier to a low bluff that reaches a height of about 150 feet. Two high radio masts painted red and white can be seen on the summit of this bluff 0.5 mile east of Goleta Pier. Seeing the two masts in transit is a clear sign that you have passed the anchorage.

The approach to Goleta anchorage is straightforward—there are no outlying dangers. From a mile or more offshore,

identify both Storke Tower and the two radio masts. Goleta Pier lies approximately two thirds of the way from Storke Tower to the two radio masts and is sometimes inconspicuous against the land; however, groves of palm trees can be seen behind it. After the radio masts and Storke Tower have been identified, steer for a position that takes you toward the lowest point of land between Storke Tower and the radio towers—this is the low ground opposite the end of the Santa Barbara Airport runway. As you close the land, Goleta Pier appears on your starboard bow. After it has been identified, steer for the end of the pier and anchor to the west, according to draft. A thick bed of kelp sometimes lies approximately 0.5 mile offshore of the beach, extending from Goleta Point east toward Santa Barbara. You can cross the kelp bed either by steering straight through it or by looking for gaps that often are cut opposite the pier and near Goleta Point.

Anchorage. Goleta Beach is smooth and sandy, and shelves gradually. Approximately ¼ mile offshore, there is 15 feet of water and a smooth, sandy bottom that, in calm conditions, is admirable for anchoring. An excellent position off the pier has the end of Goleta Pier bearing 015 deg. M and Storke Tower bearing 215 deg. M. More shelter from prevailing westerly swells may be obtained by moving up closer to the campus cliffs, where anchor can be dropped in depths of 12 to 15 feet some 200 to 300 yards offshore. In both of these positions, however, you should beware of swells refracting from the beach, which make the motion uncomfortable. Beware, also, of fouling your ground tackle on a sewer line that is often marked by kelp running perpendicular to shore near the pier.

Goleta Beach is not recommended as an anchorage in even moderate NE or SE winds, except perhaps for lunch. The kelp bed does provide some shelter from swells, but as an overnight anchorage—except under the calmest conditions or offshore winds—conditions are apt to be bumpy. When canyon winds are blowing, there are sometimes strong gusts that blow over the airport and out over the anchorage. The low beach offers little shelter in these conditions.

Landing. You can land by dinghy on the beach or at Goleta Pier, where there is a boat-launching crane and gangway. I have had consistent bad luck landing here because the breakers are usually short and steep, guaranteeing a wet landing and take-off. Wear a swimsuit and carry everything else in a waterproof bag! A small store sells ice cream at the head of the pier. A small park with toilets, water, and picnic facilities is maintained under a grove of palm trees at the head of the bay. There is an excellent beachside restaurant. There is ample parking for cars with easy access to the freeway system. There is no resident warden. Goleta Beach is an excellent place for children or a family day sail, and the bay is very busy on holiday and long weekends.

GOLETA TO SANTA BARBARA HARBOR

The coast from Goleta Beach E toward Santa Barbara Harbor is of moderate height and consists of low cliffs that run just inshore of the beach at approximately 150 feet. Near Goleta Beach are groves of eucalyptus trees that give way to the flat More Mesa area, with its white cliffs. East of More Mesa, more houses and trees are seen as you pass the Hope Ranch residential area and Campanil Hill, which is easily identified by an arch-like monument built on its summit, conspicuous from seaward. Many expensive homes are built on the hillside extending up to the monument. The beach from Goleta to Santa Barbara is sandy with only occasional rocky interruptions.

Approaching Santa Barbara from the W, the low tower of Santa Barbara Point light (Fl. 10 sec., 15 miles) is relatively inconspicuous until you are within a mile or so of the headland. The point itself is of moderate height, capped with trees and houses and sloping steeply into the ocean. Santa Barbara light is built on the cliffs immediately E of the point and is sometimes difficult to see among the houses. E of Santa Barbara light, the coast gradually declines in altitude until Santa Barbara Harbor is reached, at which point the buildings of Santa Barbara City College and the houses of the town are conspicuous behind the harbor breakwater.

There are no outlying dangers along this stretch of coast. It is possible to sail along it immediately outside the kelp bed that runs directly along the coast as far as Santa Barbara Point and beyond. At intervals, the kelp extends at least 0.75 mile to seaward. There are two racing marks normally placed off Santa Barbara Point. Wide clearance should be given to yacht races that sometimes are encountered in this vicinity. In foggy weather, the coast sometimes remains obscured when other areas are already clear. Caution should be exercised when approaching land, but you can be sure you are close to it when you encounter the kelp bed or changes in the water color. Approximately 15 to 30 feet of water is on

Lesley Newhart

Approach to Santa Barbara Point from W, a key landmark for the harbor when passagemaking inshore from Point Conception or cross-channel from San Miguel Island.

the shore side of the kelp bed, at which point a close watch should be kept for breakers. Small craft, including fishing boats, move fast just offshore of the kelp. Watch for them in foggy conditions, as well as lobster pots in the same area.

When approaching Santa Barbara Harbor from W, be careful not to approach too close to Santa Barbara Point or to the beach because both areas can be encumbered with kelp. Your vessel should pass offshore of the red-and-white-striped buoys off West Beach that mark the limit of the bathing area. Be careful also to not pass too close to the breakwater because considerable water disturbances frequently result from the swells breaking against the rocks and then rebounding offshore.

SANTA BARBARA HARBOR

Large-scale plan on Chart 18725; Chart-
Kit, p. 7
Fairway Buoy: Lat. 34°24.1′ N, Long.
119°40.8′ W

Santa Barbara Harbor lies 39 miles E of Point Conception and 24 miles NW of Ventura Marina. It offers complete shelter under all weather conditions. However, entrance should not be attempted in a southeaster, when it lies on a lee shore. The harbor is a friendly place, crowded with more than a thousand yachts, fishing boats, and a few commercial ships. The U.S. Coast Guard maintains a cutter on station here, and there is a flourishing Naval Reserve unit. Santa Barbara itself is a well-known resort city that offers every facility for the visitor.

Unfortunately, the harbor—although welcoming to visiting yachts—becomes very congested during the summer months, especially during Semana Nautica Regatta (July), Old Spanish Days Fiesta, and the King Harbor Race (both in early August). The entrance can be tricky, too, especially at low tide and when the channel has not been dredged for a while. Although a minimum depth of 15 feet is theoretically maintained, there are times—especially in the spring after winter storms—when sand buildup accelerates and the entrance shallows rapidly to as little as 3 feet. Eventually, it is dredged again, but sometimes there are considerable delays. Nevertheless, Santa Barbara is strongly recommended for a leisurely visit. Every facility for yachts is available. It is an ideal place to change crews, as it is within easy reach of Los Angeles and San Francisco.

Santa Barbara Harbor is a recent development. In the nineteenth century, the anchorage off the town could be bumpy and dangerous. Vessels visiting the mission anchored in the open roadstead, with their anchor cables ready to slip at a moment's notice. Thick kelp beds lay close offshore. "In winter," wrote George Davidson in 1858, "vessels must anchor outside of the kelp, as the gales detach and drive it shoreward in such vast quantities that, coming across a vessel's hawse, it helps to bring home her anchors." It was not until 1929 that visiting small craft could enjoy the shelter of a breakwater.

Approach. I can hardly improve on Davidson: "Vessels coming from the westward first sight La Vigia [Hill], as upon approaching the anchorage, keep outside of the line of kelp (here nearly half a mile wide), gradually rounding the point upon which is situated the lighthouse, two miles southwesterly of the landing, keep along the kelp abreast of the town and anchor in 7 fathoms; or pass through the kelp and anchor inside in 3½ fathoms, both hard bottom."

From S. Lavigia Hill, 0.6 mile NE of Santa Barbara light, reaches an altitude of 142 feet above sea level. It is conspicuous from both east and west and is the primary landmark for finding the harbor. Santa Bar-

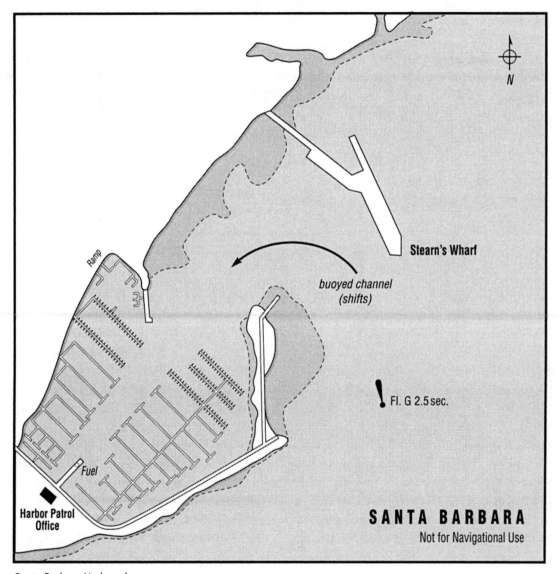

Santa Barbara Harbor plan.

Lesley Newhart

Approach to Santa Barbara from SE, distant 2 miles. The twin summits of Lavigia Hill W of the harbor stand out (arrow).

bara Point itself is 1.0 mile E of the light, a high cliff at the SE extremity of the narrow tableland that extends from Lavigia Hill. Sandy West Beach extends from Santa Barbara Point to the western end of the Santa Barbara breakwater. The white buildings of Santa Barbara City College and La Playa Stadium with its floodlight posts, a complex of tiered seats, are conspicuous on the bluff behind the breakwater and may be spotted before the gray breakwater itself, which tends to merge with the land. You probably will observe numerous yacht masts behind the breakwater before you see the 2,364-foot seawall itself. Santa Barbara Yacht Club, a

wooden building with decks on pilings and a conspicuous satellite antenna on its roof, stands on the beach immediately west of the breakwater. A racing start line, delineated by two marker buoys with fluorescent-orange markings, extends offshore of the club and should be given a wide berth when a race is in progress.

From W. Identify Lavigia Hill and Santa Barbara light. Round Santa Barbara Point, staying outside the kelp and at least 0.5 mile offshore. Then identify the City College buildings, the harbor breakwater, and the 2,040-foot-long Stearn's Wharf beyond it. Passing 0.5 mile offshore of the breakwater, there is sometimes confused water from backwash against it. Identify the fairway bell buoy (Fl. G. 4 sec.) and aim to pass midway between the marker and the next bell buoy (R. G. 2.5 sec.) that marks the beginning of the entrance channel close to the W end of Stearn's Wharf. Once you are well clear of the end of the breakwater, alter course to port to leave the second bell buoy close to port and Stearn's Wharf to starboard. Do not alter course inshore too soon.

From E. The first landmark will be the Rincon oil island off Punta Gorda, 12 miles east of the harbor. The conspicuous erosion contours on the side of the Rincon, 2 miles east, will become apparent on the starboard bow soon afterward, at the point where U.S. 101 moves inland to pass Carpinteria. On a clear day, you should be able to distinguish low-lying Lavigia Hill. The harbor lies in the dip of the land to starboard of Lavigia. At night, you should be able to pick up Santa Barbara Point light from some distance; however, it will become obscured as you move inshore.

As you approach Santa Barbara, you will see the conspicuous white buildings of the Hammond Estate development and the beachside tower of Coral Casino just E of the Santa Barbara cemetery. These landmarks lead you to Stearn's Wharf and the entrance 3.2 miles W. Following are some useful points of reference.

- Montecito Country Club, a white building with a conspicuous square white tower east of the city, visible above a wide expanse of green golf course

- the arched facade of the Red Lion Inn and the brightly colored chromatic arch (an artistic extravaganza) behind the beach a mile E of the harbor
- St. Augustine's Seminary spire NW of the harbor
- Bekins Moving and Storage warehouse behind the harbor
- the illuminated spire of the Arlington Theatre on State Street (at night)

Santa Barbara is difficult to pick up from offshore on hazy days because you only have mountaintops to go by. When coming in from Santa Cruz Island, your best guide is a gray-colored cleft in the Santa Ynez Mountains that lies directly behind the harbor and town. Three quarters of a century ago, fishermen and local sailors called this cleft "the Saddleback" or "Larco's Dip"; both names have fallen into disuse (Larco was a celebrated local fisherman of the 1920s). A course set on Larco's Dip will bring you safely in toward land until the important landmarks for the city emerge from the haze. These include the following.

- Lavigia Hill
- Santa Barbara Point light
- Montecito Country Club (square white tower)
- Santa Barbara City College buildings and stadium on a bluff above the harbor
- four oil platforms that lie 5.5 miles offshore, SSE of the harbor, in a precise line, approximately E-W; these platforms are your best guide on foggy days

Once the major landmarks are spotted, steer for the conspicuous buildings of Santa Barbara City College that lie on a bluff above the breakwater. The red-roofed Performing Arts Center is especially prominent, E of the main college campus. The squat white structure of Santa Barbara Point light can be identified to port, then soon afterward sandy West Beach W of the harbor. You may have some difficulty identifying the main breakwater that lies parallel to the shore. Look for the masts behind it and for surf breaking against its footings. The western end of the breakwater tends to merge with Stearn's Wharf when seen from offshore. The Bekins warehouse behind the harbor is conspicuous and a good landmark for finding the entrance.

The white lighthouse tower on shore immediately E and behind Stearn's Wharf is not a navigational aid, but rather part of a restaurant!

When approaching Santa Barbara from offshore in foggy weather, the four oil rigs that lie 5.5 miles SSE of the harbor are a useful checkpoint if you are approaching the land from east of Santa Cruz or Anacapa Islands. The course from the westernmost oil rig to the harbor entrance

Lesley Newhart

Santa Barbara approach from S, distant 1½ miles. Note the Saddleback (arrow), the yacht masts in the harbor, and the buildings of City College to W (arrow).

Santa Barbara entrance, with Stearn's Wharf and approach buoy. The white warehouse ashore is conspicuous—a useful signpost from some distance offshore.

is about 315 deg. M. In thick weather, approach the land with great care and watch for high-speed fishing boats. The foghorn on the breakwater is a useful reference mark (two blasts every 20 seconds). It is recommended to delay entrance until the weather clears, and to anchor E of Stearn's Wharf instead. Do not anchor there in SE conditions because steep swells run onto the beach, which is a lee shore.

Harbor Entrance. Santa Barbara Harbor entrance is notorious for its shoaling. Many yachts have grounded on the sandbar, especially at low tide or when the entrance is congested. Check conditions in the entrance by calling the harbormaster on VHF channel 16 and then switching to channel 12.

Once the entrance opens up between Stearn's Wharf and the sandbar that runs NE from the breakwater and the second bell buoy (Fl. G. 2.5 sec.) is abeam, watch for a series of green can and red nun buoys that mark the dredged limits of the entry channel. Then trend around to port, as you pass the landward end of the sandbar, and turn into the harbor proper. The buoys are often removed during dredging or severe shoaling. Do not pass outside the marker buoys or steer direct for the harbor after rounding the breakwater at high tide. First-time visitors are advised to attempt their entrance on the flood and at middle to high tide, in clear weather.

The narrow entrance channel can become congested on weekends. A depth-sounder will save you from disaster and give you room to maneuver. Monitor depths closely at slow speeds because the water can shoal rapidly. The deepest water is normally on the sandbar side of the dredged channel. Give the end of Stearn's Wharf a wide berth. Stay on the starboard side of the dredged channel when entering.

Once you are safely inside the harbor, head SW up the 225-foot-wide main fairway (10 feet) to the Navy pier at the head of the harbor. A Union 76 gas dock is at the end of the pier. The sign is conspicuous, as is the gray icehouse behind it. Visiting yachts should secure to the temporary mooring float that lies immediately S of the Navy pier near the harbormaster's orange launches. The harbormaster's office—at the head of the dock—will then assign a visitor's slip for the duration of your stay. It is not possible to secure to the Navy pier (16 feet) because it is busy with U.S. Coast Guard traffic, commercial boats, and unloading fishing boats.

In thick weather, a foghorn sounds twice every 20 seconds from the light at the end of the breakwater. Your problem is to locate the end of the breakwater and Stearn's Wharf. When you have found one of these landmarks, you should be able to feel your way up the channel from buoy to buoy using the depth-sounder. If in doubt, however, anchor east of Stearn's Wharf until the fog clears, usually by midday.

Although Santa Barbara Harbor is easy to find at night, actual entry can be confusing due to the bright lights of the town. Santa Barbara Point light (Fl. 10 sec., 142 feet) is visible for 25 miles. The harbor itself displays three lights:

- On Stearn's Wharf: Fl. R. 6 sec., 25 feet, 7 miles
- On the E end of the breakwater: equal intermittent Fl. W. 6 sec., 35 feet, 9 miles
- On the S end of the N breakwater: Qk. Fl. R.

The flashing green lights of the approach buoys offer a useful approach line. All the harbor lights are difficult to distinguish against the mass of city illuminations. Two red flashing radio-mast lights, seen east of Stearn's Wharf, provide a general guide.

Once you have identified the approach lights, you have to feel your way through the channel buoys (the green buoy at the main corner exhibits a faint Fl. G. light). Do this by using your depth-sounder, staying closer to Stearn's Wharf than to the sandbar until you pick up the first red starboard-hand buoy. The best way to spot it is to go onto the foredeck, bring your head close to the deck, and try to spot the dark mass of the buoy against the shimmering water. A spotlight helps because the buoys are marked with reflecting tape. Once you have located this mark, you should shape your course SW up the channel. There is talk (as of early 2001) of lighting the channel, so you may find lights when you arrive at night!

Cautions. It is important to observe the following cautions:

- Do not attempt to enter Santa Barbara Harbor during a strong SE storm because the entrance is a dangerous lee shore, especially at low tide.
- Beware of the dredge operating in the entrance at certain times of the year. The space for navigation is then severely restricted and the entrance is sometimes temporarily blocked. It is difficult to enter or leave at night under these circumstances. Consult *Local Notices* for information on dredging activities.
- Give the sandbar a wide berth at night. Do not steer straight for the masts in the harbor because you will go hard aground.

If you are in doubt about the entrance, call the harbormaster on channel 16.

Berths. Anchoring in the harbor is forbidden—indeed, impossible—even if you wanted to. About thirty guest slips are available, and each berth has water and electricity. The maximum permitted stay is fourteen days. Showers and heads are available; a key can be obtained from the harbormaster for a nominal refundable deposit.

Anchorage. In the event that the harbor is full, you can anchor E of Stearn's Wharf, except in SE weather. Do not try to tie up alongside the wharf (18 to 24 feet), even temporarily. The constant surge makes this an unpleasant berth and, in any case, mooring is forbidden. A launching ramp for trailer boats lies on the N side of the harbor. To approach it, turn starboard from the fairway when the north breakwater (Qk. Fl. R.) is abeam.

Facilities. Gasoline and diesel can be obtained from the Union 76 station on the Navy pier; water is available at your berth. The service station operates a small crane on the pier for a modest charge. A small-boat hoist is located near the 30-ton Marine Travelift haul-out berth south of the Navy pier. Both the Travelift and hoist are operated by the boatyard behind the harbormaster's office, which is highly recommended and undertakes all small-boat repair and maintenance work.

The harbormaster's office is located at the head of the harbor above The Chandlery, an exceptionally well-stocked marine hardware store. Other marine businesses, including a small fish market, fishing equipment store, an electronics store, yacht brokers, and another yachting hardware outlet, are a few yards away.

There is much to see in Santa Barbara, including the tenth mission founded by the Franciscans in 1786, some fascinating old adobes, and the remains of the 1782 Royal Presidio. The Santa Barbara Museum of Art and Natural History Museum are justly famous. Do not miss the Sea Center

Santa Barbara Harbor during a strong southeaster.

Lesley Newhart

Museum on Stearn's Wharf—a fascinating window on the channel—or the Santa Barbara Maritime Museum at the head of the harbor. Many people plan their visits to coincide with Old Spanish Days Fiesta in August, which is an orgy of parades, dancing, parties, and general good times. The most important sailing events of the year are the Semana Nautica Regatta in July—which offers several days of keen racing for boats of all sizes—and the Santa Barbara to King Harbor Race in early August, which is one of the most popular yacht races in Southern California with more than 150 entries most years.

Santa Barbara Yacht Club welcomes visiting members of reciprocal clubs, and has excellent bar, food, and shower facilities. It is noted for its friendly atmosphere and keen racing programs. Santa Barbara Sailing Club has less elaborate facilities, but has a very active racing program, especially for smaller craft.

Contacts.
Harbormaster
132A Harbor Way
Santa Barbara CA 93109
805-963-1737/8
www.sailorschoice.com/SBHarbor.htm

U.S. Coast Guard Patrol Boat–Santa Barbara: 805-966-3093

Courses. Given in degrees magnetic (2000). For reverse course, add 180 degrees.

Santa Barbara to

Point Conception: 255 deg., 38 miles (From Santa Barbara Point)

Cuyler Harbor, San Miguel: 224 deg., 38 miles

Becher's Bay, Santa Rosa: 203 deg., 29.8 miles

Prisoner's Harbor, Santa Cruz Island: 168 deg., 22.4 miles

San Pedro Point, Santa Cruz Island: 146 deg., 23.3 miles

Ventura Marina: 100 deg., 23 miles

Channel Islands Harbor: 108 deg., 27 miles

Arch Rock, Anacapa Island: 131 deg., 28.1 miles

MAINLAND: SANTA BARBARA TO POINT MUGU

SANTA BARBARA HARBOR TO FERNALD COVE

Chart 18725; Chart-Kit, pp. 7–8

We now sail past the eastern mainland coastline of the Santa Barbara Channel, from Santa Barbara to Point Mugu. Surprisingly, this part of the coast is little frequented by small-boat sailors, most of whom take passage directly from the Channel Islands or Ventura to Santa Barbara. When traveling E with the prevailing W winds, however, you may benefit from staying closer to land. A current of 0.25 to 0.50 knot sometimes flows E close inshore, giving you extra boat speed. Although there is only one recognized calm-weather anchorage between Santa Barbara and Ventura, the contrasting scenery of mountains, sandy beaches, and busy highway make this an interesting trip. Fortunately, modern sailing vessels do better than their nineteenth-century counterparts. "We have

known a vessel to be three days working from San Buenaventura to Santa Barbara," wrote George Davidson in 1858.

A leisurely sail down to Fernald Cove off Montecito, at the eastern end of Santa Barbara, has long been a favorite weekend excursion for Santa Barbara sailors. The backdrop of mountains, houses, and green trees can be impressive on a fine clear day. Passage down the coast can be made either inside or outside the kelp bed that bounds the shore about 0.25 to 0.5 mile off the beach. There is water at least 20 feet deep just inside the kelp, but watch for bathers and water-skiers who use the smooth water inside the kelp for high-speed runs. It is inadvisable to close the coast nearer than 100 yards. Give the rocky ledges off the Santa Barbara Cemetery and immediately W of Fernald Cove a wide berth.

East of Stearn's Wharf, the yellow beach is fringed with the tall palm trees of

Cabrillo Boulevard. Some yachts are anchored year-round E of the wharf. Avoid fishing lines off Stearn's Wharf and stay clear of the landings on the wharf, except in emergencies. The city sewer-outfall pipe runs out to deep water immediately E of the Wharf for 1.5 miles. Its outer end is marked by an orange and white striped buoy, which is used as a racing mark by local yachts. Under no circumstances should you anchor on or near this line. A red buoy (lighted at night) marks the outer end of the city desalinization water pipeline. Several large mooring buoys laid by the oil companies also lie off Cabrillo Beach, and are too large for practical use by small craft. However, it is possible to anchor east of Stearn's Wharf between the moorings and the kelp in approximately 30 feet (soft sand). The holding ground can be poor. Good scope should be laid out and you should be prepared to take shelter in the harbor if the wind swings to the SE and blows with any force in this anchorage. Many boats wash ashore when they drag here during winter storms. Anchor outside the Anchoring Forbidden zone E of Stearn's Wharf.

The white arches of the Red Lion Inn lie behind palm-fringed Cabrillo Beach. The low-lying hotel buildings can be seen from some distance from seaward, as can the bright colors of the fanciful chromatic arch that was erected by wealthy art patrons in front of the inn. The beach continues past the Cabrillo Recreation Center—a conspicuous white building with a long veranda. The white tower of a hotel rises immediately NE behind the center. White buoys laid off the center in the summer warn small craft to stay away from swimmers.

East of the recreation center, the beach ends in a low cliff, which extends E for the best part of a mile. The Clark Mansion, a square gray stone house of considerable size, stands on the western end of the cliff among low bushes and trees. The mansion grounds adjoin Santa Barbara Cemetery. As you approach the cliff from W, Montecito Country Club (with its conspicuous tower) is clearly visible inland. This important landmark can be seen far from seaward and is a useful way to identify Santa Barbara from midchannel. The brown cemetery cliff slopes down to sea level as you approach the Biltmore Hotel, the white buildings of which can be seen immediately inshore, just W of the white tower of the Coral Casino on Edgecliff Point. The tower is a conspicuous landmark from all directions, as are the multistory Hammonds Estate condominium buildings that can be seen from a long way offshore.

East of the condominiums, the tree-covered shore indents slightly N, forming a shallow bay off Miramar Beach. A row of beach houses and a seaside luxury resort bound the sandy beach. It is possible to anchor off this beach for an afternoon picnic, but an overnight stay is not recommended. There is 20 feet of water 60 feet off the beach. A comfortable landing can be made on the sand, and a road into Montecito is at the western end. The eastern end of the beach is low-lying and backed by private houses. It ends in a rocky shelf that forms the western extremity of Fernald Cove.

Fernald Cove

Fernald Cove is a convenient day anchorage 3.7 miles E of Santa Barbara Harbor that provides a pleasant day-picnic anchorage.

Approach. Fernald Cove is easy to identify from seaward, although the actual cove indentation is relatively small. Approaching from offshore, the cove is situated at the eastern end of the houses that form coastal Montecito. The spot can be readily located because it lies at the precise spot where U.S. 101 climbs from sea level up Ortega Hill (250 feet) to Summerland. As soon as the last houses are identified, steer for the eastern house until individual structures can be discerned from outside the kelp. When you are about 0.25 mile outside the kelp, identify the easternmost residence—a large, two-decked, wooden house—and steer for it on a bearing of 010 deg. M. The freeway runs at roof level behind this house. Once you are inside the kelp, proceed carefully inshore, altering the course E to steer for a red-roofed house that can be seen above the freeway.

From E or W. Steer up the coast inside the kelp in about 30 feet. From E, pick up the wooden house and sound your way to a suitable spot. From W, give the rocky shelf at Fernald Point a good berth, and stay about 200 yards offshore until the timber house is located and the anchorage is selected.

Anchorage. Sounding carefully, anchor about 250 yards offshore in about 20 feet or more (sand), depending on draft and

Fernald Cove from S, distant ⅓ mile. Arrow indicates the house referred to in the text above.

Lesley Newhart

swell conditions. At this spot, the wooden house will bear about 345 deg. M. Beware of water-skiers, surfers, and swimmers, especially close inshore. This anchorage is exposed to all southern directions and offers only limited shelter from W. It is suitable for overnight stays only in the most favorable calm conditions.

Landing. Land on the beach and use the path to the other side of the freeway or follow the seashore to Miramar Beach. There are no facilities here.

FERNALD COVE TO VENTURA

East of Fernald Cove, the cliffs rise steeply to the yellow bluff of Ortega Hill. The bluff is crisscrossed with highway and railroad grades that render it conspicuous from seaward. Ortega Hill descends into the buildings of Summerland, a small village fronted by a sandy beach that runs eastward to Carpinteria. A bed of kelp lies offshore of the beach in 30 to 35 feet; navigation close inshore is often hampered by its dense growth. The wooded, yellow-brown cliffs of Loon Point are easily identified both from offshore and when passing Summerland near the kelp. This stretch of coast has a backdrop of steep mountains. U.S. 101 passes close inshore of the beach most of the way between Fernald Cove and Ventura except at Carpinteria, where it passes through the town. The lights of passing traffic can be seen at night, and trucks can be heard far offshore in still conditions.

On its eastern side, Loon Point trends NE. The coast is low-lying from this yellow bluff as far E as the Rincon Oil Island,

low cliffs giving way to a sandy beach and the conspicuous white buildings of Santa Claus Lane, 1.7 miles E of Carpinteria. The structures at Santa Claus Lane can be seen from far offshore and are a useful landmark when approaching the coast in thick weather.

Carpinteria claims it owns the "world's safest beach," protected as it is by a kelp bed in 30 to 50 feet. It is possible to anchor off the beach for bathing in quiet weather, but not overnight. Approach with caution because breakers can occur up to 0.5 mile offshore along much of the beach.

A complex of white mooring buoys and an oil pier lie 1.6 miles E of Sand Point, a small headland with off-lying shoal just W of Carpinteria. This point should be given a berth of at least 0.75 mile because of an exposed rock 550 yards offshore. Avoid anchoring off the oil pier because pipelines run offshore from shore facilities and storage tanks to the platforms at this point. Be alert to launch traffic between the pier and the platforms at all hours of the day and night. The green oil tanks behind the pier are conspicuous.

The coastline remains low-lying E of Carpinteria, the beach being bounded by low brown cliffs that end in sandy Rincon Point. Behind lie the yellow-brown slopes of Rincon Mountain. The Rincon is conspicuous for these yellow-brown slopes and large-scale anti-erosion works that stand out as straight lines for a long distance. U.S. 101 rejoins the coast E of the Rincon, at a famous surfing spot. The coastal mountains now press on the coast, leaving only a narrow strip of land for the freeway and the Southern Pacific Railroad, with 2,000-foot peaks behind them. An obvious fold in the mountains lies immediately behind the Rincon itself. It is possible to anchor immediately E of the Rincon (sand), but it is at best a temporary anchorage and the freeway is noisy. Watch for surfers when maneuvering inshore in this vicinity; the surf can come up rapidly here.

The shoreline at the foot of the mountains now forms a series of shallow bays that run between the Rincon and Ventura. Punta Gorda is prominent because of a long pier that runs from its extremity to an artificial oil-pumping island 0.50 mile offshore (Lat. 34°20.8′ N, Long. 119°26.7′ W). Rincon Island is adorned with oil pumps and some palm trees. At night, it displays a white light (Fl. 5 sec.), sounding a horn in thick weather.

Anchorage. You can anchor in the lee of the artificial island with some shelter from W–NW winds, but an overnight stay is not recommended. Give the island a good 0.5 mile berth.

The kelp-lined coastline has few noticeable landmarks between Punta Gorda and Ventura. Houses of Seacliff Village can be seen 1.5 miles E of the Rincon. Some conspicuous oil-storage tanks lie on a ridge above Rincon Island. The facility is well lit at night—an isolated patch of brilliance that provides a useful landmark. Because of off-lying ledges and breakers, stay well off this stretch of coastline until you approach Ventura—and certainly outside the kelp. Pitas Point, 5.5 miles NW of Ventura, is conspicuous, a low spit running seaward from a steep slope. A deep arroyo appears W of the point.

Rincon Oil Island from W, distant ½ mile.

Lesley Newhart

Conspicuous freeway trestle at the foot of the hillside immediately W of Ventura.

The coastal mountains fall away into the Ventura River Valley. The isolated buildings and beach houses of the rockwall-faced shoreline give way to the dry estuary of the Ventura River and the urban sprawl of Ventura itself. An easily identifiable concrete freeway bridge and contoured freeway cutting lie on the coast approximately 4 miles W of Ventura Marina; these are your first landmarks when looking for the harbor. The coastline of the Santa Barbara Channel now begins to trend SE toward Point Hueneme and the eastern entrance of the Channel. The harbor lies close to two green oil tanks on the coast ahead.

Ventura Harbor
Large-scale plan on Chart 18725; Chart-Kit, p. 8
Lat. 34°14.8′ N, Long. 119°16.2′ W

Ventura Harbor is used frequently by visiting small craft and is an attractive and friendly harbor. Unfortunately, the entrance can be difficult in strong westerly conditions. In calm weather, Ventura provides a safe berth with all reasonable facilities for small craft. A development named Ventura Keys with waterfront homes (least depth 9 feet) lies NE of the main harbor, with an access channel leading into the harbor.

Approach. From W: The mouth of the Ventura River lies immediately east of the coastal mountains, which come down to sea level west of the city. You should be able to identify this point from a long distance on clear days. A large concrete freeway bridge at the foot of the mountains is also prominent, as well as the erosion contours on the slope behind the highway (see the photograph on page 156).

The buildings of Ventura should now be clearly visible. Look for the gray high-rise Holiday Inn on the shore, which usually can be spotted from some distance. This useful checkpoint lies 0.5 mile east of the green- and yellow-roofed buildings of Ventura County Fairgrounds near the coast. A conspicuous microwave tower on top of a hill overlooks Ventura 1.8 miles NE of Ventura Pier and can sometimes be spotted above a mantle of coastal fog and haze.

Padre Junipero Serra's cross can be seen at the summit of a 350-foot hill NE of Ventura when it is lit at night. After the Holiday Inn has been identified, it should be possible to discern the following landmarks that mark the final approach to Ventura Harbor.

- A fishing pier that extends 1,960 feet seaward just east of the Holiday Inn into Pierpoint Bay. This pier is 1.8 miles NW of the Ventura Harbor entrance and has 19 feet at the outer end.
- The SE end of a row of conspicuous trees that grow along the coast behind Ventura Harbor. The trees are a useful background to the harbor entrance.
- Two green oil tanks that lie behind the breakwater.

Ventura Harbor entrance from S, distant 1 mile (arrow) in moderate visibility. The National Park Service building just inside the entrance is conspicuous.

Lesley Newhart

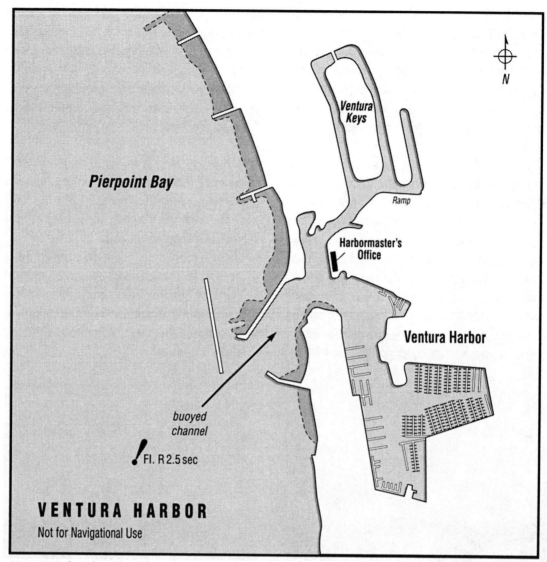

Ventura Harbor plan.

Once the pier is abeam, you should be able to see the Ventura Marina breakwater 1.8 miles SE and the gray mass of the Channel Islands National Park building. The breakwater lies parallel to the land and tends to merge against the shore, especially in foggy conditions. However, you should be able to spot the Ventura Harbor lighted whistle buoy, known as No. 2, which is painted red (Fl. R. 2.5 sec.); this marks the entrance to the harbor.

The outer breakwater is detached from land and is lit at the southern extremity by Fl. G. 2.5 sec., 5 miles.

Steer for the southern extremity of the detached breakwater and pass the Ventura Harbor whistle buoy, which lies 0.5 mile SW of the entrance. Maintain your course until the entrance of the harbor behind the detached breakwater is clearly visible. Then shape your course to pass between the detached breakwater and the south jetty of the harbor itself. Stay well clear of the small sandy beach on the southern side of the entrance inside the breakwater.

From S. Locate the conspicuous red and white smokestack of the Edison Power Plant 3 miles SW of Ventura Harbor. Follow the coastline NW, staying at least 0.5 to 0.75 mile offshore until the Ventura Harbor buoy and breakwater are located. The conspicuous trees and green storage tanks behind the harbor are also useful landmarks; so is the park headquarters. The approach lights can be confusing against the mainland at night, so approach the entrance with care.

Caution. Although the Ventura harbormaster regularly distributes duplicated plans of the shoals in the harbor entrance, the documents are only available locally. Following are some precautionary hints for visitors.

- Do not attempt Ventura entrance when high swells are running or strong NW or W winds are blowing. Shoaling can make the entrance extremely hazardous. Several vessels have been lost trying to make the harbor in bumpy conditions. Under these circumstances, divert to the Channel Islands.

- Approach Ventura Harbor with caution at night. Both the harbor and its lights are difficult to locate against the bright lights of the mainland. When entering at night, keep a close check on your position, and never attempt the entrance in marginal conditions.
- Do not enter Ventura Harbor from the northern end of the detached breakwater. There are least depths of 3 feet in this area—it is not a channel.
- If you are in doubt about conditions at the entrance, call the Ventura harbormaster's office on VHF channel 16 or 12.

Entrance. Two jetties that enclose the harbor entrance are at an angle to the detached breakwater. Approach the entrance around the SE end of the detached breakwater, keeping a close watch for breaking water in the entrance. Leave the small red buoy that marks the western edge of the sand shoal in the entrance to starboard as you enter. This shoal, with a reported least depth of 4 feet, can create dangerous conditions in rough weather.

Once abeam of the south jetty, alter course to starboard and proceed up the dredged channel (20 feet) through the 300-foot-wide entrance. Once beyond a rock groin that extends from the sand spit on the NE side of the channel, the harbor itself will open up before you. Pierpoint Basin (least depth 15 feet) lies to port, reached between two channel buoys. The dredged channel to the Ventura Keys residential development leads NE off Pierpoint Basin, with a least depth of 10 feet. There is 9 feet in the Keys channel. The main harbor lies to starboard of the entrance channel and is dredged from 10 to 14 feet in most places.

Small-boat hoists, a fuel dock, and launching ramps lie E of the harbormaster's office and National Park Service facilities at the head of the entrance channel. The marinas lie in Basin A and South Basin, and are reached by a dredged channel marked with a midchannel marker. Ventura Yacht Club lies to starboard just as you enter South Basin. Visiting yachts from other clubs sometimes may find a slip there. South Basin is a major marina development, and Basin A also has some visitors' slips. Consult the harbormaster for up-to-date information.

Berths. All three harbor marinas (listed under contacts) have guest slips and full facilities for visitors. The Port District on the NE side of the marina operates a launching ramp. Anchoring in Ventura Harbor is not permitted. You can anchor in Pierpoint Bay outside the harbor, but this is only recommended on a very temporary basis. In the words of George Davidson in 1858, "There is excellent holding ground off Buenaventura in 10 fathoms, but the landing is not good." Vancouver spent a day recovering a fouled anchor here in 1793.

Facilities. A Union 76 fuel dock lies just E of the harbormaster's office. A full-service shipyard can lift yachts up to 150 tons and perform most work. Dry storage ashore is also available. Marine hardware stores and yacht brokerages are in the harbor area. All typical city services are within a short taxi ride. There is plenty to see and do in Ventura. The Ventura County Fair in August is a popular annual event, and Mission San Buenaventura, the Ortega and Olivas adobes, and the Padre Serra Cross are worth visiting.

Contacts.
Harbormaster
Ventura Port District
16033 Anchors Way Drive
Ventura CA 93001
805-642-8538
Harbor Patrol (24 hours):
805-642-8618
www.venturaharbor.com

U.S. Coast Guard Search and Rescue
Emergency (call collect): (Oxnard)
805-985-9822

Channel Islands National Park
1901 Spinnaker Drive
Ventura CA 93001
805-644-8262

Marinas

Ventura Isle Marina
1363 Spinnaker Drive
Ventura CA 93001
805-644-5858
(Pump-out station)

Ventura West Marina
1198 Navigator
Ventura CA 93001
805-644-8266
(Pump-out station)

Village Dock Master
1449 Spinnaker Drive
Ventura CA 93001
805-644-8286

Courses. Given in degrees magnetic (2000). For reverse courses, add 180 degrees.

Ventura to

Santa Barbara: 280 deg., 23 miles

Pelican Bay, Santa Cruz Island: 224 deg., 25 miles

San Pedro Point, Santa Cruz Island: 209 deg., 18 miles

Arch Rock, Anacapa Island: 183 deg., 14.5 miles

Channel Islands Harbor: 140 deg., 6 miles

VENTURA TO CHANNEL ISLANDS HARBOR

A low-lying sandy beach stretches SE to Port Hueneme and then E to Point Mugu. Oxnard and Port Hueneme occupy much of the Santa Clara plain behind the sandy shoreline. Point Mugu Naval Air Base lies E of Oxnard, its main runway extending S to the coastline W of Point Mugu itself. The Pacific Missile Range extends offshore across the eastern entrance to the Santa Barbara Channel. All in all, the coastline is tedious, considerably developed, and exposed to dangerous swell during winter storms. We are fortunate to have a com-

fortable, all-weather, small-boat harbor at Channel Islands that offers a secure refuge in all conditions.

The 5 miles of low-lying coastline between Ventura Marina and Channel Islands Harbor consists of low sand dunes and a yellow sandy beach, with few features of interest inshore. The highway between Ventura Marina and Channel Islands follows the coast about 0.5 mile inland. It is advisable to stay at least 1 to 1.75 miles offshore, especially if a moderate or heavy swell is running.

A line of trees extends SE from Ventura Marina. A group of oil-storage tanks stands at the end of the trees. Another row of trees can be seen immediately S of the most conspicuous landmark on the coast, the Mandalay Beach power plant 3 miles SE of Ventura Marina. With its single red and white striped smokestack 220 feet high, this facility can be identified from a considerable distance. Indeed, when approaching Channel Islands from W, you may sight the power plant long before the low-lying coast comes into view. Note that this power station has only *one* smokestack, which is lit at night by a flashing red light. Nine mooring buoys lie off the generating plant, marked by buoy "2MB" 1.0 mile offshore (Fl. 4 sec. at night), as well as two privately maintained markers with orange flashing lights. The power plant is brightly illuminated and provides a useful landmark for a nocturnal approach. Six oil-storage tanks lie immediately SE, behind the power plant.

A row of beach houses and a resort hotel with a tower mark the outskirts of Oxnard and Channel Islands. The built-up area

Mandalay Bay power plant.

extends all the way to Port Hueneme. In clear weather, the Santa Monica Mountains behind the coastal Santa Clara plain provide an admirable landmark for locating Channel Islands Harbor from as far away as Santa Barbara.

Channel Islands Harbor
Large-scale plan on Chart 18725; Chart-Kit, p. 9
SE end of detached breakwater: Lat. 34°09.3′ N, Long. 119°13.8′ W

Channel Islands Harbor is a magnificent modern yacht harbor that offers every possible facility and complete shelter to visiting small craft. The entrance is safe in all but the roughest weather, and has ample space for visiting yachts. Channel Islands is an ideal stopping-off point for visiting the offshore islands or Santa Barbara, and is a comfortable day's sail from Santa Cruz Island or Marina del Rey. Santa Catalina Island is also within easy cruising reach.

Approach. Channel Islands Harbor is protected by a detached breakwater that is lit at both its northern and southern extremities with lights that are mounted on metal brackets. Both this and the north jetty are also lit. Like Ventura, the detached breakwater lies parallel to the low-lying mainland and is difficult to locate from offshore, especially in thick weather. Remember that the higher-pitched foghorn on the south jetty may be confused with that the one on Point Hueneme.

From SE. Once you are around Point Hueneme, steer NW parallel to the shore 0.75 mile offshore until the detached breakwater and south jetty are located ahead. Then shape your course for the entrance, keeping a safe distance offshore from the breakers.

From S through NW. Your best long-distance landmark is the Mandalay Bay power plant with its prominent single red and white striped smokestack. Approaching from Anacapa Island in clear weather, you should be able to obtain an accurate fix from this power plant and the equivalent Ormond Beach facility with its twin smokestacks. Both facilities are marked on Chart 18725.

As you approach the shore between Channel Islands and Ventura, leave the Mandalay Bay power plant well on the port bow and look for the N end of the row of beach houses that extends from Point Hueneme toward Ventura. The Channel Island Harbor breakwater lies about 1 mile SE of the first houses. In clear weather, you should be able to locate Point Hueneme and the detached breakwater 1 mile NW once you are within 2 miles of shore. When the 2,300-foot-long detached breakwater has been located, alter course for the S extremity. A foghorn (15 seconds) is located at the south jetty inside the detached breakwater. Unfortunately, there are no conspicuous landmarks behind the harbor to aid your daylight approach, except for some water towers. Regular visitors develop their own approach from experience.

Do not attempt to pass between the northern end of the detached breakwater and the beach in rough weather. This entrance can shoal rapidly.

A night approach from offshore is complicated by the confusing mass of lights behind the flashing harbor beacon. As you approach the land, identify the following:

- the brilliant lights of Mandalay Bay power plant to port
- Point Hueneme light [Gp. Fl. (5) 30 sec., 20 miles] to starboard

Fix your position from these points of reference, then approach land cautiously and identify these detached breakwater lights:

- North end: Fl. R. 4 sec., 7 miles
- South end: Fl. W. 6 sec., 6 miles

Then shape your course to pass to starboard of the southern extremity of the breakwater. The two harbor jetties bear the following lights at the outer ends:

- North jetty: Fl. G. 4 sec.
- South jetty: Fl. R. 2.5 sec.

If you doubt your exact position at night or in thick weather, steer for Mandalay Bay power plant or Point Hueneme. Once you have identified one of these two landmarks, alter course parallel to the shore 0.75 mile offshore and proceed until you sight the breakwater.

Approach Channel Islands Harbor with caution in rough westerly weather. A heavy swell can make conditions in the entrance bumpy and potentially hazardous. Strong NE winds occasionally blow down the Santa Clara Valley and also cause problems

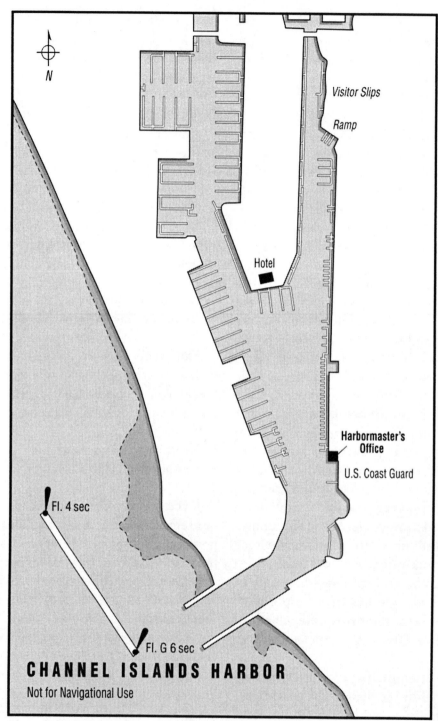

N

Visitor Slips

Ramp

Hotel

Harbormaster's Office

U.S. Coast Guard

Fl. 4 sec

Fl. G 6 sec

CHANNEL ISLANDS HARBOR
Not for Navigational Use

Channel Islands Harbor plan.

for small vessels. Sudden currents can be experienced inside the detached breakwater in rough weather, and ample engine power is advised.

Entrance. The Channel Islands Harbor entrance lies between two rock jetties 300 feet apart. The 1,650-foot entrance channel is dredged to a least depth of 13 to 20 feet; 9.5 feet is the average in most of the harbor. When entering, leave the southern extremity of the detached breakwater to port, head north midway between it and the southern jetty, leaving the red buoy well to starboard. Then turn NE as the entrance opens up. Stay just to starboard of the middle of the channel when entering or leaving. After 0.5 mile, the channel trends N, and the harbormaster's office and U.S. Coast Guard docks can be seen on the starboard bow. Make sure you stay in the middle of the channel as you start to turn N. The deepest water is in the northern entrance near the breakwater.

As you approach the harbormaster's office area, you will open up the main harbor basin, bounded to the W by extensive marina developments. The basin bifurcates at the northern end of the harbor, with the right-hand fork leading to a boatyard complex (with its large yellow crane) and the Fisherman's Wharf development. The left-hand channel passes the Casa Sirena Marina Hotel, a conspicuous building, and heads past Anacapa Island Marina, under a road bridge (clearance 29.5 feet) to the waterside Mandalay Bay and Leeward

Southern entrance to Channel Islands Harbor from SW, distant 200 yards.

Marina residential development. A lowerable mast is necessary to pass under this road bridge.

Following is a list of conspicuous landmarks as you proceed up the harbor.

To starboard:
- the harbormaster's office and U.S. Coast Guard facility
- an Arco fuel station
- Channel Islands Sport Fishing Center
- Anacapa Yacht Club (gray) clubhouse
- a boatyard complex and slips

To port:
- Channel Islands Yacht Club clubhouse
- a restaurant building

Straight ahead:
- Lobster Trap Restaurant and Casa Sirena Marina Hotel, which lead, via the port channel, to Anacapa Island Marina, surrounded by condominium developments
- To starboard, the lighthouse tower and buildings of the Fisherman's Wharf development

Night Entrance. Once the detached breakwater is to port, identify these two jetty lights:

- North jetty: Fl. G. 4 sec., 16 miles
- South jetty: Fl. R. 2.5 sec., 16 miles

Channel Islands Harbor main fairway. The harbormaster's office is to the right.

When you are in the channel, identify these two channel lights 0.5 mile inside the jetties, situated on either shore:

- Fl. G. 4 sec., 25 feet
- Fl. R. 4 sec., 25 feet

Stay midway between these lights until the brightly illuminated harbor basin opens up to port. These lights may be difficult to locate from a distance due to the bright lights onshore.

Berths. The harbormaster's office will allocate a guest slip (take your registration papers to the office); forty are available. Channel 16 is monitored around the clock. Guest berths are also available at Channel Islands Marina on the western side of the harbor, and Anacapa Isle Marina has some temporary slips, as does Peninsula Yacht Anchorage. All these marina developments offer excellent facilities including showers, electricity, and water; Anacapa Isle Marina also boasts of a fine clubhouse. Bahia Cabrillo Apartments on the western side offer apartments with slips; Casa Sirena Marina Hotel has rooms with slips. Anchoring in the harbor is forbidden.

Trailer-boatowners can launch their vessels at the county ramp on the eastern side of the harbor. The ramp is open 24 hours a day with seven lanes, free of charge—but there is a modest parking fee.

Facilities. Gasoline and diesel are available from the Arco fuel dock (Channel Islands Marine Services) in daylight hours. Three boatyards can haul your boat. Channel Islands Boatworks has a 40-ton Marine Travelift and offers every service to small vessels, as well as do-it-yourself facilities. They also build new boats. Anacapa Marine Services offers haul-out services for yachts up to 30 tons and complete boatyard facilities, including engine work. It can accommodate people who want to work on their own yachts. Channel Islands Landing has a 4-ton hoist and dry storage. All marine services, including sailmakers and diesel mechanics, can be found near the harbor. Oxnard is a 2½-mile taxi ride away, with all typical urban facilities. You can fly to Santa Barbara or Los Angeles from Ventura County Airport.

Contacts.
Harbormaster
3900 Pelican Way
Oxnard CA 93030
805-985-5544
www.channelislandsharbor.org

U.S. Coast Guard
Search and Rescue
Emergency (call collect): 805-985-9822
or 911

Yacht Clubs

Anacapa Yacht Club
3821 Victoria Avenue
Oxnard CA 93030
805-985-6003

Channel Islands Yacht Club
4100 Harbor Boulevard
Oxnard CA 93032
805-985-6091

Courses. Given in degrees magnetic (2000). For reverse courses, add 180 degrees.

Channel Islands to

Santa Barbara: 288 deg., 27 miles

Pelican Bay, Santa Cruz Island: 236 deg., 25 miles

San Pedro Point, Santa Cruz Island: 228 deg., 16 miles

Arch Rock, Anacapa Island: 205 deg., 11 miles

Santa Barbara Island: 168 deg., 42 miles

Port Hueneme

Large-scale plan on Chart 18725; Chart-Kit, p. 9

Fairway Buoy: Lat. 34°08.3′ N, Long. 119°13.0′ W

Many strangers to the Santa Barbara Channel are confused by the proximity of Channel Islands Harbor and nearby Port Hueneme, which is effectively off-limits for pleasure craft. This description of Port Hueneme is brief because few yachts visit this military port, approximately 1 mile SE of Channel Islands Marina.

This deep-water haven is maintained and operated by the U.S. Navy and the Oxnard Harbor District. Large commercial vessels, Navy craft, and oil boats use the harbor day and night. Because Channel Islands Harbor is so close, little provision is made for small craft. You are strongly advised to use Channel Islands Harbor except in a grave emergency or when the entrance of the harbor is unsafe in heavy weather. The following general notes are for emergency use only and should be used in conjunction with Chart 18725, which has a plan of the entrance.

Approach and Entrance. Port Hueneme lies at the extreme E end of the Santa Barbara Channel. To approach the harbor, identify the Mandalay Bay and Ormond Beach power stations with their conspicuous smokestacks and fix your position. Then lay a course for Point Hueneme, which is low-lying and inconspicuous. The light structure on the point is prominent. As you approach the land, you should be able to identify the two rock jetties that enclose the entrance channel. A red bell buoy (Fl. R. 4 sec.) lies 800 yards SW of the eastern jetty. There is 36 feet in the entrance channel, 31 feet inside the harbor. Other useful landmarks are as follows:

- a large yellow building 500 yards E of the entrance
- two red and white checkered elevated water tanks, one 0.8 mile, the other 1.3 miles N of the entrance
- a silver elevated water tank 1.0 mile east of the entrance

Night entrance is straightforward—the Point Hueneme light [Gp. Fl. (5) 30 sec.] and Oxnard aerobeacon (Rot. W. and G.) are both conspicuous. Two red range lights on 022 deg M lead up the fairway, visible 4 deg. either side of the range line. When entering Port Hueneme, watch out for large ships in the fairway and keep a close watch for instructions from the shore. Note that regulations surrounding shipping traffic lanes apply.

Berths and Facilities. Because this is a commercial port, there are no facilities for yachts. Berth temporarily at Wharf 1 and request instructions from the berthing master at the landward end of the dock. Leave for Channel Islands Harbor as soon as conditions permit.

We repeat, Port Hueneme is *not* recommended for yachts. One can anchor outside the harbor east of the entrance in 35 feet (sand and shale), but this berth is bumpy and little more than a temporary stopping place.

Contacts.
Port Hueneme Naval Construction Battalion Center
Base Information Officer:
805-982-4711
Officer of the Day: 805-982-4571

Beyond Channel Islands Harbor, the coastline continues without major change to Port Hueneme 1.0 mile E. Point Hueneme itself is low-lying and sandy. The land turns abruptly east at the point, lit by a 52-foot-high light (and fog signal) located on a conspicuous square building [Gp. Fl. (5) 30 sec., 20 miles]. This foghorn can be confused with the one on the south jetty at Channel Islands Harbor, which seems, however, to have a higher pitch.

East of Point Hueneme, the coastline remains low and sandy as far as rocky Point Mugu, which can be located from a long distance west. Ormond Beach power plant is located on the coast 2.4 miles SE of Port Hueneme Harbor. In contrast to the Mandalay Bay power plant, Ormond Beach has *two* red and white striped smokestacks, which display red flashing lights at night. The runway of the Point Mugu Naval Air Base ends at the shore E of the power plant. Low-flying jets sometimes give you quite a shock as they pass overhead.

Caution. A passage to Los Angeles along the coastline E of Point Hueneme takes you across the Pacific Missile Range. Call "Plead Control" on channel 16 to avoid delay. Also consult *Local Notices* for notifications of firings. Information on firings is also broadcast on 2638 kHz and 2738 kHz at 0900 and 1200, Monday through Friday.

A lagoon lies inshore of the beach S of the air base. A rifle range is situated at the E end of this long beach about 1 mile W of Point Mugu. Red flags are displayed and a depressing sign reads: DANGER LIVE FIRING. They mean it!

You should stay about 1.0 mile off this desolate coast, and 2.0 miles off the rifle range to avoid unnecessary surge and ricochets when firings are in progress. A launch patrols the fire path of the Pacific Missile Range S of the beach.

Point Mugu is the seaward end of the Santa Monica Mountains. California Route

Lesley Newhart

Ormond Beach power plant (arrow) photographed in hazy, offshore conditions with a 25-knot NW wind blowing. Point Mugu is in the distance.

1 passes through a blasted roadway back of the point, leaving an isolated rock as the outer extremity of the headland. Two aluminum-colored tanks 1.5 miles NW of Point Mugu and radar-warning installations on the peak behind the headland are conspicuous and a useful lead to the position of the point in thick weather. The tanks are marked by flashing red lights.

You can encounter windy conditions off Point Mugu and W to Point Hueneme, especially in the late afternoon. Under sail, the W wind can give you a bumpy ride to windward as you tack toward Channel Islands Harbor along the sandy wastes of the Santa Clara Valley to starboard.

SAN MIGUEL AND SANTA ROSA ISLANDS

San Miguel and Santa Rosa Islands are the westernmost of the Channel Islands and are among the most remote national park properties in the nation. Their very remoteness makes them a favorite destination for people cruising the islands, and San Miguel's elephant-seal rookeries are famous.

Few Chumash Indians lived on either of the islands. In 1850, a local sealing captain named George Nidever settled on San Miguel. He imported cattle and sheep and ran a ranch on the island until 1870, when he sold out. The island became sheep-grazing land until 1892, when Captain James Waters leased the island for eight years. He claimed that San Miguel was still in Mexican territory and refused to let U.S. coast surveyors land on the island. Waters's stance was overridden by an order signed by President Cleveland. His greatest claim to fame was the construction of a remark-able house built from driftwood and shipwreck materials.

New Englander Herbert Lester and his family were the last ranchers on San Miguel. They arrived on the island in the late 1920s and had only sporadic contact with the mainland by boat and private plane. The Lesters' two daughters were educated in a tiny schoolhouse, using books and curricula supplied by the Santa Barbara Board of Education. Depressed over his health, Lester committed suicide when he learned that the Navy was about to take over San Miguel and his family would have to evacuate after the outbreak of World War II. The island served as an air gunnery range until it became part of the Channel Islands National Park.

Santa Rosa was awarded as a Mexican land grant to Carlos and José Antonio Carrillo in 1834. By the 1850s, the island was on its way to becoming a prosperous sheep

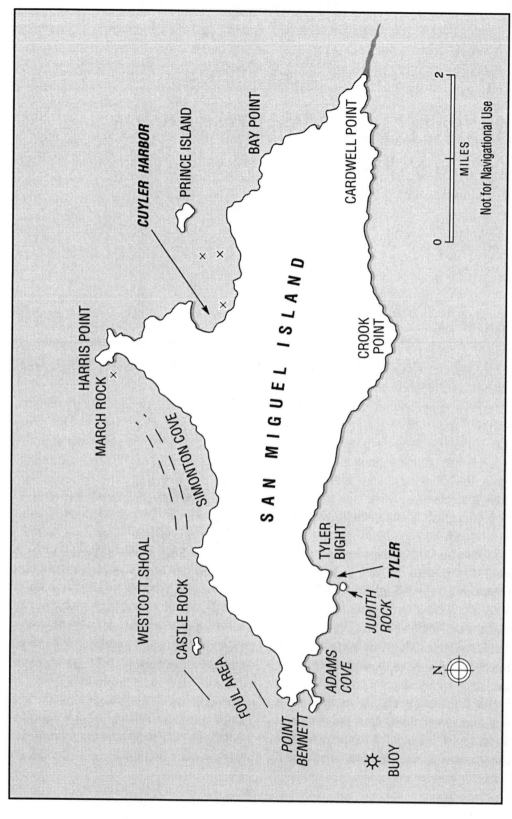

San Miguel Island, showing major features and anchorages mentioned in the text.

ranch. The island passed into the hands of L. Vickers and J. V. Vail in 1902. In 1986, the Vail and Vickers Company sold Santa Rosa Island to the federal government, and it is now part of the Channel Islands National Park. The U.S. Air Force maintained a small Nike missile base on the southern coast of the island near Johnson's Lee in the 1950s, long since abandoned.

SAN MIGUEL ISLAND

San Miguel Island, part of the Channel Islands National Park, is an Ecological Reserve and is in the Channel Islands National Marine Sanctuary. The island currently is open to the public on a limited-access basis, both to protect the large seal and sea-lion rookeries and to avoid accidents with the unexploded bombs and ammunition from the abandoned air gunnery range that occasionally turn up underfoot. San Miguel has a resident ranger for most of the year. A permit to visit must be obtained from the Channel Islands National Park office in Ventura (805-644-8262), where appointments for a guided tour of the island must also be made—well in advance. You cannot obtain permits at the island. Overnight anchorage is permitted *only* at Cuyler Harbor and Tyler Bight.

For all the difficulties of access and unsettled weather, San Miguel is well worth a visit just to see the rookeries and unusual vegetation in the company of a knowledgeable guide. There are navigational restrictions at the western end of the island; first-time visitors are advised to use Cuyler Harbor.

Approaches to San Miguel Island
Chart 18727; Chart-Kit, p. 10

San Miguel is the most remote of the Santa Barbara Channel Islands, a desolate and windy place that has a charm all its own. The island is 7.6 miles long and up to 4 miles wide. On clear days, you can see the two hills on San Miguel as far as 20 miles away because the 800-foot humps stand out on the horizon even when the lower slopes of the island are invisible. San Miguel is notorious for its strong northwesterlies, which often spring up at night. Even in moderate NW weather offshore, the local winds can reach 50 knots. Once covered with dense brush, the island was denuded by drought and decades of sheep-ranching. The western part is now sand dunes; stunted grass and scrub cover the remainder.

Do not visit San Miguel until you have had considerable experience cruising in the Channel and with heavy-weather sailing. San Miguel's weather is unpredictable and sometimes dangerous. Even in calm conditions, heavy Pacific swells can roll into seemingly sheltered anchorages and seriously impede progress under power. The golden rules of cruising San Miguel are simple.

- Choose your weather and monitor weather forecasts constantly.
- Avoid the western end of San Miguel. There are many off-lying dangers and often heavy swells.

This said, I should mention that it has been flat calm the last eight times I have been at San Miguel!

Approach. From N: Approaching San Miguel from north of Point Conception takes some care. Plan to stay well off the mainland, clear of strong winds that funnel around Point Conception. As you approach San Miguel, keep a sharp watch for the following outlying dangers:

Richardson Rock.

- Richardson Rock, 5.5 miles NW of Point Bennett. This isolated rock is 53 feet high and white-topped. A lighted whistle buoy (Lat. 34°06′ N, Long. 120°31.2′ W) (Fl. R. 2.5 sec.) lies 0.5 mile NW of the Rock. To avoid the foul areas closer inshore, do not pass between this lighted rock and San Miguel at night.
- Wilson Rock, 2.2 miles NW of Harris Point, only 19 feet high. A reef extends about a mile WNW from the black rock.

Point Bennett and the western end of San Miguel Island. Give this area a wide berth.

This shoal is covered with breaking water even in a slight swell. Further foul ground lies S and SW of Wilson Rock.

- Castle Rock, a three-headed outcrop 1.6 miles NNE of Point Bennett. This 180-foot landmark is usually surrounded with dense kelp. The nearby shoals break in moderate swells.

Although San Miguel itself is unlit, the following lighted buoys mark off-lying hazards:

- Richardson Rock whistle buoy (Fl. R. 2.5 sec.)
- Whistle buoy off Point Bennett (Lat. 34°01.3′ N, Long. 120°27.7′ W) (Fl. R. 4 sec.)

Wilson Rock is unlit, so a NW approach at night could be foolhardy. Neither of the San Miguel lighted buoys is visible from any great distance. Do not attempt to approach the western end of San Miguel in thick weather even with GPS in hand. Soundings give no warning of the hazards described herein and there are many unmarked rocks.

You cannot approach within 300 yards of the area between Judith Rock and Castle Rock at the western end of the island without a permit. Further restrictions apply between March 15 and April 30 and between October 15 and December 15. There is no beach access allowed within this area.

Mainland Approaches. Passage to San Miguel also can be made from Cojo, Sacate, Refugio, and Goleta—an easy, if sometimes bumpy, reach across the western end of the Santa Barbara Channel. Beware, however, of a westerly set offshore that can push you a considerable distance off course. If you use this crossing strategy, make your miles to windward from Santa Barbara or points E in the calmer water inshore.

As usual in the Channel, the quietest conditions for a crossing are in the early morning or at night. Many Santa Barbara vessels leave harbor after sundown and motor directly to San Miguel, arriving there by early morning. If the sea is calm, this is a straightforward passage except for the shipping lanes. An autopilot makes everything more comfortable for all hands, provided a good lookout is maintained. The return home is a different matter. One time we set our spinnaker just outside Cuyler Harbor and ran all the way down to Santa Barbara on the afternoon westerly with an ideal breeze. As the sun set, we lowered the spinnaker off Santa Barbara Point, then broad-reached to the harbor entrance. The W wind dropped at Stearn's Wharf and then a gentle SE air took us to our slip without using the engine—talk about ideal passagemaking!

If you plan to sail to San Miguel against the prevailing wind, prepare yourself for a long, often wet beat to windward. Only truly hardy types or serious ocean racers should try this particular passage under sail.

From Neighboring Islands. When bound for San Miguel from Santa Cruz or Santa Rosa Islands, plan to motor to windward in the early morning, leaving at first light. On most days, you should reach San Miguel before the westerly fills in. Although South

Refuge Anchorages: San Miguel and Santa Rosa Islands

N–NW WINDS

N–NW Wind 12 to 29 Knots

San Miguel: Cuyler Harbor, Tyler Bight, Crook Point

Santa Rosa: Johnson's Lee, Becher's Bay, Eagle Rock

N–NW Wind 20 to 29 Knots

San Miguel: Cuyler Harbor, Tyler Bight

Santa Rosa: Johnson's Lee, Becher's Bay N of pier, Eagle Rock

N–NW Wind 30 to 39 Knots

San Miguel: Cuyler Harbor, Tyler Bight

Santa Rosa: Johnson's Lee, Becher's Bay N of pier

N–NW Wind More than 40 Knots

San Miguel: Cuyler Harbor

Santa Rosa: Johnson's Lee

NE WINDS

NE Wind 15 to 19 Knots

San Miguel: Cuyler Harbor, Tyler Bight

Santa Rosa: Johnson's Lee, Becher's Bay, Eagle Rock

NE Wind 20 to 29 Knots

San Miguel: Cuyler Harbor, Tyler Bight, Crook Point

Santa Rosa: Johnson's Lee, Southeast Anchorage

NE Wind 30 to 45 Knots

San Miguel: Crook Point, Cuyler Harbor, Tyler Bight

Santa Rosa: Johnson's Lee, inside Talcott Shoal (shallow-draft powerboats only)

NE Wind 45 to 60 Knots

San Miguel: Cuyler Harbor, Tyler Bight

Santa Rosa: Inside Talcott Shoal (shallow-draft powerboats only) in lee of W end (watch for submerged rocks)

SE WINDS

SE Wind 12 to 19 Knots

(All wind speeds: watch for NW shift as storm passes and be prepared to move on short notice)

San Miguel: Cuyler Harbor

Santa Rosa: Southeast Anchorage

SE Wind 20 to 29 Knots

San Miguel: Cuyler Harbor

Santa Rosa: Inside Talcott Shoal (shallow-draft powerboats only)

SE Wind 30 to 50 Knots

San Miguel: W side of Harris Point, keep clear of breakers and rocks; when the wind shifts to NW, move inside Cuyler Harbor

Santa Rosa: Inside Talcott Shoal (shallow-draft powerboats only)

Point on Santa Rosa is lit, San Miguel is not, so night passages are not recommended unless you have GPS and reliable radar. There are many outlying rocks and unlit dangers. Even with a full moon and perfect conditions, navigation can be hazardous.

For a first visit to San Miguel, you are best advised to approach the island from Becher's Bay or Johnson's Lee on Santa Rosa Island or Forney's Anchorage on Santa Cruz Island, choosing perfect conditions to venture westward. For planning purposes, assume that weather patterns W of South Point on Santa Rosa will be similar to those of San Miguel—frequently boisterous.

Northwest Coast and Simonton Cove

The extreme western end of San Miguel is readily identified by the long, jagged bluff of Point Bennett (see the bottom photograph on page 174). The 74-foot-high cape rises to 337 feet farther east. A lighted whistle buoy lies 0.8 miles SW of the point (Fl. R. 4 sec.). The W end of San Miguel is mantled by extensive sand dunes that extend across the island. The NW coast is backed by low cliffs and trends NE to a low-lying spit that extends NW. A patch of rocks and shoals heavily infested with kelp runs NW of the spit for nearly a mile. This area is known as Westcott Shoal, and much of it is covered with a minimum depth of 28 feet; 0.6 mile farther N lies a natural oil spring with a minimum depth of 15 feet. The entire coastline between Westcott Shoal and Point Bennett is foul with rocks and kelp. Castle Rock and its off-lying boulders are conspicuous. Kelp beds and breaking water often extend a mile or more offshore of Castle Rock.

Simonton Cove

East of Westcott Shoal, the coast forms a gradual bight 2.4 miles long and 0.6 mile wide. This bay, known as Simonton Cove, is blanketed with kelp. Some covered rocks lie up to 0.3 mile offshore just W of the center of the bay. If you must go inshore, approach the beach with great care and only in calm sea conditions, watching for subsurface rocks and kelp.

Simonton Cove is fully exposed to NW and W winds, and a lively surge commonly enters the bay. Shelter from SE and Santa Ana winds can be found by anchoring under Harris Point. To anchor in Simonton Cove, identify Harris Point and March Rock immediately on the western side of this conspicuous landmark. Then steer toward shore, keeping a close watch for kelp and breaking water. Anchor (rock and sand) according to draft, tucked in under the cliffs for maximum shelter according to prevailing conditions; 15 feet can be found at a considerable distance from the beach. Simonton Cove is preferable to Cuyler Harbor in SE and NE conditions. If anchored in SE conditions, be prepared to move to Cuyler Harbor if the wind shifts to NW. Overnight anchorage is not allowed.

Cuyler Harbor
Chart 18727; Chart-Kit, p. 10
Lat. 34°03.3′ N, Long. 120°22.6′ W
Harris Point is the most prominent landmark on the San Miguel coast, a bold and

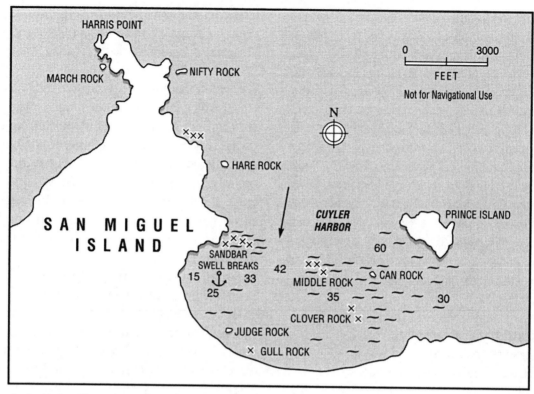

HARRIS POINT

MARCH ROCK

NIFTY ROCK

HARE ROCK

SAN MIGUEL ISLAND

N

0   3000

FEET

Not for Navigational Use

CUYLER HARBOR

PRINCE ISLAND

SANDBAR
SWELL BREAKS

15   33

25

42

60

MIDDLE ROCK   CAN ROCK

35

30

CLOVER ROCK

JUDGE ROCK

GULL ROCK

Cuyler Harbor. Plan redrawn from Chart 18727.

precipitous promontory that is connected by a saddle to a 485-foot peak 1.0 mile S of the headland. Harris Point can be identified from far offshore, a dark and menacing symphony of rock and stunted grass. You can safely approach Harris Point to within 0.5 mile. Cuyler Harbor lies immediately SE of the point, one of the most famous anchorages in the Santa Barbara Channel.

The explorer Juan Cabrillo may have died in Cuyler in 1543. The harbor, named after its original government surveyor, has been a favorite anchorage for explorers, sealers, fishermen, and cruising people ever since. The anchorage is sheltered from NW to SW, but is exposed to strong NE and SE winds. A fine sandy beach extending around the anchorage is formed by a bight of volcanic cliffs that are a shoulder of the 485-foot hill behind Harris Point. The cliffs are mantled by sand dunes on the S side of the anchorage. Prince Island guards the eastern approach to Cuyler and is often alive with hundreds of sea birds. Cuyler Harbor is a comfortable and uncongested anchorage with good holding ground. However, a nasty surge can roll in and the strong winds sweeping over the cliffs have to be experienced to be believed.

Approach. When approaching from any direction, identify Harris Point, which is unmistakable with its conspicuous hill,

shoulder, and steep cliffs. Steer for the point until the other landmarks are spotted. When approaching Cuyler from the NW, give wide berth to Wilson Rock, which is often difficult to see. Approaching from any direction between E and NW, identify the following landmarks.

- *Prince Island*, at the E side of Cuyler, 288 feet high. The seaward face of this huge rock is precipitous and black, and lies 0.4 mile offshore
- *Nifty Rock*, 39 feet, 250 yards offshore, 1,000 yards SE of Harris Point
- *Hare Rock*, a 56-foot pinnacle 300 yards offshore, 1,110 yards SSE of Nifty Rock
- the conspicuous *sand dunes behind Prince Island*

- *Judge Rock*, a small black rock near the western end of the sandy beach. A smaller outcrop, *Gull Rock*, lies on the beach 0.3 mile ESE of Judge Rock; do not confuse the two
- *Middle Rock*, 0.5 mile WSW of Prince Island, dries at low tide—a shoal area

Entrance to the anchorage lies one third of the distance between Prince Island and Harris Point cliffs. Shape your course to stay about 300 yards E of the Harris Point cliffs. When arriving from the E, steer for a point somewhat inshore of Hare Rock until you are close to the cliffs; this course keeps you clear of the kelp and foul ground that lies inshore of Prince Island. Once close to shore, shape your course to stay at least 0.4 mile offshore. A reef extends over

Approach to Cuyler Harbor from NE, with Prince Island to port and anchorage indicated (arrow).

Lesley Newhart

Approach to Cuyler Harbor from NE, distant 1 mile. Arrows indicate anchorage (right) and approach course (left).

300 yards E of the NW extremity of the anchorage. Use your depth-sounder to avoid this danger. Breaking water is found on this shoal even in moderate weather; give it a wide berth. Once clear of the shoal, alter course W toward the beach.

In thick weather, or when you are uncertain of the minor landmarks, follow these directions from the *U.S. Coast Pilot*:

Bring Harris Point to bear 261 degrees true (246 degrees M), distant 1.7 miles, and the west point of Prince Island to bear 181 degrees true (167 degrees M), distant 1.3 miles; thence steer 209 degrees true (194 degrees M), heading midway between Mid-dle Rock and the west point of the entrance, and when the south point of Prince Island bears 084 degrees true (069 degrees M), anchor in five to seven fathoms.

You can also approach Cuyler through a channel S of Prince Island, passing between the island and San Miguel itself. However, the area is sometimes heavily overgrown with kelp and can be difficult to negotiate. Minimum depth is about 18 feet. Clover Rock (awash at low water) and Can Rock (4 feet high) lie SW of Prince Island (see the harbor plan on page 178). They should be given a wide berth—a course shaped to pass midway between Can Rock and Prince Island and offshore of Middle Rock brings you to the main entrance channel. Do not try to pass between Can and Clover Rocks without local knowledge and perfect visibility.

Anchorage. Inside the anchorage, the bottom shoals gradually toward the beach. Anchor according to draft; 15 to 20 feet of water is found up to 200 yards offshore (soft sand). Watch out for the foundation of an old pier at the S corner of the anchorage. Choose your anchorage with care, paying particular attention to current swell and surge conditions and the strength of the gusts funneling down the cliffs.

Some people lay two anchors at 45 degrees from the bow when winds are blowing strongly through the anchorage. You can sometimes anchor at Cuyler Harbor in the calmest conditions and then find yourself rolling wildly in a dangerous surge. Make sure you give yourself enough space to swing and to leave on short notice if necessary. Don't forget to lash your inflatable dinghy aboard in strong winds. Heavy swells can break in the entrance in rough weather. Entering or leaving Cuyler Harbor in these conditions is crazy.

Landing and Facilities. The best place to run a dinghy ashore is at the NW corner of the bay. To land opposite the path to the ranger camp is to invite a dunking—and it's a long row to get there. There are no facilities except for a small freshwater spring on the beach. Anyone can land on the beach, but an advance appointment for a guided tour with the park ranger is needed to go farther ashore. Apply to park headquarters in Ventura (805-644-8262).

Parties are usually met at 0900 near the four palm trees on the beach, which were planted by a movie company in the 1920s. If you are scheduled for a shore excursion, take sturdy walking shoes.

Cuyler Harbor to Tyler Bight

A government-designated Military Danger Area connected with Vandenberg Air Force Base extends over the eastern half of San Miguel Island. Check the regulations in chapter 2 of the *U.S. Coast Pilot*.

East of Cuyler, the coast tends SE past Bay Point to Cardwell Point. The black-gray bluffs at the E end of Cuyler Harbor gradually fall away to sea level, and the scrub-covered coastline slopes into the water. A sandy beach masks low-lying Cardwell Point, fronted by a conspicuous low sand spit that extends ESE for about 0.5 mile. This area is constantly shoaling and underwater dangers extend almost a mile offshore. Fortunately, the sand spit is fairly obvious because its white-yellow sand can be seen from some distance. Even in calm weather, Pacific swells break with great force on the spit, throwing cascades of spray into the air. Further breaking water is caused by clashing currents in San Miguel Passage that meet the prevailing swells. Cardwell Point is treacherous in heavy weather. Use your depth-sounder for warning of rapidly shoaling water in thick weather.

Give Cardwell Point a berth of at least a mile. When bound through San Miguel Passage, stay closer to the Santa Rosa shore. Two outlying rocks are located 400 yards S of Cardwell Point, and extensive

Approach to San Miguel Island from E on a gray day, with breaking water on Cardwell Point (left) and Prince Island (right).

kelp beds are found on both sides of the point. From Cardwell Point, San Miguel slopes gradually to the shore. A yellow-white sandy beach bounds the surf, wrapping around inconspicuous Crook Point, the southern promontory of the island. Keep well offshore to avoid the kelp growth along this stretch of coast.

The low-lying coastline, bounded by high bluffs, trends WNW beyond Crook Point; there is little to interest cruising yachts in this area. Fishermen anchor E of Crook Point along the inner edge of the kelp and 0.5 to 1.0 mile E of the point. This area provides good shelter in moderate NW and NE winds, but beware of the breaking reef a mile E of Crook Point.

Give the coast a wide berth to avoid Wyckoff Ledge, 1.4 miles W of Crook Point. This ledge and its associated kelp beds lie 0.5 mile offshore with a least depth of 9 feet. The kelp beds provide an excellent boundary beyond which it is dangerous to navigate inshore; a number of submerged rocks lie between Wyckoff Ledge and Tyler Bight, which opens up on your starboard bow. The entrance to the Bight is typically mantled with dense kelp beds that mask submerged rocks, some lying as close as 3 feet from the surface.

Tyler Bight Anchorage
Lat. 34°02.0′ N, Long. 120°24.9′ W
This is a useful and little-known anchorage with good protection from W and NW

winds. Even when winds are blowing more than 40 knots offshore, Tyler Bight is relatively calm, partly due to the off-lying kelp beds that filter the swell.

Approach. Tyler Bight is bounded by a high bluff at the NW end of the anchorage, which protects the bay from W to NW winds. The bluff is streaked with yellow dune sand and has a sandy beach at its foot. Once you have identified this conspicuous bluff, look for white-topped Judith Rock, which lies at the western entrance of the bight, close inshore. Then shape your course to bring the rock N of your vessel, distant 0.5 mile, or farther offshore if the kelp beds are dense inshore. Then alter course shoreward, aiming to pass between the kelp patches, and leave Judith Rock 200 yards to port.

Do not approach Tyler Bight Anchorage from the ESE because there are dense kelp beds and subsurface rocks.

Anchorage. Although the U.S. Coast Pilot recommends anchoring in 40 feet with Judith Rock bearing 250 degrees M, 500 yards distant, you can also move as close inshore as seems prudent in prevailing wind and swell conditions. However, government regulations forbid anchoring closer than 300 yards from the shore because of the elephant-seal rookeries on the beach (see the photograph below). Sound your way to a berth in 18 to 25 feet (sand), tucked in under the cliff and as

Tyler Bight Anchorage from SE, distant ½ mile. Judith Rock lies just to port of the photograph. The anchorage is under the white patch on the cliff to starboard (arrow).

Lesley Newhart

much in the lee of Judith Rock as possible. Watch for kelp and be prepared to leave if weather conditions deteriorate.

Tyler Bight to Point Bennett

From Tyler Bight, the coastline remains low-lying and is covered with extensive patches of sand dunes. This can be a windy corner and should not be approached except on a calm day. Low rocky outcrops bound the shore and form the last small cove before merging with a sandy beach and low spit that join Point Bennett to the island. Two rocky islets lie close inshore S of the point. Approaching this coast within 300 yards is forbidden.

Adams Cove

This small indentation lies immediately E of Point Bennett and gives some shelter from W to NE winds. However, a nasty surge can roll into the anchorage even in calm weather. Adams Cove is at best a temporary berth in fine weather or in an emergency. Overnight anchorage is not allowed.

Approach and Anchorage. Identify Point Bennett and its sand spit. Adams Cove lies at the E end of the sandy beach that extends E from the point, a sloping bluff of rocks and sand that forms the indented cove.

Once the indentation has been identified, feel your way in with your depth-

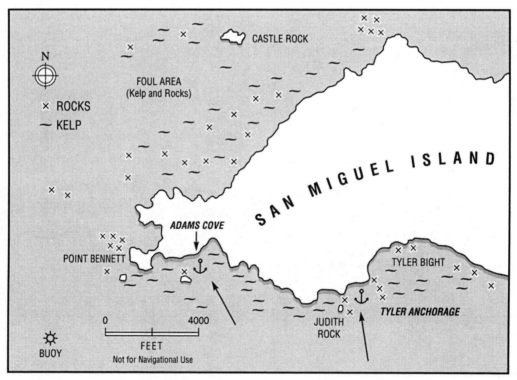

Western end of San Miguel Island showing anchorages and hazards. Note: Approaching within 300 yards of the shore is forbidden between March 15 and April 30 and between October 1 and December 15.

sounder and an alert lookout on the foredeck. Anchor in 30 feet off the beach (rock and sand), but be prepared to leave at a moment's notice if winds come up. Again, government regulations restrict anchoring within 300 yards of the shore. Elephant seals and sea lions can be observed on the spit to the east.

SANTA ROSA ISLAND

Santa Rosa Island has had a colorful history as both a hunting ground for sea otters and a cattle ranch. The second largest of the offshore islands, Santa Rosa is about 15 nautical miles long from E to W and 9 miles across at its widest point. Unlike Santa Cruz Island, Santa Rosa Island lacks natural harbors and has a generally steep-to coast with extensive offshore kelp beds. The highest point of the island is 1,589 feet above sea level. On a clear day, Santa Rosa usually can be seen from the mainland, although its profile is less spectacular than that of its larger easterly neighbor. Like San Miguel, Santa Rosa is not an island to be trifled with because sudden gale-force downslope winds and strong westerlies can easily catch a small-boat sailor unaware. Once, while beating from Gull Island off the southern coast of Santa Cruz to Johnson's Lee on Santa Rosa, we were caught by a sudden NW blow that funneled through the Santa Cruz Channel. Fortunately, the sea was flat and we enjoyed an exhilarating sail with spray blowing horizontally. We came to anchor at Johnson's Lee with considerable difficulty against the strong

wind. The wind screamed through the rigging until 0200, when it dropped as suddenly as it had risen. The unpredictability of Santa Rosa weather makes it unwise to take chances with faulty gear or inadequate preparation.

The island is now part of the Channel Islands National Park and the Channel Islands National Marine Sanctuary. Landing permits are available through the Channel Islands National Park Headquarters in Ventura (805-644-8262).

Sandy Point to Becher's Bay
Charts 18727, 18728; Chart-Kit, pp. 11–12

Sandy Point is a conspicuous rocky point that forms the western extremity of Santa Rosa Island. White sand dunes more than 400 feet high extend inland from Sandy Point and are conspicuous from seaward. A small rock, 4 feet high, lies off the point. Two peaks, 465 and 485 feet high, rise inland off Sandy Point. The 10-fathom line extends N from the western end of Santa Rosa 1.5 to 2.0 miles offshore. Irregular swells and breaking water may extend a considerable distance offshore, even in moderate weather. Talcott Shoal, a mile NE of Sandy Point, has a minimum depth of 10 feet (rock). This entire area—indeed, the whole northern coast of Santa Rosa— should be given a berth of at least 3 miles to avoid shallow water, confused seas in rougher weather, and kelp beds that can extend up to 3 miles offshore.

The northern coast trends E to Brockway Point, a low spit with high bluffs behind it 300 to 500 yards inland. A peak 534 feet

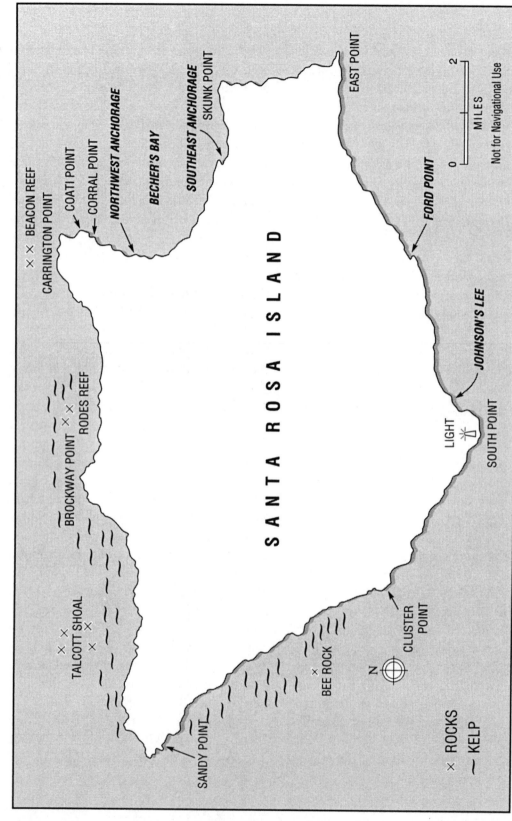

Santa Rosa Island, showing major features and anchorages mentioned in the text.

high rises 2.2 miles SE of Sandy Point at the W end of the island. Beaches on this stretch of coast have nothing to offer small-boat sailors and are obstructed by kelp.

Rode's Reef, a patch of three submerged kelp-covered rocks with a minimum depth of 7.5 feet, lies 1.2 miles ENE of Brockway Point, 0.8 mile offshore. The swell breaks on this reef. If you stay 3.0 miles offshore, you will be well clear of Rode's Reef and other off-lying dangers. The northern coast continues in a shallow bay of steep cliffs that trend NE to Carrington Point, the NE extremity of Santa Rosa Island. This shoreline should also be given a wide berth.

Carrington Point rises to a peak 452 feet high, 0.75 mile inland. The seaward face of the point is bold and rocky and 0.8 mile long. Beacon Reef lies 0.4 mile N off Carrington Point, with a minimum depth of 14 feet. To avoid concealed rocks, stay at least a mile off the land.

The eastern shore of Santa Rosa Island is dominated by Becher's Bay, a large open bight 4.5 miles across. Becher's Bay is backed by low cliffs that are highest near Carrington Point. The bluffs are 100 feet high at Coati and Corral Points just S of Carrington, but the 100-foot contour recedes behind the low cliffs. A ridge of higher ground extends E from the high spine of the island down to sea level at the southern end of Becher's Bay. The cliffs taper away and end in the sandy spit known as Skunk Point. Becher's Bay is generally steep-to, with kelp beds lying up to 0.5 mile offshore. Shallower water extends farther from land off Skunk Point, which should be passed at least a mile offshore.

Becher's Bay Anchorages: Northwest Anchorage

Lat. 34°0.7′ N, Long. 120°2.6′ W

Becher's Bay has been a favorite anchorage since the time of the conquistadors. This large bay offers shelter from the prevailing westerlies, even when they are blowing strongly.

Northwest Anchorage is an open roadstead with a pier that services the park. The Bay provides fairly good shelter from the prevailing NW winds, but it can blow hard at night. Strong winter swells can swing around Carrington Point and break in the anchorage, sometimes with little warning.

Approach. Approaching from N or NW, identify Carrington, Coati, and Corral Points by their bold cliffs. The land appears somewhat featureless until you are within a mile or so of the anchorage, because the pier tends to merge with the cliffs when viewed at a distance, especially when approaching just before sunset. However, once the trestles of the pier are identified against the brown cliff, steer for the pier and select your anchoring spot. A white bunkhouse just north of the pier is also conspicuous. When approaching from S, steer inshore from Carrington Point about 1 mile to where the cliffs become lower, until you can identify the pier. At night, you can sometimes use the lights of the buildings that lie inshore of the pier as a leading mark for the anchorage.

Anchorage. Some vessels anchor under the cliffs about 0.5 mile N of the pier, where sometimes smoother water and fair shelter may be found in an opening between the kelp beds. This is the best shelter in winds

Northwest Anchorage, Becher's Bay. The pier from ESE, distant 0.25 mile. Anchor north of the pier, clearing the mooring buoy and approach.

more than 30 knots. If you are anchoring off the pier in 30 feet or more, position yourself well clear of any mooring buoys in a berth where you gain maximum shelter from the cliffs consistent with a kelp-free anchorage. Do not anchor near shore, especially in the winter, because of the extensive disturbed breaker zone. There is about 16 feet at the end of the pier.

Gusty winds can blow through Northwest Anchorage, especially at night. Rough weather brings heavy surge, but Becher's Bay is a wild and interesting spot for an overnight stay. The holding ground is good, but clear out if the wind fills in from NE or SE.

Landing and Facilities. Landing is at the pier, by permit only. There are no facilities available.

Becher's Bay: Southeast Anchorage
Lat. 34°33.8′ N, Long. 120°0.7′ W

Southeast Anchorage lies 1.5 miles W of Skunk Point but is little more than a shallow bay offering limited shelter from SE winds. The anchorage is typically bumpy and not recommended for an overnight stay except in perfect conditions.

Approach. From the N or NW, identify Skunk Point with its sandy spit. Shape your course to close with the land 1 mile W of the point. Southeast Anchorage lies near an inconspicuous indentation in the land, which can be identified from a distance by steering for the eastern edge of a patch of trees on the hills that slope down to the cliffs above the indentation. Patches of kelp may lie offshore.

Anchorage. Anchor off the beach in 20 to 30 feet (sand). Although holding ground is good, there is always a surge. Beware of recent shoaling in this anchorage. Anchor in a good least depth at low tide to avoid bumpy breaker swells, or even the danger of bouncing on the sand.

Skunk Point to Ford Point

The southern coast of Santa Rosa offers a number of fair-weather anchorages, but can be uncomfortable when swells roll in from Mexican tropical storms during the summer months. A passage eastbound along this coast during SE conditions is not recommended either. The last time I tried it, we battled 20-knot headwinds and a sea that had to be experienced to be believed.

The coastline between Skunk Point and East Point, the SE corner of Santa Rosa Island, is low-lying with a sandy beach. Higher ground behind the low sandy spit trends SE to end in East Point, a fairly bold rocky headland. East Point should be given a wide berth because there are off-lying dangers, including a rock in the kelp; minimum depth is 16 feet 0.7 mile north of the point. A shoal with a minimum depth of 22 feet lies just SE of Skunk Point. Stay at least 1.5 miles offshore of the SE corner of Santa Rosa unless you are anchoring close inshore. It is possible to anchor off the beach between Skunk Point and East Point, sheltered by the coastline and kelp beds in 12 to 25 feet (sand). This is better than Becher's Bay in heavy winter swell

Graham Pomeroy

Southeast Anchorage (arrow) in Becher's Bay from NE, distant 1 mile.

conditions. A first visit with someone who has local knowledge is recommended. The shore between Skunk Point and East Point is sometimes difficult to identify at night. Breaking water occurs off Skunk Point even in moderate conditions, where strong currents can sometimes set you NW or inshore. Give this dangerous spot a wide berth.

The southern coast of Santa Rosa slopes steeply into the Pacific, with a series of dry canyons flowing into the ocean. Low cliffs and sandy beaches occur along most of the distance between East Point and Ford Point, but rocks are found close inshore. You should stay at least 0.5 mile offshore in 30 feet or more. Two anchorages—Eagle Rock and Ford Point—are frequented by fishermen.

Eagle Rock Anchorage

This is a useful anchorage under the cliffs with good shelter in moderate NW and NE conditions.

Approach. Eagle Rock lies 1.9 miles W of East Point, off a conspicuous green-yellow bluff. Another rock lies close inshore just W of the bluff. After Eagle Rock and the bluff have been identified, alter course to close with the shore E of the Rock. Do not attempt to pass between Eagle Rock and the shore without first exploring the area in a dinghy.

Anchorage. Anchor in the lee of the bluff and cliffs in 15 to 30 feet (sand) clear of kelp and other obstructions. This is a surprisingly sheltered anchorage in NW winds up to 30 knots.

Lesley Newhart

Eagle Rock Anchorage from S, distant ½ mile. Best anchorage is immediately E of the conspicuous bluff, close to the beach (arrow).

Lesley Newhart

Ford Point anchorage from E (arrow), distant ½ mile.

Ford Point Anchorage

This is a temporary anchorage in the lee of a small point that offers little shelter for a prolonged stay. A pleasant sandy beach is nearby.

Approach. Ford Point is a low rocky promontory that lies 4.2 miles west of East Point. Once the point is identified, steer to pass just inshore of the headland. Give the rocks off the point a wide berth (at least 200 yards) and sound your way into the anchorage.

Anchorage. Anchor off the beach in 15 feet or less (sand) where maximum shelter can be obtained. Do not set yourself too close to the breaker line, and be prepared to clear out if the surge gets up.

Johnson's Lee

Lat. 33°54.10′ N, Long. 120°06.3′ W

The coastline between Ford Point and Johnson's Lee is somewhat featureless, with low cliffs and steep slopes and canyons behind them. The bottom is rocky. Some kelp lies close inshore, which thickens as you approach conspicuous South Point. Johnson's Lee lies immediately NE of South Point.

Many people claim Johnson's Lee is the best anchorage on Santa Rosa Island, but it can be uncomfortable in winter and spring. The open roadstead faces SE and offers considerable shelter from W to N winds. An abandoned military base overlooks the anchorage, complete with empty barracks and a severed Navy pier that becomes more dangerous through disuse every year. The

Johnson's Lee. Approach from the S, with South Point to port and buildings of the abandoned base right of center (arrow shows anchorage).

Johnson's Lee anchorage from S, distant ½ mile.

Lesley Newhart

former base is now the park service head-quarters on the island. A thick kelp bed provides some shelter from the swells that roll toward the beach. The anchorage is fairly comfortable in moderate weather.

Approach. Johnson's Lee is easy to find because the anchorage lies immediately NE of South Point, the southernmost extremity of Santa Rosa Island. Approaching from San Miguel Island, simply identify South Point and its light, then pass 0.5 mile off and alter course into Johnson's Lee to the E. The buildings on the slopes above the anchorage are visible from a long distance. Steer for the pier immediately below them. (These same buildings and South Point are your landmarks for approaching Johnson's Lee from Santa Cruz Island.) Stay outside the kelp beds as you approach the anchorage, then thread your way through the seaweed toward the pier. Do not attempt this anchorage at night without local knowledge.

Anchorage. Anchor just inside the kelp bed in 25 to 35 feet (sand). Avoid anchoring close to the northern shore of Johnson's Lee; the bottom is rocky and holding poor. Also do not try to secure alongside the pier, all parts of which are sadly decayed and extremely hazardous in the surge. It is also inadvisable to pick up the mooring buoy SE of the pier because it is in constant use.

Strong downslope winds can blow in Johnson's Lee, and you should clear out at the slightest sign of a southeaster.

Fair anchorage can be obtained off the beach 0.5 mile E of Johnson's Lee in settled conditions, if the main anchorage is congested.

South Point, a conspicuous rocky promontory 100 feet high that rises steeply to a height of 460 feet, can be identified from a long distance. A 603-foot peak lies behind the point. Steep brown cliffs several hundred feet high and about 0.5 mile long extend SW from the point. An automated light (Fl. 6 sec., 9 miles) is situated 540 feet above sea level on the point; you cannot see it from Johnson's Lee. Extensive kelp beds can form off South Point.

In 1962, SS *Chickasaw* ran aground W of South Point during a rain squall. For many years, the wreck sat almost intact on the shore, but the hull has broken up in El Niño storms and there is nothing to see anymore.

The high ground slopes down to the shoreline as you approach Cluster Point, 3.5 miles NW of South Point. Rocks and ledges make Cluster Point dangerous to approach closer than 0.75 mile. Shape your course for San Miguel Island or Sandy Point to pass offshore of Bee Rock, 2.5 miles NW of Cluster Point. Bee Rock is only 5 feet high and normally surrounded by dense kelp beds that extend offshore between Cluster Point and the western end of Santa Rosa Island. Another 10-foot-high outcrop lies close SE of Bee Rock. The entire area is rock-studded and smothered with breaking water in even moderate weather. You can pass safely inside Bee Rock, but the passage can be thick with kelp and rocks lie close inshore.

The coastline, with its low vertical cliffs, gradually slopes to the NW, ending in the dunes of Sandy Point. Stay well offshore as San Miguel Passage opens in front of you and only head inshore if you plan to visit Sandy Point anchorage.

Sandy Point Anchorage
Lat. 33°59.9′ N, Long. 120°14.8′ W

This is a small little-known anchorage at the extreme western end of Santa Rosa Island that offers shelter from N and NW winds. Few people visit this exposed landing, which is both remote and desolate; at best, it is a fair-weather day anchorage.

Approach. First identify Sandy Point, then a small bight formed by a dark brown-gray headland that extends about 400 yards seaward from the general NW–SE trend of the coast. Always approach this anchorage from S. Sound your way carefully toward the bight, steering to pass into the middle of the bay. Watch for submerged rocks and have someone con the ship from the bow.

Anchorage. Once you are inshore, anchor in the bight in 12 to 18 feet (sand), avoiding kelp and rocks. The protected swinging area is very limited. Be prepared to leave in a hurry if swell or wind comes up.

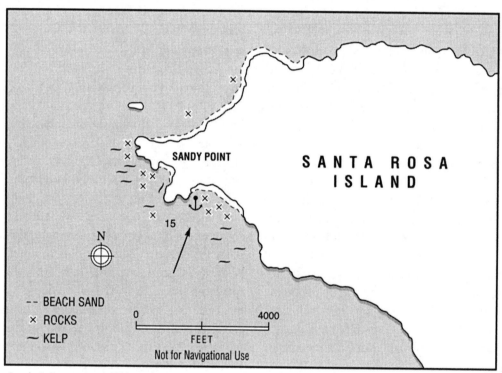

Sandy Point approach. This anchorage is not recommended except in very smooth conditions.

SANTA CRUZ ISLAND: NORTH COAST

SANTA CRUZ ISLAND is 20.5 miles long and 5.5 miles across at its widest point. The eastern and much of the central portions of the island are part of the Channel Islands National Park; the Nature Conservancy, a private nonprofit organization, owns the remainder. Landing rights on its property are controlled. The island's deeply indented coastline offers dozens of anchorages to the discerning skipper. Some coves are secure in any weather, others are merely fine-weather picnic spots. Although the winds can blow hard off Santa Cruz Island, its weather seems more predictable than that of its more remote neighbors. The biggest dangers are strong nocturnal canyon winds and very occasional NE storms. Most of the time, however, the weather is benign and the anchorages are secure. A Santa Cruz anchorage is a world of its own—the placid beaches, the barking of sea lions and gulls soaring over the steep cliffs that enclose the anchorages. Santa Cruz offers a momentary glance at another less hasty world, miraculously intact in a polluted twentieth-century world. Long may it offer such a contrast!

Santa Cruz Island, once known as San Lucas, was so named in 1769 by Spaniard Gaspar Portola's supply-ship captain, Juan Perez. The origin of the name is uncertain, but it may be connected with either the Feast of the Holy Cross (May 3) or the Feast of the Exaltation of the Holy Cross (September 14). Another legend states that the name commemorates the Native Americans' return of a lost crucifix. The island first appeared on British Admiralty charts after George Vancouver recorded the name in the late eighteenth century. Sea-otter, seal, and sea-lion hunters, as well as fishermen and contraband traders, used its coves during the early nineteenth century. In 1839, Mexican Governor Juan Alvarado granted Santa Cruz Island to Spanish-Mexican Andres Castillero, who probably kept cattle, sheep, and pigs. In 1857, Castillero sold the island to William E. Barron, an Englishman in the Mexico–California trade. However, the land title was contested before the Land Claims Commission after the annexation of California in 1850. It was not until 1859 that the Santa Cruz Island case was settled by a judgment of the U.S. Supreme Court, signed by the celebrated Chief Justice Roger Taney.

Barron sold Santa Cruz Island in 1869 to a group of ten investors connected with the French Bank in San Francisco. They incorporated the Santa Cruz Island Company in 1869. But the bank fell on hard times, so one of the original incorporators—an assayer and hardware merchant named Justinian Caire—obtained control of the company. Caire himself never visited the island until 1880, when he developed an old-style family ranch there, staffed by Italian immigrants and local vaqueros. Caire's wife was Genoese, so he used her connections to recruit farmhands, who were allowed to work off their travel expenses as part of their wages on the island.

Caire reorganized Santa Cruz Island into a viable, large-scale sheep and cattle ranch. Once his stock operations were prospering, he then turned to the dry cultivation of vines, almonds, and olives. Soon Santa Cruz wines became popular on the mainland. After 1880, Caire built a network of dwellings throughout the ranch from which the cattle business was controlled. In 1891, he constructed a Roman Catholic chapel in the central valley. The chapel was

recently re-consecrated and is now part of the Parish of San Buenaventura.

Caire died in 1898. Twelve years later, some family members dissolved the Santa Cruz Island Company through litigation that continued until 1927. During this period, the island was partitioned into seven lots by the courts. Caire's widow remained in control of the largest portion. She and four of her children re-formed the Santa Cruz Island Company when the law cases ended, joining five of the lots into a single property; the two remaining parcels at the eastern end of the island went to another faction within the family.

By this time, the ranch was in trouble, partly because of prolonged litigation, but also because of the Depression and the effects of Prohibition. In 1937, Edwin Stanton purchased approximately 90 percent of the island, the assets of the newly re-formed Company. The Gherini family, descendants of Justinian Caire, continued to hold the remaining 10 percent: the two parcels in the eastern part of the island. Stanton maintained a cattle ranch on his acreage until his death in 1983. Five years earlier, he had made an arrangement with The Nature Conservancy whereby it would acquire the Stanton land after his death. The federal government has acquired the Gherini property, which is now part of the Channel Islands National Park. In 2000, the Nature Conservancy deeded part of its land, including Prisoner's Harbor (the main landing spot) to the National Park Service. It's reasonable to assume that there may be more transfers in the future.

Cautions. *Landing Permits:* Santa Cruz Island is owned by the National Park Service and the Nature Conservancy. The latter controls some of the central and all of the western portions of the island. Thus, much of Santa Cruz Island is NOT part of the Channel Islands National Park. However, the entire island is in the Channel Islands National Marine Sanctuary. Public access is restricted and landing on any portion of the Nature Conservancy's property is forbidden without a landing permit, which must be obtained on the mainland. You can apply for one by contacting the

Nature Conservancy, P.O. Box 23259, Santa Barbara CA 93121, 805-962-9111.

An application form can be obtained from either this address or harbormasters' offices, yacht clubs, or chandleries. An annual or monthly fee is charged. Allow at least a week to ten days for your application to be processed.

The anchorages are patrolled by Santa Barbara County Sheriffs and the Department of Fish and Game, as well as Channel Islands National Park rangers, who

Refuge Anchorages

N–NW Wind 12 to 29 Knots
North coast: Anchorages E of Fry's Harbor.
South coast: Forney's Cove, Malva Real, Willow's Anchorage, and anchorages from Coches Prietos E.

N–NW Wind 29 to 39 Knots
North coast: Fry's Harbor or Pelican Bay, also protected coves E of Scorpion.
South coast: Malva Real (windy but safe), Albert's, Yellowbanks, Smuggler's Cove, and Hungryman's Gulch.

N–NW Wind More than 40 Knots
North coast: Pelican Bay.
South coast: Albert's, Yellowbanks, and Smuggler's Cove.

NE Wind 15 to 19 Knots
North coast: Protected anchorages from Pelican Bay to Lady's Harbor.
South coast: Forney's Cove, Malva Real, Willow's Anchorage, and Coches Prietos.

NE Wind 20 to 40 Knots
North coast: None.
South coast: North parts of Christy Canyon and Forney's Cove, also Fraser Cove (N of Forney's).

NE Wind More Than 40 Knots
South coast: Between Christy Canyon and Forney's Cove if you cannot move, or Johnson's Lee on Santa Rosa Island; at more than 60 knots, there is no shelter.

SE Wind 12 to 30 Knots
North coast: E side of Chinese Harbor; Potato Harbor offers the best shelter in SE conditions up to 50 knots.
South coast: Fraser Cove, N of Christy Canyon.
• In all cases, look out for a rapid NW shift as the front passes and be prepared to move.

Sunniest Anchorage in Foggy Conditions
North coast: None.
South coast: Gull Island to San Pedro Point.

supervise inshore marine sanctuaries. These rangers are deputized as deputy sheriffs in Santa Barbara County, so they also fulfill a law-enforcement function in the area.

Hazardous Winds. Santa Cruz Island is an isolated landmass, far from the comforts of the mainland and its safe harbors. It requires good judgment and careful monitoring of weather forecasts to decide whether to visit the island. Conditions in Windy Lane are extremely dangerous when post-frontal northwesterlies are blowing in the winter and spring; avoid crossing to the island under these circumstances. You can, however, find safe refuge in both north- and south-coast anchorages in this weather condition.

Northeasterly (Santa Ana) conditions are quite a different matter. The winds howl offshore from the Oxnard–Ventura area and sweep into normally sheltered anchorages with vicious intensity. Sea conditions are confused, the wind is changeable; few anchorages, except Coches Prietos, Potato Harbor, and Chinese Harbor, are safe. Since writing the first edition of this book, I have been caught over at the islands several times in Santa Ana conditions. Each time, they have scared me; each time, I have returned to the mainland. There is only one golden rule: *Avoid Santa Cruz Island (and the other islands, for that matter) when Santa Ana conditions are forecasted.*

If you are at the island in such weather, you will enjoy fantastic visibility and calm water. However, if a swell starts rolling in from the mainland, *get out of your anchorage at once*—a strong NE wind may arrive soon afterward, leaving you on a lee shore. It is much better to clear out in good time and to give yourself adequate sea room. At worst, your crew may curse you for disturbing their sleep for nothing; at best, you will have avoided potential shipwreck.

Once clear of your anchorage, your best strategy on the north coast is to head into midchannel in a NW direction, a course that will take you out of the main NE wind pattern that flows from the Oxnard Plain (see photograph on page 170). On the south coast, head SW and heave-to when you have adequate sea room. Do not attempt to shift to another anchorage; almost none are secure in these conditions.

Telltale signs of NE conditions at the islands are layers of smog and dust lying offshore when they are usually over the mainland, exceptional visibility, and—believe it or not—restrictions on freeway travel in the Southern California area for campers and trailers!

You may be tempted to sail to Santa Cruz Island under the sort of idyllic conditions that often occur in NE weather. Resist the temptation and stay home—these are possibly the worst circumstances for visiting the islands.

APPROACHING SANTA CRUZ ISLAND FROM SANTA BARBARA

The distinctive skyline of Santa Cruz Island makes landfalls easy on clear days because several of the best north-coast anchorages lie below conspicuous hills or mountain profiles that can be identified from the mainland.

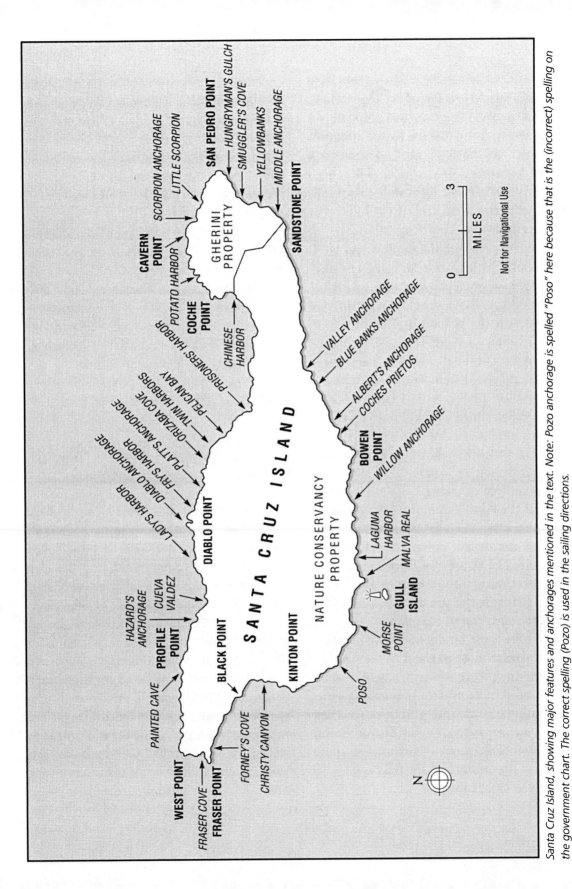

Santa Cruz Island, showing major features and anchorages mentioned in the text. Note: Pozo anchorage is spelled "Poso" here because that is the (incorrect) spelling on the government chart. The correct spelling (Pozo) is used in the sailing directions.

APPROACHING SANTA CRUZ ISLAND FROM SANTA BARBARA

Santa Cruz Island lies slightly more than 20 miles off Santa Barbara. On a clear, sunny day, you can see the low slope of San Pedro Point at the eastern end as it climbs gradually to the high ground that rises above Scorpion Anchorage. This high ground undulates for some miles, then falls away behind a deep fold in the hills—the lowest point on the north coast.

Prisoner's Harbor, the main island landing, lies in the nick of this fold. The skyline rises again E of Prisoner's Harbor where Pelican Bay lies below a distinctive conical hill, the second in a series of six humps that run from E to W along the summit of the island. Once past these humps, the mountain ridge rises to the highest point of Santa Cruz Island. Fortunately, it lies above Diablo Point, an excellent leading mark for Fry's and Lady's Harbors and other close-by anchorages. Another distinctive conical hill W of this high point marks Cueva Valdez. The backbone of the island slopes away gradually until the steep cliffs of the west end are reached. An ancient beach line, millions of years old, can be seen as a distinctive platform extending about 3 miles E of West Point. It forms the precipitous cliffs that mark the west end of the island.

Steer for these landmarks—we mention and illustrate most of them in connection with the anchorages described herein—and you should have no trouble finding your destination on a clear day. In thick weather, lay off a compass course for Diablo Point, West Point, Prisoner's Harbor, or some other conspicuous feature that is easy to identify at close range.

Steer only toward prominent landmarks in foggy weather unless you have an intimate knowledge of Santa Cruz Island. You may not see anything as you close the land, often not until you are less than a mile offshore. Although there are no outlying dangers, an accurate DR plot is essential in fog, even if you are using GPS.

A night approach to Santa Cruz Island is not recommended without local knowledge. The island is lit by Gull Island light on the south coast (Fl. 4 sec.). The only other night landmark is a conspicuous patch of lights marking a radar station high above Valley Anchorage, visible from both sides of the island on clear nights.

Our sailing directions proceed clockwise around the island from the west end.

WEST END TO CUEVA VALDEZ
Charts 18728, 18729; Chart-Kit pp. 13, 14

The west end of Santa Cruz Island is steep-to, the abrupt end of a 3-mile terrace of cliffs that fall precipitously into the Pacific (Lat. 34°04.3 N′, Long. 119°55.2′ W). You can approach close inshore between West and Profile Points for a look at some fascinating rock formations and soaring sea birds. The cliffs are particularly impressive on a foggy day when the mist comes and goes in delicate wraiths along their dark faces. Stay well clear of this coastline in rough weather. In calm conditions, there are some wonderful nooks and crannies under the forbidding cliffs where you can stop for lunch. However, the bottom is usually rock and holding ground is poor.

Strong winds can funnel down over the cliffs, dumping grit and sand on your decks and blowing you against the cliffs.

A possible fair-weather anchorage lies in an unnamed cove just over a mile E of West Point, where anchorage may be obtained in 40 feet (sand, kelp, and rock) sheltered close to the cliffs. Beware, however, of strong down-cliff gusts and surge. This can be a good spot in the summer when popular anchorages are congested. The sea lions are worth watching and often swim near your boat.

Spectacular cliffs lead E to Profile Point, so called because of its distinctive shape when viewed from the east or west. Painted Cave, just W of Profile Point, is a favorite excursion for small craft visiting the north coast of Santa Cruz Island. You can also enter three caves that lie 1.1 mile W of Painted Cave, where the cliffs are steep-to. It is possible to anchor temporarily under the shelter of the land off the middle cave in a patch of sand among the rocks and kelp that litter the bottom. These caves have large entrances and fascinating rock formations. Lights are unnecessary. The water is calm except when channel swells are up.

Painted Cave

Painted Cave is not an anchorage, merely a fascinating spot to lie off and visit by dinghy. It is easily reached on a calm day from Cueva Valdez. The area should be

Lesley Newhart

Painted Cave from the N, distant ⅓ mile. The entrance is immediately astern of the yacht lying off the cave (arrow).

avoided if a heavy surge or strong westerly is blowing. It is best to visit Painted Cave in the morning, when conditions are calm.

The cave lies in the second indentation W of Profile Point, the entrance being relatively inconspicuous. Many people confuse it with a larger-mouthed sea cave just to the E. Although some crews take large power-boats into the mouth of the cave and secure them to the rocks inside, it is better (and more socially responsible) to lie off the cave and go in by dinghy in relays; of course, a sailing yacht can do nothing else.

The walls of the cave are about 80 feet high at the entrance, and flanked by boulders. The ceiling rises to more than 125 feet inside and slopes down to about 20 feet at the rear. Magnificent greens, yellows, and reds can be seen on the walls as you row your dinghy into the cave. Row to the end of the first section, more than 600 feet into the cave. Then alter course hard to starboard into the side chamber, which extends 150 feet in total darkness. You will find rock shelves and a beach where seals and sea lions lie ashore. As your flashlights light up the chamber, the sea lions will scramble into the water and leave you in possession of their home.

Under no circumstances should you try to enter Painted Cave in a heavy surge. The best time to visit Painted Cave is in the calmer morning hours. And—please . . . do not take your powerful and noisy power-boat into the entrance. The din of your engine scares the sea lions and the unfortunate sailors in their dinghies inside the cave, to say nothing of choking them with exhaust fumes.

E of Painted Cave, the coastline trends slightly SE beyond Profile Point, but continues precipitously with few outlying dangers. Some trees appear on the hillsides as you reach the classic anchorages of the north coast.

Hazard's Anchorage
Hazard's Anchorage is a sandy beach and slightly indented cove 0.75 mile W of Cueva Valdez anchorage that offers limited shelter in prevailing westerlies. The cove is easily identified because it is the only conspicuous sandy beach between Cueva Valdez and Profile Point. There are no offlying dangers. Anchor in 25 to 30 feet (sand) off the beach and lay plenty of scope. For some reason, this pleasant calm-weather anchorage has been neglected in recent years, although it was well known in the 1950s. It becomes sloppy in even moderate west wind or surge.

The steep cliffs are now less precipitous as we near Cueva Valdez with its reddish slopes and fine caves.

Cueva Valdez Anchorage
NOAA Chart spelling is Cueva Valdaze
Lat. 34°03.1′ N, Long. 119°49.2′ W
Cueva Valdez is a popular anchorage for family cruises. Many boats congregate here on fine summer days. For those with landing permits, the magnificent sandy beach is a paradise for children, and the caverns are well worth exploring. However, a nasty surge can roll into the anchorage without warning, making Cueva Valdez uncomfortable.

Graham Pomeroy

Cueva Valdez from 5 miles offshore. Left arrow indicates anchorage directly below the conical peak. Right arrow shows Hazard's Anchorage (the white beach is conspicuous).

Graham Pomeroy

Cueva Valdez anchorage, showing caves at the W side of the cove, distant 1 mile.

Approach. Cueva Valdez is easy to identify from some miles offshore because it lies immediately below a sharp, pointed, conical hill on the skyline of the island. Once this hill is identified, keep the ship's bow on the summit until the details of the coastline are visible 2 or 3 miles offshore. The sandy beach of the anchorage can now be spotted immediately below the pointed hill, bound on the west by a steep hillside. Caves are in the base of this hillside and can be located from about 1.5 miles offshore. Steer for the midpoint of the sandy beach, about halfway between the two sides of the cove, and sound carefully because it shelves rapidly.

From W or from Painted Cave. Skirt the coast about a ½ mile offshore, clear of all dangers as the coast recedes slightly SE. Cueva Valdez opens up and the caves become visible W of the beach, once abeam. When the caves are in sight, steer for the middle of the anchorage, staying at least 100 yards off the western shore of the cove.

From E. Start looking for the anchorage once Arch Rock W of Lady's Harbor is abeam. Cueva Valdez is the first sandy beach beyond the rock, and lies 1.75 miles W of this landmark. The north cave can be identified in a fold in the cliff when you are about a mile out of the anchorage. Course may be safely set for the caverns, leaving the eastern promontory of the anchorage at least 0.25 mile to port. Once this point is abeam, head for the center of the anchorage.

Anchorage. The most sheltered anchorage in prevailing westerly conditions is off the cave entrances in 20 to 25 feet (sand) under the shelter of the cliff. However, be aware of a huge rock (least depth 5 feet) that lies just below the surface about 150 feet from the mouth of the cave and approximately the same distance from the beach; it is a serious danger to even the smallest yachts. Sometimes a float marks the rock, but it is often washed away by swells rolling into the anchorage. A lookout on the bow can often spot the rock in advance in the clear water.

Everyone typically lies in a parallel line stern-to the beach, each new arrival anchoring E of its neighbor. The best berth is about 100 yards E of the caves. Be sure to lay considerable scope, for the bottom shelves rapidly. There is 60 feet of water only 100 yards from the beach. Holding ground is generally good, but watch for patches of kelp and sea grass. Anchorage on the E side of Cueva Valdez should be avoided if possible in westerly conditions. There is often bad surge, as well as patches of slippery kelp and rock on the bottom. A second anchor is recommended throughout the anchorage to reduce motion at anchor.

Cueva Valdez is open to the NW, and an uncomfortable surge can set into the anchorage. Get out when the swell comes in or when a strong NW or NE wind is forecasted. The swells often develop in midafternoon and become most uncomfortable at sunset, after which they commonly decrease. However, this lovely spot is usually idyllic in the summer.

Landing. Landing is by permit only. Land by dinghy in the south cave entrance and on the beach.

The landscape E of Cueva Valdez is considerably less precipitous than the W end of the island. The eastern promontory of the anchorage slopes gradually into the ocean, and the northern slopes of the high spine of the island fall away more gradually to cliffs that are about 75 feet high.

The stretch of coast between Cueva Valdez and Arch Rock can be approached to within 0.25 mile with impunity, but there is little to attract a small vessel other than some fine scenery.

The next landmark is Arch Rock, a conspicuous outcrop that lies immediately offshore of another flat-topped rock. The two rocks form a conspicuous point of land that should be given a berth of about 400 yards. Lady's Harbor lies 0.5 mile E of Arch Rock, immediately E of the steep cliffs that face the two outlying rocks.

CUEVA VALDEZ TO FRY'S HARBOR

Lady's Harbor
Lat. 34°03.2′ N, Long. 119°47.4′ W

Lady's Harbor consists of two parts: the main anchorage and a smaller cove to the east, often called Little Lady's. The main anchorage is a magnificent spot for one or two yachts in calm conditions. Lady's Harbor tends to be congested in the summer and can experience bad surge when the swell offshore is still relatively moderate. The main anchorage is reported to be surprisingly calm in strong NE winds. Little Lady's (Baby's) is only a fair-weather anchorage that is potentially suicidal in rough westerly conditions because the pre-vailing wind and swell head right into the entrance.

Approach. Lady's Harbor can be difficult to find from offshore. You are best advised to steer for the pointed hill above Cueva Valdez and to identify both that anchorage and Arch Rock when you are 2 or 3 miles out. The entrance to the cove lies 0.5 mile east of Arch Rock.

From W. Leave Arch Rock 0.25 mile to starboard. Diablo Point can be seen to the E in the far distance, with the sloping profile of the eastern promontory of Lady's Harbor in the middle distance. This promontory can be identified by a conspicuous patch of gray soil that caps the ridge as it slopes into the water. The W side of the anchorage is less prominent, lying 200 yards S. Set your course midway between these two points, and hold it until the land is close ahead and the main Lady's Harbor anchorage opens up to starboard. Little Lady's Harbor lies 100 yards S of the easternmost promontory. The course midway between the two points takes you to the entrance passage for the latter.

From E. Leave Diablo Point 0.25 mile to port and pick up Arch Rock. Aim to approach the land 0.5 mile E of the Rock, and identify the E side of Lady's Harbor by its gray capping when 0.5 mile W. Leave the promontory 200 yards to port and alter course inshore when the main anchorage opens up to port.

Anchorage. Main Anchorage: Once the main cove is open, steer for the beach midway between the two cliffs. Kelp grows off the E side of the entrance and sometimes extends across the cove. There is between

Lesley Newhart

Graham Pomeroy

Top: *Lady's Harbor from NE, distant ½ mile. Left arrow indicates entrance, right marks Arch Rock to the W of the anchorage.* Bottom: *Lady's Harbor and Little Lady's Harbor from NW, altitude 2,000 feet.*

45 and 50 feet of water in the narrowest part of the entrance. Sound your way in, keeping midway between the cliffs, until the depth-sounder reads 25 to 30 feet; then choose your anchorage spot. It is probably best to lie in the middle of the cove or nearer the western cliff in 15 to 20 feet, but beware of getting too close to the rocks where backwash can be uncomfortable. The bottom is generally sandy, but good scope should be laid. A second anchor is essential, even if no other boats are present; there is barely enough room to swing safely.

Little Lady's (Baby's). This lovely spot has a more hazardous approach because the narrow passage into the anchorage is often bumpy, with some breaking water and sometimes daunting surge. Also, there is little room to turn once you are inside. Bear this is mind for boats over 35 feet, especially if other vessels are already anchored in the cove. The entrance is midway through the rock-girded passage, where a least depth of 30 to 35 feet is found, as well as some isolated rocks. The bottom is rocky and care must be taken to avoid a 20-foot patch immediately N of the passage where thick kelp is sometimes found. When going through the passage, maintain sufficient speed to provide steerageway in the steep

Lesley Newhart

Lady's Harbor entrance from 200 yards offshore. The beach at Lady's Cove is visible in the center of the photograph.

swells that can run into the entrance. Once you are through the passage, slow down in 25 feet and prepare to anchor off the beach in 15 to 20 feet (sand). The most sheltered place is on the SW side, under the cliff, but watch for swell and rocky patches. This small anchorage can only accommodate a few boats.

Little Lady's is exposed to westerly winds and swell. You should clear out at once if it shows any sign of becoming a difficult lee shore. Do not sail in with a leading wind because there is little room to turn. The entrance can be rough for dinghies, even if conditions both inside and outside are quiet.

Strong canyon winds can blow through both anchorages at night. Your second anchor should be laid carefully to guard against swinging.

Landing (both anchorages). Those with permits can land on the sandy beaches in both coves. A small stream with refreshing bathing pools runs down to Little Lady's Harbor.

The coastline from Lady's Harbor to Diablo Point is steep-to with sheer cliffs. Most people head straight for Diablo Point, the most conspicuous headland on the north coast of Santa Cruz Island. Diablo Point slopes steeply into deep water and lies immediately north of the highest point of the island. Give the point a berth of at least 0.25 mile because irregular swells often form off Diablo Point from the effects of waves breaking against the steep cliffs and the offshore current.

Diablo Anchorage lies immediately W of the point; Fry's Harbor is 0.5 mile E. Two large islets lie off the western shore of Diablo Anchorage and are conspicuous when approaching from the W.

Diablo Anchorage
Lat. 34°03.3′ N, Long. 119°46.0′ W

Diablo Anchorage, a relatively large anchorage, is a viable alternative to Fry's Harbor in quiet conditions. Because Diablo suffers from uncomfortable surge in moderate W to NW conditions, it is rarely congested.

Approach. From Santa Barbara: Set course for Diablo Point. When a mile offshore, the anchorage opens up immediately W of the point. The two off-lying islets mentioned previously can be seen W of the beach. Steer midway between them and the cliffs of Diablo Point.

Western from Lady's Harbor. This approach is straightforward. Steer for Diablo Point with the two rocky islets that form the W side of the anchorage close on the starboard bow. Once they are abeam, distant about 300 yards, the anchorage opens to starboard. Shape your course midway between the islets and Diablo Point, and proceed to the anchorage.

Anchorage. There is 70 feet of water in the entrance to Diablo Anchorage, 50 feet as the inshore islet is abeam. Proceed toward the beach and anchor nearer the western cliff, close to a cave in 20 to 25 feet (sand) with sufficient room to avoid backwash from the rocks. Use a second anchor to minimize the effects of surge. The beach shelves rapidly inshore of a cave in the western wall of the cove, halfway between the beach and the W tip of the

Lesley Newhart

Diablo Anchorage from NE, distant ¼ mile. Note the two conspicuous rocks (arrows) to starboard, a distinctive sign-post to the entrance.

land. A loose gravel bottom is found inshore of the cave.

Fry's Harbor

Lat. 34°03.2′ N, Long. 119°45.4′ W

Fry's Harbor is one of the most famous anchorages in the Santa Barbara Channel and is rarely empty. The cove provides adequate shelter in all but extreme conditions. I have ridden out westerlies exceeding 40 knots without discomfort in this cozy berth; however, surge can be a problem under these conditions. Strong down-canyon winds can blow in the late afternoons and at night. Fry's Harbor is suicidal in strong NE winds. In 1929, the stone for the Santa Barbara harbor breakwater came from the cliff immediately SE of the beach, and remains of the quarrying operations can still be seen. Several Chumash settlements once flourished here.

Approach. The anchorage is easily found when approaching from either direction along the north shore.

From Diablo Point. The scar from the quarry operations in the 1920s can be seen on the eastern cliff of the anchorage, above the beach, once you are well E of the point. A platform of boulders extends seaward from the beach below this steep cliff—the

Lesley Newhart

Top: *Fry's Harbor. Diablo Point from ENE, distant 2 miles. Arrow indicates Fry's Harbor entrance.* Bottom: *Fry's Harbor from N, distant ¼ mile. The two yachts are anchored in excellent places. Note the conspicuous cliff scar from quarrying operations and the tree at the base of the E end of the cliff.*

remains of the loading area for the quarried stone. A simple wooden derrick once stood at the northern end of the platform, but it has since collapsed, forming an underwater obstruction. The beach is tucked behind a shoulder of land and does not appear until you are close to the entrance.

From E. Aim to steer about 300 yards inshore of Diablo Point. When Fry's Harbor opens up—it lies at the eastern root of the point—alter course to port and steer for the beach.

Diablo Point lies under the highest point of land on the western half of Santa Cruz Island (Diablo Peak at 2,434 feet). When approaching from the mainland, lay off a course for Diablo Point, then identify the anchorage when a mile offshore and alter course accordingly. Like other popular anchorages, Fry's Harbor can often be identified offshore by the white hulls of yachts anchored in its shelter.

Anchorage. When approaching the anchorage, watch for kelp lying off the cliffs of Diablo Point. Sudden shifting gusts can blow off these cliffs, so use care when lowering sail in the entrance.

Enter Fry's Harbor by steering for a point midway between the two sides of the cove, sounding carefully. Once you have a depth of 50 feet, choose your anchoring spot off the beach according to draft. The best spots are tucked in under the western cliff (kelp and sand), as close to the beach as your boat can safely allow. A second anchor is usually laid and should be well dug in. Strong canyon winds can spring up in the anchorage without warning, causing some yachts to anchor bow to shore. For this reason, stay well clear of the eastern side of the cove, because the canyon winds tend to blow you onto the rocks.

Fry's Harbor is a popular spot and several boats are found here on most weekends; I have counted at least thirty-five yachts on occasion. Under these circumstances, go elsewhere. Many fishing boats anchor under the high cliffs just outside the bay, which offer protection from the N in depths of more than 60 feet. There is little surge here. If you anchor in a more exposed position or in deeper water than usual, be prepared to leave at once if conditions deteriorate.

A small cove lies immediately E of Fry's Harbor. Although yachts sometimes anchor, there is often surge. Dinghy expeditions to this beach are fun, as well as to the cave 600 feet W of Fry's Harbor.

A second cove E of Fry's Harbor, although fairly deep (50 to 60 feet, rock and sand), is a good, seldom-used alternative anchorage known as the Grotto. Beware of fouling your anchor on the rocks, however.

Landing. Landing is by permit only on the sandy beach, safe under normal conditions. The smoothest landing is at the western end. A hike to the summit of Diablo Peak takes about 4 hours for the return trip, but a superb view of the coast can be enjoyed from the top. You can spend hours in your dinghy here exploring caves and communing with seals and other wildlife. The kayaking is superb.

The 4 miles between Fry's and Prisoner's Harbors is the best-known portion of Santa Cruz Island. We describe the coast first, then the anchorages.

East of Fry's Harbor, you pass some spectacular cliffs. Deep-water anchorages under these cliffs are used by commercial diving and fishing boats. A mile E of Fry's Harbor, the coastline slopes more gradually, giving way to low-lying cliffs capped by undulating ridges that can be spotted from a long distance by the patches of gray soil that mantle the hillsides. This low shoreline is indented with tiny coves, most of which are unsuitable for overnight anchoring—except Platt's Anchorage, which lies a mile E of Fry's Harbor, and tiny Orizaba Cove, immediately E of a low island 0.6 mile farther E. Do not approach the coast much closer than 0.25 mile because dense kelp beds flourish in depths of 30 to 50 feet close inshore.

The point at Twin Harbors is conspicuous from both directions and can be identified by the small arch in its outermost end. A low promontory extends seaward a few hundred yards W. The coves on either side of this point form Twin Harbors anchorage.

From Twin Harbors to Pelican Bay, the coast is somewhat steeper because a ridge of hills runs down to the coastline. The shoreline is deeply indented in places, but there are no suitable overnight anchorages for small craft. Pelican Bay opens up behind a low bluff with several conspicuous clumps of trees on its western side; the far side of this popular anchorage is marked by a low promontory with a small sandy beach on its eastern shore. The high rocky cliff at the back of Pelican Bay is conspicuous from some distance to seaward.

From Pelican Bay to Prisoner's Harbor, the coastline trends SE for just over a mile. Sloping cliffs fall steeply into the ocean, and you can skirt the coast about 200 yards offshore. Prisoner's Harbor, with its conspicuous pier and small buildings, opens up on the starboard bow. Long before the pier appears, you can identify the deep fold in the hills that leads to the interior of the island.

This coast is at its best in spring, especially after late rains. The hillsides are lush green and ablaze with the bright yellow flowers of the giant coreopsis. This is the time of year to hike ashore, when the streams are flowing; you may be lucky enough to see an island fox resting in the shade. The hills around Orizaba are especially inviting because they are not precipitous and the walking is somewhat easier than hiking up virtually inaccessible hillsides.

Platt's Anchorage
(Dick's on older charts)
Lat. 34°02.8′ N, Long. 119°44.3′ W
A large, open roadstead with a small beach, steep cliffs, and deep water, Platt's Anchorage is much frequented by divers and commercial fishing boats. It is exposed to prevailing winds and swell.

Approach. Platt's Anchorage lies 1.0 mile E of Fry's Harbor. The anchorage is easily identified because it is surrounded by

Lesley Newhart

Platt's Anchorage (arrow) *from the NE, distant 1 mile.*

dark cliffs. The land falls away sharply on the eastern side of the bay and the sandy beach is conspicuous. More precise directions need not be given because the approach is completely safe under normal conditions.

Anchorage. The best anchorage is off the small beach in the SW portion of the roadstead (sand). Anchor according to draft and clear out if the wind comes up. Surge can be uncomfortable. The SE corner of Platt's Anchorage is heavily infested with rocks and kelp, and should be given a wide berth.

Orizaba Cove
Lat. 34°02.7′ N, Long. 119°43.4′ W
Orizaba Cove is a charming spot, but should be visited with care in anything but very calm conditions. It is sometimes used by diving and fishing boats. There is excellent shelter from S and W in quiet weather.

Approach. When approaching Orizaba Cove from offshore, make a landfall on Diablo Point or at Twin Harbors. If you intend to spend the night in Orizaba, check on prevailing weather conditions before making the anchorage. In anything but settled conditions, anchor elsewhere.

Orizaba Cove lies immediately E of Mussel Rock, a conspicuous low-lying rock whose highest point lies inshore. The Rock, stained with white bird droppings, was featured in many shipwreck scenes in early Hollywood movies. Considerable kelp growth is found around this outcrop. When approaching Orizaba Cove from either direction, steer to pass 200 yards offshore of Mussel Rock. Once opposite the eastern

Top: *Orizaba Cove. Approach from the W. Entrance is behind Mussel Rock* (arrow). Bottom: *Orizaba Cove entrance from the N, distant 300 yards.*

Lesley Newhart

end of this landmark, you can spot the anchorage. The entrance lies between a low bluff covered with conspicuous gray soil to the E and a rocky cliff, the right-hand side of which is capped with similar gray deposits. A small canyon overgrown with trees empties into the rocky cliff at the back of the anchorage. Once you have spotted these landmarks, steer slowly into the mouth of the cove, some 150 yards E of the offshore rock, sounding carefully.

Anchorage. The two sides of the tiny cove close in on you as you steer inshore. Dense kelp lies off the eastern side of the anchorage and can fill much of the cove as well. Enter the middle of the cove in 30 feet and anchor in deep water. A second anchor is essential because the amount of sandy bottom is limited and swinging is severely restricted. Beware of anchor-grabbing rocks on the bottom. The best spot is slightly W of the center of the cove, but your anchorage should be governed by surge and kelp conditions. You will almost certainly have harbor seals as interested spectators. This is a spectacular location in quiet weather.

The sandy beach inshore of the entrance rock W of Orizaba Cove offers no shelter from surge and W–NW winds, and it is not recommended.

Landing. Landing is by permit only. Land on rocks and pull your dinghy clear of the water's edge.

Twin Harbors
Lat. 34°02.7′ N, Long. 119°42.9′ W
Twin Harbors is a small anchorage that can be idyllic in quiet conditions, except when an uncomfortable surge rolls in. There are two anchorages; the western one offers little shelter.

Twin Harbors from NNE, distant ⅓ mile. Arch Rock to the W is conspicuous; yachts are anchored in the best position.

Lesley Newhart

Approach. This anchorage is best approached from E or W. The eastern cove lies immediately on the E side of a small arch rock that can be spotted from more than a mile away from W.

Once this conspicuous landmark is in sight, aim to pass 100 yards offshore until the sandy beach of the eastern anchorage opens up to port or starboard. Then alter course inshore, giving a wide berth to a rocky ledge on the eastern shore of the arch rock. A small rock that lies just offshore of the arch also should be avoided.

Anchorage. East Anchorage: Enter the cove and steer for the middle of the beach; there is 60 feet of water in the entrance off the arch rock. Sound your way toward the beach and anchor in 20 to 25 feet (sand and some rocks) some 150 feet off the beach near the western cliff. A second anchor is essential, especially if you are in the company of other boats. The western side is most sheltered.

West Anchorage. It is somewhat larger and has limited shelter from swell or wind. The sandy beach cannot be seen W of the arch rock. Sound your way into the beach and anchor according to draft, but for no more than a lunch stop. Island ironwood trees abound in the nearby canyon.

Pelican Bay

Lat. 34°02.3′ N, Long. 119°42.2′ W

Although many people regard Pelican Bay as the best anchorage on Santa Cruz Island, I have to say that I disagree with them. The scenery is magnificent—especially in spring when the flowers are in bloom—but the anchorage can be bumpy, holding ground is patchy, and landing is tricky. There are smoother anchorages at Fry's Harbor and elsewhere nearby. Pelican Bay does have the definite advantage of generous size and it is a favorite destination for yacht-club and power-squadron cruises from the mainland. Yacht races from Santa Barbara occasionally end in Pelican Bay or round a temporary mark off the entrance. Ira and Margaret Eaton ran a resort hotel at Pelican Bay 75 years ago, the remains of which overlook the Bay. Eaton used to ferry his passengers across the channel in his boat, *Sea Wolf*, until she blew ashore at Santa Barbara in a December 1927 southeaster. Many famous people stayed with the Eatons. Jan Timbrook has edited *Diary of a Sea Captain's Wife*, a fascinating and widely available account of those early Pelican Bay days.

Pelican Bay can be located far offshore by setting course for a conspicuous pointed hill with a step to the E, and a steep, conical profile to the W. This landmark lies W of the lowest point of Santa Cruz Island behind Prisoner's Harbor. Identify the hill and steer for it until you can identify the Pelican Bay landmarks 1 or 2 miles offshore. The yellow cliffs that form the western side of the anchorage are conspicuous, especially when the sun shines on them in the early morning. White hulls of yachts are often more prominent than the anchorage landmarks, and you may spot your future neighbors first. The low bluff with two summits and a patch of trees that form the western side of Pelican Bay is the first landmark identified from offshore. Steering to pass 100 yards E of this landmark takes you into the anchorage. A sandy cove close E of the anchorage can sometimes be spotted offshore.

This same bluff is the best landmark when approaching along the island coast. The patch of trees referred to helps identify the bluff from W, as does a distinctive notch in its base. Conspicuous yellow rocks on the western cliff of Pelican Bay are visible when arriving from the E. Approaching from either direction, steer for the bluff until both sides of the anchorage can be identified or it opens up on the port or starboard bow. There are no off-lying dangers and you can safely alter course inshore at this point.

The eastern shore of Pelican Bay ends in a low point marked by the tall spines of century plants on its summit. These plants were part of the landscaping of the resort hotel that flourished at Pelican Bay in the late 1920s.

Anchorage. There is more than 50 feet at the entrance. Most vessels drop anchor in 25 to 35 feet farther inshore. The favorite anchorage is in the shelter of the western cliff, sufficiently distant to avoid back-surge from the rocks. Stay at least 50 feet off to avoid loose rocks on the bottom. Later arrivals often anchor in the middle of the Bay close inshore. The bottom is littered with patches of kelp and some sea

Graham Pomeroy

Pelican Bay to Potato Harbor from the NNE, altitude 2,000 feet. Left to right (arrows): *Potato Harbor, Chinese Harbor, Prisoner's Harbor, and Pelican Bay.*

Lesley Newhart

Top: *Approach to Pelican Bay from W, distant 1 mile. Arrow shows entrance to the E of the bluff protecting the entrance.* Bottom: *Pelican Bay from NE, distant 1 mile. The yacht is anchored in an excellent position.*

grass that can cause a badly set anchor to drag if the wind comes up. It is said that the best holding ground is in the center of the anchorage, but opinions differ. Make sure your anchors are well dug in, in case they slip on a patch of kelp.

An irritating easterly chop can fill in during the night, the result of a gentle mainland breeze. The best shelter from this "Pelican Roll" is on the eastern side of the anchorage, but there is slightly more exposure to western surge here. A single anchor enables you to swing to the chop. In calm weather and when Pelican Bay is congested, you can anchor in the so-called Hole-in-the-Wall anchorage immediately W of the main bay. This snug inlet, named after the arch rock on its eastern side, offers anchorage for one or two boats. However, be careful of rocks on the bottom and be prepared to leave if the surge comes in. You can traverse the arch-rock passage in a dinghy at mid to high tide. This is a wonderful spot for short dinghy excursions.

Another inlet that may tempt you lies immediately up the coast, but there are submerged rocks in the entrance, making the potential anchorage impassable to all but the smallest craft.

Landing. Landing can be accomplished at a set of ruined steps that once led to the hotel on the cliff in the SE corner of the anchorage. Fortunately, the Nature Conservancy has installed handrails here. Beware of surge and slippery rocks. Lift your dinghy out of reach of waves and rising tides, leaving enough room for others to do the same. In calm weather, you can also land on the sandy beach in the cove

(Tinker's Harbor or Little Pelican) immediately E of Pelican Bay. The canyon behind the main anchorage opens into this bay; however, it is not a suitable overnight anchorage because it is unsheltered. Even on quiet days, a steep chop can break on this steeply shelving beach, and you may get wet. There are fascinating walks through nearby canyons and the coast is worth exploring by dinghy. You can admire a rare stand of Santa Cruz pines and read the names of yachts that visited Pelican Bay in yesteryear on the Ship Tree above the southern end of the bay (please do not add your name!).

Caution. When anchored in potential Santa Ana conditions in Fry's Harbor, Pelican Bay, Prisoner's Harbor, or any of the anchorages between them and San Pedro Point, monitor Point Mugu weather with great care. In the event that a steep swell runs into your anchorage from NE in calm conditions, on a day with perfect visibility and a very dry atmosphere, get out at once. Strong onshore winds may be on the way in a short time, and these anchorages are absolutely exposed under these conditions. However, do not be alarmed by a gentle, late night NE breeze that often drifts through Pelican Bay without raising any swell.

Prisoner's Harbor
Lat. 34°01.5′ N, Long. 119°41.1′ W
This is one of my favorites because of its attractive surroundings and also because it is rarely congested. Prisoner's Harbor is the main landing for the island and is now under National Park Service jurisdiction, as

are all anchorages E of this bay. A Navy boat brings supplies to Prisoner's Harbor each week. The buildings, pier, and tall eucalyptus trees give this spot a unique feeling—the rocky coves elsewhere on Santa Cruz Island seem to be in a different world. Prisoner's Harbor is, however, less sheltered than some other anchorages, especially from the E.

Approach. *From the mainland:* Prisoner's Harbor lies below the lowest point of land on Santa Cruz's north coast, where a fold of land gives access through a large canyon to the central valley. When approaching from the NE or NW, simply steer for this low point until the pier and buildings can be identified. From that point, head for the pier.

From E or W. The approach is just as straightforward. Once around Cavern Point, west of Scorpion Anchorage, you should be able to see the pier. The pier and buildings behind Prisoner's Harbor bear about 240 degrees M from Coche Point. When skirting the coastline from the west, keep 200 yards offshore from Pelican Bay until the coast recedes SE more sharply and the cliffs fall dramatically into the ocean. The pier then opens up on the starboard bow as you follow the coastline SE. Head for the pier, leaving the cliffs at least 200 yards to starboard. The metal roofs of the barns inshore are conspicuous from a considerable distance. A small lookout building can be seen on the hillside behind the landing.

Prisoner's Harbor (arrow). Piers and barns from the NW, distant 0.5 mile. The buildings can be detected from as far as 5 miles offshore on a clear day because the roofs glint in the sun.

Lesley Newhart

The National Park Service has replaced the old Navy pier with a new one. You can land people from your dinghy at a stage on the east side.

Anchorage. Steer for the pier head until you are in 50 feet, then shape your course for your chosen anchoring spot (see photograph on page 220). There is 12 feet along an imaginary line extending W of the pier head (sand). Depths between 15 and 35 feet are found N of this line, in sand, mud, and silt. Do not anchor inshore of the pier head because the bottom shelves rapidly. Choose your position according to surge and wind conditions and make sure you lay plenty of scope because the holding ground can be a little weak. Your anchor may slip on the hard sand or eelgrass. The most sheltered berths are close under the western cliffs. Securing alongside the pier is forbidden. Anchoring E of the pier is possible but more exposed. Mooring buoys off the pier are in constant use.

Landing. Land on the beach, and be prepared to get your feet wet.

PRISONER'S HARBOR TO SAN PEDRO POINT

The western side of Prisoner's Harbor consists of a steeply sloping hillside, with red-brown rocky cliffs shelving steeply into the anchorage. East of the canyon that gives access to the interior at Prisoner's Harbor, the coast again rises steeply. The shoreline is indented, but sloping cliffs prevent easy access on shore. It is possible to anchor off the isolated beaches between Prisoner's and Chinese Harbors in moderate westerly weather. Do not anchor too close to the gradually shelving beach because of swells. At Chinese Harbor, the steep coast turns NE and trends E toward Cavern Point. High rocky cliffs fall sheer into the water, and it is possible for divers and fishermen to work close inshore. The only landing between Chinese Harbor and Scorpion Anchorage is at Potato Harbor, described later in this section. Seen from a distance and from the west, the cliffs dip steeply 2 miles SW of Cavern Point, and just north of Potato Harbor, giving way to the lower topography of the eastern part of Santa Cruz Island. But the coastline itself remains steep and inhospitable for landing.

Cavern Point is steep-to and leads to a high, sheer, red-brown cliff that marks the western extremity of Scorpion Anchorage. A fold of hills behind Scorpion gives way to the steep cliffs and rocky outcrops that back Little Scorpion Anchorage; a conspicuous beach extends along the back of Scorpion. After Little Scorpion, the coastline is markedly lower and cliffs bound gentle grassy slopes that lead inland to high ground. San Pedro Point forms the easternmost extremity of Santa Cruz Island.

The stretch of coast from Little Scorpion Anchorage to San Pedro Point is steep-to, but should not be approached closer than 200 yards. Patches of kelp can occur off the point and close inshore, and interesting blowholes and colorful spring flowers are features of this stretch of coast. Seals are still common off the many rocks near the water's edge. When approaching San Pedro Point, beware of sudden wind increases as you round the point and enter

E end of Santa Cruz Island from NE; altitude 2,000 feet. Left to right (arrows): Smuggler's Cove, Little Scorpion, and Scorpion Anchorages.

the windy Anacapa Passage that separates Santa Cruz Island from Anacapa Island. In the 1858 *Sailing Directions*, we learn that "a site for a lighthouse at the eastern end of the island has been reported upon and recommended by the Superintendent of the Coast Survey to the Lighthouse Board." It was never built.

Chinese Harbor

Chinese Harbor is little more than a large, open roadstead that was used by passing ships in the nineteenth century, when it was somewhat magnificently known as Contrabandista Bay. Oil boats sometimes use it today. Few yachts or fishing boats spend the night off this open and exposed beach

in an anchorage that is bumpy in almost any conditions. A fumarole, the only one on the offshore islands, can be seen smoking in the NE cliff of the anchorage several hundred feet above the beach. Chinese Harbor offers moderate shelter in NE winds.

Approach. The approach is straightforward. From W, identify Prisoner's Harbor pier and follow the coastline to the white-brown cliffs that slope to Chinese Harbor 3 miles SW of Cavern Point, which can be identified from a long distance even on misty days. The best anchorage lies in the NE corner of Chinese Harbor. Steer for the NE end of the beach to reach this spot. Approaching from Potato Harbor or Scorpion Anchorage, stay 200 yards offshore until the shoreline indents at Coche Point toward the beach that forms Chinese Harbor anchorage. The fumarole usually can be identified when you are 0.5 mile from the anchorage. Aim to have the smoke trail on the starboard bow as you approach the beach.

Anchorage. Anchor according to draft, sounding your way to the beach and avoiding patches of kelp. The best anchorage appears to be in a position where the fumarole cliff bears about SE, in 25 to 30 feet (sand), but use your judgment in choosing the best spot. A second anchor is unnecessary except to control boat motion.

Landing. Landing is on the beach. Take careful note of swell conditions before landing, which should not be attempted except in calm weather.

Potato Harbor

(Potato Harbor was once known as Tyler's)
Lat. 34°02.9′ N, Long. 119°35.7′ W

This is one of my favorites, a picturesque anchorage in a narrow bay in the steep cliffs east of Prisoner's Harbor—which, however, is exposed to the prevailing westerlies. Potato Harbor offers shelter from NE and SE winds that can blow down from the cliffs in strong gusts, and provides complete protection from swells out of these directions. Be prepared to move out quickly if the wind shifts to NW and strengthens significantly.

Approach. From W: Locate a patch of white cliffs west of Cavern Point; Potato Harbor lies just E of those white slopes. The narrow entrance can be identified as you

Potato Harbor from the W, distant ½ mile. Yacht (arrow) is anchored in a good place.

Lesley Newhart

close with the land, with a prominent rock lying off the southern side of the indentation.

From E. Round Cavern Point and identify the northern side of the Potato Harbor entrance, the second prominent headland beyond Cavern Point. A patch of white cliffs can be seen halfway up the slope immediately behind this low, sloping headland. Pass 0.5 mile offshore until the entrance opens up to port. Enter Potato Harbor by steering midway between the entrance headlands for the beach, sounding carefully.

Anchorage. Sound your way toward the beach staying slightly to the N of the center of the bay, which gives you some shelter behind the outcrop on the S side of the entrance. Anchor off the beach in 25 to 30 feet (sand), avoiding rocks and kelp in the NE corner of the anchorage and the shallower water on the S side.

Potato Harbor is a lee shore in prevailing westerly winds and swells. Clear out at the first sign of stronger winds. This anchorage is recommended for an overnight stay except in settled weather.

Scorpion and Little Scorpion Anchorages

(Known as East End Anchorage on 1882 chart)

Scorpion: Lat. 34°03.0′ N, Long. 119°33.4′ W

Two well-known anchorages—Scorpion and Little Scorpion—lie E of Cavern Point and are especially popular with vessels from Ventura or Channel Islands. Little Scorpion is the better of the two because it offers more shelter than its western neighbor. Also, the holding ground in Scorpion is sometimes

unsatisfactory. Scorpion Anchorage is a major public landing for the eastern end of the island. A pier extends seaward at the NW side of the anchorage. You will encounter numerous kayaks on weekends.

Approach. From Santa Barbara: Both anchorages are readily identified at a distance by finding low-lying San Pedro Point and the distinctive hump of the hill behind Cavern Point. You should then be able to identify a saddle of land between the easternmost peak of high ground and the summit of the foothill ridge to the east. Scorpion lies in front of a conspicuous cleft in the cliff below the saddle. Steer for this cleft until the pier and rocks W of Little Scorpion can be identified.

From E. Identify Cavern Point and two detached rocks lying inshore and to the east that shelter Little Scorpion. Steer to pass 200 yards offshore of these rocks, a course that takes you into Scorpion Anchorage.

From W. Simply follow the coast E from Cavern Point until the rocks of Little Scorpion are identified and the anchorage opens up ahead.

These two anchorages can be congested in the summer, but you can always find room at Smuggler's Cove at the eastern end of the island.

Scorpion Anchorage. Approach the anchorage by steering for the pier, giving the offshore rocks at the E end of the bight a wide berth. Avoiding the kelp to the W and off the bay, sound your way to the anchorage S or E of the pier in 35 feet (mud, sand, and kelp). Anchor between the pier and a pyramid-shaped rock to the east for the best kelp-free berth. Anchorage can also

Lesley Newhart

Scorpion and Little Scorpion Anchorages. Approach to the anchorages is from NE, distant 1 mile. Little Scorpion is indicated by the left arrow, lying to port of the white rock. The right arrow marks the distinctive cleft that signposts these anchorages from far offshore.

Lesley Newhart

Scorpion Anchorage from NNE, distant 1 mile. Yachts are anchored in the best position, sheltered from the swell by Cavern Point.

be obtained W of the pier, but beware of extensive kelp beds under the steep cliffs. Lay plenty of scope and a second anchor. Clear out if the wind fills in strongly from NW or NE, or if the odor of bird droppings becomes unbearable. Anchorage in Scorpion can be insecure due to kelp and sea grass on the bottom. Make sure your anchor is well dug in.

Landing. Land on the beach or at the pier. The entire coast, especially the cliffs and caves, is worth exploring by dinghy in the calm early morning.

Little Scorpion Anchorage. As you approach, give the two white-stained rocks W of Little Scorpion a berth of at least 100 yards to avoid kelp beds; enter the anchorage midway between steep cliffs to the east and these outcrops. There is 60 feet in the entrance. A sandy bottom gives excellent shelter in 22 to 45 feet in the lee of the two rocks. Anchor as close to the rocks as you can, consistent with your draft. A second anchor is essential, both to minimize surge and to prevent swinging into the kelp south of the clear water and immediately W of the rocks. Little Scorpion is often congested, and is dangerous in strong NE winds. Afternoon winds can gust strongly between the rock outcrops in summer.

Landing. Landing is not recommended, but you can explore the cliffs, caves, rocks, and kelp beds from a dinghy. This is a paradise for gunkholers and kayakers.

SANTA CRUZ ISLAND: SOUTH COAST

MANY PEOPLE VISITING Santa Cruz Island for the first time cross from Channel Islands Harbor, stopping at Anacapa Island on the way. This route provides convenient access to the attractive anchorages on the south coast of Santa Cruz Island—easier access than is possible by approaching them through the bumpy Santa Cruz Channel. In this section, we describe the coasts of Santa Cruz Island from San Pedro Point along the eastern, southern, and western shores, as far as West Point (Chart 18728; Chart Guide, pp. 1–4; Chart-Kit, pp. 13–14). (For location of anchorages, see the map on page 199.)

Approaching from the Channel Islands or Anacapa, Santa Cruz Island appears as a steep mountain chain, tailing off to the low-lying NE corner. When crossing to Santa Cruz Island from these directions, expect a strengthening of the afternoon breeze in the Anacapa Passage. Much stronger NW winds funnel through this passage on many days, so much so that you may have to reduce sail. Beware of the effects of current against wind in the passage, which can result in short, steep seas. Smaller craft, especially outboard fishing boats, are best advised to make this crossing in the calmer hours of morning, although it can blow in Anacapa Passage at any time.

Caution. All south coast anchorages are subject to heavy surge from tropical storms off the Mexican coast that can come in without warning, especially in the summer.

SAN PEDRO POINT TO YELLOWBANKS

San Pedro Point is low but steep-to, with some outlying kelp and rocks. Give the E end of Santa Cruz Island a berth of 0.5 mile. East of San Pedro Point, the steep, red-brown cliffs are indented with small rocky

Lesley Newhart

Hungryman's Gulch anchorage from E, distant ¼ mile. Anchor off the beach clear of the kelp (arrow).

caves, the most prominent of which lies 0.5 mile SW of the point.

Hungryman's Gulch terminates in this cove, which can provide shelter from NW winds in 15 feet (sand and rock). But beware of rocks and kelp lying off the beach in the middle of the bay. Late nineteenth-century charts describe this as a "small boat landing," but surprisingly few vessels use it today. The shore trends SW into Smuggler's Cove, the major anchorage at the E end of the island, 1.25 miles SW of San Pedro Point.

Smuggler's Cove
(Called Anacapa Bay on the 1858 chart)
Lat. 34°01.3′ N, Long. 119°32.6′ W
A large, open roadstead that provides shelter for large numbers of small craft in calm

weather, Smuggler's Cove has the advantage of being easy to find but suffers from frequent heavy surge and strong offshore (NW) winds at times. I have spent the night in Smuggler's Cove riding to a 35-pound Hi-tensile Danforth, 90 feet of chain, and 90 feet of heavy-duty Dacron hawser in an offshore wind of at least 45 knots, gusting even higher (far stronger gear than most people typically carry). We stayed put, but people around us were dragging all night. Without adequate ground tackle, this anchorage can be uncomfortable and hazardous. In calm weather, Smuggler's Cove is an attractive place with groves of olives and fine eucalyptus trees overlooking the Cove.

Approach. Approaching from Anacapa or the Channel Islands, the yellow-brown cliffs of the SE shore of Santa Cruz Island can be seen from a long distance on a clear day. Identify the northernmost of these light-colored bluffs that lie immediately SW of Smuggler's Cove, as well as low-lying San Pedro Point. Steer for the point on the coast where yellow cliffs merge with the lower shoreline. Smuggler's Cove opens up on your starboard bow as you approach the land.

When looking for the anchorage on passage along the island, from the south coast follow the yellow cliffs into the open bay, staying a sufficient distance offshore to avoid the extensive kelp beds off the coastline. As the roadstead opens up to port, you'll see the serried rows of olive trees on the NW slope of the bay. Once Smuggler's Cove is identified, shape your course for the middle of the cove until you are near the head of the anchorage. Smuggler's Cove is found from N by following the coastline from San Pedro around into the bay.

Anchorage. Anchorage can be obtained almost anywhere in Smuggler's Cove on a sandy bottom in 25 to 40 feet. The best shelter lies under the cliffs on the NW side of the bay. Make sure you anchor sufficiently far enough offshore to minimize the effects of ground swell. Beware of shallowing at the head of the anchorage, and be sure that you anchor clear of other people in case they drag when a downslope wind blows. Lay plenty of scope.

At the first sign of a swell from NE on calm, dry, clear days, or of smog offshore— both warning of an impending Santa

Lesley Newhart

Smuggler's Cove from SE, distant 2 miles. The best anchorage lies off the olive grove on the hillside behind the bay.

Ana—leave this anchorage at once. Also leave if a SE swell and dark clouds indicate an approaching southeaster.

Yellowbanks Anchorage
Lat. 34°00′8″ N, Long. 119°32.8′ W
Yellowbanks is another open roadstead that provides an attractive alternative to Smuggler's Cove in both calm and heavy NW weather. Yellowbanks is usually less congested than its neighbor, but provides much greater protection from NW winds. However, it is slightly more exposed to prevailing swells, which wrap around the island from N or NW, or from Mexican tropical storms to the S.

Approach. The approach is the same as for Smuggler's Cove, but the anchorage lies under the yellow-brown cliffs to SW of the former. As you approach the NE extremity of the yellow bluffs, identify the steep, high cliff that marks the SW side of Yellowbanks and the steep, V-shaped canyon that runs into the head of the anchorage. Yellowbanks is separated from Smuggler's Cove by a low-lying cliff and point. A shallow reef and some kelp lie off this spot, which should be given a 0.5-mile clearance. Watch for kelp in the entrance as you steer for the canyon mouth. Beware of an isolated rock in 18 feet that uncovers at low tide off the S side of the bay.

Yellowbanks anchorage from E, distant 1 mile. The best anchorage is close under the cliffs (arrow), clear of beach surge.

Lesley Newhart

Anchorage. Anchor off the beach in 20 to 35 feet (sand, rocks, and pebbles). To avoid disturbance from ground swell, do not anchor too close in. A second anchor is advisable. Clear out at the first sign of a NE or SE wind. Watch for rapid shallowing near the beach. The amount of sheltered water for anchorage is relatively small.

YELLOWBANKS TO ALBERT'S ANCHORAGE

SW of Yellowbanks, the island turns W at a conspicuous yellow-brown cliff formed by a ridge that runs down to the shore from the center of the island. Sandstone Point is visible from a long distance offshore. Extensive kelp beds extend out to sea from Sandstone Point for at least a mile. You are best advised to keep outside them, unless you plan to anchor off the beach at Middle Anchorage or W of the point. There are several anchorages along this stretch of coast, none of them exceptional.

Middle Anchorage
Little more than a slight indentation in the cliffs, Middle Anchorage is only a calm-weather, temporary landing. Even in quiet conditions, a slight swell runs into the beach. Identify Sandstone Point and steer through the kelp, leaving the point 0.75 mile to port. The anchorage lies inside the kelp off the beach. Watch for isolated rocks near the shore on either side of the anchorage. Anchor off the beach in 15 to 35 feet (sand), according to draft.

Sandstone Point Anchorage
You can also anchor 0.5 mile W of Sandstone Point inside the kelp in 30 feet (rock and sand) in an open bay that offers shelter from NW winds. I do not recommend this as an overnight stop.

The easternmost stretches of the south coast of Santa Cruz Island consist of attractive yellow-brown cliffs that fall steeply into the ocean. Fine sandy beaches lie at the foot of the cliffs, but dense kelp can mantle the coastline.

Steep canyons run down through the cliffs from the central spur of the island. A conspicuous radar-tracking station lies high above the coast and can be seen from a long distance when it is brightly lit at night. It is not marked on the chart. Keep outside the kelp until you approach a conspicuous yellow bluff, 800 feet high, which lies 1.5 miles E of Valley Anchorage. A rock (10 feet) lies offshore below the bluff, the most conspicuous feature of the foul rock and kelp area off the coast in this location. This foul ground extends W of the bluff. Do not approach the coast too closely until you are within 0.75 mile of Valley Anchorage.

Valley Anchorage
Lat. 33°59.2′ N, Long. 119°39.8′ W
Valley Anchorage is an exposed, calm-weather berth, uncomfortable in a surge or strong winds. Low-flying aircraft sometimes come in overhead because the island airstrip lies upslope of the anchorage. Cliffs immediately E of the bight are white and conspicuous. A reef and sometimes dense kelp beds extend SE from the shore. Anchor in 34 to 40 feet (sand) off the beach. Avoid

Lesley Newhart

Valley Anchorage from S, distant 1 mile. Arrow indicates the best anchoring spot.

anchoring too close inshore; stay clear of the NE area of the anchorage that is kelp- and rock-infested. A flopper stopper is useful to reduce movement from the constant surge into the anchorage.

The deep indentation that runs inshore from Valley Anchorage forms the central valley of Santa Cruz Island. It is here that the island airstrip is located, so sometimes you will see a light aircraft swooping down for a landing or taking off downhill across the anchorage. Landing by plane on Santa Cruz Island is an experience not to be missed if you have the opportunity—the airstrip is truly an adventure.

The cliffs W of Valley Anchorage are precipitous and fall sheer into the Pacific.

Blue Banks Anchorage is the next indentation in this steep coast, 0.5 mile W of Valley Anchorage. The shoreline is very steep all around the anchorage, with bands of brown, yellow, and reddish-brown that can be identified at some distance.

Blue Banks Anchorage

A shallow indentation in the coast that provides some shelter from W and NW winds, Blue Banks Anchorage has a constant surge problem and is at its best in calm summer weather. No conspicuous landmarks mark the Blue Banks approach. Look for the indentation in the land 1.5 miles E of Albert's Anchorage and 0.5 mile W of Valley Anchorage. The banded brown-yellow coloring of the cliffs sometimes stands out near the shore, and sometimes appears blue; hence, the name "Blue Banks." Once the anchorage is identified, plan to enter the cove midway between the two extremities of the indentation. Anchor in 25 to 30 feet, 35 yards or more off the beach in the center of the cove, or just SW of a conspicuous green rock outcrop. Blue Banks is uncomfortable in any surge and should be avoided in strong winds, even if it provides some shelter from W and NW winds.

Precipitous cliffs continue to trend SW toward the prominent sloping promontory that forms the western side of Albert's Anchorage. This conspicuous and unnamed headland has a characteristic sloping profile readily identifiable from a considerable distance. As you approach, the tilted geological strata stand out on the cliffs. A recent rock fall can be seen on the E side of the cliff near Albert's Anchorage. High cliffs between Blue Banks and Albert's Anchorage end at the beach behind the anchorage, where the headland, a steep slope from the spur of the island, and the cliffs meet.

None of the anchorages at the SE corner of Santa Cruz Island are truly all-weather berths. They are best used in the settled summer months, especially on crowded holiday weekends.

Albert's Anchorage
For the headland between Albert's and Coches Prietos: Lat. 33°58.0′ N, Long. 119°42.5′ W

History does not reveal who Albert was, but he may have been a nineteenth-century surveyor. His anchorage is a comfortable berth in settled weather with good shelter from W through N winds. The steep cliff to the W puts the cove in shadow in the late afternoon. A small beach lies at the head of the anchorage. Albert's Anchorage can be bumpy with surge and is completely exposed to the SE. You have a fine view of the SE coast of the island and distant Anacapa Island from this cove, but Albert's Anchorage is dark in late afternoon and you may feel closed in.

Approach. From E: Identify the conspicuous sloping headland and shape your course to pass 200 yards inshore of the tip of the promontory. The anchorage, with its small beach, opens up to starboard, immediately inshore of the headland. Once it is identified, steer into the cove and choose an anchorage spot.

Anchorage. Smaller vessels typically anchor 35 to 40 yards off the beach in 25 to 35 feet (sand). Good shelter can be found under the steep cliffs in 35 feet (sand) off a recently collapsed slab of rock. Watch out, however, for underwater rocks and kelp. When the anchorage is congested, anchor in deep water with plenty of scope. A second anchor can be used to minimize surge effects. Landing is on the beach, by permit; there is limited access inshore.

When bound W past the headland, give the end a berth of at least 300 yards to avoid isolated rocks and kelp. Once you are around the headland, Coches Prietos anchorage opens up on your starboard bow.

Graham Pomeroy

Coches Prietos and Albert's Anchorages from S, distant 1 mile. Left arrow indicates Coches Prietos; right arrow indicates Albert's. Albert's Anchorage is in the shadow because this photograph was taken in the afternoon.

Lesley Newhart

Albert's Anchorage from SSE, distant 1 mile. Left-hand yacht is in the best position for smaller vessels (arrow).

Coches Prietos

A charming cove, Coches Prietos (which means "Black Pigs") is probably the best anchorage on the southern side of Santa Cruz Island. Coches Prietos has a fine sandy beach, good shelter from W to N winds, and offers some protection in Santa Ana conditions; Albert's Anchorage is best in strong NW winds. This beautiful location is typically crowded with visitors, especially in the summer.

Approach. The cove is formed by a beautiful, semicircular, sandy beach at the foot of a valley that extends inland. Approaching from W and once beyond Bowen Point, identify the sloping strata of the headland just beyond the anchorage. Steer for it until Coches Prietos bay opens up to port; then head for the beach, keeping within 40 yards of the cliffs to starboard and watching for kelp. You are inside the anchorage once the curving point at the W side of the anchorage is well abeam.

Anchorage. Anchor in 10 to 25 feet (sand) off the beach. Tuck in behind the kelp and the W cliff as much as possible. There is a bed of slippery algae on the bottom just inside the reef. Your anchor may slide on it, so choose your spot with care. Do not anchor too close to the beach; a second anchor is normal. Coches Prietos is usually relatively smooth and a comfortable berth if you lay adequate scope. If the anchorage is congested, you may need to anchor near the E cliffs.

Coches Prietos can be very uncomfortable when the swell is running. If there is heavy surge on the beach, anchor outside

Coches Prietos and Albert's Anchorages from SSE, altitude 2,000 feet. The best berths in Coches Prietos are off the beach, well clear of the reef and surf.

Lesley Newhart

Coches Prietos anchorage approach from the WSW, distant 0.3 mile. The best anchorage is to the W of the small boats in the photograph (arrow), tucked behind the reef if possible.

the kelp or, better still, go to another anchorage. The bay soon fills up on calm summer days so you may have to anchor outside, enjoying only slight shelter from the swells in the distant lee of Bowen Point. Many people prefer doing this rather than finding an alternative berth at somewhere like Morse Point to the west, which is never crowded. If you do anchor outside, it is better to lie to one anchor, letting out a great deal of scope. Be ready to leave at once if the weather gets up. Strong winds can blow down the Coches Prietos canyons at night and during Santa Ana conditions.

Precipitous gray cliffs descend into the ocean between Coches Prietos and Willow's Anchorage 2.75 miles W. Bowen Point, a mile W of Coches, drops steeply into the Pacific. A small white rock lies off the end of the point. Dense kelp beds can be found off Bowen Point. This brown-gray point has sloping geological strata. The shoreline between Coches Prietos and Bowen Point is much fouled by rocks and kelp, and should be given a berth of 0.5 mile. At night, the flashing light on Gull Island comes into view as you round Bowen Point.

Steep, gray cliffs continue 1.75 miles W to Willow's Anchorage, which lies just east of a 669-foot peak near the shore.

Willow's Anchorage
(Alamos Anchorage on 1882 chart)
Lat. 33°57.7′ N, Long. 119°45.3′ W
A popular anchorage, protected from W to N winds, Willow's Anchorage is a pretty spot. Surge conditions can be dangerous if even moderate wind comes in from the SW. Avoid anchoring here when high swell is running offshore.

Approach. From E: Identify the 669-foot peak with its precipitous cliffs and look for two conspicuous detached rocks, each 87 feet high, which lie about 100 and 200 yards from the shore. The offshore rock is stained white; the inshore pinnacle is brown-black. These landmarks guide you to the anchorage, which should not be approached until the outer pinnacle rock is on the starboard quarter. Give this offlying danger a berth of at least 0.3 mile. Dense kelp and hidden rocks lie offshore. Then steer for the beach midway between the cliff and the two rocks.

From W: Follow the coastline from Gull Island E until you spot the two pinnacle rocks and Bowen Point 1.75 miles E. A course shaped to approach the land 1.0 mile W of Bowen Point opens up the landmarks on a safe bearing.

This can be a hazardous coastline when the Mexican swell is up, so keep well offshore under these conditions.

Lesley Newhart

Willow's Anchorage from the ESE, distant 0.6 mile. Left arrow indicates main anchorage; right arrow indicates the berth E of the pinnacle rocks.

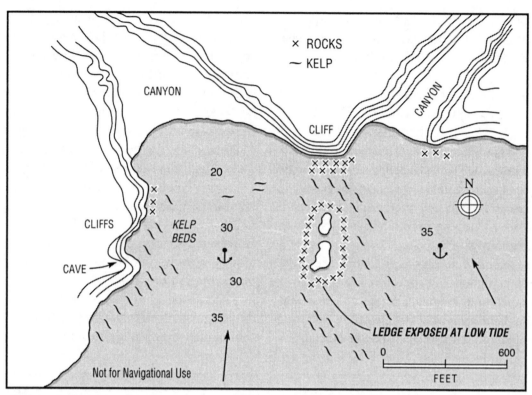

× ROCKS
~ KELP

CANYON

CANYON

CLIFF

CLIFFS

KELP BEDS

CAVE →

20

30

30

35

35

N

35

LEDGE EXPOSED AT LOW TIDE

0   600

FEET

Not for Navigational Use

Plan of Willow's Anchorage adapted from Chart 18728. The arrows show the best courses to steer.

Anchorage. The most popular anchorage lies in the middle of the cove off the beach in 20 to 35 feet (sand); larger vessels anchor under the W cliff in 35 to 50 feet. Lay plenty of scope and a second anchor to minimize surge movement and to leave space for others. The surge in Willow's Anchorage can build up rapidly, so be prepared to move on if the anchorage becomes intolerable.

You can also anchor in calm weather E of the pinnacle rocks in 35 feet (sand), clear of the kelp, or closer to shore. Watch out, however, for the off-lying and awash rocks close inshore SE of the beach. This berth is sometimes quieter than Willow's Anchor-

age itself, but neither the cove nor this spot are recommended in bad weather.

Strong NW or NE winds can funnel down the canyons at Willow's Anchorage. Be prepared for sudden changes in wind direction and site your anchor(s) accordingly.

WILLOW'S ANCHORAGE TO GULL ISLAND AND PUNTA ARENA

Between Willow's and Laguna Harbor 2 miles W, the steep cliffs are relieved by two conspicuous sandy beaches with 30 feet close inshore. Neither are realistic overnight anchorages, however. Kelp beds lie inshore along this stretch of coast. Laguna Harbor is immediately W of an unmistakable precipitous sloping point 574 feet high.

Laguna Harbor

Chart 18728 calls this a harbor, although it is difficult to understand why—perhaps nineteenth-century surveyors were tougher than we are! Laguna Harbor consists of a long sandy beach below a conspicuous canyon. A steep yellow-brown cliff and a high rock lie just W of the beach, and can be identified from a considerable distance. Anchor off the beach in 35 to 40 feet (sand) and be prepared for a bumpy stay. Laguna Harbor is not recommended as an overnight berth.

The SW and W coasts of Santa Cruz Island can be dangerous in unsettled W and NW weather. Even on relatively calm days, the afternoon westerlies pick up strength as you approach Gull Island. A westbound yacht often finds herself beating or motoring into a much stronger breeze than is the case farther east. Under normal conditions, eastbound sailing vessels enjoy a fast run from West Point, but tend to lose the wind as they leave Gull Island astern and conditions quiet down.

When bound westward, monitor weather forecasts carefully, especially for strong NW or down-canyon winds and heavy offshore swells. Under these conditions, you are best advised to stay clear of the area between Bowen Point on the south coast and Cueva Valdez on the north.

As you pass Bowen Point, Gull Island and its light appear about a mile offshore of low-lying Punta Arena. You now have the choice of passing offshore or inshore of the island. On a first visit, we recommend that you pass offshore, giving the lighted rock a berth of 0.5 mile.

Gull Island (Lat. 33°57.0′ N, Long. 119°49.5′ W) is 65 feet high and 0.2 mile across. It is a popular sunning place for sea lions and many sea birds, whose droppings have stained the rocks white. A light (Fl. W. 4 sec. 73 feet, 6 miles) is exhibited from a white pyramid-shaped structure on the summit of the island. Dense kelp beds and both exposed and subsurface rocks surround Gull Island. When bound past the island offshore, you can pass safely 0.5 mile outside the kelp.

The inshore passage requires caution, a good depth-sounder, and calm weather: it can be very overgrown with kelp growing on foul ground. When bound between Gull Island and Santa Cruz Island, identify the following landmarks (see map page 241):

- low-lying Punta Arena, which looks like a low ridge extending seaward with a conspicuous pointed peak sloping steeply upward inshore of the headland
- Gull Island and its kelp beds
- kelp beds lying SE of Punta Arena when approaching the narrowest point of the passage, or N from Gull Island
- breaking water and rocks awash near Punta Arena

Once you clear these features, steer carefully between Gull Island and the main island, sounding often. The clear passage lies about one third of the way between Gull and Santa Cruz Islands, close to Gull

Gull Island from SSW, distant ½ mile. Beware of swells breaking on the reefs off the E end of the island.

Lesley Newhart

Island in about 35 feet or slightly less. You should steer for Gull Island until kelp beds and smooth water are seen, then shape your course through the passage. Do not attempt this passage at night, in fog, or in rough weather.

The kelp-protected coast of Santa Cruz Island between Laguna Harbor and Punta Arena is steep and barren with little of interest for small craft. However, Malva Real anchorage lies in the lee of Punta Arena tucked behind the kelp and rocks off the headland.

Malva Real Anchorage

Malva Real is a temporary anchorage that is often uncomfortable with surge in the lee of a desolate and rocky promontory. It offers shelter from W to NW winds, especially if you take advantage of the flattening effects of kelp on swell.

Once Punta Arena is identified from E, pass inside of the kelp beds, sounding carefully, steering to bring your vessel inshore 250 yards N of the point. From W, you will have to pass inshore of Gull Island, giving the rocks and kelp off Punta Arena a wide berth before heading through the kelp to the anchorage. Anchor inside the kelp (if possible) off the pebble beach in 30 to 35 feet (rock and sand). Be prepared to leave quickly if swell or wind conditions deteriorate. This is a fair-weather anchorage but is often used by fishing boats. You can experience bumpy swell even in calm weather.

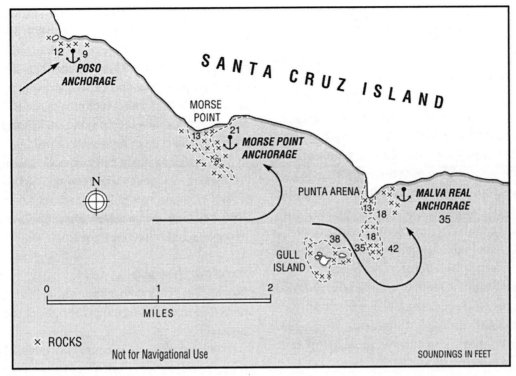

Poso Anchorage to Malva Real, including Gull Island passage. Adapted from Chart 18307. Note: The extent of the kelp bed varies greatly over the years. (The chart spelling of "Poso" is used here.)

Malva Real Anchorage from SE (arrow), distant 1 mile.

PUNTA ARENA TO FORNEY'S ANCHORAGE

West of Punta Arena, the immediate shoreline is lower lying than farther E, terminating in low brown sandy cliffs that are creased by innumerable water gullies. Punta Arena itself is capped with yellow dunes and gray soil. Unless you want to anchor in the lee of Morse Point, stay at least 1 mile offshore until this headland is well astern to avoid a zone of kelp and rocks extending SE of the point for 0.75 mile. The bight to the E is called Johnson's Lee—not to be confused with the anchorage of that name on Santa Rosa Island. These off-lying dangers break heavily in any swell and are dangerous in a gale. Morse Point has a conspicuous yellow cliff on its eastern side.

Morse Point Anchorage
Lat. 33°57.9′ N, Long. 119°50.7′ W
You can anchor in the lee of Morse Point, a steep-ended promontory with a high rocky ridge inshore of the coast. Anchor in 25 feet (sand), well off the beach between the inner and outer kelp beds to avoid rocks in shallow water. Approach the anchorage from the E, skirting the off-lying ledge SE of Morse Point. This is a wonderful anchorage in fine summer weather, even in winds up to 15 knots—but you should go elsewhere in unsettled conditions. Watch your tides here; the topography and depths can change dramatically, especially during spring tides.

Morse Point runs down to the coast to end in 150-foot-high yellow-brown cliffs. Viewed from the W, the headland has a dis-tinct stepped profile that is easily identified from some distance. The coast now trends NW into the Santa Cruz Channel and the gray-brown hills of the SW corners of the island slope down to the shore, ending in low steep cliffs that front the ocean. A dense kelp bed lies off this coast and should be given a berth of at least 0.75 mile.

The shallow bight between Morse and Pozo Points and the anchorage 1.4 miles NW is exposed to the full onslaught of the SW swell. Larger breakers make the beach unapproachable in any surge.

Pozo Anchorage
(Note: The NOS Chart spelling is "Poso," which we use on the charts for navigational clarity.)

A temporary anchorage in the lee of a steep promontory with a rock at its extremity and conspicuous from NW, Pozo Anchorage can be bumpy. Anchor off the beach in 30 to 35 feet (sand), giving both the end of the point and the kelp a wide berth. This anchorage is dangerous in any swell because waves break for a considerable distance off the point.

Kinton Point is the next landmark, a precipitous and conspicuous headland with rocks at its foot. The promontory offers no protection from the prevailing winds. It forms one side of the large bay that marks the W end of Santa Cruz Island. This huge bight curves around to end in Forney's Cove and Fraser Point. The central valley of the island ends in the Christy Canyon Anchorage, the low-lying head of the bay. The coastline is steep-to around Kinton Point and slopes downward to the floor of the canyons that empty into the shore. Low cliffs trend around the bay toward Fraser Point.

As you sail NW through Santa Cruz Passage, you will see a mountain chain that forms the northern spur of Santa Cruz Island on the starboard bow, an impressive background to Forney's Cove at the NW corner. Black Point is the only conspicuous headland in the bight, about midway between Kinton and Fraser Points. Because there is little to attract visitors to this large bight, most people sail directly across toward Forney's Cove or West Point.

Christy Valley Anchorage

You can anchor off the mouth of the valley in 18 to 35 feet (hard sand). The best anchorage lies a little N of the valley mouth, close inshore S of the awash rocks, where there is more protection. The anchorage can be identified from a long distance by the white buildings behind the beach; a course for these buildings brings you to the anchorage. Stay at least 0.5 mile off either shore of the bay to avoid kelp and outlying rocks. Christy Valley is a bumpy anchorage and is not recommended for a long stay, except as a refuge from strong NE winds when the land N of the canyon offers some protection.

Forney's Cove

Lat. 34°03.2′ N, Long. 119°55.0′ W

Forney's Cove is one of the more popular anchorages on Santa Cruz Island, offering a desolate and fascinating berth amidst spectacular scenery. There is excellent skin diving and fishing nearby. Forney's Cove provides some protection from W and NW winds, but cannot be recommended if a heavy swell is running. If a strong offshore wind blows up after sundown and you are lying at the W end of Forney's Cove, leave the anchorage at once—you are on a lee shore. I once got caught there in a 45-knot downslope wind and nearly lost my ship, snapping a 1-inch anchor line in the small hours of the night because we failed to get out.

Approach. *From N or S:* Identify Fraser Point, a long low-lying peninsula that protrudes like a detached islet from the main island. Fraser Point can be approached within 0.5 mile. Once you are within a mile of Fraser (from S) or with the headland abaft the beam (from N), identify a series of off-lying rock islets that are 0.5 mile E and inshore of the end of the headland. These islets are surrounded by isolated sub-surface dangers and extensive kelp beds that extend SE for 0.5 mile. Forney's Cove lies behind these rocks, which provide much of the shelter in the anchorage.

From W or N. Give the S side of the headland and these rocks a 0.75-mile berth, staying clear of the kelp, as you steer SE into the bight beyond Fraser Point. When the rocks and kelp are well astern, alter course to the N to pass through the gap in the kelp between the rocks—which is only about 100 feet wide—and the steep cliffs of the shore.

From S. Leave the rocks and kelp broad on the port bow and steer for a point a little more than halfway between the cliffs and the rocks, just outside the kelp beds. This course (probably just W of N) brings you into the cove safely. Note that Fraser Point is easily identified from offshore in the Santa Barbara Channel, lying 1.5 miles S of West Point.

Anchorage. Forney's Cove is formed by a semicircular sandy beach that ends in steep cliffs to the NE and in Fraser Point to the W. The off-lying rocks and reefs mentioned previously provide some protection from prevailing swells. As you enter the cove, steer for the beach until rocks and kelp to port are abaft the beam. Then sound your way into an anchor berth between the beach and rocks, tucked as far W into the anchorage as conditions and your draft per-

mit. The smoothest water is at the head of the cove. Anchor in 15 feet (sand, kelp, and rocks). Lay plenty of scope and a second anchor to minimize effects of surge.

Although people do anchor off pebbly Fraser Beach immediately NE of Fraser Point, this berth is a lee shore in prevailing NW conditions and is usable as a day anchorage only in the calmest weather. Fraser Cove is a refuge anchorage in Santa Ana and SE conditions, but be prepared for a sudden shift to the NW (see sidebar page 197).

You are best advised to avoid Forney's Cove when Santa Ana conditions are pre-

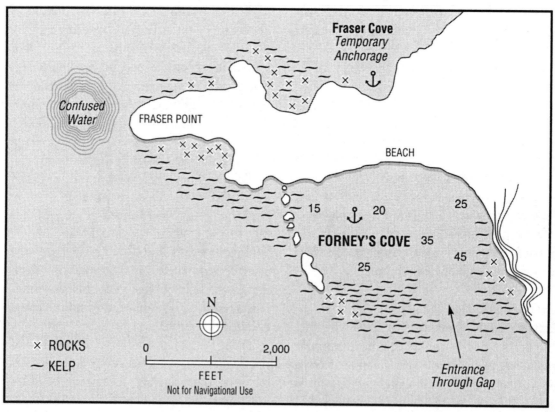

Plan of Forney's Cove. Anchor according to draft, with as much shelter from the rocks as possible.

Lesley Newhart

Forney's Cove from SE, showing approach (arrow). The yacht is anchored in shallow water behind rocks and kelp beds. There is more protection at low water.

vailing over the mainland. The downslope winds in this area have to be experienced to be believed. If you must anchor under these conditions, your best berth is tucked under the cliffs at the E end of the anchorage. Even there, you will experience strong gusts—and you have the rocks and kelp of Forney's Cove as a lee shore.

Landing. The dinghy landing can be tricky because of the shallow water and irregular wave sets. Be prepared to get wet!

Forney's Cove is a paradise of color when the spring wildflowers are in bloom. They are like a carpet underfoot, but their vegetable dye will stain your clothes! There is a magnificent (if steep) walk up to the crest of the ridge overlooking the north coast, with spectacular views.

N of Fraser Point, the steep cliffs of the rugged NW corner of Santa Cruz Island fall directly into the ocean. Although you can approach West Point within 0.3 mile (watch out for the rocks awash at the point), the water inshore can be rough, because of underwater dangers as well as wave refraction from the cliffs.

The so-called "Potato Patch" (no relation to the Golden Gate beast) extends 2 miles W of West Point, and is a zone of turbulent water caused by opposing currents in the Santa Cruz Channel and the main channel. In heavy weather, westerly swells are confused by these opposing currents, creating an extensive area of dangerous and turbulent seas. Even on calm days, overfalls caused by the currents can cause the sea to seethe and ripple. In any wind or swell, the Potato Patch comes alive with steep-sided chaotic seas, moving in all directions. The wind spills from your sails; waves can break aboard at any time.

Beware, also, of a spot of breaking water 0.25 mile SW of Fraser Point, where swells can build suddenly even in quiet weather. In anything but the calmest conditions, give West Point a wide berth—up to 2 miles if necessary—to avoid disturbed water.

ANACAPA, SANTA BARBARA, SAN NICOLAS, AND SAN CLEMENTE ISLANDS

ANACAPA ISLAND

Anacapa Island has a remarkable profile, visible for miles on a clear day. The 4.5 miles of Anacapa, nowhere much more than 0.5 mile wide, is actually three islands separated by two very narrow passages blocked with rocks and sand. Vela Peak at 932 feet forms the W extremity of the island, visible from a long distance—so much so that Portola's supply-ship captain Juan Perez named it Falsa Vela (False Sail). Vancouver subsequently renamed the island Anacapa after a Chumash word for mirage: *'anyapah*. The Chumash never lived on Anacapa for any length of time because the island is waterless. Instead, they visited it in search of shellfish, seals, and seal lions. There were no European settlers for the same reason.

In a dense fog on December 2, 1853, the 225-foot side-wheel steamer *Winfield Scott* struck the rocks near the present Anacapa lighthouse. All the passengers and $800,000 of gold bullion from San Francisco were rescued safely. The following year, the federal government sent a survey party to look for a lighthouse site. A young man named James Whistler accompanied the survey crew and made a sketch of the island for publication. It has been said that he was fired because he put seagulls in his sketch, which was intended as a chart diagram; Whistler later achieved international fame as an artist. In 1912, fifty-six years after the original request to Congress, an automatic light was finally built on Anacapa Island. A lighthouse with resident keepers replaced the original pyramidal skeleton tower in 1932. The keepers lived near the light in four white houses with red-tiled roofs. These buildings and the water reservoir can be seen from a considerable distance away. The light was recently automated for a second time. The

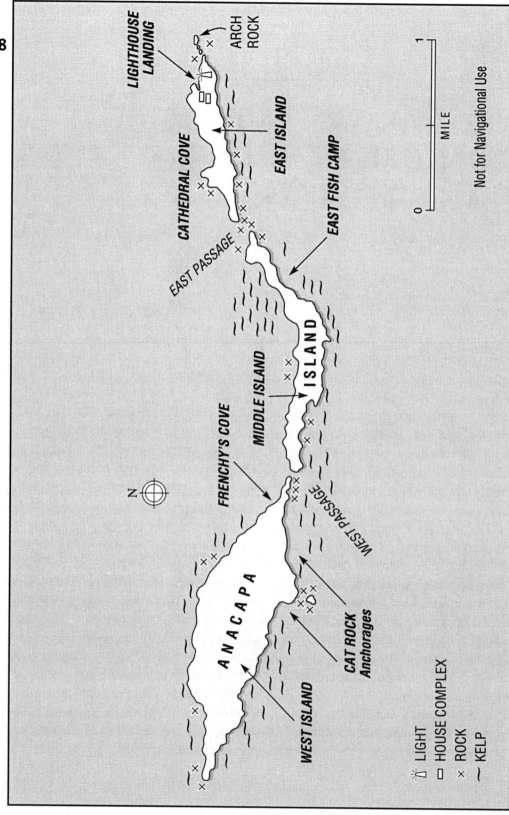

ARCH
ROCK

LIGHTHOUSE
LANDING

EAST ISLAND

CATHEDRAL COVE

EAST FISH CAMP

EAST PASSAGE

MIDDLE ISLAND

I S L A N D

FRENCHY'S COVE

WEST PASSAGE

N

A N A C A P A

CAT ROCK
Anchorages

WEST ISLAND

LIGHT
HOUSE COMPLEX
× ROCK
~ KELP

0   MILE   1

Not for Navigational Use

Anacapa Island, showing major features and anchorages mentioned in the text.

U.S. Coast Guard now controls its operation from Port Hueneme on the mainland. Anacapa and Santa Barbara Islands became the Channel Islands National Monument (now Channel Islands National Park) in 1938. Anacapa has remained uninhabited except for government personnel and one remarkable individual—Frenchman Raymond Ledreau. He dwelt at Frenchy's Cove (named after him) from 1928 to 1956, surviving off the bounty of visitors and fishing.

Vela Peak falls rapidly to the east, giving way to a narrow spine of land that extends for 1.5 miles and is 0.2 mile wide, although 325 feet high. Anacapa Island ends in a mile-long, 250-foot-high level landmass that terminates in 80-foot-high Arch Rock at the E end. The sides of the island are steep and precipitous, so landing can be difficult. Thick beds of kelp hug the shore.

The most significant manmade structure on Anacapa Island is the cylindrical white tower of the lighthouse on the eastern end (Lat. 34°01.0′ N, Long. 119°21.6′ W). Now automated, the light [Gp. Fl. (3) 60 sec.] is one of the most powerful on the California coast, visible from 26 miles away in clear weather. The light is 277 feet above sea level and sounds a foghorn every 15 seconds in thick weather. The light is a vital signpost for navigating this general area at night.

From a distance, Anacapa appears as a single hump, the lower-lying eastern segments of the island not appearing until you are 10 to 15 miles away. Mirage effects can play strange tricks with Anacapa. On warm days, the island can appear to be swimming on a bed of haze, its peak magnified to strange and distorted shapes. The western end is imposing to approach, a precipitous, desolate peak that tumbles into deep water. I once approached Anacapa from NW in the Santa Barbara to King Harbor Race on a magnificent, calm August evening. More than 120 yachts were running down to Anacapa, passing close inshore on its southern side. Their multicolored spinnakers, glowing in the soft yellow evening light, were reflected in the mirror-like water. I sailed close to

Arch Rock, Anacapa Island, from the U.S. Coast Survey, *1853.*

the cliffs, hoping to pick up some advantage close inshore. The steep sides of Anacapa Island fell into 60 feet of water or more, the Pacific barely breaking on the island shores. I had never seen the area so calm.

Caution. Anacapa Island is part of the National Park System and the Channel Islands National Marine Sanctuary. You may land on the island, but the western part of the island is off-limits because of its important brown-pelican rookeries. Stringent regulations protect the island. You may not

- mutilate or interfere with submerged features or wrecks

- take abalone or lobsters for commercial purposes on the northern side of the island; use fishing nets inside the kelp beds (fishing licenses are required)
- interfere with the wildlife or archaeological remains on the island

Overnight camping on the island is by permit only and is limited to no more than fifty campers. All accidents at the National Park must be reported to the National Park Service within 24 hours. For further information, contact

Channel Islands National Park
1901 Spinnaker Drive
Ventura CA 93003
805-644-8262

Profile of Anacapa Island from NNW, distant 15 miles on a hazy day with Santa Ana conditions.

Lesley Newhart

Refuge Anchorages at Anacapa Island

N–NW Winds 12 to 29 Knots
East Fish Camp, Frenchy's Cove (up to 20 knots only); no refuge in stronger conditions

NE–SW Winds
E of Cat Rock is tenable in NE winds up to 19 knots; otherwise, no refuge anchorages

General Sailing Directions
Chart 18729; Chart-Kit, p. 15

If you are unfamiliar with local conditions when crossing to Anacapa Island from the mainland, you are best advised to cross in the early morning when conditions are often calmer. Afternoon westerlies can blow strongly near Anacapa and at times near the mainland as they funnel through the E end of the Santa Barbara Channel. If a NE wind is blowing at the mainland, extreme care in crossing to Anacapa is required—such winds can blow with great force near the island, especially on clear, dry nights.

Anacapa should be approached with caution. Although most of the island is steep-to, thick beds of kelp impede navigation close to the shore. Be particularly careful when coming up to Anacapa in thick weather or on a dark night. Deep water extends close inshore and you could literally collide with the land in zero-visibility conditions. Many small craft visit Anacapa, but relatively few spend the night in its anchorages because they are somewhat exposed.

From some distance offshore, the north coast of Anacapa looks like a bastion of cliffs with a steep peak at the western end. Indeed, the long-out-of-print Southern California *Sea Guide* by Leland R. Lewis (charts by Peter E. Ebeling) refers aptly to the profile as "several segments of an outsize freight train." Notches in the land that mark the two passages can be identified some distance off and are helpful in locating the two possible anchorages on the north coast.

Extensive kelp beds surround both shorelines of the high western extremity of Anacapa Island. An isolated rock lies immediately off the extreme western end. Stay at least 0.5 mile offshore and outside. The western end of the north shore is steep-to and of no particular interest, except for its precipitous cliffs. Extensive kelp beds can grow off this part of the island. The area around the East Passage and the cliffs of Middle Island are heavily infested with kelp.

East of the passage, steep cliffs form Cathedral Cove. It lies 0.5 mile W of the National Park Service landing. Sailing E toward Arch Rock, your best landmark is a cluster of houses that formerly housed lighthouse personnel. Four white houses with red-tiled roofs, a communications center, and other structures are situated on the summit of the cliff. They are connected to the lighthouse by a short road. A white-painted concrete wall marks a small indentation in the cliff used as a landing place, where a platform is reached by means of two vertical iron ladders. Although you can bring a sizable vessel alongside, it is inadvisable due to surge. If you want to leave a dinghy at this platform, hoist it up 11 feet onto the platform—the surge and a blowhole are certain to bang the dinghy against the pier. National Park Service personnel now live in the U.S. Coast Guard houses, and there is a small museum. Provisions and supplies for the lighthouse are hauled up the cliffs with a crane, easily spotted close inshore. Two mooring buoys lie off the landing. This unsheltered spot is not recommended as an overnight stop because it's often bumpy after noon.

Anacapa Island ends in a sloping promontory and the celebrated 80-foot-high Arch Rock, with a 50-foot natural archway in the middle. Arch Rock is separated from Anacapa itself by a large flat-topped rock. Give this end of Anacapa a berth of at least 0.5 mile because of the kelp and outlying rocks. The white tower of Anacapa Light is conspicuous above Arch Rock, 277 feet above sea level. Kelp beds can extend along the easternmost part of Anacapa, providing a protective barrier against coastal rocks for small boats. The cliffs of the flatter East Island overlook the ocean and fall steeply into the Pacific.

Steep cliffs of Middle Island rise to a 320-foot peak just W of East Fish Camp anchorage. The anchorage is a conspicuous bight in the land about 0.5 mile W of East Passage. Filled with rocks, the East Passage

Approach to the lighthouse landing from the NE (arrow), distant 0.5 mile.

Graham Pomeroy

The lighthouse landing.

Arch Rock from N, distant ⅕ mile.

is somewhat wider than its western relative. Kelp beds lie off this passage and may congest the approach to East Fish Camp anchorage.

Kelp beds extend up to 0.5 mile offshore along the middle of the south side of the island. The West Passage, which separates the highest part of Anacapa Island from its central portion, is little more than a sand spit, although a chart of 1856 records it as a "Boat Passage" with 3 feet. Isolated sub-surface rocks, some exposed at low tide, lie W of this passage and should be given a wide berth on this side of the island. Even moderate swells can break on the beach with considerable force. I once had a dinghy swamped here.

Cat Rock, a 71-foot isolated outcrop, is the only outlying danger on the SW side of Anacapa Island.

The 1856 chart records "boat landings" at the extreme NW corner of Anacapa, also 0.3 mile E of the West Passage on the north coast, but they are no longer commonly used and, in any case, are subject to restrictions.

Frenchy's Cove
Lat. 34°00.6′ N, Long. 119°24.5′ W

Frenchy's Cove is the most sheltered anchorage on Anacapa Island, but it is far from ideal in anything but the calmest conditions. The bay is completely open from NW to NE. The anchorage is famous for its

Approach to Frenchy's Cove anchorage and the W end of Anacapa Island from NE, distant 1.5 miles. Arrow indicates anchorage off the beach.

Graham Pomeroy

tide pools and for caves in the cliffs NW of the cove, but their entrances are opposite often-dense kelp beds.

Approach. When headed for Frenchy's Cove from the mainland, steer for the E end of West Island, where the higher ground ends in the confused rocks of West Passage. Shape your course for the narrow passage that will bring you into the wide bight of the anchorage. Frenchy's Cove lies immediately W of the passage, off a rock and sand beach. Approach the anchorage with care, avoiding the kelp beds that may grow offshore.

Anchorage. Sound your way toward the beach and anchor according to draft in the most sheltered spot possible under the cliffs in 20 to 30 feet (sand and small rocks). To minimize surge movement, lay a second anchor. The National Park Service sometimes maintains a mooring buoy in Frenchy's Cove to which you can tie temporarily, using the rope bridle attached. You can land on the beach, where there are no facilities. Landing may be tricky in a surge.

Cathedral Cove

Cathedral Cove is a marginal fair-weather anchorage in one of the most beautiful parts of the island, with partial shelter from N to NW. Anchoring is restricted. For more information, inquire of National Park Service personnel.

Approach. From the mainland, steer for the conspicuous building in the lighthouse complex. As you close the land, identify the landing place and crane, then look for a spire-like rock, which in fact is a N–S rock wall, extending at right angles to the beach. This forms a barrier that gives some shelter from prevailing wind and surge in settled conditions. There is 18 feet between this rock and the beach, but the passage is heavily congested with kelp. Once the spire-like rock is identified, sound your way into the anchorage E of the rock.

Anchorage. Aim to anchor on a line that places your boat E of the highest point of the spire-like rock, parallel to the rocky wall. This is the most sheltered berth, in about 25 feet (sand and rock). A second anchor is essential, but beware of placing it too close to shore. The bottom shelves steeply and becomes rocky with poor holding ground. Kelp growth will probably keep you at least 35 feet from the wall of the spire-like rock. Also be aware of sunken wire cable on the bottom, NE of the spire rock. You could foul your anchor on this obstruction, but on calm days, you can usually spot the cable on the bottom.

Anchorage may also be obtained W of the spire-like rock, with some limited shelter from a protruding headland, in 20 to 25 feet (sand). The surge in this spot, however, is a nuisance, and it cannot be regarded as anything more than a temporary anchorage. Cathedral Cove is untenable in a NE wind. National Park Service rangers patrol this area and may call on you.

Lighthouse Landing

Many yachts anchor off the Lighthouse Landing while visiting ashore. Anchor in 60 feet off the cliffs clear of the mooring buoys. There is little shelter, so this is definitely a calm-water anchorage.

Graham Pomeroy

Approach to East Fish Camp from E, distant 1.3 miles. Arrow shows the anchorage.

East Fish Camp
Lat. 34°00.6′ N, Long. 119°23.2′ W

This anchorage is frequently used by fishing boats. East Fish Camp provides shelter from N and W winds, although surge sometimes rolls into the anchorage. It is an adequate overnight anchorage in quiet conditions and a refuge spot in unexpected strong westerlies.

Approach. First identify Cat Rock and East Passage. East Fish Camp lies 0.6 mile W of the passage. A conspicuous bluff visible from either end of the south side of the island and a minor indentation in the land form the bight of the anchorage. Once the bight is identified, shape your course for the middle of the bay, finding the clearest route through the kelp.

Anchorage. Anchor in 30 to 35 feet (sand and rock) as close to the shore as you deem safe, clear of the rocks to minimize the effect of surge and to maximize shelter. A second anchor should not be necessary in this anchorage unless it is congested. There is only 18 feet of water or less off the beach. East Fish Camp is often heavily overgrown with kelp.

Cat Rock Anchorages

The anchorages lie on the south side of West Island, about 0.75 mile W of the West Passage, and provide shelter from NW to NE winds. Allegedly, the rock was named after Frenchy's cats, which were stranded there by incoming tides.

Approach. Identify Cat Rock, an outlying rock surrounded by other smaller rocks. For the western anchorage, alter course to pass inshore 200 yards W of the rock itself. A mooring buoy sometimes lies 200 yards offshore at the anchorage. Aim to anchor as close to shore as possible to gain maximum shelter of the land—yet far enough out to avoid backwash. Provided you stay 200 yards W of Cat Rock, there are no outlying dangers except for kelp.

Anchorage. Anchor according to draft as close as possible to the beach in 30 feet (sand). You can also anchor under the lee of the land E of Cat Rock. There is deep water close inshore. Thread your way through the kelp and choose a sheltered spot. This is a protected area for pelicans, and should be avoided.

Cat Rock from E, distant 0.6 mile, with the wind blowing in excess of 45 knots. Anchorage may be obtained on both sides of the Rock in calm conditions, but certainly not on days like this!

SANTA BARBARA ISLAND

Light: Lat. 33°29.3′ N, Long. 119°01.8′ W
A visit to Santa Barbara Island can be somewhat of an adventure because this small and desolate landmass lies 42 miles SW of Los Angeles Harbor, on the outer approaches to the Santa Barbara Channel. Even from Santa Cruz Island, you have a 40-mile passage over open water in front of you. But this tiny speck of land is well worth the journey, for it is truly unique. Sebastián Vizcaíno landed there on December 4, 1602, to find no permanent residents due to the lack of water. Native Americans periodically visited the island by canoe on their way to other islands. The native vegetation was badly damaged after the first settlement in the 1920s. The island has never been settled permanently, despite sporadic efforts to grow crops there. In 1938, President Franklin Roosevelt declared the island, with Anacapa Island, as a National Monument. The U.S. Navy used it as an aircraft early-warning outpost in World War II. The National Park Service now administers the 639-acre island as part of the Channel Islands National Park.

Santa Barbara Island is only 1.5 miles long and about 1 mile wide. There are 5.5 miles of trails to explore and the bird watching is superb. From a distance, Santa Barbara Island appears as two landmasses because the two peaks are 635 and 562 feet high, with the higher of them to the south. These peaks can be seen from more than 25 miles away on clear winter days. The island is waterless and devoid of trees, but it is covered with succulents and interesting shrubs. The flora include the giant coreopsis, which blooms yellow in the spring and can reach a height of 8 feet. Santa Barbara Island is famous for its sea-lion colonies and occasional elephant seals, as well as thousands of sea birds. The fishing grounds around its shores are celebrated for abalone and lobsters.

Cautions. A passage from Channel Islands or the Santa Barbara Channel to Santa Barbara Island involves crossing the Pacific Missile Range, which is in frequent use. Call Plead Control on channel 16 for information before leaving or consult Local Notices for firing times. Information on firings is also broadcast on 2638 and 2738 kHz at 0900 and 1200, Monday through Friday (Range Officer: 805-982-8841).

Santa Barbara Island can be very windy. If a strong NE (Santa Ana) wind fills in, get out immediately. The anchorage becomes a lee shore. Strong W to NW winds occur mostly in the fall and winter, when the anchorage offers some shelter, but it is very gusty. There are no refuge anchorages on the island.

General Sailing Directions
Chart 18736; Chart-Kit, p. 15
When making a passage from the Santa Barbara Channel, check with the Range Officer at Point Mugu before setting out to avoid a time when missile firing is in progress (805-982-8841). Your course takes you across the range. It is always disconcerting to be turned back by an aircraft with an extremely loud hailer ordering you to return to port. This happened to me one fine summer day, and an interesting cruise

Graham Pomeroy

Santa Barbara Island from the S, with Sutil Island.

had to be aborted on short notice. Such restrictions don't apply when you are bound from Catalina Island or the Los Angeles area. When on passage from the mainland to Santa Barbara Island, keep a sharp lookout for shipping vessels as you cross major shipping lanes into San Pedro and Long Beach.

Because Santa Barbara Island is a relatively small target after an open-water passage, lay a compass course, even in clear weather and even with GPS aboard. Your first sight of the island will probably be one or two prominent peaks. The lower portions of Santa Barbara Island come into view when you are less than 10 miles out.

In thick weather, approach the island with great care because soundings shoal rapidly from 60 feet into shallow water. However, the island is surrounded by dense kelp beds, which warn of the land. The kelp can extend as far out as the 10-fathom line in many places, and on the western side of the island for more than a mile.

A night approach is simple because the Santa Barbara Island light acts as a signpost for commercial shipping vessels bound for Los Angeles. Situated at the NE corner of the island on Arch Point, the light is 195 feet high (Fl. 2.5 sec., 6 miles). But, be warned—the light is obscured from 342 to 053 deg M by high ground. The main

F. C. Hochberg

Santa Barbara Island from the N, distant 2 miles.

island lies 700 yards W of the light. Be careful when navigating close to shore at night—there are numerous unlit off-lying dangers.

The cliffs of Santa Barbara Island are steep, dark-colored, and bold. Arch Point, the NE corner, is low-lying and steep cliffs on the E side of the island merge with dry slopes of the higher ground that drains into the ocean. The main anchorage at Santa Barbara Island lies off these cliffs.

Santa Barbara Island Anchorage
Lat. 33°28.9′ N, Long. 119°01.8′ W
An open roadstead that extends from Arch Point to the middle of the eastern shore of the island, the main landing and anchorage of Santa Barbara Island comprise little more than an indentation in the shoreline and offering limited shelter from the prevailing westerlies. The kelp beds off Arch Point provide some protection from the surge, but the anchorage can be quite bumpy.

Approach. From N, E, or SE: Identify Arch Point and shape your course to the headland until just outside the kelp beds. Then look for the National Park Service huts on the top of the cliffs. The main anchorage lies N of the huts and the landing spot below it. Sometimes a gap in the kelp is found; otherwise, you'll have to thread your way through the seaweed growth.

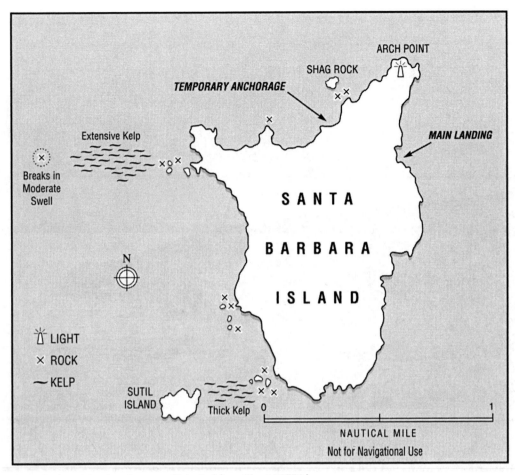

Santa Barbara Island anchorages. (Adapted from Chart 18756.)

Anchorage. Anchor off the landing in 30 feet or more, but watch for solid rock on the bottom. Lay a second anchor if swinging room is restricted. This anchorage is a dangerous lee shore in Santa Ana winds.

Landing. Landing is by dinghy, on the flat rocks E of the landing platform. Take care when stepping onto the rocks and judge the moment so that the dinghy is on the crest of a wave. There are no facilities on the island, but you may camp ashore, bringing water with you. A ranger is often in residence. The Canyon View self-guided tour, which starts near the ranger station and campground, is a good place to start. The sea lion rookeries are on the NW corner of the island, also about 0.5 mile SE of the landing. Stay well clear of the herds—they are easily frightened and have been known to bite humans.

The southern half of the island slopes steeply into the ocean, a 250-foot contour high above the ocean. Extensive kelp beds mantle this portion of the shore. Sutil

Main anchorage at Santa Barbara Island.

Peter Howorth

Island, 300 feet high, lies 0.4 mile W of the southernmost point of the main island and is surrounded by dense kelp. Although some bold ocean racers do it, it is best to resist the temptation to pass between Sutil and the main shoreline; the passage is congested with kelp. Although there is 20 feet in the channel, isolated subsurface rocks make navigation hazardous. The western coastline is very precipitous with high dark cliffs. Again, dense kelp mantles the shore. Stay well offshore at the NW corner to avoid both kelp and rocks off the point. Beware also of an unmarked rock 0.7 mile W of this corner. Swell breaks on this rock in moderate weather, but you can easily come on it without warning in a calm. Shag Rock, 145 feet high, lies 200 yards off the NE coast, 0.2 mile W of the light. Stay clear of the Rock and the kelp beds around it.

Anchorage. Anchor in calm weather off the northern coast in 30 to 35 feet (sand). The anchorage is kelp-free and lies below the highest cliff on the north coast. When moving into this temporary anchorage, leave Shag Rock well to port and maneuver through the kelp, sounding carefully. High cliffs provide considerable shelter in SE weather, but this should never be regarded as an overnight anchorage, even if it is a good base for viewing sea lions playing in the water.

In calm weather, you can have an energetic day exploring the island's fascinating coastline by dinghy or kayak. The northern and western shores can be alive with sea lions, gregarious and companionable as they pause to peer up at you.

Further information on Santa Barbara Island and its fascinating wildlife can be obtained from

Superintendent
Channel Islands National Park
1901 Spinnaker Drive
Ventura CA 93001
805-644-8262

SAN NICOLAS ISLAND

Chart 18755; Chart-Kit, p. 20

San Nicolas is located 54 miles W of Port Hueneme and 24 miles SW of Santa Barbara Island. The outermost of the California islands, San Nicolas was discovered by Juan Cabrillo in 1541 and has been U.S. Government property since 1848. Although some enterprising sheep ranchers attempted to graze their herds on the island in the early years of the last century, San Nicolas remained almost deserted after the Spanish removed its Native American inhabitants to the mainland. The U.S. Navy took over the island in the 1930s. Few yachts but many diving and fishing boats venture to San Nicolas, which is off-limits to the public, serving as part of the Pacific Missile Range. For this reason, the sailing directions that follow are somewhat attenuated.

From a distance, 8-mile-long San Nicolas has a gently rounded profile, rising to 905 feet at its highest point. The middle of the island is visible from a long distance, especially at night, when an aerobeacon (Rot. W & G) flashes brightly. Once you close the land, you will see that the western end of the island is mantled with drifting sand. An airstrip has been built at the E end of San Nicolas and naval buildings are concentrated in this area. Deep arroyos cut into the high ground of San Nicolas. The entire island is surrounded by dense kelp beds up to 3 miles offshore at the western end. Give this extremity of San Nicolas a wide berth because there are dangerous reefs under the kelp beds.

Begg Rock, a 15-foot off-lying rock, rises abruptly from deep water in 300 feet 8 miles NW of the western end of San Nicolas. It is named after the ship *John Begg*, which struck a reef nearby on September 20, 1834. Reefs associated with Begg Rock extend 100 yards N and S. You can come on this danger without warning in thick weather, missing the red whistle buoy (Fl. 4 sec.) 500 yards 330 deg M from the rock. A lighted target ship is sometimes located 6.5 miles NW of Begg Rock, and exhibits Fl. W. lights at bow and stern and a Fl. R. at the masthead. A bell onboard sounds 24 hours a day. The target is sometimes removed for repair, in which case a bell buoy (Fl. W.) marks the spot. Another target is usually anchored 2 miles N of the middle of the northern coast of San Nicolas, and is marked by a lighted bell buoy.

San Nicolas Island is lit by the following three major lights:

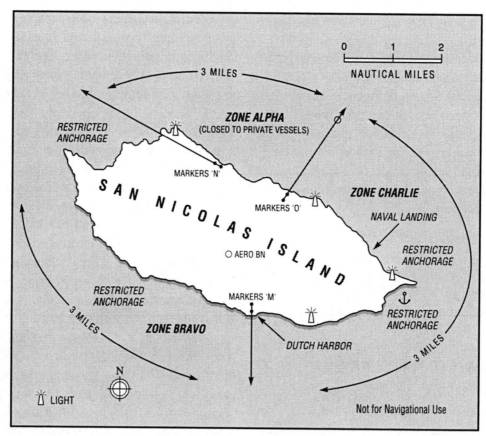

San Nicolas Island, showing anchorages mentioned in the text.

- North Side light, on the northern shore, Fl. 6 sec., 8 miles, 33 feet (visible from 102° to 293° M)
- South Side light, on the southern shore, Fl. 6 sec., 6 miles, 50 feet (visible from 247° to 086° M)
- East End light, on a point on the eastern extremity, Fl. 2.5 sec., 6 miles, 55 feet (visible from 140° to 355° M) (Lat. 33°13.8′ N, Long. 119°26.1′ W)

However, the aerobeacon mentioned previously is the best long-distance signpost at night.

This remote island is usually a very windy place. The prevailing NW winds sweep around both shores and over the summit of the island, especially in the spring and when the Catalina Eddy is in force. However, if you leave the mainland in the evening, you should have a calm passage, reaching San Nicolas in the morning.

San Nicolas is a Naval Restricted Area, and you are only allowed in certain designated areas of the coastline. Specific written permission from the Commander of the Pacific Missile Range at Point Mugu is needed to land. The waters off San Nicolas are divided into three zones designated by lines of onshore markers: pairs of triangular RW beacons on 80-foot poles 100 yards apart. Zones Alpha, Bravo, and Charlie (shown on the map) extend 3 miles offshore. Only official craft may use zone Alpha, while privately owned vessels may enter the other two zones unless naval operations are in progress. Call 805-982-7567 before leaving for the island to check whether the zones are open.

Anchorages. The restricted anchorages at San Nicolas are clearly shown on Chart 18755. You may anchor in these berths only with written permission or, in a grave emergency, with the authority of the senior officer on the island. These areas are sometimes under bombardment. If you attempt to enter them, you will be told to leave. Nevertheless, the main anchorages are described as follows.

On the S side of a 0.6 mile sand spit at the eastern end of the island, 30 to 50 feet (hard sand). Anchor about 200 yards off the sand spit and about the same distance off the mainland, in the protection of the kelp. This can be an uncomfortable spot because the westerly swell breaks on the sand spit with great force. If you anchor too far inshore, ground swells can be dangerous. Strong land breezes can sweep over the anchorage. In rough weather, Santa Barbara Island is preferred.

Dutch Harbor, on the southern side of the island. This harbor, 1.0 mile W of South Side light, is a long open bay foul with rocks and kelp that is entered through a gap in the kelp (Lat. 33°13.1′ N, Long. 119°29.4′ W). Anchor in 30 feet (hard sand) as far in as possible. This anchorage is available only with permission.

Other possible anchorages exist (see Arthur R. Sanger, "How to Land on San Nicolas Island," *Sea,* Oct. 1951), but local knowledge is essential to use them.

Facilities. There are no facilities available on San Nicolas except in the gravest emergency. San Nicolas Island has little to offer small craft. There is little to see or do there, except for the fishing; indeed, few pleasure craft make the long passage out to this windswept landmass.

SAN CLEMENTE ISLAND

Charts 18762, 18763; Chart-Kit, pp. 38–39

On a clear day, you may be able to see San Clemente Island offshore. Like San Nicolas, San Clemente is off-limits to the public. The island, owned by the federal government since 1848, lies 43 miles SSW of Point Fermin, 19 miles beyond Catalina Island across the outer Santa Barbara Channel. San Clemente is 18 miles long NW to SE, 4 miles wide at its widest point, and 1,965 feet high. From a distance, San Clemente looks like a table mountain. The NE coast is bold and precipitous. A conspicuous white radar dome is located on the highest part of the island and can be seen from both sides of San Clemente Island. The SW shore is more irregular and has more gentle slopes. Kelp beds extend out to the 60-foot line, masking outlying rocks for several hundred yards offshore. George Davidson was unenthusiastic about San Clemente:

"Very few trees were found, and the aspect is sterile."

Approaching San Clemente is straightforward because its bold topography is visible from a considerable distance even in restricted visibility. The island is well lit by the following lights:

- West shore, south of Wilson Cove, two lights:
  - Fl. G. 6 sec., 8 miles, 125 feet (visible 14° to 302° M)
  - Fl. W. 2.5 sec., 7 miles, 140 feet (visible 305° to 135° M)

- Pyramid Head, E. Int. G. 6 sec., 6 miles, 226 feet (visible from 135° M to 080° M); Pyramid Head is 900 feet high, jagged, and conspicuous
- China Point, E. Int. 6 sec., 6 miles, 12 feet (visible from 245° to 113° M)
- a flashing red light (4 seconds) exhibited at a height of 886 feet at the southern end of San Clemente

Northwest Harbor

Northwest Harbor, at the NW corner of the island, provides shelter from S and W winds. The anchorage is protected by a

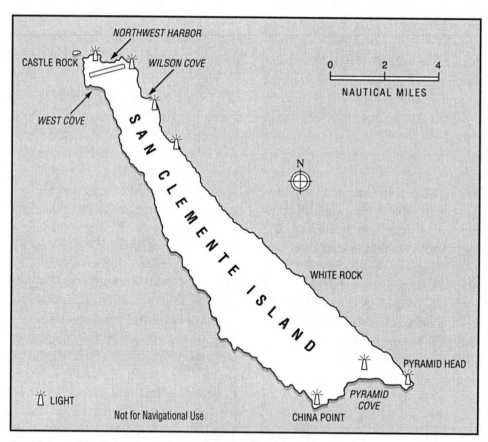

San Clemente Island, showing anchorages mentioned in the text.

low islet and dense kelp beds to the N. A military pier extends from the head of the cove. You can anchor close to the western shore just outside the kelp in 18 to 30 feet (sand). The S side is less sheltered; the NW side is dangerous in strong NW winds. Be warned that a danger area for live firing extends 300 yards around Castle Rock, at the extreme NW corner of the island, near this anchorage.

Wilson Cove

Wilson Cove, 2 miles SE of Northwest Harbor, serves as the major military anchorage on the island. You can anchor there if military activity is not in progress. A 550-foot Navy pier extends seaward from the center of the Cove. The buildings on the hill above the pier are conspicuous from offshore and provide a useful landmark. Approach Wilson Cove from the NE because there are numerous military buoys N and S of it. The best anchorage for small craft is up to a mile NW of the pier in the lee of the kelp in 30 feet or more (sand). This berth provides some shelter from W winds, but the surge can be uncomfortable and strong. Winds may blow downslope in the afternoon. You cannot land at Wilson Cove without official permission.

Wilson Cove can be approached at night by identifying the following lights:

- Wilson Cove North End light (Fl. W. 6 sec., 60 feet, 7 miles) is visible from 124° to 315° M. The white pyramid-shaped structure can be seen from some distance offshore by day. A large sand dune is visible behind the light.

- Wilson Cove light (Fl. G. 6 sec., 125 feet, 8 miles) is visible from 140° to 302° M. A huge radar dish is behind this light.
- Navy Anchorage South End light (Fl. 2.5 sec., 140 feet, 7 miles) is visible from 305° to 135° M, and is exhibited 2 miles S of Wilson Cove.

Once these lights are identified, look for the two Fl. R. lights for the Navy pier on the bearing of 183° M from seaward. These lights are exhibited from two small houses 27 and 40 feet above sea level, respectively.

Pyramid Cove

Located at the extreme SE end of San Clemente Island, Pyramid Cove provides shelter from NW winds. When approaching the Cove, identify Pyramid Head, a jagged headland 900 feet high; and China Point, lower-lying with several detached rocks close offshore. Give China Point a wide berth to avoid off-lying kelp and submerged rocks. The approaches are lit by the following lights:

- Pyramid Head light (E. Int. G. 6 sec., 226 feet, 6 miles) visible from 132° to 080° M
- Pyramid Cove Anchorage light (Fl. R. 4 sec., 10 miles, 886 feet), visible from 113° to 205° M
- China Point light (E. Int. 6 sec., 6 miles, 112 feet) visible from 245° to 113° M

Give Pyramid Point a wide berth to avoid off-lying dangers and kelp close inshore, and steer for the head of the Cove. Watch for patches of kelp that may hide shallow dangers. Anchor at the W end of the Cove under the cliffs and away from the beach in 25 to 40 feet. Numerous fishing boats use this anchorage. The best shelter is found by careful observation of wind patterns and local currents.

The Commandant of the 11th Naval District writes: "Any unoccupied anchorage can be used in Pyramid Cove except during periods when shore bombardment exercises are scheduled."

West Cove

West Cove is 1.5 miles SE of Castle Rock (3 feet) at the NW corner of the island and provides some shelter from Santa Anas. Extensive sand dunes lie behind the anchorage, which is entered through a gap in the kelp. Anchor in 30 feet (rock and sand) inside the kelp. Anchorage is currently prohibited in West Cove due to sensitive underwater cables. Because of live firing during military exercises, a danger area extends 1.5 miles offshore and 3.5 miles south of this anchorage.

Facilities. No facilities are available on San Clemente Island except in the gravest emergency. If you visit the island, be aware that the Navy controls everything within 300 yards of the shore. For information on restricted anchorages, contact

The Commander, Amphibious Force, Pacific Fleet
Naval Amphibious Base
Coronado CA 92118
619-545-8167

For exercise schedules, consult www.scisland.org.
or 11th U.S. Coast Guard District
400 Oceangate
Long Beach CA 90822

POINT MUGU TO ENSENADA, MEXICO
(INCLUDING SANTA CATALINA ISLAND)

It was like coming to anchor on the Grand Banks, for the shore, being low, appeared to be at a greater distance than it actually was. . . . The land was of a clayey quality, and as far as the eye could reach, entirely bare of trees and even shrubs; and there was no sign of a town—not even a house to be seen.

San Diego is decidedly the best place in California. The harbor is small and landlocked; there is no surf; the vessels lie within a cable's length of the beach, and the beach itself is smooth, without rocks or stones.

RICHARD HENRY DANA
Two Years before the Mast,
on San Pedro and San Diego

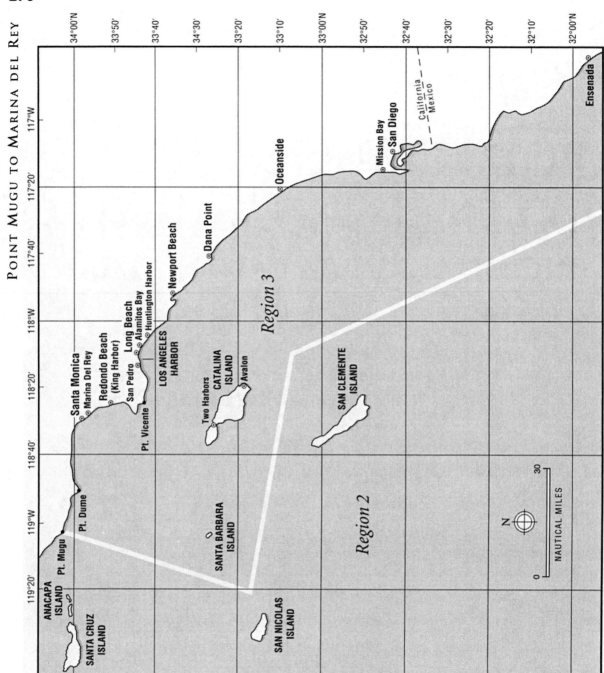

Mainland coast from Point Mugu to the Mexican border and Catalina Island, showing major ports described in the text.

MAINLAND: POINT MUGU
TO HUNTINGTON HARBOR

South of the Santa Barbara Channel, you enter some of the most crowded cruising grounds on earth. The marine environment on the mainland is now largely artificial, with few anchorages to attract a small boat with a yen for privacy. Even the coves at Catalina Island are congested with moorings, which are among the most expensive in the world. Nevertheless, there is some spectacular scenery and something special about navigating off an enormous metropolitan area, especially at night when the lights of Los Angeles and Orange County sparkle on the horizon, or their loom can be seen reflecting in the high overcast or against a starry sky.

The southern border of the Santa Barbara Channel is at Point Mugu, where the afternoon westerlies funnel southward past this conspicuous headland and Point Dume into the much calmer waters of Santa Monica Bay.

The coastline between Point Mugu and Redondo Beach Harbor (King Harbor) in Santa Monica Bay is heavily traveled by watercraft of all kinds. Santa Monica Bay is a major yacht-racing area. Many day-fishing boats also operate in these waters.

POINT MUGU TO MARINA DEL REY

Chart 18740; Chart-Kit, pp. 3, 16

Point Mugu is easy to recognize at a distance because it appears as an island, cut through by Highway 1, which runs along the cliffs. The low-lying Oxnard Plain with its military structures and firing range (see page 170) gives way to the rugged Santa Monica Mountains, which press close to the beach between here and Point Dume. A conspicuous sand dune visible from a long distance, even on a clear day, lies 1.5 miles S of Point Mugu. This may be your first sight of the land if you are tacking inshore, northbound, on your way from Catalina to Channel Islands Harbor.

Point Dume, 200 feet high (off-lying buoy: Lat. 33°59.6′ N, Long. 118°48.3′ W), is a conspicuous reddish headland, whose distinctive profile with its flat top and reversed back slope is easily identified when approaching from either direction. The summit of the point was flattened to accommodate a gun emplacement during World War II. Approaching from Point Mugu and points N, Point Dume can be identified in clear weather from many miles away. A line of cliff-top houses, one with a prominent white observatory tower, leads toward the point, with red-tiled buildings at intervals at the foot of the cliffs beneath them. Off-lying rocks and kelp extend out from the SE edge of the point. Point Dume is unlit, but a red buoy (12) (Fl R. 4 sec.)

Conspicuous sand dune S of Point Dume from SSE, distant 1 mile.

Point Dume from SW, distant 1 mile.

lies 0.5 mile offshore. It is best to shape your course outside this mark on a first-time visit.

Most people head directly from Point Dume to Marina del Rey and points beyond, which is unfortunate because there is plenty to see along the coast—especially the innovative beach architecture. Winds tend to be light close to land, so this is usually powerboat country. If you do sail inshore, watch for a gentle S-flowing current, which occasionally induces a slow, counterclockwise eddy inshore.

Once you are beyond Point Dume, the coastline trends E down to Santa Monica, with a series of steep bluffs intersected by canyons and beaches at their feet. The coastline forms Dume Cove, a shallow indentation that offers little shelter from prevailing swell. The 10-fathom (60-foot) line usually lies about a mile offshore. Anchorage may be obtained anywhere off the coast between Point Dume and Paradise Cove; however, surge is a constant problem and rare is the day when you have completely smooth water. Anchor in about 50 to 60 feet (sand), clear of kelp patches, watching out for surfers and kayakers. One good spot lies about 100 to 200 yards off a blue-tiled house just above the beach, just E of the prominent headland beyond Point Dume. Many people stop for lunch or a swim in this area. Some of the houses above the cliffs are spectacular.

274 *Paradise Cove*

Paradise Cove is a popular beach spot with a 300-foot pier, whose white railings can be identified from some distance. There is a prominent restaurant building at the back of the beach and a white house immediately E of the pier.

Although you can anchor in many spots, one place is opposite the fourth arroyo in the cliffs, counting from Point Dume, in 35 to 45 feet (sand), with the point bearing about 240 deg. Wherever you anchor, stay well clear of the pier traffic in 40 feet or more, and watch for water-skiers in the summer and kayakers. Surge can be a problem off Paradise Cove so plan to anchor with two anchors to head your boat into the swell. Many people stop for lunch here.

Out of consideration for beach users, please row ashore rather than use an outboard dinghy. Landing on the beach is straightforward under normal conditions, but hazardous when Mexican swells are entering Southern California. There are no boating facilities ashore, but there is a popular restaurant.

Paradise Cove to Marina del Rey

The coastline between Paradise Cove and Santa Monica is backed by hills and low mountains, with often densely populated beachfront property. In places, rows of beach houses line the shore, with occasional breaks where Highway 1 is close to the ocean. The traffic on the highway is an excellent landmark at night. If you are

Paradise Cove from S, distant 0.5 mile.

familiar with the highway, you can readily identify the raw scars from landslide repairs at Red Rock and other locations from a long distance offshore.

There is little to attract even the smallest outboard runabout here. It is best to stay about a mile offshore, staying well clear of kayaks and other small inshore traffic, as well as kelp and a few outlying rocks. Notable landmarks include the red-tiled buildings of Pepperdine University, located just W of Malibu and set on a bluff above the town. These buildings are most conspicuous from E, but are easily seen from the opposite direction.

Keller's Shelter offers temporary anchorage 9 miles W of Santa Monica at Malibu Beach.

With its weathered white buildings, the 700-foot Malibu fishing pier is prominent, as is the brick-facade clock-tower structure immediately E. A kelp-marked reef and a shallow bight offer some shelter from W and NW winds. Anchor about 0.5 mile E of the pier in 30 feet or more (sand). Watch for private moorings, as well as kayakers and surfers, in this vicinity. The anchorage is exposed and not recommended for overnight. Constant traffic from Highway 1 is another distraction.

Santa Monica

Santa Monica is easily identified by the conspicuous high-rise buildings that sprout from the cliff top, notably one tall white tower with dark windows in the center of town. This structure is an excellent landmark until you can identify Santa Monica pier, with its colorful buildings and the Fl.

G bell buoy close offshore. Unless you are bound inshore, stay outside the marker.

A damaged and mostly submerged stone breakwater just SW of the city pier protects the pier and small-craft mooring area. Give this area a wide berth and do not approach it at night because the markers are unlit. You can anchor inside the breakwater in 25 feet or so, but the protection is minimal and the landing is such that you have nowhere to leave your dinghy protected. It is best to go to Marina del Rey.

Santa Monica pier is a short distance from the Marina del Rey breakwater and has a large American flag, which you can usually see close offshore even in overcast conditions, as well as Venice Pier, which lies to the W of the harbor entrance.

Santa Monica's artificial fishing reef is at Lat. 34°00.6′ N, Long. 118°31.8′ W. The reef in Santa Monica Bay is at Lat. 34°00.8′ N, Long. 118°32.55′ W.

MARINA DEL REY

Chart 18744; Chart-Kit, p. 19
N entrance: Lat. 33°57.9′ N, Long. 118°27.7′ W
S entrance: Lat. 33°57.6′ N, Long. 118°27.5′ W
www.marinadelrey.com

Marina del Rey, the largest humanly constructed yacht harbor in the world, is home to more than six thousand pleasure craft. A combination of busy racing programs and numerous arrivals and departures can make entering and leaving somewhat of an ordeal for those unused to traffic jams at sea. The congested entrance channel is so busy that the harbormaster has laid out traffic-separation zones to control traffic in the dredged channel. If you are a stranger, you might want to plan a first-time arrival for a weekday, when things are quieter. Nevertheless, Marina del Rey offers complete shelter in all weather and every facility imaginable for visiting craft.

Approach. *From offshore:* The major landmark for Marina del Rey is Los Ange-

les International Airport, whose runways lie immediately SE of the harbor. Huge jetliners rush out every few minutes during peak hours, appearing suddenly over a low ridge. A conspicuous tract of barren and undeveloped land marks the flight path. If you shape your course to pass close N of the airport, you will find yourself in the vicinity of the harbor entrance.

Two prominent striped smokestacks at

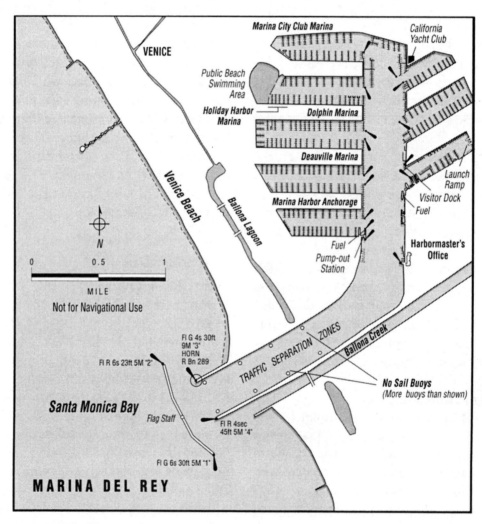

Plan of Marina del Rey.

El Segundo, 3 miles S of the entrance, also provide an excellent landmark, to the left on the starboard bow.

Two white high-rise buildings behind the harbor are also conspicuous from a long distance offshore, as is a tall apartment building in back of the marina areas.

A foghorn on the N jetty sounds in thick weather (2-second blasts every 20 seconds).

From N. Identify the following approach landmarks:

- *Santa Monica pier*, with the conspicuous high-rises of the city on the bluff above it
- *Venice Pier*, with its distinctive rounded end: The pier is 1 mile W of the Marina del Rey entrance. In thick weather, Venice Pier sounds a foghorn (2 seconds at 10-second intervals). Do not confuse this with the horn on the Marina del Rey jetty, which sounds at 20-second intervals.

Run about a mile offshore in deep water, identifying these landmarks and the entrance between the offshore breakwater and the N breakwater that will appear ahead. The houses of Venice run right up to the edge of the entrance channel behind the beach.

From S. Identify the following landmarks:

- *the El Segundo smokestacks* 3 miles S of the entrance
- *bell buoy "2ES" (Fl. W. 4 sec.)*, which is 3 miles offshore, from which the breakwater bears about 344 deg. M

- *the detached harbor breakwater*, which is often difficult to spot, especially on hazy days. Fortunately, a large American flag atop the center of the breakwater, illuminated at night, provides a useful landmark.

Shape your course for the S end of the detached breakwater, then alter course to pass down the middle of the S entrance.

In foggy conditions, it is easy to confuse the Ballona Creek jetty SE of the harbor breakwaters for your destination. Approach with caution and double-check your position.

Night approach. A night approach can be tricky because of the bright and sometimes confusing lights behind the harbor. Identify the following landmarks:

- *the LAX flight path*, marked by the constant taking off of airliners
- *approach buoy "2ES"* and its Fl. W. 4 sec. light, which should be easy to spot on clear nights against the dark of the Pacific
- *light "3"* (Fl. W. 5 sec.) on the N jetty, which is visible for 9 miles
- *the lights of the detached outer breakwater and illuminated flag* (N end: Fl. W. 6 sec.; S end: Fl. R. 6 sec.)

These reference points should guide you safely to the entrance.

Entrance. The N entrance is deeper because the S channel tends to shoal more aggressively. Turn on your depth-sounder if you are using the S entrance, which is the most logical route for arriving or leaving from that direction. Shoaling exists about

100 feet off the end of the N jetty and 300 feet off the S. Give a good berth to the inside of the N jetty, which is also shallow. Buoys mark the extent of shoaling in either entrance and are moved constantly. If you have concerns, contact the harbor patrol on channel 16. Foghorns sound from the detached breakwater in thick conditions.

Use the N entrance at night because the shoal buoys are unlit. There is an 8-knot speed limit in the entrance, which is strictly enforced. The entrance channel between the jetties carries 14 to 15 feet in the center, but is shallower near the edges. Once in the channel, you are subject to the following traffic-separation scheme:

- Unlighted buoys marked No Sail delineate the traffic zones within the channel. You *must* leave these to *port* and pass along the outer sides of the entrance channel if you are under power.
- Vessels under sail alone going in either direction use the central lane.

I strongly recommend that you enter under power on your first visit, especially if you are in a larger yacht. During summer weekends, use caution and keep a sharp lookout for aggressive skippers, who sometimes exercise the marine version of road rage. I have been set aground here by inconsiderate captains.

A pink apartment-building complex and pseudo-lighthouse are prominent to starboard as the channel turns slightly to port into the harbor fairway. A 5-knot speed limit and no wake restrictions are enforced in the harbor.

Berths. Guest slips are available at both county-owned and private marinas in the harbor. Anchoring is not permitted in Marina del Rey. Slip fees for visitors vary dramatically from one marina to the next, but nothing in Marina del Rey is cheap, with a minimum of $9/foot per day.

Burton Chase Park, which is Los Angeles County–owned, lies to starboard immediately beyond the New England village–style buildings of Fisherman's Village. The harbormaster's office, a sheriff's station, and a U.S. Coast Guard facility lie immediately S of the village. Vessels up to 100 feet overall can stay at Burton Chase for a maximum of seven days a month, with forty-five slips available. Slips are assigned on a first-come, first-served basis; reservations are not accepted. There is a 4-hour free guest dock. Contact the community building in the park between 0600 and 2200 (310-305-9595). You will have to show your registration papers and an ID.

Private Marinas. There are no less than twenty private marinas in the harbor, and it would be tedious to mention all of them here. The Beaches and Harbors Office can guide you to those likely to have vacant slips. Major marinas like Deauville (310-305-9595), Dolphin (310-578-6666), Holiday Harbor (310-821-4582), Marina City Club (310-822-5375), and Marina Harbor (310-822-1659) all require advance reservations (for locations, see the plan on page 276).

Facilities. Marina del Rey has every facility imaginable, although they are well spread out and it takes some time to become familiar with such a large harbor.

Marina del Rey north entrance, distant ½ mile.

Marina del Rey south entrance, distant ½ mile.

Marina del Rey. Top: *Mock lighthouse on starboard side of the main fairway.* Bottom: *The main fairway, showing high-rise buildings behind the harbor.*

All marinas have showers and there is a wide array of marine services, including a West Marine store (310-823-5357) and Windward Yacht and Repair (310-823-4581). A fuel dock with pump-out facilities lies to port of the entrance channel opposite Fisherman's Village.

With its hospitable yacht clubs and many restaurants, Marina del Rey has much to offer. However, be aware that distances are longer than in most harbors and you may have to rely on taxis (or—if you have one aboard—a bicycle).

Taxis

Independent Cab: 800-473-2896

Yellow Cab: 800-540-1199

Boat-Launching Ramp. Burton Chase Park has a public launching ramp. There are small-boat hoists at basins G and H.

Artificial Fishing Reefs. Reef 1 is at Lat. 33°57.9′ N, Long. 118°29.2′ W. Reef 2 is at Lat. 33°58.1′ N, Long. 118°29.2′ W.

Contacts.
Emergency: 911

Harbor Patrol: 310-823-7762 or channel 16, then working channel 12

Beaches and Harbors: 310-305-9595

Fuel Dock: 310-823-244

Local Weather: 310-554-1212

Courses. Given in degrees magnetic (2000). For reverse course, add 180 degrees.

Marina del Rey to

Point Dume buoy: 263 deg., 17.4 miles

The Isthmus, Catalina: 170 deg., 30.0 miles

REDONDO BEACH HARBOR (KING HARBOR)

Chart 18744; Chart-Kit, p. 18–19
Entrance bell buoy: Lat. 33°50.3′ N, Long. 118°23.8′ W

Like Marina del Rey, Redondo Beach Harbor was built during the 1960s, before the days of coastal commissions and restricted development. With its 1,748 slips, the harbor lies 7.6 miles SSE of Marina del Rey and is famous for its pier and waterfront area, as well as the Santa Barbara to King Harbor Race, which finishes here in early August.

The low-lying coastline between Marina del Rey and Redondo Beach is heavily developed. First you pass the sterile slope before the LAX runways, where airliners fly overhead every few minutes. El Segundo's conspicuous oil refinery with its smokestacks, and the densely packed residential communities of Hermosa Beach and Manhattan Beach with their prominent fishing piers, occupy the shoreline back of the sandy beach. Oceangoing tankers are often moored close offshore by the El Segundo pipeline and oil-loading area. Give a wide berth to this area. When coasting S, I usually stay in at least 10 fathoms (60 feet) of water to avoid underwater obstructions, while watching the passing landmarks ashore. Watch for fishing barges

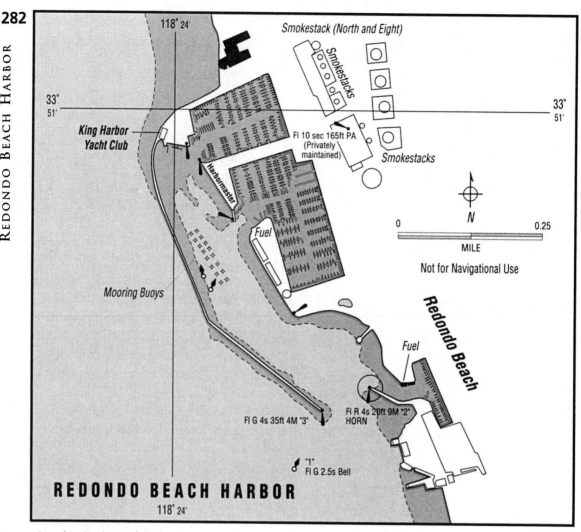

Smokestack (North and Eight)

Smokestacks

33°
51'

King Harbor
Yacht Club

Fl 10 sec 165ft PA
(Privately
maintained)

Harbormaster

Smokestacks

33°
51'

Fuel

0   N   0.25

MILE

Not for Navigational Use

Mooring Buoys

Redondo Beach

Fuel

Fl G 4s 35ft 4M "3"

Fl R 4s 20ft 9M "2"
HORN

"1"
Fl G 2.5s Bell

REDONDO BEACH HARBOR

118° 24'

Plan of Redondo Beach harbor.

that operate close offshore during the summer months.

Approach. Redondo Beach is easy to spot from a considerable distance, thanks to the enormous power plant with its seven black-tipped smokestacks and blue-whale mural immediately behind the harbor.

From N. Pass well offshore until the long harbor breakwater running parallel to the shore is seen. The yacht masts in the harbor are easily spotted. Leave the breakwater at least 0.5 mile to port until the entrance opens up at the S end. The water can be rough for small craft in this vicinity due to the "bounce-back" effect of waves rebounding off the breakwater. Light bell buoy "I" (Fl. G. 2.5 sec.) lies about 230 yards SSW of the outer breakwater.

When turning into the harbor, give the breakwater a wide berth because speedboats and personal watercraft sometimes careen out to sea without keeping a close lookout.

From S. Identify and steer well offshore of the power plant until the outer breakwater, bell buoy, and entrance open up ahead.

The entrance is lit (Fl. G. 4 sec., 4 miles; Fl. R. 4 sec., 9 miles), but the lights are sometimes difficult to discern against the lights ashore. The flashing lights on the power-plant smokestacks are visible from a considerable distance.

Entrance. The entrance is straightforward, with plenty of water in the main fairway. A bank of mooring buoys lies to port at the upper end of the channel, with the Portofino building complex to starboard.

Watch for small boats tacking back and forth in the deeper water.

The entrances to the marina areas lie to starboard, immediately inside the harbor, two thirds of the way up the channel, and at the far end of the fairway.

Berths. Redondo Beach Harbor has four private marinas that have guest slips available. The harbor patrol does not allocate slips, but is glad to assist outside business hours. The marinas, all of which accept reservations, are as follows:

King Harbor Marina: 310-376-6926

Port Royal Marina: 310-376-0431

Portofino Marina: 310-379-8481

Redondo Beach Marina: 310-374-3481

King Harbor entrance from SE, distant ¼ mile. Note the power-plant smokestacks.

Anchoring. Unusually, Redondo Beach allows anchoring in the harbor, which is controlled by the harbor patrol. You may anchor free just inside the breakwater, W of the green channel markers. However, a permit is required from the harbormaster's office, and no more than a three-day stay is permitted. You must anchor fore and aft to avoid swinging into the fairway. Dinghies can be left at the harbor-patrol dock at the entrance to basin 2.

Facilities. All day-to-day facilities are readily available and there are many restaurants within a short distance. Fuel can be obtained at the fuel dock, opposite the harbormaster's office, on the starboard side of the entrance to basin 2. Showers are available at all marinas and the King Harbor Yacht Club is very hospitable. King Harbor Marine Center (310-374-8923) and Redondo Marine Hardware (310-376-0512) provide many maintenance needs. There is much to do in the harbor area, but taxi service may be needed for reprovisioning (Beach Cities Yellow Cab, 310-376-4336; South Bay Yellow Cab, 800-399-1921).

Launching Ramp. There is a launching ramp at Redondo Beach Marina. Call 310-374-3481 for information.

Artificial Fishing Reef. An artificial fishing reef is located at Lat. 33°50.2′ N, Long. 118°24.53′ W.

Contacts.
Emergency: 911

Harbor Patrol: 310-318-0632
or channel 16

Harbor Hotline: 310-318-0648

Local Weather: 213-554-1212

Harbor Web Site:
www.redondo.org/harbor/

Course. Given in degrees magnetic (2000). For reverse course, add 180 degrees.

Redondo Beach to

The Isthmus, Catalina: 164 deg., 27.6 miles

REDONDO BEACH HARBOR TO SAN PEDRO BAY

Charts 18744 and 18746; Chart-Kit, pp. 18, 21

The coast trends SW and the coastal topography changes at Flat Rock Point, just over 2 miles S of King Harbor. Flat Rock is a spur that protrudes from a rounded point, with two detached rocks off its end. Bluff Cove, immediately S of the point, does not offer adequate anchorage even in calm weather. Palos Verdes Point, 1.7 miles SW, marks the S extremity of Santa Monica Bay. The point is a 120-foot-high bold headland that rises to the western end of the Palos Verdes hills. Extensive kelp grows inshore, so keep at least 0.75 miles offshore, passing outside the bell buoy off the point (Fl. R. 4 sec.) (Lat. 33°46.4′ N, Long. 118°26.6′ W). Lunada Bay under Palos Verdes Point forms a small bight and an unsatisfactory berth even in calm conditions.

Point Vicente, 2 miles SSE, is steep and rocky, with distinctive red and white cliffs rising 120 feet above the ocean. The light (Lat. 33°44.5′ N, Long. 118°24.6′ W) [Gp.

Fl. W. (2) 20 sec., 185 feet] is visible from a distance of 24 miles. Stay well clear of the land because there is a rock 250 yards SW of the point. Extensive kelp lies outside this rock, which breaks even in calm conditions.

At Point Vicente, the buildings of the Oceanarium, with its white observation tower, come into view 0.7 mile SE of Long Point. Stay clear of the ruined pier in this vicinity. The coastline trends SE past the white radar domes on San Pedro Hill and into the outskirts of San Pedro. Point Fermin, a bold headland, is easy to identify with its prominent pavilion: "The Korean Bell of Friendship" lies on high ground about 0.3 mile N of Point Fermin light (Fl. W. 10 sec., 120 feet, 16 miles).

Point Fermin marks the W extremity of San Pedro Bay. Pass outside the whistle buoy (Fl. R. 4 sec.) that lies off the point (Lat. 33°41.9′ N, Long. 118°17.5′ W).

SAN PEDRO BAY

Chart 18751; Chart-Kit, pp. 21, 26–28
San Pedro Bay was not one of Richard Henry Dana's favorite anchorages. The bay was wide open to fierce winter southeasters, the water so shallow that ships lay 3 miles or more from shore. Even strong northwesters set up a sea in the bay because the breeze whistled over the low-lying treeless land. "What brought us to such a place, we could not conceive," he wrote. The nearest ranch was 3 miles from the beach and there were no conspicuous landmarks to be seen. The deserted bay described by Dana is now one of the major commercial harbors along the West Coast. In his day, the empty roadstead teemed with migrating whales, which even rubbed against ships' anchor chains. Rowing small boats at night could be hazardous, too, for a sounding whale could easily capsize even a large gig.

I would be dishonest if I said San Pedro Bay and its busy commercial harbors was one of my favorite cruising grounds. However, there is plenty to do and see, especially in Long Beach, and the local marinas and yacht clubs are very friendly.

George Davidson was not effusive:

"This bay is well protected in every direction, except against the winter gales from the southeast round to the southwest. During the spring, summer, and winter, it is an excellent roadstead. . . . Vessels must anchor a mile off to get five fathoms. . . . In winter anchor further out, and more to the southward, in order to be able to slip the cable and go to sea should a strong southeaster spring up. . . . Wood and water are not readily obtained, and the charges are high. The beef raised here is remarkably tough."

Today, long breakwaters protect Long Beach and San Pedro harbors from severe gales, but the area of open water inside the breakwaters is such that quite rough seas can build up in strong winds.

Traffic-Separation Zones and Commercial Shipping
Merchant ships rule in San Pedro Bay. Container ships, tankers, warships, and oceangoing fishing boats are on the move day and night. Quite apart from the *Rules of*

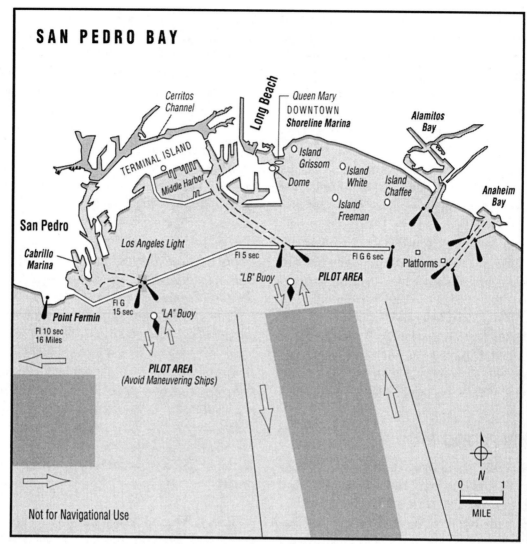

SAN PEDRO BAY

Cerritos
Channel

Long Beach

Queen Mary
DOWNTOWN
Shoreline Marina

Alamitos
Bay

TERMINAL ISLAND

Island
Grissom

Island
White

Island
Chaffee

Anaheim
Bay

Middle Harbor

Dome

Island
Freeman

San Pedro

Cabrillo
Marina

Los Angeles Light

Fl 5 sec

Fl G 6 sec

Platforms

Point Fermin

Fl G
15 sec

"LB" Buoy

PILOT AREA

Fl 10 sec
16 Miles

"LA" Buoy

PILOT AREA
(Avoid Maneuvering Ships)

0   1

N

MILE

Not for Navigational Use

Plan of San Pedro–Los Angeles Harbor and the Long Beach area.

the Road, any vessel displacing more than 300 tons is under a pilot's direction in the restricted waters of the approach to San Pedro Bay, within the breakwater, and in deep-water fairways.

Stay clear of all commercial shipping, even vessels at anchor waiting for a berth.

Two traffic-separation zones converge in the approaches to San Pedro Bay. The west-erly scheme is a continuation of the one running through the Santa Barbara Channel and Santa Monica Bay. The lanes turn E 4 miles S of Point Vicente—running toward the Los Angeles Approach Lighted Buoy [Mo (A) W], where pilots board and disembark, sometimes as far as 3 miles off-shore. The N–S traffic-separation scheme passes E of Catalina Island and ends in the same general area. Exercise extreme caution when you cross the traffic lanes, especially in the approaches to the harbor entrances. If possible, pass inshore or cross the traffic zones at near-right angles as you are legally required to do so.

Approaches to San Pedro Bay and Its Breakwaters

The following three breakwaters protect the enormous harbor area.

San Pedro Breakwater extends in a bight E from Point Fermin, with Los Angeles light (Fl. G. 15 sec., 73 feet, 20 miles) at its extremity. The San Pedro breakwater entrance (Lat. 33°42.6´ N, Long. 118°14.8´ W) lies between this light and the Middle Breakwater.

Middle Breakwater, which is detached from land, runs E from the western entrance for 3 miles and provides most of the protection for the harbors inside. The W end (the Long Beach entrance) is lit (Fl. R. 2.5 sec., 42 feet, 5 miles) with a fainter light than the Long Beach light at the E extremity (Fl. W. 5 sec., 50 feet, 24 miles), which is a major light by any standard. The Long Beach entrance is at Lat. 33°43.5´ N, Long. 118°11.0´ W.

Long Beach breakwater runs E 2 miles farther, and is also lit at both ends with lights visible from about 5 miles away (W end: Fl. R. 2.5 sec.; E end: Fl. G. 6 sec.). A pair of markers provides you with a measured mile on a course of 090 deg. T in the center of this mole.

As discussed previously, from offshore, San Pedro Hill—with its two white radar domes 3.5 miles NW of Point Fermin—provides the best landmark, but it is

Los Angeles light.

Bob Greiser

Bob Greiser

San Pedro entrance, from S, distant ½ mile.

sometimes obscured on hazy days. However, the Korean Bell of Friendship at Point Fermin is usually visible from some distance, even on foggy mornings. High-rise buildings in Long Beach appear S of these landmarks as you approach land, by which time the long gray breakwaters should be in sight.

You can enter San Pedro Bay by three routes—two of them through the main breakwater entrances—a straightforward matter provided that you time your entry for when no commercial vessels are entering or leaving. If necessary, heave-to and wait until ship traffic is gone before attempting the entrance, especially in heavy weather. Most small craft arriving from the N or Catalina Island and bound for Los Angeles Harbor or Long Beach use these entrances.

The southern entrance, between the Long Beach breakwater and the mainland, offers a convenient route from Newport Beach or leeward ports. When entering from S, pass well outside the breakwaters of Huntington Harbor and Alamitos Bay, and give the breakwater end a wide berth. Oil platform *Esther* is a convenient landmark in the approaches. You can pass on either side of oil island *Chaffee*, with its lighted markers.

Once inside San Pedro Bay, you have plenty of water until you approach shore. Be sure to have chart 18751 in hand as you navigate these congested waters. Much of the central part of the bay is a busy merchant-vessel and commercial anchorage. Adjust your course to avoid anchored ships as necessary and stay clear of the main entrance fairways unless you must cross them or use them to enter a commercial port area.

LOS ANGELES HARBOR

Chart 18751; Chart-Kit, pp. 26A–C

Los Angeles Harbor is primarily a commercial port, but also an important recreation center. More than four thousand yachts are berthed within the administrative confines of the harbor, and there are long waiting lists for permanent slips. Visiting yachts may have trouble finding berths here, even in private marinas. You can sometimes use a slip on an overnight basis if the user is away, but it is probably best to try Long Beach or Alamitos Bay. There is a 5 mph speed limit throughout the harbor, which offers wonderful small-boat sailing away from the main shipping areas.

California Yacht Marina, Cabrillo, or Cabrillo Marina

Lat. 33°42.4′ N, Long. 118°17.2′ W

Most visiting yachts head for Cabrillo Marina at the SW corner of San Pedro Bay. This is a modern yacht harbor, built by the Port of Los Angeles in 1986. It forms part of an extensive beach and marine recreational complex, where sport fishing and whale-watching are important activities. For a nominal fare, the San Pedro electric trolleys provide an excellent way to get around to nearby attractions such as the

O' Call Village. They run from Thursday through Monday from 1000 to 1800 in the summer and to 1600 in the winter.

Approach. Immediately after entering the western breakwater entrance, turn to port out of the shipping lanes and identify the marina breakwater, which lies beyond some moorings off Cabrillo Beach, where there is a boat-launching ramp. The entrance is straightforward. The marina channel, which is dredged to between 30 and 35 feet, lies just NW of a commercial wharf and is easily spotted with the many yacht masts behind it. Watch for moorings and anchored yachts to the S of the channel.

Berths and Facilities. The Marina Operations Building, a fancy name for the harbormaster's office, is at the head of the first slip basin. Contact this office for berths during working hours or harbor security after hours. Advance reservations are accepted on a first-come, first-served basis. Even large yachts up to 124 feet overall can find berths here. Be aware that visitors' slips are in short supply during the summer months. There is a fuel dock close to the office and a well-established boatyard. All typical facilities are available at the marina and large supermarkets are within a short taxi ride.

Anchorage. Anchorage may be obtained just beyond the marina breakwater in 15 to 20 feet (sand and mud). However, you must get authorization from the port police (310-732-3500).

Launching Ramp. Cabrillo Marina has superb launching facilities, for which a

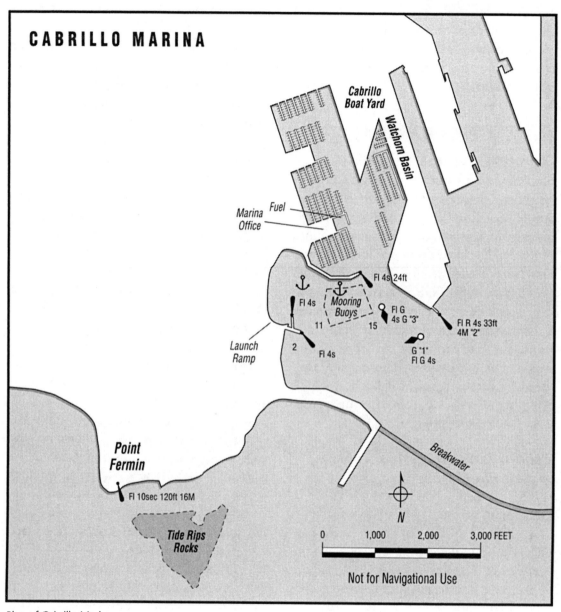

CABRILLO MARINA

Cabrillo
Boat Yard

Watchorn Basin

Marina
Office

Fuel

Fl 4s 24ft

Fl 4s

Mooring
Buoys

Fl G
4s G "3"

11

15

Fl R 4s 33ft
4M "2"

Launch
Ramp

2

Fl 4s

G "1"
Fl G 4s

Breakwater

Point
Fermin

Fl 10sec 120ft 16M

Tide Rips
Rocks

N

0   1,000   2,000   3,000 FEET

Not for Navigational Use

Plan of Cabrillo Marina.

modest fee is charged. This is a convenient jumping-off spot for Catalina Island.

Contacts.
Emergency: 911

Los Angeles Port Police: 310-732-3500 or channel 16

California Yacht Marina Security: 310-732-2249 or channel 68

Marina Office: 310-732-2252

Taxi: 310-533-6800

Local Weather: 310-554-1212

LONG BEACH HARBOR

Chart 18751; Chart-Kit, pp. 26–27
Apart from being a major commercial port, Long Beach is a major pleasure-boating center with important attractions ashore, among them the *Queen Mary* and the state-of-the-art Aquarium of the Pacific, which is well worth going a long way to see. There are excellent shops and restaurants at the harbor, as well as a convention center and a thriving downtown within a short distance. Long Beach is an excellent base for re-provisioning before taking off for Catalina Island. The free Runabout Shuttle Service makes getting around a breeze and even runs as far S as Alamitos Bay Marina.

Downtown Shoreline Marina
Lat. 33°44.2′ N, Long. 118°11.2′ W
This modern facility is convenient to everything ashore and is usually congested in the peak summer months. Nevertheless, it is a friendly place.

Long Beach Downtown Shoreline Marina.

Bob Greiser

Approach. The approach to Long Beach Harbor is straightforward, thanks to the conspicuous *Queen Mary.*

From N and offshore. Long Beach Harbor lies 4 miles E of the Los Angeles Harbor entrance, E of the massive harbor facilities of Terminal Island. The most direct access is through the entrance between the Middle and Long Beach breakwaters; avoid entering and departing commercial shipping vessels. (This can be interesting: the last time I entered, we were competing with two inbound and one outbound container ships!) Once inside, steer NE out of the main channel, which leads toward Terminal Island, passing between Pier J (to port) and Island Freeman (to starboard). The *Queen Mary* and the white dome that once housed the legendary Howard Hughes flying boat, the *Spruce Goose,* come into view as you steer outside a row of lighted buoys (Qk. Fl.), which lead to the Queensway Bay area. The breakwaters of the Downtown Shoreline Marina and Island Grissom, which form part of it, will appear ahead, perhaps slightly on the starboard bow.

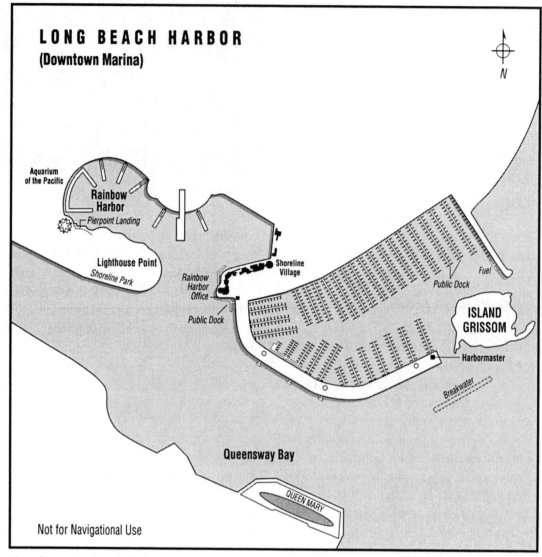

LONG BEACH HARBOR
(Downtown Marina)

Aquarium
of the Pacific

Rainbow
Harbor

Pierpoint Landing

Lighthouse Point
Shoreline Park

Rainbow
Harbor
Office

Public Dock

Shoreline
Village

Public Dock

Fuel

ISLAND
GRISSOM

Harbormaster

Breakwater

Queensway Bay

QUEEN MARY

Not for Navigational Use

Plan of Long Beach yacht harbors.

From S. Enter San Pedro Bay between the Long Beach breakwater and the mainland, then steer to pass 0.25 mile inshore of Island Chaffee. Once Chaffee is abeam, set a course 0.3 mile offshore of Island White. By the time Island White is close, you will have picked up the *Queen Mary* and Island Grissom, which form part of the Downtown Shoreline Marina.

Islands Chaffee, Grissom, and White are named after NASA astronauts who died in a 1967 accident.

Entrance. A detached breakwater protects the marina entrance. *Incoming boats must pass around the E side; departing vessels pass around the W end.* The detached breakwater is lit, but I sometimes find the light difficult to see against the city lights in the background. Just as at Santa Barbara, the lights are easier to see if you lie on deck and look forward from near deck level. Enter the Downtown Shoreline Marina (16 feet) between the curved breakwater that forms the SW side of the marina and Island Grissom.

Do not enter through the eastern entrance between Island Grissom and the E breakwater, which is obstructed.

Berths and Facilities. The harbormaster's office is at the head of the W breakwater. There is a slip for you to tie up at while they assign you an end tie or another berth. Reservations are accepted from visiting yachts berthed at least 100 miles away, with two weeks' notice. You must pay the first night with your reservation. If the office is closed when you arrive, contact the marine patrol, which will assign you an end tie until you can check in the next day. A fifteen-day limit applies. (Don't even think of trying for a berth on either Long Beach Grand Prix Day in April or the Fourth of July weekend, when higher charges apply!) There is a fuel dock E of the entrance with every marine service available, as well as the typical marina facilities.

Anchorage. You can anchor in the lee of Island White in 15 to 25 feet (mud and sand). There are also private marinas in the Long Beach area that can sometimes accommodate visitors.

Launching Ramp. There is no launching ramp in the marina; however, there is one at Alamitos Bay a few miles away.

Contacts.
Emergency: 911

Downtown Shoreline Marina:
562-570-1815

Fuel Dock: 562-436-4430

Taxi: 562-435-6111

Local Weather: 213-554-1212

Courses: San Pedro and Long Beach Entrances. Given in degrees magnetic (2000). For reverse course, add 180 degrees.

San Pedro entrance to

The Isthmus, Catalina: 210 deg., 18.5 miles

Avalon: 179 deg., 22.1 miles

Long Beach entrance to

The Isthmus, Catalina: 209 deg., 23.4 miles

Avalon: 184 deg., 24 miles

The Queensway Bay Moorage
Across the channel from the Downtown Shoreline Marina, the Queensway Bay Moorage offers forty mooring buoys, which are convenient for visiting the *Queen Mary*. Make reservations by contacting

Queensway Bay Marina
700 Marina Drive
Long Beach CA 90801
562-436-0411

There is a thirty-day limit; charges vary according to boat length.

ALAMITOS BAY MARINA

Chart 18749; Chart-Kit, pp. 27–28
Lat. 33°44.2′ N, Long. 118°07.2′ W

Alamitos Bay is 3.25 miles S of the Long Beach Downtown Shoreline Marina, opposite the end of the Long Beach breakwater. The two harbor jetties can be seen from a considerable distance.

Approach. From Long Beach and Other San Pedro Bay Locations: Pass between Island Freeman and Island White, aiming to pass close inshore of Island Chaffee. The coast is heavily built up, but you will see Belmont Pier 0.5 mile E of Island White. The Alamitos Bay jetties are clearly seen slightly on the port bow as you come up on Island Chaffee.

From S. Identify the end of the Long Beach breakwater. The twin jetties of Alamitos Bay Harbor are a mile NE and can be seen projecting from the mainland. The angled breakwaters of Huntington Harbor lie a mile SE, but are easily distinguished from Alamitos Bay's jetties, which run straight into the ocean. Pass inshore of oil platform *Esther*, steering for Island Chaffee until the entrance is open and clearly in sight. Then alter course to pass between the jetties.

From offshore. Pass inshore a safe distance from the end of the Long Beach breakwater, then identify the harbor jetties a mile ahead.

Night approach. A night approach is straightforward after the Long Beach break-water light has been identified. The jetty ends are lit [Gp. Fl. (2) G. 6 sec., 5 miles; E jetty Fl. R. 2.5 sec., 5 miles]. Late at night and when I have been tired, I have confused the Anaheim Bay lights for those of Alamitos Bay. *Remember that red and green flashing entrance lights mark Alamitos Bay.*

Entrance. The Alamitos Bay entrance channel (17 to 20 feet) leads straight into the harbor. Keep to starboard when entering or leaving. A 5 mph speed limit applies.

Berths and Facilities. The harbormaster's office (Marine Bureau) is on the E side of the main channel into the harbor as you turn NE into the marina area. There is a slip for tying up while you obtain a guest slip. If you arrive after hours, contact the marine patrol, which will be glad to help you. Reservations can be made in advance (the first night is payable ahead of time) and a fifteen-day stay is permitted. You will probably be allocated an end tie.

Alamitos Bay has all typical facilities and excellent marine services. A fuel dock is located on the S side of the main channel just beyond the harbormaster's office. Marina Shipyard is at the NE corner of the main basin.

The areas upstream of the Davies Bridge (32-foot clearance) form the Upper Alamitos Bay and are suitable for smaller craft and powerboats. Sometimes more than 10 to 15 feet is found in these areas, which are fun to explore in a dinghy. Watch your vertical clearance! The Appian Way Bridge has 13 feet at zero tide; the 2nd Street Bridge has a mere 4 feet.

Anchorage. There is no anchorage in the harbor.

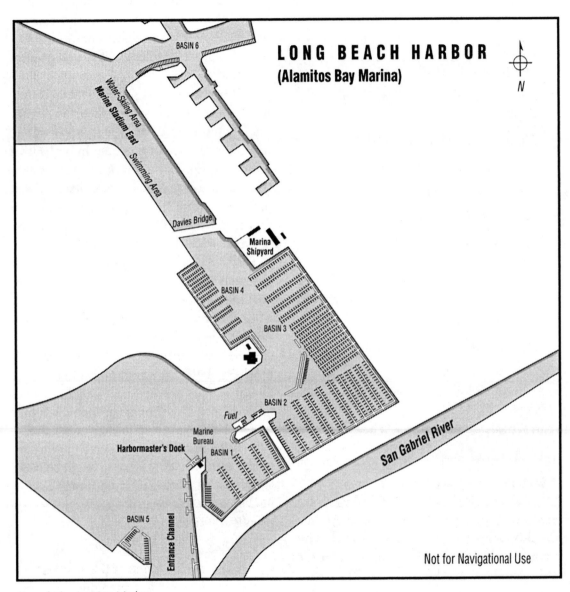

Plan of Alamitos Bay Marina.

Launching Ramp. The Davies launching ramp lies immediately above the bridge of that name on the E side of the channel.

Contacts.
Emergency: 911

Marine Patrol: 562-570-3217 or channel 16

Alamitos Bay Marina: 562-570-3215

Marina Shipyard: 562-594-0995

Taxi: 800-400-7313

Fuel Dock: 562-594-0888

Local Weather: 213-554-1212

Courses. Given in degrees magnetic (2000). For reverse course, add 180 degrees.

From Alamitos Bay to

The Isthmus, Catalina: 216 deg., 25.6 miles

Avalon: 193 deg., 25.4 miles

HUNTINGTON HARBOR (ANAHEIM BAY)

Chart 18749; Chart-Kit, p. 28
Lat. 33°43.6′ N, Long. 118°06.0′ W
Seal Beach pier lies 0.5 mile SE of Alamitos Bay, with 9 feet at its outer end. The twin, angled jetties of Huntington Harbor are 1.5 miles S of Alamitos Bay. The jetties protect Anaheim Bay, site of the U.S. Naval Weapons Station; you enter the harbor through restricted waters. State-registered and -documented vessels may enter under power, subject to special military controls when the Navy moves explosives. No per-mission is needed to pass through these waters under normal circumstances. A 5-knot speed limit is in effect and there is only a 23-foot vertical clearance in the harbor because of a fixed bridge that crosses the main fairway.

Approach. The approach is straightforward, once you have identified the Alamitos Bay jetties and the curved breakwaters of Anaheim Bay. Two lighted buoys (Fl. G. 4 sec. and Qk Fl. R.) mark the approaches to Anaheim Bay. The channel itself is well marked, with a lighted range for day and night use. Shape your course for the entrance once the piers are open.

Entrance. To enter, follow the marked channel, which turns sharp E once you are into the harbor.

Berths and Facilities. A fixed bridge with 23-foot clearance crosses the main channel beyond the main basin. Green markers delineate the S boundary of the channel. This bridge effectively limits the harbor to small sailboats and powerboats.

The harbormaster's office is on the N side of the main channel above the bridge, where marina development begins. Guest slips can be obtained by contacting the harbor patrol or one of the following two private marinas:

Peter's Landing Marina (714-840-1387) is on the S side of the channel. Reservations are accepted during working hours. The maximum stay varies.

Sunset Aquatic Marina (714-846-0179) is on the N side of the channel. Reservations are sometimes accepted during working hours, depending on vacancies.

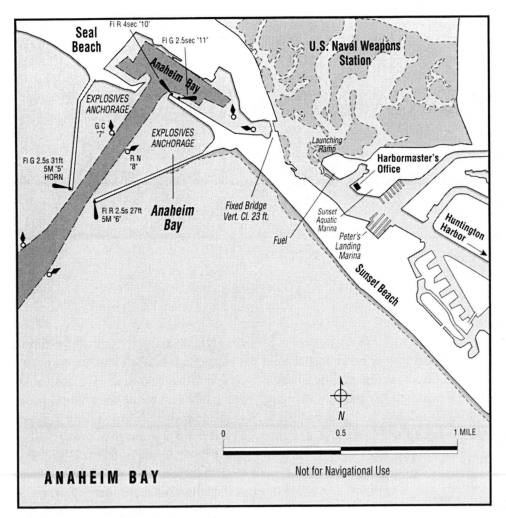

Plan of Huntington Harbor (Anaheim Bay).

All typical marina facilities are available, including a fuel dock.

Anchorage. There are no anchorages in Huntington Harbor.

Launching Ramp. There is a launching ramp at Sunset Aquatic Marina; the modest fee includes parking.

Contacts.

Emergency: 911

Harbor Patrol Dispatch: 949-723-1002 or channel 16

Fuel Dock: 562-592-4975

Taxi: 714-373-6996

Local Weather: 714-675-0503

SANTA CATALINA ISLAND

Santa Catalina Island, 18.5 miles long and a mere 7 miles across at its widest point, is a submerged mountain chain, whose peaks hover offshore above the haze on a summer's day. About 25 miles separate island and mainland, but the two are a world apart.

BACKGROUND

Catalina's isolation goes back millions of years, creating a unique environment. Only about 12 inches of rain fall annually, but frequent summer fogs ameliorate the dryness. Moderate ocean temperatures lessen the impact of even unusually wet and cool winters. The 54 square miles of the island is rugged, with dramatic changes in topography that create a great variety of local environments and microclimates—sometimes confined to a single canyon or a few hillsides. Catalina's remoteness—even at

the height of the Ice Age twenty thousand years ago, when sea levels were as much as 300 feet lower than today—meant that relatively few plant and animal species made it across the channel. Some tiny seeds arrived on air currents; others, like the holly-like toyon, in birds' beaks. The Pacific created such an effective barrier that only about four hundred native plant species have become established on the island, many of them in local plant communities. During the past ten thousand years, humans have introduced the wild oats that dominate the island's grasslands and many other plants.

GEOLOGY

Catalina began as part of the seabed, but a series of complicated plate movements created the island at least twenty million years ago. A chain of volcanic islands rose from the seabed off the California coast. Between

24 million and 5.3 million years ago, complex earth movements shifted the island some 150 miles northward from near the Mexican border to its present position. A spectacular ancient shoreline, complete with sunken river valleys, lies 80 feet below the Pacific a mile W of the island.

Catalina's cliffs are a giant geological enigma, with ancient sea levels lifted high above the modern ocean and rugged volcanic peaks. Some of the most spectacular formations lie in the cliffs at the southwestern corner of the island, where rock is still mined in the quarries.

PLANT AND ANIMAL LIFE

The complicated geology of Catalina has created great botanical diversity that can be enjoyed within a short walk. North-facing slopes and deep canyons are home to island oaks, cottonwoods, and willows, with dense groves of Catalina ironwood and cherry. The ubiquitous California chaparral covers many of the north ridges and east- and west-facing stream drainages. Chaparral gives way to grassland, where wildflowers abound in the winter and spring. Efforts are underway to restore the hardy native bunch grasses that almost vanished as a result of more than 150 years of pig and goat husbandry. Bunch grasses have a pale-green appearance year-round, in contrast to the familiar yellow grasslands of today's dry season.

Much of the more exposed western parts of the island is covered with drought-

Bob Greiser

Patrick Short

observed. Unfortunately, the island's Mediterranean climate has made it easy for species from other subtropical lands to flourish, among them the ubiquitous eucalyptus tree. Many native species have lost ground to imported forms, but long-term restoration projects by The California Conservancy offer hope that such precious rarities as the Catalina ironwood will survive for future generations to enjoy.

The island's animal life is also impoverished, but the native animals are unique, many of which evolved to adapt to the island environment. Humans have introduced goats, pigs, sheep, and—more recently—bison. The avian diversity of the mainland is conspicuously absent; fewer bird species flourish on Catalina. Indigenous birds include the Catalina quail—larger and darker than its mainland relative—and the tiny Bewick's wren. Bald eagles and peregrine falcons have recently been reintroduced to the island. Various gulls and other sea birds feed off the rich marine life. Reptiles and amphibians include rattlesnakes and a distinctive aquatic garter snake. Rotten tree stumps floating across the channel may have brought lizards and frogs to the island.

The most famous mammal is the elusive island fox, a distant relative of the mainland gray fox. A chance encounter with these small, intensely curious animals is a memorable experience. Native Americans may have introduced pet foxes many millennia ago. Unfortunately, the Catalina fox population is now sparse because of their vulnerability to attack by domestic cats and other feral animals.

resistant maritime desert scrub, including cacti and other arid species that can resist constant westerly winds, salt-laden air, and strong sunlight. Prickly pear, cholla, and other cacti burst into flower in the rainy season, even on the driest slopes. Upslope, the desert scrub gives way to low-growing sages with their characteristic aroma. The north side of the island displays greater variety, including dense patches of the distinctive and drought-resistant St. Catherine's lace.

Catalina's plant life is unique and botanically significant, much of it only recently

Bob Greiser

Humans introduced animals to Catalina with the best intentions, but often with catastrophic environmental consequences. Pigs were brought ashore to eat rattlesnakes, but they habitually root for grubs and tubers; as a result, the growth of forest trees has suffered drastically. Feral goats stripped native grassland and eroded steep slopes before these voracious eaters were controlled. Sheep, cattle, and bison have also inflicted serious damage to the island's delicate ecology.

MARINE LIFE

The waters off Catalina form a transitional zone where the cold, nutrient-rich California current mingles with warmer water from the south. A remarkable diversity of marine life flourishes off Catalina's 54-mile shoreline in water that is often surprisingly clear, making it a paradise for divers and snorkelers. The shallow waters off the island with their rich kelp beds and eelgrass and surfgrass meadows provide a wonderful spawning area for many fin fishes, such as the colorful goldfish-like garibaldi, which nearly became extinct during the twentieth century due to overfishing. Glass-bottomed boats at Lover's Cove near Avalon offer visitors the chance to see garibaldis, kelp bass, and other species, including skates and rays and even the occasional larger open water fish and sharks. Abalone, lobsters, and sea urchins once abounded, but overhunting decimated these populations. The deeper waters offshore are famous for marlin, tuna, and larger sharks.

It is common to see seals and sea lions sunning themselves on the rocky outcrops and sandy beaches of Catalina. California sea lions visit in the spring, and seem to prefer the eastern end of the island. Harbor seals frequent the kelp and, because of their insatiable curiosity, seem unafraid of divers. They breed on deserted beaches, and the mothers often leave their young while they fish nearby. Please do not disturb the pups on the beach.

Migrating gray whales are sometimes seen close offshore, and pilot whales are said to breed in Ironbound Cove at the northwestern corner of the island. Porpoises are one of the great thrills of crossing to Catalina in a small boat. These friendly mammals cavort around your bow for several minutes, then—as if on signal—inexplicably depart. Sea otters were once a common sight at Catalina, but were hunted out for their pelts more than a century ago.

The marine life around Catalina is but a shadow of its former self, due first to intensive exploitation by Native Americans, then modern-day commercial and recreational fishing. Today, we face the challenge of living with a drastically impoverished marine environment at a time when there are more fishing boats than ever before.

HISTORY

The date of the first settlement of Native Americans in North America is debated and still uncertain, but there are traces of human occupation dating back at least twelve thousand years in California. No one knows how long people have been paddling out to Catalina Island, but it may have been as early as seven thousand years ago. The Native Americans of Southern California exploited coastal waters with great skill from their planked canoes. They were expert kelp fishers and also ventured offshore for swordfish and other deep-water species.

When the first Europeans arrived in the sixteenth century, Native American groups known as Gabrilieños lived on Catalina and the adjacent mainland. They were part of a complex series of coastal- and island-based hunter-gatherer groups that clustered along seacoasts. Chumash communities with as many as a thousand people flourished in the Santa Barbara region. The Pimugnans, the indigenous people of the island (which was then called Pima) had major villages at Avalon, Little Harbor, and the Isthmus, some with as many as five hundred inhabitants. Including several smaller settlements along the shore, the island population totaled as many as twenty-five hundred people.

The highly variable rainfall, the effects of periodic El Niño and La Niña events, and dramatic changes in water temperatures had drastic effects on marine and human populations. Deep-sea cores and ancient tree rings indicate that Southern California suffered through prolonged and often severe droughts a thousand years ago, causing widespread hunger. For this reason, ancient Californians maintained close links with mainland trade networks that extended far into the American Southwest. Pima was an important source of soapstone, or steatite, which was used to manufacture stone bowls. This valuable material was traded to the mainland, probably for foodstuffs and other commodities.

Gabrilieño villages were small clusters of thatched, dome-shaped dwellings fabricated with a willow sapling framework, each housing several families. The people used bone harpoons attached to wooden shafts to hunt sea mammals and larger fish, and also were experts with hook and line. Their diet included shellfish, especially in leaner times of the year. The women gathered acorns and various wild plant foods, such as prickly pears.

Life on the island was only possible because of planked canoes called *tiats*, which were probably derived from similar vessels developed by the Chumash of the Santa Barbara Channel to the north, with whom the Gabrilieños traded. These seaworthy craft, fashioned from a hollowed tree trunk as keel and built-up plank sides, enabled skilled crews to cross from the mainland in about four hours in calm conditions—a remarkable time by any standard.

The Gabrilieños enjoyed a rich symbolic and religious life, and their culture would have continued to evolve and flourish indefinitely, had not foreigners arrived. On October 7, 1542, Portuguese navigator Juan Rodríguez Cabrillo landed on the island and named it San Salvador, claiming it for Spain. The visitors were received peacefully by the Pimugnans, who traded eagerly for iron tools. Sixty years later, Spaniard Sebastián Vizcaíno arrived at the island and named it Santa Catalina in honor of the saint's feast day, under the impression that it was undiscovered.

For 250 years, Catalina was neglected and never missionized, although occasional ships landed there: one of the earliest recorded was the American otter-trading brig *Lelia Byrd*. The rare visitors brought infectious diseases. In 1805, a measles epidemic killed two hundred Native Americans on the island, just as Aleuts on Russian ships began hunting the otters that abounded in Southern California waters. The rapacious hunters preyed mercilessly on the islanders, most of whom soon perished. A few fled to San Gabriel Mission on the mainland. By 1832, there were probably no Native Americans on the island.

During the mid-nineteenth century, Catalina was inhabited by fishermen and squatters who grazed a few cattle. Yankee traders called at the island to make repairs in Avalon Cove and sometimes offloaded valuable cargo to avoid paying tariffs to the Spanish authorities on the mainland. Illegal Chinese immigrants were frequently landed on the island to await transshipment elsewhere in smaller craft. In 1846, Pío Pico, the last Mexican Governor of Alta California, is said to have deeded the island to Thomas Robbins of Santa Barbara in exchange for a horse and a silver-decorated saddle with which to escape from advancing American troops. Robbins established a large ranching operation on the island; by the early 1860s, sixty head of cattle, eight thousand goats, and twenty thousand sheep were roaming Catalina, with disastrous effects on the native vegetation.

Rumors of gold caused a minor gold rush at the Isthmus in 1863. The U.S. Army had established a garrison there during the Civil War (the barracks are now the clubhouse of the Isthmus Yacht Club). Eventually, the military ordered all goldminers off the island, but abandoned claims and mines can still be seen.

Catalina Island passed through several owners, among them the eccentric James Lick—philanthropist, real estate speculator, and founder of the observatory near San Jose that bears his name. In 1887, George Shatto purchased the island from Lick's trustees for $200,000. He founded and subdivided the town of Avalon. Shatto defaulted on his mortgage payments, so the trustees repossessed Catalina and sold it to George Banning for $128,740 in 1892. Four years later, he deeded the island to the newly formed Santa Catalina Island Company, a Banning family enterprise that attempted a major development of Avalon; however, a disastrous fire leveled the town in 1915. In 1919, chewing-gum millionaire William Wrigley Jr. purchased a majority interest in the company for $3 million, and soon after acquired the entire company. He and his heirs invested millions in Avalon, building the famous circular casino and an elaborate bird park with "the largest birdcage in the world," and installing a modern utility system. Between the two world wars, Catalina became a world-class tourist destination. To this day, Avalon remains in the control of the Santa Catalina Island Company.

William Wrigley bought Catalina with the specific intention of developing Avalon.

As the town grew, the interior remained off-limits to anyone except residents and privileged visitors. So it remained until 1972, when William's son Philip formed the Santa Catalina Island Conservancy "to preserve and protect open space, wild lands, and nature-preserve areas for future generations." Two years later, Los Angeles County and the conservancy entered into a fifty-year easement agreement that allowed unlimited public access to 41,000 acres of the coast and interior. In 1975, 86 percent of the island passed from the Santa Catalina Island Company into the hands of the Santa Catalina Island Conservancy. Since then, this organization has been responsible for the interior roads and beaches, the famous Airport in the Sky, and a variety of educational programs at its nature center and other facilities. The conservancy relies on membership dues for much of its work in restoring and protecting the fragile island ecosystems. There are two membership support programs: Catalina Marineros are interested in boating activities; Catalina Caballeros are horse trekkers in the interior. Every fall, an annual Buffalo Wallow sponsored by these organizations combines island tours with a festive barbecue and dance in a hangar at the airport. Apply for membership by contacting

The Santa Catalina Island Conservancy
P.O. Box 2739
Avalon CA 90704
213-510-1421
www.catalinaconservancy.org/

Avalon Casino.

WHAT TO DO ON CATALINA

Most people arrive at Catalina by boat, some come by air. This book is for people who travel on their own boats, but there is easy access to the island by ferry from ports between Redondo Beach and San Diego. Once you arrive, there is an almost bewildering array of choices of sea- and shore-based activities, which we can only summarize here. The many people who just relax aboard their boats miss a unique and very special place.

HIKING AND MOUNTAIN BIKING

Hiking in Catalina's rugged terrain adds a nice dimension to a boating excursion to the island. A complex network of both developed and undeveloped trails criss-crosses the island, more than enough to satisfy all but the most fanatical hikers. These few simple rules make hiking on the island a joy for everyone:

- Please stay on designated trails to help protect the fragile island ecology.
- Be self-sufficient: carry enough food and water with you because there are no facilities on the trail. Also carry a first-aid kit.
- Carry a free hiking permit with you, obtainable at the Department of Parks and Recreation in Avalon, at the airport, and in Two Harbors.
- Travel light and wear good hiking boots. Carry layers of clothing because temperatures vary with the terrain and evenings can be cool, even in the summer. Sunblock, sunglasses, and a good hat are essential.

We think the best hikes are from the Isthmus area. Some visitors prefer the organized nature hikes conducted at Two Harbors during the summer, but most people strike out on their own. Trail maps are available in Avalon and at Two Harbors. Two of our favorite trails from Two Harbors are the following:

- *Two Harbors to Parson's Landing*: 6.8 miles, along a dirt road that follows the coastline past the scout camps and popular coves (this trail is not particularly arduous, but it offers spectacular views of the Pacific)

- *Silver Peak Trail*: a strenuous 10.1-mile trail that leaves Well's Beach at Catalina Harbor and reaches an altitude of 1,802 feet atop Silver Peak before descending to Starlight Beach and Parson's Landing Campground (definitely for the experienced hiker)

You can also hike from Two Harbors to Little Harbor, a distance of about 5 miles, along either relatively straightforward or arduous routes. The trail combinations are almost endless throughout the island.

The dirt roads of the interior island offer challenging bicycle rides for all levels of expertise. A helmet rule is enforced. You can ride for free within Avalon Township or in the Two Harbors village area, but an annual permit is required for interior rides (currently $50 for an individual, $75 for a family); the fee insures you while on the conservancy's property. Some ferries will carry bicycles if you reserve in advance, or they can be rented on the island.

BEACH CAMPING

Although it is possible to hike to Parson's Landing and some other coastal campgrounds, your best access is by boat. Twelve coves along the eastern shore are available for what the authorities call "boat-in camping," a nice way to explore the island from an outboard runabout or small sailboat. The sites are undeveloped without picnic tables, barbecues, and fire rings. Bring your own portable toilet and firewood. All trash must be carried out. You can light a fire close to the water, but not close to nearby shrubs. The campsites are asterisked on pages 322, 328, and 331, and include such well-known coves as Parson's Landing and Ripper's Cove. Check-in time is 1400, check-out is 1100. Advance reservations are required and there is a cancellation fee. Call 310-510-2800 for information.

There are also developed coastal campgrounds at Parson's Landing, Two Harbors, Little Harbor, and Avalon. The most spectacular inland site is Black Jack, 1,500 feet above sea level in a pine forest on the slopes of the peak of that name.

Beach camping is a marvelous way to spend a quiet weekend, especially in the fall when the weather can be magnificent and the summer crowds are gone.

KAYAKING

There is no better way to enjoy Catalina's magnificent coastline than from a kayak, which provides a sea-level view of everything. You glide along in still water, making almost no sound, as sea lions play near rocky outcrops and pelicans swoop overhead. Kayaking has enjoyed explosive growth in recent years due to the advent of mass-produced fiberglass single and double kayaks that can be handled by even the inexperienced.

Before setting out on your own, we strongly advise first-time kayakers to obtain some formal instruction, which is available at both Avalon and Two Harbors. The naturalist-led kayak tours at Twin Harbors are an excellent way to obtain experience and to see some wildlife. You can rent kayaks at both locations, both the "sit-on" types that are best for beginners and intermediate paddlers, and the more advanced touring kayaks used by more experienced people. Be sure to take waterproof bags to store your clothing and other essentials while afloat.

Another way to experience the delights of Catalina kayaking is to sign up for a tour that includes transportation from the mainland in addition to a day's time on the water. These fun tours are closely supervised and take in the best spots. They are an excellent way to decide if you want to get serious about kayaking.

Safe kayaking on your own means careful attention to advance preparation. Also keep in mind the following safety rules:

- Unless you are highly experienced, never go kayaking alone; arrange for a buddy kayak to go with you.
- Make sure that someone back at base knows where you are going and when you expect to return.
- Wear a lifejacket at all times, have adequate waterproof clothing, tie your paddle to the boat, and know how to right a capsized kayak.
- Never travel a farther distance than you can paddle back, take a chart in a plastic bag, and check the weather forecast.

The best kayaking at Catalina is on the eastern shore facing the mainland, where the water is smoother and ocean swells are rarely troublesome. Just exploring the coves around the Isthmus or the shores of Catalina Harbor will occupy many hours. We always enjoy excursions toward Parson's Landing, where the scenery is

especially spectacular and there are numerous beaches and steep cliffs to explore. Exercise care if you round the western end of the island, where steep ocean swells can be experienced. Another fun trip is from Avalon to Long Point, but you will need to watch for busy summer boat traffic.

If you have a larger yacht, anchor off the coastline anywhere you can find shelter, then launch your kayak and explore. We guarantee that you will experience Catalina from an entirely different perspective. The sailing directions in this book provide some guidance.

Please respect wildlife and don't go too close to the sea lions basking on the rocks; they have as much right to privacy as you do.

DIVING

Catalina is a diver's paradise. The western end of the island and the Two Harbors area are recognized as two of the world's best dive locations. Many excellent dive spots are within easy reach of Avalon, with all the local expertise needed to make the most of your experience. You can explore shipwrecks and kelp beds swaying in the swell, float over steep underwater pinnacles, and swim into deep caves. Water temperatures range from 64 to 73 degrees in the summer and from 54 to 59 degrees in the winter. Diving is possible year-round, with fewer crowds in the winter when the water is sometimes crystal clear.

Excellent full-service diving facilities are located in both Avalon and Two Harbors, all of which either own or have access to day-charter boats. You can rent or buy any equipment you need on the island or bring your own. Your equipment should be in first-rate condition because you will be diving in open waters. For your first visit, it is probably better to go on a charter boat with a skipper who knows the water and local conditions.

Diving at Catalina offers several fascinating options. Many shipwrecks await your exploration. Spanish galleons allegedly were wrecked near the island on their way back from Asia to Mexico, but they have never been found. Early Hollywood moviemakers burned lumber schooners and other abandoned merchant ships for their shipwreck scenes. The most famous Catalina wreck is the *Valiant*, a 163-foot, 444-ton steel motor yacht, built in 1926—one of the largest privately owned yachts in the world at the time. *Valiant* exploded and burned off Descanso Beach near Avalon on December 17, 1930, reportedly taking $67,000 of jewels with her. The wreck lies perpendicular to the shore, listing to port with the stern in 80 feet and the bow in 110 feet. A free permit to dive on her is required from the Avalon harbormaster's office. You may find a brass coin inscribed "Yacht Valiant/Good for One Drink"—not that it will do you any good!

The keel and ribs of Catalina's most notorious wreck, the 110-foot junk *Ning Po*, can be seen at Ballast Point in Catalina Harbor at low tide. Built in 1753, this extraordinary and often rebuilt vessel was once a pirate and slave ship—legend has it that 158 pirates were beheaded on her decks. She was seized by Colonel Peter "Chinese" Gordon in 1861 and was sailed to San Pedro from Shanghai in fifty-eight days in 1913. *Ning Po* became a tourist attraction and movie prop until she sank at Ballast Point during the 1930s.

Kelp-diving is popular off Catalina and is best mastered by first going on a guided tour, then exploring with a buddy. The dense fronds can be somewhat daunting, so move slowly through the forest, look for gaps, and try to keep your profile as streamlined as possible so that diving tanks, cameras, and other impedimenta do not catch on the kelp. If you do get caught, relax and carefully disentangle yourself, using a knife only as a last resort. Expert divers recommend that you have ample air reserves on hand to allow the time needed to get clear of dense kelp. If you have to surface within a kelp bed, locate a gap in the canopy, and then use your arms or exhaust bubbles to part the fronds. It is a good idea to master kelp-diving before you try reefs because clinging fronds are encountered almost everywhere you dive.

Catalina abounds in interesting dive sites, too many to describe fully here. Bruce Wicklund's *Boating and Diving Catalina Island* (Black Dolphin Diving, Two Harbors, Santa Catalina Island, 2000) is highly recommended and provides expert definitive information on all the major dive locations. The book also provides excellent advice on spearfishing, lobster-hunting, and shellfish-collecting. Wherever you dive, watch for boat traffic and avoid damage to reefs when anchoring. Following are a couple of our favorite spots:

Farnsworth Bank lies 1.5 miles, 235 deg M, from Ben Weston Point at a depth of 55 to 90 feet. The highest pinnacles are between 55 and 70 feet. Farnsworth Bank is a marine preserve with fine purple hydrocoral and abundant white sea bass, yellowtail, rockfish, and calico. Look out for surge and subsurface currents. Avoid the torpedo rays that flourish here; they emit powerful electric shocks and can be aggressive.

Eagle Reef on the NE shore of the island W of the Isthmus is a large area of pinnacles in three sections—the highest is only 4 feet below the surface. White sea bass, yellowtail, and calico can be seen here. Currents may run strong and there is significant boat traffic.

Lover's Cove Marine Preserve is for beach-diving and snorkeling only; scuba is not permitted. There are numerous large and friendly fish, among them calico and sheepshead. There also is heavy boat traffic.

FISHING

The sportfishing off Catalina is world-famous—marlin, sea bass, yellowtail, and halibut are just a few of the fish awaiting angling enthusiasts offshore. Although many people fish off their yachts with considerable success, it is wise to take a first-time excursion with a local captain who knows where the fish are currently biting. Day-long and shorter excursions from the Isthmus, Catalina Harbor, or the mainland are readily available.

Fish abound close inshore—including sea bass, rock cod, sand dabs, button perch, and sheepshead—although many areas are protected. Unless you have fished there before, be sure to obtain up-to-date information when you arrive on the island.

Some of the best fishing for open-water fish, such as white sea bass and yellowtail, is in the spring when the fish move into shallow water to spawn. They frequent the edges of kelp beds and the margins of rocky points. Skilled divers can take them with a speargun, but they also offer excellent sport with rod and line.

Some of the best and most challenging fishing is in and around kelp beds, by reefs and rocky points, and near subsurface pilings and submerged wrecks. Calico bass are a favorite prey that frequent kelp and rocky crevices. Sheepshead are good eating when they are less than 18 inches long—they can reach great size. A variety of rockfish live on the bottom, including rare cabezon and ling cod.

Bottom fish dwell in sand, especially the tasty and much-prized halibut, which moves inshore from February to July to spawn and breed. They remain in water between 5 and 15 feet deep until early fall. Halibut like long sandy beaches, channels leading to sandy bays, and areas bordered by rocks and eelgrass, but they move aggressively off the bottom to feed. Their average weight is between 5 and 20 pounds, which may mean a fight when you hook one.

Whatever your fishing interest, please obtain the correct permits and respect size and catch limits, as well as protected areas. The future of everyone's fishing pleasure depends on all of us doing our part.

Contacts.
Santa Catalina Island Conservancy: 310-510-2595

Santa Catalina Island Chamber of Commerce: 310-510-1520

Two Harbors Visitors Center: 888-510-7979

Avalon Visitors Center: 310-510-1520

Web Sites:
www.catalina.com
www.catalinaconservancy.org/
www.sailorschoice.com/catalina.htm

GENERAL SAILING DIRECTIONS

Catalina (Chart 18757; Chart-Kit, pp. 24–25), a comfortable day passage from the mainland, is Southern California's favorite boating destination. Many beginning skippers are somewhat daunted by the crossing, mainly because they are apprehensive about open water and the difficulties of finding their destination at the other end. Except during midwinter storms, thick fog, and Santa Anas, the passage is straightforward across calm seas.

CROSSING STRATEGIES

Catalina is 18.5 miles long and 7 miles across at its widest point. The rugged peaks of the highest points of the island can be seen from a long distance away on a clear day, which enables you to eyeball your way across the channel from your port on the mainland. The greatest elevation is 2,125 feet near the middle of the E end. A deep canyon about 6 miles from West End nearly severs the island. Two deep coves, forming the Two Harbors

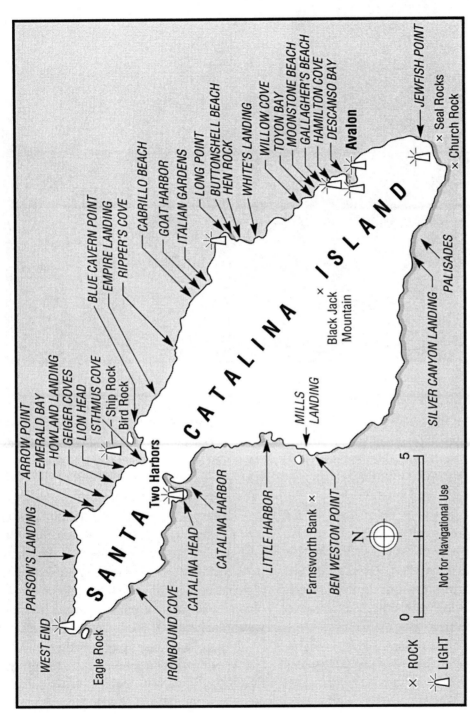

Santa Catalina Island, showing major ports and coves mentioned in the text.

Patrick Short

area, almost divide Catalina, their bights being only 0.5 mile apart. The shorelines are precipitous, with steep cliffs falling into deep water. There are few outlying dangers, except off Isthmus Cove on the NE coast.

It is best to time your departure from the mainland for relatively early in the morning to avoid the wind waves set up by the afternoon westerly. For a passage under power, the morning hours are definitely best, especially for vessels that can cruise at 15 knots or more.

Most people take at least 4 hours for the crossing and aim to arrive in midafternoon. Do not make your first passage at night because Catalina is not well lit—unless you

are planning on entering Avalon, the lights of which can be seen from miles away. Whatever time you leave, keep your eyes open for commercial shipping vessels in the traffic-separation zones that lead to San Pedro Bay—ships move fast in these areas.

The return passage to the mainland is more benign, especially for sailors, who will enjoy a freer wind particularly when bound to downwind ports like Newport Beach. To have as enjoyable a sail as possible, plan to leave in midmorning when the wind fills in.

Passages during foggy weather and at night require a sharp watch for shipping. Be especially careful when making a night passage from San Diego to Avalon because frequent cruise-ship departures can complicate your navigation. Fortunately, these vessels are lit up like Christmas trees and can be seen from miles away.

APPROACHING CATALINA

From N. Catalina is difficult to see when approaching from the N on a hazy day. You will probably be within 5 miles of West End before seeing the high ground behind the light. Soon afterward, conspicuous Eagle Rock with its white top appears.

West End light, a white pyramid-shaped structure (Lat. 33°28.7′ N, Long. 118° 36.3′ W) (Fl. W. 10 sec., 76 feet, 16 miles), provides a useful day landmark when close inshore, but it is surprisingly faint at night. You will probably be quite close to the island before you see it.

From the Mainland. This approach is straightforward, once you have identified the low ground that is the Isthmus. A radio tower on Black Jack Mountain, midway between Long Point and Avalon, also can be seen from some distance. The flashing red light on the tower is invaluable at night. Once you are within 10 miles, the city of Avalon—with its huddle of buildings, condominiums, and the circular casino building—are easily visible. The city lights make an excellent nocturnal landmark.

Shape your course for Avalon or the Isthmus, then fine-tune your approach for the cove of your choice when you are close inshore.

From S. Hazy conditions may prevent you from seeing the island until you are as close as 5 miles. A conspicuous rock quarry 1.5 miles E of Avalon will probably serve as

Catalina Island Refuge Anchorages

In NW conditions over 20 knots, the western coves at the Isthmus are well sheltered, as is Catalina Harbor.

Santa Anas: Big Fisherman Cove (if space is available) up to 40 knots, Ironbound Cove, or make your way to open water.

a landmark before the buildings of the town come into sight.

Once close inshore, you can safely navigate the coast at a distance of 0.5 to 0.75 mile offshore; there are few outlying dangers, except as marked on the chart or described in these pages.

GENERAL NOTES ON CATALINA BOATING

Catalina is a boating paradise that is remarkably unspoiled, considering it lies off one of the largest metropolitan areas in the United States. Inevitably, the intense boat traffic and many summer visitors have resulted in the development of the major coves as summer camps. Many of them are leased by mainland yacht clubs for the use of their members. Moorings are a way of life at Catalina and command very high prices. The accompanying drawing shows the typical Catalina mooring setup. At Avalon and Twin Harbors, a patrol boat will assign you a mooring if one is available, on a first-come, first-served basis. Owners have until 24 hours before to notify the authorities that they'll be using

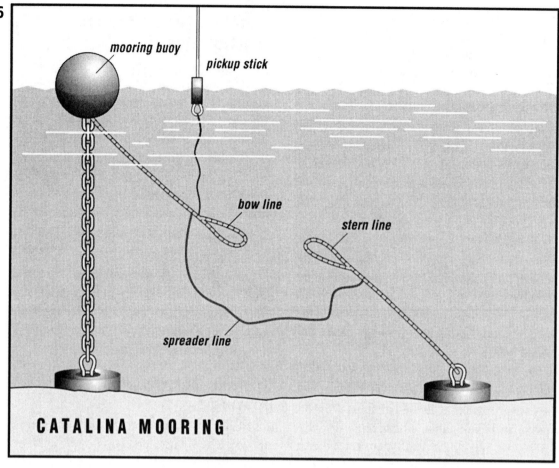

mooring buoy

pickup stick

bow line

stern line

spreader line

CATALINA MOORING

their mooring; otherwise, the early bird gets the worm!

The weather at Catalina is generally benign, except after the passage of winter fronts, when strong postfrontal westerlies can blow. Winter Santa Anas can blow very strongly, making most of the island coves untenable for small craft. If such conditions are forecast, return to the mainland or leave port for open water. Even the coves on the offshore side of the island experience very strong winds.

AVALON TO ISTHMUS

The sailing directions that follow cover the island in a counterclockwise direction. Asterisks (*) indicate camping coves. *Remember that there is a 5-knot speed limit and no wake is permitted inshore off Moonstone Beach to Long Point.*

Avalon Harbor

Chart 18757; Chart-Kit, p. 25
Lat. 33°20.8′ N, Long. 118°19.4′ W
Avalon, incorporated as Los Angeles

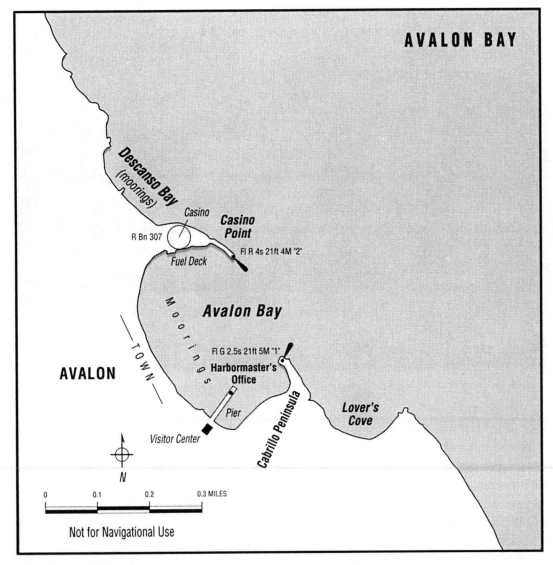

AVALON BAY

Descanso Bay
(moorings)

Casino

Casino
Point

R Bn 307

Fuel Deck

Fl R 4s 21ft 4M "2"

M
o
o
r
i
n
g
s

Avalon Bay

Fl G 2.5s 21ft 5M "1"

AVALON

Harbormaster's
Office

T
O
W
N

Pier

Cabrillo Peninsula

Lover's
Cove

Visitor Center

N

0   0.1   0.2   0.3 MILES

Not for Navigational Use

Plan of Avalon Harbor.

County's thirtieth city in 1913, is named after the poet Alfred, Lord Tennyson's paradise in his *Idylls of the King*. The bay is a fine base for a Catalina cruise.

Approach. Avalon Bay lies beneath the southernmost dip in the skyline of the island seen from the mainland. Steer for this dip or to port of Black Jack Mountain until the main landmarks appear. The white circular casino building is conspicuous on the northern side of the harbor entrance, and the Hamilton Cove condominium development ½ mile N of the bay can be seen from a long distance offshore.

Patrick Short

Approach to Avalon from NW, distant 1 mile. The casino building is prominent.

These landmarks will bring you in sight of the harbor moles. Keep a close watch for arriving and departing ferries.

Entrance. Steer midway between the two breakwaters, keeping a close watch for ferry traffic. There is a 5 mph speed limit in the harbor. At night a Fl. R. 4 sec. light marks the north mole, a Fl. G. 2.5 sec. marks the south.

Berths. Avalon is always crowded in the summer, especially on weekends, and moorings are assigned on a first-come, first-served basis. Wait in the fairway leading to the pier for a mooring assignment from the patrol boat. Call the harbormaster's office on channel 16, then 12, or sound three horn blasts or flash a light near the pier.

The patrol boat will assign you a mooring in the harbor or in Descanso or Hamilton Bay. You cannot be guaranteed the same mooring every night. However, you will be advised of the need to move between 0730 and 0900. Check-out time is 0900. The best time to visit here is midweek in the fall, when temperatures are still warm and the crowds are gone.

Avalon Boat Stand SE of the pier accepts reservations for boats up to 22 feet overall. The harbormaster's office is on the pier.

Anchoring. You may anchor outside the harbor breakwater, W of the casino, but you must be at least 300 feet outside the mooring areas. Anchor in Descanso Bay outside a line extending from Casino Point

Bob Greiser

General view of Avalon Harbor.

and White Rock. This is not a particularly attractive anchorage; go elsewhere if there is no mooring available. Anchor lights are required.

Facilities. Avalon is a closely managed harbor, with strict policies on noise (no generators between 2200 and 0730) and discharge. The harbor patrol may place dye tablets in your heads; if you refuse, you will not be permitted to moor. A trash-pickup service operates twice a day; place your trash bags on your stern. Fuel is available from a dock near the casino during morning and afternoon hours (310-510-0046).

Avalon's shore-boat service is very civilized and will pick you up from your mooring. Call on channel 9 or 310-510-0409.

You can land your dinghy without charge at Avalon Pier floats, but your stay is limited to 10 minutes. Dinghies can be left at the docks throughout the harbor for up to 72 hours, but remove loose items and lock the engine.

Avalon is a tourist town, often visited by cruise ships, with many bars, restaurants, gift shops, and ample provisions. Propane can be obtained from the Edison Plant at Pebbly Beach (310-510-0932). There are three marine service companies (see harbormaster's office).

A permit from the harbormaster's office is required to dive in Descanso Bay, where the 444-foot vessel *Valiant* was wrecked in 1930.

Avalon Pier.

Bob Greiser

Contacts.
Emergency: 911

Avalon Harbor Patrol: 310-510-0535 or channel 16, then working channel 12

Avalon Sheriff's Station: 310-510-0174

Local Weather: 213-554-1212

Catalina Taxi: 310-510-0025 (pick up at Island Market)

AVALON TO LONG POINT

The coastline between the condominiums at Hamilton Cove and Long Point is mostly steep-to with a few coves, and is popular with both boaters and divers. The cliffs are generally gray-brown; the few beaches stand out clearly from offshore. The most conspicuous landmarks are of human origin: buildings at the back of beaches and, more importantly, landing piers, often with white superstructures. Following are the major stopping points.

Gallagher's Beach
Lat. 33°22.2′ N, Long. 118°20.9′ W
Palm trees and a conspicuous white house on the E side of the beach, as well as a prominent pier and float, mark Gallagher's Beach, which is leased to the Intervarsity Christian Fellowship. Moorings belong to the camp. There is anchoring space for up

to five boats in about 40 feet. Gallagher's Beach is quiet in settled summer weather.

Moonstone Beach
Lat. 33°23.4′ N, Long. 118°22.0′ W
The white pier maintained by the Newport Beach Yacht Club, which leases the beach, is an excellent landmark—as is the green building at the E end of beach. Anchor outside the moorings in 40+ feet. Moonstone Beach offers some shelter in the summer.

Toyon Bay
Lat. 33°22.5′ N, Long. 118°21.2′ W
Toyon can be identified by the cream-colored Catalina Island Marine Institute buildings behind the beach, as well as by its large pier. This is a busy place, and the moorings belong to the Institute. You can anchor offshore in sheltered conditions, with minimal surge, in about 40 to 50 feet (sand). Watch out for kayaks, rafts, and other on-water activities. There is excellent photographic diving on both sides of the cove for divers of all skill levels in up to 50 feet.

Willow Cove
Lat. 33°22.6′ N, Long. 118°21.4′ W
Willow Cove is a small bay with summer anchorage in 20 to 40 feet (sand) 0.3 mile W of Toyon. This is a better berth than Toyon in the summer.

White's Landing
Lat. 33°23.5′ N, Long. 118°22.2′ W
White's Landing boasts of palm trees visible from offshore. The Balboa Yacht Club building at the W end is conspicuous. At least seventeen moorings lie off this beach,

with anchorage for additional boats 300 feet outside the buoys in 50+ feet. White's Landing offers moderate shelter in W winds. The pier at the E end is busy in the summer with Los Angeles Girl Scout activity.

Hen Rock
Lat. 33°24.1′ N, Long. 118°22.0′ W
Hen Rock is basically an open roadstead with shelter from Long Point immediately W of White's Landing. Moorings lie in rows offshore. There is no safe anchorage.

Buttonshell Beach
Lat. 33°24.3′ N, Long. 118°22.2′ W
This fine bay lies in the lee of Long Point with its conspicuous light beacon and derrick. The buildings of Camp Fox and the pier are visible well offshore. Steer for the pier and anchor clear of moorings in excellent shelter. This is an ideal overnight anchorage when bound on passage for points north or south. You can set an anchor here in the small hours when bound from San Diego to the Santa Barbara Channel, sleep for a few hours, then go on your way well rested.

BUTTONSHELL BEACH TO THE ISTHMUS
A little developed coastline follows, much of it steep-to with yellowish cliffs. The terraces of the abandoned quarry just E of the Isthmus are easily identified. The area between Blue Cavern Point and Big Fisherman Cove in the Isthmus is a State Marine Life Refuge: no fishing allowed!

Italian Gardens*
Lat. 33°24.6′ N, Long. 118°22.6′ W

A long beach named after an Italian fisherman who once dried his nets here, Italian Gardens is backed by steep cliffs between Long Point and Twin Rocks, a headland with two small rocks just offshore. Anchor off the beach in the best available shelter in 30 to 90 feet (sand and gravel). There is some shelter here in the summer, and it is an excellent place when other spots are congested. There are no facilities ashore. There is excellent diving in the kelp, also off Long Point and Twin Rocks, but watch for strong currents. Good fishing is close offshore.

Goat Harbor
Lat. 33°24.9′ N, Long. 118°23.7′ W

Goat Harbor is 0.4 mile W of Twin Rocks and offers anchorage in 15 to 40 feet (sand), with some shelter. It is identifiable by the beach, the first beyond Twin Rocks.

Cabrillo Beach (or Harbor)
Lat. 33°25.3′ N, Long. 118°24.0′ W

Long Beach Boy Scouts use this beach with its conspicuous landslide, which offers limited protection from WNW. Anchor off the beach, tucked as much as possible behind Little Gibraltar Point in 30 to 50 feet (sand). There is good sea-bass fishing here.

Ripper's Cove*
Lat. 33°25.6′ N, Long. 118°26.0′ W

Ripper's Cove is a small bay with an easily identifiable beach 1.6 miles W of Little Gibraltar Point. This is one of the shallowest anchorages in Catalina Harbor, with good holding off the beach in 15 to 30 feet (sand and grass patches). Watch for the shallows on the W side of the bay. Use two anchors to combat the afternoon surge. There is excellent diving and fishing here.

Empire Landing
Lat. 33°25.7′ N, Long. 118°26.5′ W

Once used for loading cattle, Empire Landing is a beach immediately W of Ripper's Cove. There are no moorings and exposed anchorage; landing is not recommended. The foundations of the stock-loading pier lie just W of the buildings behind the beach and serve as a convenient landmark.

THE ISTHMUS (TWO HARBORS)

Chart 18757; Chart-Kit, p. 24

The Isthmus is a major year-round rendezvous point for boats of all kinds and a favorite destination of yacht-club cruises from throughout Southern California. Ferries run from here to the mainland, so it's a good place to change crews. Doug Bombard Enterprises (Catalina Cove and Camp Agency) is headquartered here and runs the facilities.

Sailboats are not permitted to enter Isthmus Cove under sail. There is a 5 mph speed limit and a no-wake restriction throughout the area.

Approach. From the Mainland: Your course for the Isthmus is easily shaped in clear weather. Simply steer for the lowest point of land at the western end of the island. About 5 miles out, the high cliffs of Catalina Head on the southern side of the island become prominent. Shape your

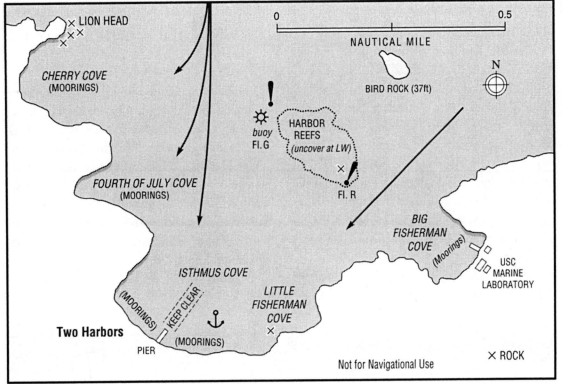

0
0.5
NAUTICAL MILE

Plan of the Isthmus area.

course to pass between white-topped Ship Rock (Fl. W. 4 sec.) and Bird Rock, a low-lying outcrop brilliant white from myriad bird droppings. Once past Ship Rock, you should be able to identify landmarks ashore: a water tank high on the hillside on the western shore of Isthmus Cove, and the buildings and pier at the head of the bay. Identify the buoys that mark Harbor Reefs immediately inshore of Bird Rock, and give them a wide berth, shaping course for the fairway leading to the pier.

From NW. Pass along the island shore. Once Howland Landing is abeam, identify Eagle Reef, marked by a buoy, and pass well inshore or outside the reef and associ-

ated kelp beds. Pass 0.5 mile off Lion Head and Isthmus Cove will open up ahead.

From E. Bird Rock is conspicuous from E. Steer between Bird Rock and the island, making sure you leave the lighted buoy that marks the Harbor Reefs to the right.

Isthmus Cove
Entrance: Lat. 33°26.5′ N, Long. 118°29.8′ W

Isthmus Cove is a major landing with heavy ferry and yacht traffic in the summer.

Approach. The approach is straightforward once you are inshore of the Harbor Reefs. Identify the pier and shape your course to pass down the mooring-free fairway that leads to it. Watch for arriving and departing ferries.

Berths. About 250 moorings lie in lines off the beach. To obtain a mooring, heave-to in the fairway approach to the landing pier. A harbor-patrol launch will assign you a mooring if one is available; sometimes side-tying to others is permitted. Call on channel 9 for information about availability. Moorings are assigned on a first-come, first-served basis, but owners have priority. You can stay for 2 hours free if a mooring is available; the maximum stay is fourteen days.

Anchoring. Anchorage may be obtained SE of the moorings, but it is controlled by the harbor patrol, which will be glad to give advice. You may also anchor off all coves 300 feet off the moorings except Big Fisherman Cove, which is a reserve.

Facilities. Land at the pier, where there is a summer dinghy dock. There is a shore-boat service (call channel 9 or sound three horn blasts) serving all Isthmus coves. The Two Harbors General Store has a wide range of provisions; fuel and marine mechanics are also available. Water is in short supply, so plan to arrive with full tanks. Dump trash ashore in the cans provided; pickup from your boat costs $1/bag. A free harbor guide is available by calling 310-510-0303.

The pier at Two Harbors.

Patrick Short

Contacts.
Emergency: 911

Two Harbors Harbor Department:
310-510-0535, or channel 16, then
working channel 9

Avalon Sheriff's Station: 310-510-0174

Shore Boat: 310-510-2683 or channel 9

Local Weather: 213-554-1212

Catalina Taxi: 310-510-0025

www.scico.com/twoharbors/

ISTHMUS COVES: EAST

Two coves on the eastern side of the Isthmus area offer possible shelter, and one of them is an excellent Santa Ana refuge.

Big Fisherman Cove
Lat. 33°26.7′ N, Long. 118°29.0′ W
This is a large cove dominated by the University of Southern California Marine Science Center, with its own dock and ramp (which can be used by USC invitation only). The Center buildings are a conspicuous landmark and easily identified. The moorings in the bay belong to the Center and are for emergency use only. Anchor clear of the moorings in 30 to 50 feet. Big Fisherman Cove is an excellent Santa Ana refuge, but is exposed to the N; it is good in normal settled conditions. There is a diver's recompression chamber at the Center.

Little Fisherman Cove
Lat. 33°26.6′ N, Long. 118°29.5′ W
This shallow bay lies at the SE corner of

Isthmus Cove and is backed by a nice beach and the Two Harbors campground. The beach is a good landmark. You can anchor outside moorings off this cove within easy reach of the Isthmus dinghy dock, but an outboard engine for your dinghy is advisable; there is some swell on windy days. This is a good landing.

ISTHMUS COVES: WEST

The coves on the western shore of the Isthmus are among the most popular on the island. They are busy even off-season with Catalina Island Marine Center camps and other activities. A speed limit of 5 knots, with no wake, extends along the shoreline between Isthmus Cove and Lion Point.

Fourth of July Cove
Lat. 33°26.8′ N, Long. 118°30.0′ W
Fourth of July Cove is the first bay NW of Isthmus Cove and lies immediately NW of a prominent brown water tank on the hillside above the Cove. The road cut on the S side of the bay, the buildings back of the beach, and the moorings are good landmarks. Fourth of July Cove is very busy during the summer and all moorings are often full. Anchor 300 feet outside them in 50 feet of water (sand), allowing sufficient swinging room. This berth is often disturbed by the wake of passing boats. There are quieter anchorages, but there is shoreboat service and excellent facilities at Two Harbors. Fourth of July Cove commemorates many years of family reunions by the Banning family in this beautiful place.

Patrick Short

Fourth of July Cove.

Patrick Short

Cherry Cove from E, distant 1 mile.

Cherry Cove
Lat. 33°27.1′ N, Long. 118°30.2′ W

This bay is named after cherry trees in the canyon and is readily identified by a modern lighthouse-like structure on the beach and the Boy Scout camp buildings inshore. Again, the road cuts on the hill are prominent. Lion Head offers the best landmark for identifying the Cove, which lies immediately S. Beware of the off-lying rock SE of the Head; stay at least 0.25 mile offshore. Moorings fill Cherry Cove; few are available in the summer. Anchor 300 feet outside, clear of traffic, in 50 to 60 feet (sand). The best shelter is on the S side, clear of any surge around Lion Head.

ISTHMUS TO CATALINA HARBOR

Lion Head to West End
The western third of the north shore offers spectacular cliffs and some popular coves east of Arrow Point. West End is the departure point for passages north to the Channel Islands and the Santa Barbara Channel. Close offshore along the coast, watch for semisubmerged rocks that break at low water. Pass inshore or offshore of Eagle Reef, which is marked with a buoy.

Identifying individual coves along this stretch of coast is a matter of experience, but you should be able to find them easily, given the moorings and other features ashore.

Eel Cove
Eel Cove is basically unsheltered, but has excellent diving for beginners. It is identi-

fied by the buildings behind the small beach.

Little Geiger Cove
Lat. 33°27.5′ N, Long. 118°31.0′ W

This cove is a small anchorage for one or two boats and a single mooring. Big Geiger Cove is preferable.

Big Geiger Cove
Lat. 33°27.3′ N, Long. 118°30.8′ W

Big Geiger Cove has a conspicuous beach and anchorage (30 feet, sand) for up to ten boats with reasonable shelter. The shore is leased to the Blue Water Cruising Club. Do not anchor here except in sheltered summer weather.

Howland Landing
Lat. 33°27.7′ N, Long. 118°31.3′ W

Howland Landing is a large well-sheltered roadstead protected by a low headland. Rows of moorings off the beach are busy in the summer because the Los Angeles Yacht Club has a base and private beach here. You can anchor 300 feet offshore in 25 to 50 feet (sand and kelp).

Patrick Short

Howland Landing from NE, distant ½ mile.

Emerald Bay and Sandy Beach
Lat. 33°27.9' N, Long. 118°32.0' W

A water tank on the hill and the conspicuous buildings, as well as landing piers and a flagpole, are good landmarks. Rows of moorings congest these popular coves with their prominent and excellent beaches, which serve as good landmarks. There is limited anchorage offshore W of Indian Rock and reef (give this a wide berth) in 25 to 50 feet, but there is some surge; lay two anchors. Shore facilities are leased to the Corsair Yacht Club and Great Western Boy Scouts. Indian Rock is famous for its kelp forests and is a popular diving spot.

Parson's Landing*
Lat. 33°28.42' N, Long. 118°33.00' W

Parson's Landing is an anchorage in kelp, 30 to 50 feet, immediately W of foul ground close inshore. Identify the beach and move cautiously inshore. Landing is excellent, but the beach is reserved for campsite users only. Anchor here only in settled summer weather because shelter is limited.

West End, the western extremity of Catalina, is lit with a surprisingly faint light on a short pole (Fl. W. 10 sec., 10 miles). Watch for swells and downslope winds.

West End to Catalina Harbor
The coastline between West End and Catalina Harbor is rugged and spectacular. Once you are around West End, pass offshore of Eagle Rock with its distinctive white cap. Strong downwind gusts can blow in this vicinity, even on calm days. Look for kelp patches extending some distance offshore.

Ironbound Cove
Lat. 33°26.9' N, Long. 118°34.0' W

There are no really sheltered anchorages between West End and Catalina Harbor except for a Santa Ana refuge in Ironbound Cove. It is little more than an indentation in the high cliffs, and offers little or no protection from prevailing westerlies. You can identify the cove with its dark cliffs from about a mile W of Catalina Harbor. It lies behind Catalina Head.

Ironbound Cove comes into its own when Santa Anas are howling through Catalina Harbor. The cliffs offer some shelter from the gusts, even if the ground swell is a little troublesome. Anchor in 60 feet or more (rock and sand). There is nothing to bring you here under prevailing summer conditions.

From Ironbound Cove, the coast recedes ENE to Catalina Head, which looks like the head of a dog lying on the ground.

Catalina Harbor
Chart 18757; Chart-Kit, p. 24
Lat. 33°25.6' N, Long. 118°31.0' W

This is a favorite Catalina berth—completely sheltered and quiet—yet close to the action at Two Harbors, a mere half-mile walk. However, it can be rough here in Santa Anas; 70-knot winds have been reported. Under these circumstances, clear out to sea or go around to Ironbound Cove.

Catalina Harbor is an ideal starting point for a cruise to Santa Barbara Island, 25 miles offshore. The anchorage is usually relatively uncrowded, except on major holiday weekends.

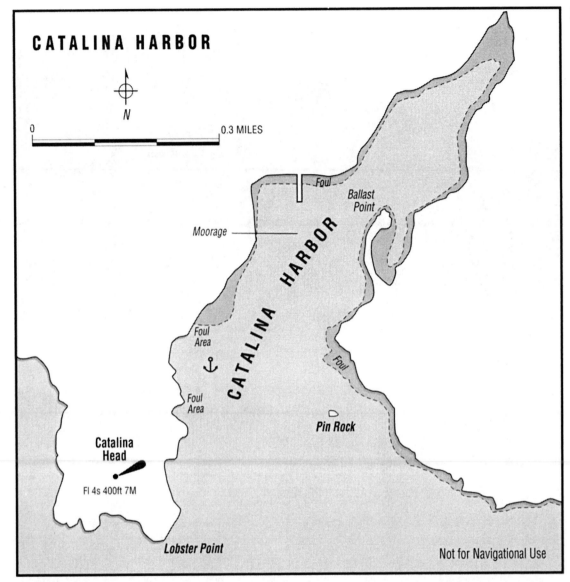

Plan of Catalina Harbor.

Approach and Entrance. Identify Catalina Head, prominent from the E and W and seaward, and which is also lit by a light on a white pole (Fl. W. 4 sec., 7 miles). As the entrance opens up, low-lying Ballast Point, the pier at Wells Beach, and yachts on moorings come into view. Shape a course midway through the deep entrance and head inshore. Give the foul ground off the E side of the entrance a wide berth.

Moorings. Moorings are controlled by the Catalina Harbor Department and are

Bob Greiser

Catalina Harbor, Catalina Head, and the entrance in the background. Ballast Point is located mid-ground left.

Patrick Short

Catalina Harbor anchorage.

often available even in high summer. Apply for a space at the Isthmus or contact a patrol boat if one is operating.

Anchorage. There is ample anchoring room outside the seventy-seven moorings in 30 feet or more, with good shelter except in (very rare) southerlies. Two anchors are advisable to prevent swinging. As many as two hundred yachts can anchor here at one time. This is a suicidal anchorage in Santa Ana winds.

Facilities. Land your dinghy at the pier in the NW corner of the cove. Two Harbors is a short walk away, where provisions can be obtained. If you want to be quiet and away from the crowd, this is the place for you. Of course, there is the additional passage time to reach the far side of the island.

CATALINA HARBOR TO AVALON HARBOR

Allow a full day to travel east from Catalina Harbor to Avalon around the E end of the island. The scenery and excellent fishing and diving make a leisurely passage mandatory! If you are proceeding close inshore, watch for kelp beds and semisubmerged rocks that break at low water.

Little Harbor*
Lat. 33°23.0′ N, Long. 118°28.4′ W
This is probably the best anchorage on Catalina Island, simply because there are no moorings.

Approach. From W: Identify the mesa-like cliff to the E of the bay and close it until the bay opens up to the left.

Little Harbor. The yacht is anchored in a good spot.

Bob Greiser

From E. Follow the coast around until you identify the conspicuous beach at the back of the anchorage.

Entrance. On entering, trend to starboard, staying well clear of the unmarked and submerged reef that extends offshore on the W wide. Once inside, turn to the W into the anchorage, and anchor tucked in under the headland in 15 to 40 feet (sand, gravel, and rock). The bottom can be tricky, so make sure that you have anchored securely.

There are camp facilities ashore, and the landing is good. Diving and fishing are excellent here. Do not anchor in Little Shark or Shark Harbor, which are the eastern portions of the bay—the surge is often bad and there is little shelter.

There are no good overnight anchorage spots E of Little Harbor, but there is good diving and fishing off much of the coast in calm weather when the swell is down.

Farnsworth Bank (54 feet), 1.5 miles SW of Ben Weston Point, is an ecological preserve with excellent visibility in quiet winter weather for intermediate and advanced divers (Lat. 33°21′ N, Long. 118°31′ W).

Mills Landing
Lat. 33°22.0′ N, Long. 118°29.0′ W
Mills Landing, 1 mile W of Ben Weston Point, is an easily identified beach without

Tile work at Avalon.

Bob Greiser

any good anchorage or landing. Diving is excellent offshore immediately to the W.

Silver Canyon Landing
Lat. 33°19.3′ N, Long. 118°23.4′ W

Silver Canyon Landing, in the rugged Palisades area, is a beach with relatively exposed anchorage in 30 to 70 feet (sand) at the foot of a prominent canyon 3 miles W of Church Rock. Landing is difficult. This location is frequently used by fishermen and divers as a day anchorage.

The E end of the island is marked by offlying Church and Seal Rocks, as well as by the major quarry with moorings and waiting barges at Jewfish Point (Lat. 33°19.2′ N, Long. 118°18.2′ W), so named after a 500-pound fish caught there many years ago. Give the quarrying activities a wide berth.

Lover's Cove

No anchoring is allowed in this glass-bottom-boat preserve immediately E of Avalon Harbor. Snorkeling is permitted, however, but not scuba.

Once you are off Lover's Cove, the Avalon casino will be in clear view and you will have completed your circumnavigation of the island.

MAINLAND: NEWPORT BEACH TO ENSENADA, MEXICO

HUNTINGTON HARBOR TO NEWPORT BEACH

Chart 18749; Chart-Kit, p. 29

Anaheim Bay lies 14 miles NW of Newport Beach, the major yacht harbor between Los Angeles and San Diego. The intervening coast is low-lying, with California Highway 1 passing behind the sand. A somewhat continuous ribbon of urban development backs the beach. Stay outside the 10-fathom line along this stretch of coastline to avoid tanker moorings and other industrial paraphernalia. Two conspicuous smokestacks of a power plant lie 5.5 miles N of the Newport Beach entrance. There is nothing to detain you along the shoreline, but I remember a fast northbound passage along here years ago, hard on the wind against a strong Santa Ana. *Chabuka* heeled to strong gusts, a double-reefed main and storm jib carrying us effortlessly through the smooth water close inshore. The air was crystal clear. You could see Catalina Island far offshore—the only sound the creak of the rigging and the hiss-hiss of the hull coursing through the blue water.

Newport Beach Harbor

Chart 18754; Chart-Kit, p. 28
Entrance: Lat. 33°35.3′ N, Long. 117° 52.6′ W

Newport Beach Harbor was once a coastal lagoon, a quiet place where passing ships occasionally collected hides and grain. The peace and quiet did not last long—efforts to dredge the shallow entrance began as early as 1876. The current harbor with its two jetties, well-dredged channel, and turning basin dates to 1936. More than nine thousand pleasure craft make their home here. Newport Beach is now a major yachting center with seven yacht clubs and comprehensive facilities.

The annual Newport to Ensenada yacht race in May is one of the great spectacles of the Southern California sailing year. Hundreds of yachts—large and small—charge across the starting line off Newport in a frantic dash for Ensenada. The fastest racing catamarans and ultralight sleds often arrive at the finish in early evening, if the winds oblige. In other years, the entire race is a drifting match past the Coronado Islands. A hard core of competitors takes the racing seriously, but many boats just go along for the ride and the parties. Stories abound of pornographic movies shown on mainsails and multi-course gourmet dinners served at midnight. The parties in Ensenada are famous. An Ensenada Race is a worthwhile experience

Plan of Newport Beach Harbor.

at least once, although the long motor homeward can be excruciating, especially with a hangover.

Newport Beach offers every facility imaginable for the sailor and powerboater, with endless possibilities for smooth-water sailing inside the harbor itself. Like Long Beach, Newport is an ideal base for a cruise to Catalina Island.

Approach. From N: Identify the power plant 5.5 miles NW of Newport Beach, then follow the coastline at a distance of 0.75 mile until the harbor breakwaters are sighted.

From offshore. The power plant N of the harbor and the high-rise buildings of Newport Center, 1.4 miles inland from the harbor, are excellent landmarks even in poor visibility. Steer for the Newport Center buildings until the harbor entrance comes into view.

From S. The dense urban sprawl of Newport Beach and neighboring communities offers the best general landmark until the high-rise structures of Newport Center come into view. Thereafter, stay 0.75 mile offshore until the harbor entrance is sighted.

Night approach. A night approach is straightforward, confused only by the bright city lights that blaze out from the coast. The harbor lights can usually be

Newport Beach Harbor entrance from land.

Bob Greiser

spotted from 2 or 3 miles away, and the power plant is a good general landmark.

Entrance. Enter the main channel (15 to 20 feet) between the two jetties, which are 825 feet apart. Both are lighted (W jetty: R. G. 5 sec., 44 ft., 10 miles; E jetty: Fl. R. 4 sec., 25 ft., 6 miles). A 5-knot speed limit is enforced. Newport Beach Harbor entrance is very congested during summer weekends, especially in the early evening when everyone wants to get home for the evening cocktail. Try and avoid rush hours during your first visit and exercise caution because of aggressive skippers. Keep to starboard when entering or leaving. On weekends, I do not recommend tackling the entrance under sail, except in a small boat. Once at the Corona Del Mar Bend, follow the fairway up the Balboa Reach to your destination. Watch for the ferries that cross the channel between Balboa and Balboa Island and elsewhere.

Berthing and Facilities. Newport Beach Harbor is enormous and confusing to the first-time visitor. Everywhere, affluent, well-manicured houses crowd the water's edge, many with private docks. Thousands of yachts lie to fore-and-aft moorings here, so a dinghy is essential. For various channels, governing depths, and other details, consult Chart 18754. Our plan gives a general impression of the harbor layout.

The Orange County Harbor Patrol and Harbormaster's Office is on the NE side of the entrance channel opposite Corona Del Mar Bend. They will be glad to help you find a guest slip. Guest slips are often in short supply, but are available as follows (note that most marinas—with locations

Newport Beach Harbor ferry.

Bob Greiser

noted on the harbor plan—require reservations, although they may be more flexible in the winter):

Orange County–owned slips and moorings (949-723-1002). These are assigned on a first-come, first-served basis and reservations are not accepted. You can stay for only five days a month at a slip and for ten days a month (sometimes longer) at a mooring.

California Recreation Company (949-644-9730). This organization administers slips for the Balboa, Bay Shore, Bayside, and Villa Cove Marinas. Reservations are required and may be made during working hours. The *minimum* stay is fourteen days and the length of your tenancy depends on available vacancies.

Lido Peninsula Marina (949-673-9330). This marina is located between Balboa Peninsula and Lido Island, and requires reservations made during working hours.

Newport Dunes Marina (949-729-1100). This marina lies in the Back Bay above a fixed bridge with a 24-foot clearance, which means that most visitors are powerboaters. Reservations are required and may be made up to sixty days in advance.

Members of recognized yacht clubs can often obtain slips or moorings at local clubs, but such berths are in short supply. Space is difficult to find during the buildup to the Ensenada Race and during long summer weekends.

Newport has fine shops and restaurants and every marine service imaginable. There are three fuel docks: one on Balboa Island, one across the channel from it, and one at the top of the harbor. If you have a larger yacht, you might want to visit with bicycles aboard to explore the harbor area in comfort.

Anchorage. You can anchor E of Lido Island in a free, designated anchoring area for no longer than five days with permission of the harbor patrol. If you anchor here, one member of the crew must be aboard at all times. You must anchor in such a way as to not swing out of the anchoring area. The harbor patrol enforces these rules strictly. The anchoring area is far from convenient for provisioning or even getting ashore because most of the surrounding shore is privately owned. You may be able to get permission to land at a club dock. Most waterside restaurants have dinghy docks where you can tie up while eating.

Launching Ramps. Newport Dunes Launching Ramp on the S side of the harbor is busy during the summer. A fee is charged; note that all harbor parking is metered. There is a second ramp to starboard, above the Balboa Island Bridge.

Artificial Fishing Reef. Lat. 33°16.2′ N, Long. 117°57.8′ W.

Contacts.
Emergency: 911

Harbor Patrol: 949-723-1002 or channel 16

Harbormaster: 949-723-1003

Taxi: 800-469-8294 or 888-829-4874

Weather: 949-675-0503

Fuel Docks: 949-675-0740, 949-673-1103, and 949-673-7878

www.ocsd.org/harbor.html

www.sailorschoice.com/nb/

Courses. Given in degrees magnetic (2000). For reverse course, add 180 degrees.

Newport Beach to

The Isthmus, Catalina: 243 deg., 31.6 miles

Avalon: 224 deg., 26.4 miles

NEWPORT BEACH TO DANA POINT

Chart 18746; Chart-Kit, p. 29

Twelve miles separate Newport Beach from Dana Point, named after the great Richard Henry himself. Dana Point is conspicuous and juts out from a coastline of low bluffs and sandy beaches fronting on low hills that roll down to the cliffs. The houses of Laguna Beach south of Newport finger out toward Dana Point. The Spanish Mediterranean structures of the Ritz-Carlton Hotel are prominent on a coastal bluff just N of Dana Point. From offshore, Santiago Peak, 17.5 miles NE of Dana Point, has an unmistakable double-headed peak.

Dana Point lies at the seaward end of a long ridge, ending in a 220-foot-high sandstone cliff with a precipitous face. Rocks and ledges extend at least 350 yards offshore. Pass outside the lighted buoy (Fl. R. 2.5 sec.) 0.5 mile off the point. A rock covered 2 fathoms 2.4 miles SE of the point sometimes breaks in strong winds.

Dana Point is famous for its associations with Dana and the crew of the *Pilgrim*. Dana wrote "no animal but a man or a monkey could get up it." They loaded hides by the simple expedient of throwing them one by one over the cliff. "As they were all large, stiff, and doubled, like the cover of a book, the wind took them, and they swayed and eddied about, plunging and rising in the air, like a kite when it has broken its string." The men at the bottom picked up the hides and carried them to the boat on their heads. When a hide caught on the cliff, they threw others at it to dislodge it from its perch. On one occasion, Dana was lowered down on a pair of topgallant studding-sail halyards to free stubborn hides that had lodged in cavities on the cliff face. He wrote: "It really was a picturesque sight: the great height; the scaling of the hides; and the continual walking to and fro of the men, who looked like mites, on the beach." Thus: Dana Point.

Dana Point Harbor
Chart 18746; Chart-Kit, p. 29
Lat. 33°27.3′ N, Long. 117°41.5′ W
Dana Point Harbor is a modern structure that takes advantage of the lee created by this famous point. Built in the 1970s, it is the epitome of a well-designed small-boat harbor: efficient, comfortable, and thoroughly sanitized. Dana Point Harbor is a convenient stop on the long transit up and down the coast.

Approach. From all directions, identify Dana Point, then shape a course immediately to its south, passing outside the whistle buoy. The main harbor breakwater runs parallel to the land, running out S from Dana Point. White yacht masts behind the breakwater and the buildings on the bluff behind the port are visible from a considerable distance. A light (Fl. G. 4 sec.) marks the S end and the harbor entrance, which is also protected by a shorter breakwater from land (Fl. R. 4 sec.). Give a wide berth to the rock 300 yards NE of the southern breakwater light, marked by a buoy.

Entrance. Enter the harbor midway between the breakwaters, taking care not to swing too close to the seaward breakwater in order to allow for departing traffic. A 5 mph speed limit is in effect throughout the harbor, which carries 19 feet throughout. The harbor consists of two basins separated by a low bridge.

Access to the East Basin can be gained by turning to starboard immediately inside the entrance and following the inshore

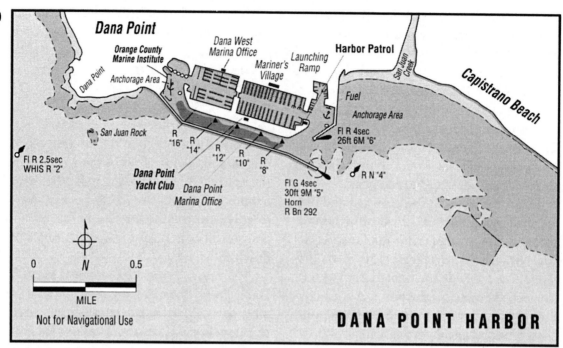

Plan of Dana Point Harbor.

Dana Point Harbor from land, showing main fairways and entrance in the background.

breakwater around until the entrance opens up ahead.

The West Basin is accessible at the head of the harbor, opposite the Orange County Marine Institute, where a replica of Dana's brig *Pilgrim* is often moored. A statue of Richard Henry Dana can be seen to starboard midway up the main fairway. This long channel is a nice place for dinghy sailing, but watch for traffic, especially on weekends.

Berths and Facilities. County-Owned Slips: The harbormaster's office lies at the head of the inner breakwater protecting the marina area. Make a sharp starboard turn once the N breakwater is abeam, and shape your course to tie up at the emergency dock behind the office. You must apply here for a slip assignment; take your registration papers and driver's license. County-owned guest slips are available on a first-come, first-served basis, with a maximum stay of fifteen days a month in the summer, sixty days a quarter in the winter. Reservations are not accepted.

Dana Point Marina Company (949-496-6137). This facility has some visitor slips available. The office is on the S side of the East Basin. Apply to the marina during office hours, Monday through Saturday. Reservations are accepted, but the length of stay depends on the season and availability.

Facilities at Dana Point Harbor are excellent, with a fuel dock and pump-out station in the basin N of the entrance, and numerous small shops and restaurants in Mariner's Village behind the harbor. From there, it is an easy walk to the shops along Highway 1 inland. A shuttle sometimes runs between the harbor and the main shopping area during the summer. You can get most repairs done here and the harbor patrol will be glad to refer you. Showers and self-service laundries are available at both marinas.

There is currently much discussion about future development in the harbor, which may result in changes in the near and more distant future.

Anchoring. There are two designated anchoring areas inside the harbor; both are free, with a maximum five-day stay. The first area lies at the head of the main channel, the other is in the East Basin on the breakwater side of the yellow buoys. Obtain the harbormaster's permission before anchoring.

Boat-Launching Ramp. A boat-launching ramp is available at the end of Embarcadero Place and next to Dana Wharf. The minimum fee is $11 and the fee for rigs over 42 feet is $16.

Contacts.
Emergency: 911

Harbor Patrol: 949-723-1002
or channel 16

Taxis

California Yellow Cab: 949-261-9096

Yellow Cab: 949-364-2000

Weather: 949-496-2210

Web Sites

www.danapointharbor.com

www.sailorschoice.com/DPHarbor.htm

Dana Point Marina; Dana Point in the background.

Bob Greiser

Course. Given in degrees magnetic (2000). For reverse course, add 180 degrees.

Dana Point to

Avalon: 244 deg., 32.4 miles

DANA POINT TO OCEANSIDE HARBOR

Chart 18746; Chart-Kit, p. 31

South from Dana Point to San Mateo Point 6.5 miles away, the rugged shoreline is still fairly high, with both the railroad tracks and Highway 1 running close to shore. San Mateo Point, just south of San Clemente's red roofs, rises 60 feet high. The point (Lat. 33°23.3′ N, Long. 117°35.8′ W) is lit (Fl. W. 10 sec., 63 ft., 16 miles) and makes a fairly prominent landmark, but the most conspicuous signposts are the white domes of the San Onofre nuclear-power generating plant, 2.5 miles S. When brilliantly lit at night, the plant stands out like a bright beacon on the coastline. Stay at least 1.5 miles offshore between Dana Point and Oceanside to stay clear of outlying dangers and kelp.

The low-lying coastal plain between San Onofre and Oceanside Harbor is part of Camp Pendleton Marine Base. A military restricted area extends from San Clemente 3 miles seaward along the coast to Del Mar Basin in Oceanside Harbor. *Local Notices to Mariners* gives details of exercise times, or you can call the Oceanside Harbor Police (760-966-4580). If you pass outside the 3-mile limit, you have nothing to worry about, but be alert to amphibious craft and military exercises. Stay outside the 10-fathom line on this 12-mile passage.

Oceanside Harbor
Chart 18774; Chart-Kit, p. 31
Lat. 33°10.7′ N, Long. 117°24.0′ W
Oceanside Harbor is the only port between Dana Point and Mission Bay along a long, low-lying stretch of coast without good anchorages. This modern harbor, completed in 1963, is a favorite port of call for north- and south-bound craft, and is also an excellent weekend destination. The harbor is also a good jumping-off point for Avalon and Catalina.

Approach. From N: The area immediately N of Oceanside forms the Camp Pendleton Marine Base exercise area and is sometimes the scene of amphibious assault exercises and helicopter landings with support ships offshore. The 5 freeway is immediately behind the beach and low coastal bluffs.

The concrete domes of the San Onofre power station at the northern edge of the camp, which are brilliantly lit at night, are a conspicuous landmark 12.5 miles N of the harbor. Once you have identified the domes, head along the coast at least 1.5 miles offshore (more if so directed by military personnel) until you pick up the following landmarks for Oceanside Harbor:

- conspicuous freeway and railroad trestles over the Santa Margarita River just N of the harbor
- an elevated water tower 1.7 miles NE of the harbor
- the harbor breakwaters that project seaward

From S. Identify the following landmarks:

- the Oceanside city pier, conspicuous from some distance; the harbor breakwaters are 1.2 miles NW
- a seventeen-story apartment complex painted white with blue trim, just SW of the harbor entrance

In case you get lost, some considerate person has placed a lighted Oceanside sign on a grassy ridge just behind the harbor entrance! A lighted tower on the SE side of the harbor resembles a lighthouse, but it isn't one.

At night, the lights of the town provide an excellent landmark from a great distance, lying as they do S of the dark mass of Camp Pendleton's undeveloped land.

Entrance. Identify the approach buoy (Fl. W. 2.5 sec.) 1,000 feet SE of the entrance and steer a safe course well offshore until the entrance opens up ahead. The opening faces SE.

Give a wide berth to the end of the offshore breakwater because there are underwater obstructions. Also stay clear of the E jetty where there may be a sandbar and breaking waves. An orange and white special buoy marks a submerged jetty

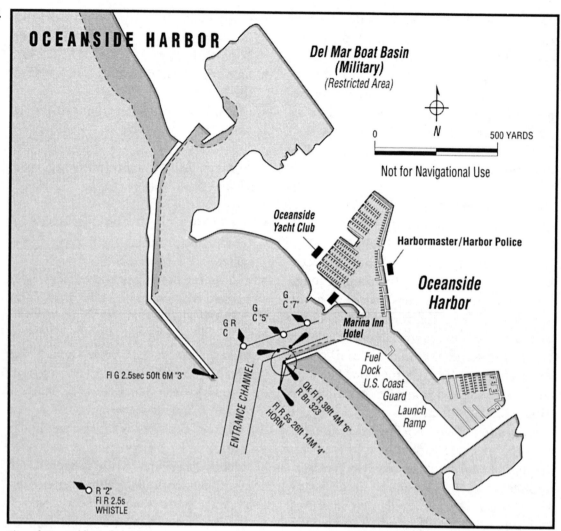

Plan of Oceanside Harbor.

200 yards NW of the junction buoy. Rocks extend out from the Mission Inn on the N side of the harbor's inner entrance.

Two breakwaters enclose the entrance. The E jetty bears a light (Fl. R. 5 sec., 26 ft., 14 miles), visible for a considerable distance. The W jetty is also lighted (Fl. G. 2.5 sec., 50 ft., 5 miles).

Oceanside Harbor consists of two parts:

- *The Del Mar Boat Basin*, reached by following the channel NNE from the entrance, is a military facility and off-limits to civilian craft.

- *Oceanside Harbor* proper lies to the E of the main entrance and is reached by a buoyed and lit channel, whose position shifts according to shoaling conditions. More than nine hundred yachts are

Oceanside Harbor from the air.

Bob Greiser

berthed there. For Oceanside Harbor, identify the channel buoys and turn to starboard immediately after passing through the breakwaters.

Caution. The Oceanside Harbor approach is dangerous in strong SE conditions due to steep waves and shoaling; do not attempt an entrance in such weather. If you have any doubt, call the harbormaster on VHF channel 16 for a report on entrance conditions.

Berths and Facilities. You cannot anchor in Oceanside Harbor. The harbor headquarters building is on the NW side of the turning basin in the northern marina area. Visitors should tie up there while applying for a guest slip. Reservations are accepted for twenty-four transit slips, the rest are available on a first-come, first-served basis. Fees must be paid in advance. and there is a thirty-day maximum stay for visitors. The friendly Oceanside Yacht Club has guest-slip space on a reciprocal basis for members of other yacht clubs.

Please note that generators and engines cannot be operated in slips between 2200 and 0800 and that laundry cannot be hung out to dry.

There are numerous small stores and several restaurants in the harbor area, as well as a wide range of marine services. A

346 U.S. Coast Guard facility and a fuel dock are located on the S side of the entrance channel to the southern marina area. Showers and self-service laundries are conveniently located nearby.

Boat-Launching Ramp. A boat-launching ramp is located on the SW side of the entrance channel to the southern marina area—there is no charge for use, just for parking.

Artificial Fishing Reefs. Reef 1 is located at Lat. 33°10.9′ N, Long. 117° 25.0′ W; Reef 2 is located at Lat. 33°12.6′ N, Long. 117°25.8′ W.

Contacts.
Emergency: 911

Harbor Police: 760-435-4050
or channel 16

www.ci.oceanside.ca.us/Harbor/
default.html

Course. Course given in degrees magnetic (2000). For reverse course, add 180 degrees.

Oceanside Harbor to

Avalon: 267 deg., 47.2 miles

The Butler did it.

Bob Greiser

OCEANSIDE HARBOR TO POINT LOMA

Charts 18774 and 18765; Chart-Kit, pp. 31–32

I always find this stretch of coast somewhat monotonous. From Oceanside Harbor, you pass mile after mile of low tableland with steep and low, usually brownish, cliffs that range between 60 and 130 feet high. Numerous canyons dissect the cliffs and break the monotony of the bluffs. The railroad and U.S. 5 run parallel to and just inshore of the beach. On a still night, you can hear the traffic for miles to seaward.

The few landmarks on this long stretch of coast are as follows:

- *Carlsbad*, 30 miles N of Point Loma: a conspicuous power-plant smokestack with fixed and flashing red lights at night. A lighted bell buoy (Qk. Fl. W.) (Lat. 33°0′8″ N, Long. 117°21.2′ W) and a complex of mooring buoys lie about a mile offshore. Your course should pass well offshore of the light buoy.
- *Del Mar*, 18 miles N of Point Loma: a conspicuous smokestack and resort buildings.
- *A measured nautical mile*, 13.5 miles N of Point Loma: marked by two pairs of steel towers.
- *Scripps Institution of Oceanography*, 12 miles N of Point Loma: This famous institution is 5 miles S of where the coastal cliffs rise to about 300 feet and U.S. 5 diverts inland. The Scripps build-

ings and its privately maintained pier are prominent from a considerable distance. A restricted area lies off the pier and is clearly marked on the chart.

Point La Jolla is a ridge of Soledad Mountain, a rounded 822-foot-high promontory that lies 9 miles N of Point Loma. Point La Jolla is the first high ground you see as you approach San Diego. The mountain has two TV towers on its summit. The buildings of Point La Jolla and Pacific Beach are prominent. When bound between Point La Jolla and Point Loma, stay at least 2 miles offshore to avoid extensive kelp beds that mask the rocky shoals inshore. A safe course along this 11-mile stretch takes you well outside the 10-fathom line.

Mission Bay
Chart 18765; Chart-Kit, p. 33
Entrance: Lat. 32°45.3′ N, Long. 117° 15.4′ W

Mission Bay is a popular yacht harbor with extensive areas of shallow water where dinghy sailing is a delight. Sea World, on the southern border of Mission Bay, and Belmont Park are major attractions. All of San Diego's many attractions are within a short taxi ride.

Caution. Swells can break in 20 feet of water in the entrance, even in moderately rough weather. Avoid Mission Bay in rough onshore weather and divert to the all-weather harbor at San Diego.

Approach. With its twin jetties, the Mission Bay entrance is 5.5 miles N of Point Loma. Approach from well to seaward—because of kelp—even when coming from San Diego.

From N. Locate the U.S. Navy Electronics Tower a mile NW of the entrance jetties. By this time, you should see the 338-foot Sea World tower 1.8 miles E of the entrance.

From S. The Ocean Beach fishing pier extends from the shore 0.3 mile S of the entrance and may be sighted before the Mission Bay jetties. The white high-rise Hyatt Islandia Hotel on the N shore of Quivira Basin inside the entrance is another excellent landmark.

Approach the jetties from seaward and stay closer to the N jetty if any swell is running; breaking can occur on the S side of the channel.

Entrance. The dredged entrance channel between the jetties carries 14 to 19 feet (shallower at the edges) and leads to Quivira and Mariner's Basins on the E and W sides of the fairway. The jetties are lit from low metal towers (N jetty: Fl. G. 6 sec., 36 ft., 7 miles; S jetty: Fl. R. 2.5 sec., 11 ft., 5 miles). The Ventura/Glen A. Rick Bridge, with a minimum clearance of 38 feet, crosses the main fairway 1.3 miles from the entrance above Quivira Basin, limiting access for larger vessels to the inner bay.

The easily identified and lit entrance to Quivira Basin, where the main marinas are located, lies on the starboard side of the main channel, just below the Islandia Hotel.

Berths and Anchoring. Contact the harbor police on VHF channel 16 for berthing information or visit the office, just to starboard inside Quivira Basin, where

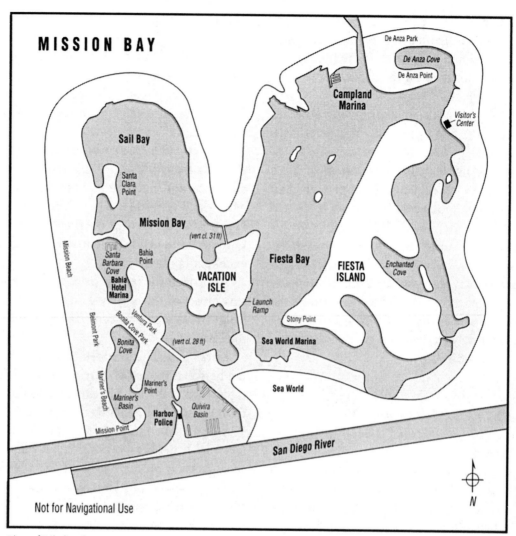

Plan of Mission Bay.

there is a temporary guest dock. Four private marinas in Quivira Basin itself offer transient slips, with convenient access to fuel and restaurants, as well as all typical facilities.

Quivira Basin Marinas. None of these marinas are cheap, and space depends on vacancies. An advance reservation is almost essential, especially in the summer.

Driscoll Mission Bay Marina (619-221-8456). In the SW corner of the basin. Reservations required. Length of stay depends on vacancies.

Islandia Marina (619-224-1234). N side of the basin near the hotel. Reservations are recommended. Maximum 72-hour stay.

Mission Bay entrance. The high-rise Hyatt Islandia Hotel is conspicuous.

Mission Bay main channel, with road bridge opening to port.

Marina Village Marina (619-224-3125). In the SE corner of the basin. Reservations are required and depend on vacancies.

Seaforth Marina (619-224-6807). NE side of the basin. No reservations accepted. Berths are allocated on a first-come, first-served basis. The maximum stay is thirty days.

The harbor police will give you permission to anchor in Mariner's Basin, where there is 9 to 12 feet (mud and sand). The best anchorage lies in the W part of the basin, opposite the entrance. You can remain there for 72 hours. I have spent hours exploring Mission Bay in my dinghy from this comfortable spot. There are public restrooms on the beach at Bonita Cove to the NW, a busy spot for small craft.

Marinas in the Upper Reaches. If you want to explore the inner reaches of Mission Bay, do so from your dinghy. Depths above the fixed bridge rarely exceed 6 to 10 feet. Access is limited by the 42-foot span of the Ventura/Glen A. Rick Bridge, just above Quivira Cove. However, you can have a lot of fun exploring the calm and extensive waters of Mission Bay in a dinghy. This is a small-boat sailor's paradise.

Dana Inn Marina (619-222-6440) and *Dana Landing Marina (619-224-2513)* are in the Dana Landing Cove to starboard of the bridge as you head up-

Bob Greiser

channel in 7 to 8 feet. There are some guest berths available, but reservations are required.

Bahia Hotel Marina (619-539-7695) lies to port around Bahia Point in Santa Barbara Cove. Slip reservations are recommended and taken during office hours. There is 6 to 8 feet in the marina, but give a wide berth to Bahia Point; enter Santa Barbara Cove in the center of the fairway to avoid shoaling off the point.

Sea World Marina (619-226-3915) lies to starboard in Perez Cove above the South Ingraham Street Bridge, which has a minimum clearance of 38 feet. The Aerial Tramway across the entrance to Perez Cove has a 42-foot clearance. You can carry 9 feet into the marina. Reservations are recommended. The maximum stay is thirty days. This is an ideal location for visiting Sea World.

Campland Marina (619-581-4224) lies immediately W of Rose Island, at the NE corner of Mission Bay in Fiesta Bay. You can carry 7 to 8 feet to the marina entrance, but exercise care and/or call ahead before entering. Reservations are required and length of stay depends on vacancies.

There is a clockwise vessel-circulation pattern in Fiesta Bay. A surge can run into the harbor and the yacht basins in rough weather.

Boat-Launching Ramps. Free boat-launching ramps are at Dana Landing, De Anza Cove, Santa Clara Cove, Ski Beach, and South Shores.

Facilities. Mission Bay is a wonderful place for family cruises. Most of the shoreline and all of the islands are part of a large San Diego city park. The marinas have all daily facilities, with large supermarkets and other stores within a short taxi ride.

Anchor Yacht Care, Driscoll Marine, and Neilson Beaumont Marine offer maintenance services. Fuel docks operate year-round at Islandia Marina and Dana Landing during daylight hours. Pump-out facilities are located at Islandia Marina, Marina Village Marina, and Sea World Marina.

Contacts.
Emergency: 911

Harbor Police: 619-686-6272, 619-223-1133 (evenings), or channel 16, then working channel 12

Harbormaster: 619-686-6272

Local Weather: 619-289-1212

www.sannet.gov/park-and-recreation/parks/missbay.shtml

Course. Course given in degrees magnetic (2000). For reverse course, add 180 degrees.

Mission Bay to

Avalon: 290 deg., 65 miles

352 *Mission Bay to Point Loma*
Chart 18765; Chart-Kit, p. 33

The 5.5-mile coast between Mission Bay and Point Loma is rocky and heavily infested with kelp. Stay at least 2 miles offshore to enjoy clear water. Your first landmark is the Y-shaped Ocean Beach fishing pier 0.3 mile S of the Mission Bay entrance. From there, simply run along the land until Point Loma is clear ahead—an easy landmark to find even in thick weather.

Approach to San Diego Harbor. From N: When approaching Point Loma from N, give a wide berth to the coast NW of the point, and approach at least 2 miles offshore to avoid kelp beds and New Hope Rock, 2.25 miles NW of the headland.

Point Loma is a major landmark in clear weather. In the mid-nineteenth century, George Davidson wrote: "Vessels bound from the northwest make the ridge of Point Loma as a long, flat-topped island when about 25 miles distant." His description holds true today. The low-lying ground behind the point will become apparent as you close San Diego. Point Loma is about 400 feet high, a rugged peninsula bare of trees but covered with sparse vegetation. According to the *U.S. Coast Pilot*: "The tanks and buildings of a sewage treatment plant are conspicuous about 0.9 mile N of the point."

Point Loma light is displayed from a skeleton tower (Lat. 32°39.8′ N, Long. 117°14.5′ W) (Fl. 15 sec., 88 ft., 23 miles).

Point Loma light.

Bob Greiser

Bob Greiser

Approach buoy for San Diego main channel from S, Point Loma to port.

From S. The S approach brings the low-lying coastline S of San Diego to starboard, and the higher ground of Point Loma between the Coronado Islands and the coast ahead. The high-rise buildings of downtown San Diego are visible from the S a long way offshore. A course toward the higher ground enables you to identify the approach buoys from a comfortable distance. The powerful lighthouse and well-lit entrance channel ensures an easy night approach.

SAN DIEGO HARBOR

Charts 18772 and 18773; Chart-Kit, pp. 34–37
Approach Whistle Buoy 1: Lat. 32°37.3′ N, Long. 117°14.7′ W

Harbor Entrance: Lat. 32°39.1′ N, Long. 117°13.5′ W

San Diego has been a favorite haven since Juan Rodríguez Cabrillo sailed into the entrance in 1542. The Presidio and Mission were established as early as 1769. George Davidson waxed lyrical about the place: "Next to San Francisco, no harbor on the Pacific coast of the United States approximates in excellence to that of the bay of San Diego." A generation earlier, Richard Henry Dana spent several months living on the beach in a hide-processing house. In his day, San Diego was just a quiet backwater. He described the back-breaking work of hide-curing and wood-cutting in the bush accompanied by a pack of howling dogs. It was a tough life, but there were barely broken horses to ride and occasional visitors to ease the monotony of the passing days. Early visitors to the bay, like Vancouver, anchored "in ten fathoms water, fine sandy bottom. . . . The Presidio of San Diego bore N21E distant 3.5 miles, and the nearest shore northwest, within a quarter of a mile of our anchorage." The entrance was first lit with a lighthouse on Point Loma on November 15, 1855, with a fixed white light of the "third order of Fresnel." Augustin-Jean Fresnel (1788–1827) developed polarized lights for lighthouses. Three orders (magnitudes) of these beehive-like lights were used in lighthouses. San Diego is, quite simply, one of the finest natural harbors in the world, offering complete shelter in any weather and slight tidal streams in the bargain. Today, San Diego is a major naval and commercial port, as well as a world-famous yacht-racing center, where several America's Cup challenges have run their course.

Many people spend a few days in San Diego and never really explore this most magnificent of harbors. With so much to do ashore and afloat, you could spend three months exploring and not see everything. Despite anchoring restrictions, the harbor is a wonderful place for a family vacation afloat. Dozens of yachts pause here before venturing south to Mexico during the winter months. If you're bound on a long cruise to Mexico or farther afield, make sure you contact the people at Downwind Marine (2804 Cañon Street, 619-224-2733). They are famous for their service to both cruising and racing sailors and run both a VHF Radio Net and a parts-ordering service, which are invaluable to people in Mexican and local waters.

Entrance. From N: Give Port Loma a wide berth and aim to pass just outside the kelp, which can extend as far out as 2 miles. Whistle buoy "Y" and bell buoy "3" mark the outer limits of the seaweed under normal conditions. Once past buoy "3," Ballast and Zuniga Points will open up. The limits of the dredged channel are marked by red and green flashing buoys (see Chart 18773).

From S. Steer for the higher ground of Point Loma, which stands out from a distance, until less conspicuous landmarks come into view. The light tower is prominent from some distance in clear weather. Then alter course for the entrance channel as the buoys come into sight and Zuniga Point is identified.

The entrance itself is straightforward. Tidal streams ranging from 0.5 to 3 knots set through the channel, depending on the state of the tide. To time your entrance most effectively, make use of the Daily Current Predictions published annually in NOAA's *Tidal Current Atlas.* You can stay outside the channel buoys all the way up and down the channel, which will keep you clear of the largest ships. However, be alert to traffic of all kinds and give a wide berth to the lighted jetty on the E side of the channel, which extends a mile S from Point Zuniga. There are often thick kelp beds on the port side close to shore.

The Point Zuniga jetty is partially submerged at high tide. Give yourself plenty of room because you may experience a set toward the jetty on the ebb. The jetty is a

Plan of San Diego Harbor.

real hazard in foggy weather, when you can come upon it without warning when the set catches you without reference points on the land. On two occasions, I have nearly collided with it in such conditions, but I did not have GPS aboard, which helps under such circumstances.

Also watch for a crosscurrent off Ballast Point that can deflect you into the channel. Steep swells can form in the channel during SE gales, but they are not life-threatening.

In Davidson's day, the entrance was less developed. You entered by watching the breakers on the shoals S of Zuniga Point. His sailing directions for a summer transit cannot be bettered for a yacht drawing 6 feet: "During the summer, keep as close to Point Loma as the draught of the vessel will permit, and lay on the wind up to Ballast Point, of which four fathoms can be carried within a ship's length, with ten fathoms in midchannel."

Every naval vessel needs protection against magnetic mines; therefore, many are demagnetized on a degaussing range near Point Ballast. Be alert to ships working the range in this vicinity and stay well clear.

Past Ballast Point, the entrance slowly trends to the NE, with naval facilities to port and a measured mile to starboard. The channel is well marked day and night, and presents no problems for small craft. At night, keep the Point Ballast light (Fl. W. 4 sec., 16 ft., 10 miles) on the port bow and follow the channel buoy lights.

The main channel continues N and E, turning SE at buoy 21 (QG) past the high-rise buildings of downtown San Diego, then under the Coronado Bay Bridge (clearance ranges from 156 to 195 feet). The channel narrows rapidly in South San Diego Bay, ending in a small dredged approach channel for Chula Vista Small Boat Harbor.

There is a 5 mph speed limit in the entrance to San Diego, except where posted otherwise.

Course. Course given in degrees magnetic (2000). For reverse course, add 180 degrees.

From San Diego fairway buoy to

Avalon: 295 deg., 70 miles

Formalities. You'll see the dredged channel to the marina area opposite channel buoy "16." San Diego is a major port of entry for yachts returning from Mexico and farther afield. You must go to the police or municipal docks near their office at the W end of Shelter Island (to starboard of the marina entrance) until all entry formalities (i.e., customs, immigration, public health, and agricultural inspection) are completed. You can moor at the municipal dock for up to ten days, but this berth is usually crowded.

I recommend that you contact the harbor police whether you have come from Mexico or simply from a windward port. They will brief you on available transient berths, private marinas, and anchoring regulations. Their Web site, www.sdhp.com, is exceptionally useful.

Visitors' slips can be difficult to find in San Diego. The best advice is to contact a private marina or to make arrangements with one of the yacht clubs on the basis of reciprocal privileges.

With high marina prices, many people want to anchor off in San Diego Harbor. This practice has long been controversial with both locals and visitors, many of whom forget that San Diego is a very busy commercial and naval port from which large ships enter and leave in all hours of the night. If you want to anchor, please contact the harbor police, which will be delighted to share the designated areas with you (see anchoring areas in San Diego Harbor, pages 363–64).

San Diego Harbor is so large that we cannot possibly cover every detail. Following is a summary of every major facility.

Facilities below Coronado Bay Bridge

Shelter Island. Shelter Island is the first marina facility located on the N shore where the channel trends NE. The entrance channel lies opposite buoy "16." Identify the entrance marker that delineates the starboard side of the entrance, and then follow the 20-foot channel into the marina area. Prestigious, crowded, and expensive, Shelter Island is an excellent base when preparing for a Mexican cruise. There are five marinas located there:

Gold Coast Marina (619-225-0588). First-come, first-served; no reservations accepted.

Half Moon Anchorage (619-224-3401). Reservations accepted during office hours. Length of stay dependent on vacancies.

Island Palm Marina (619-222-0561). Reservations required. Maximum stay is thirty days.

Kona Kai and Kona Marinas (619-224-7547). Reservations required and may be made during business hours. Length of stay is vacancy-dependent.

Shelter Island Marina (619-224-2471). Reservations required, with the length of stay depending on vacancies.

Shelter Island marinas.

Bob Greiser

Cruising yachts may ask for the thirty-day special.

Five marinas and three yacht clubs form the nucleus of Shelter Island's elaborate infrastructure. Some of the West Coast's best boatyards, among them Driscoll's and Shelter Island Boatyard, are in this area. There is a fuel dock and all typical facilities are available, with ample stores nearby.

Harbor Island. Harbor Island is a modern facility located close to the downtown area. Two basins and four private marinas comprise this enormous marina area. The masts of yachts in the marina and low-lying, red-tiled buildings are conspicuous landmarks from the main channel.

The approaches are straightforward.

West Basin: Identify channel buoy "19" on the port side of the main channel; then steer inshore, leaving the Commercial Basin entrance to port and passing outside buoy "V." The entrance to the West Basin lies straight ahead, with a least depth of 13 to 15 feet. A low fixed bridge lies at the head of the entrance, before which you turn hard to starboard into the West Basin channel.

East Basin: The entrance lies opposite channel buoy "21," behind the eastern peninsula of Harbor Island. Steer for the end of the headland, passing 0.25 mile off, then turn to port into the buoyed channel.

Harbor Island Marinas. The Harbor Island marinas are as follows:

Cabrillo Island Marina (619-297-6222). No reservations; first-come, first-served basis. Maximum stay is thirty days. Call ahead for availability.

Harbor Island West Marina (619-291-6440). Reservations are required; the maximum stay is vacancy-dependent.

Marina Cortez (619-291-5985). First-come, first-served; no reservations. There is 4 hours of free berthing for lunch and dinner guests.

Harbor Island marinas.

Bob Greiser

Sheraton East Marina (619-291-2900). Reservations required by calling during business hours. Length of stay is vacancy-dependent.

Sunroad Resort Marina (619-574-0736). Reservations are required. The maximum stay is thirty days.

Harbor Island is a modern facility with many yacht brokers, restaurants, and all typical amenities. Its main advantage is its proximity to downtown. Unless I am anchoring off, I usually berth here. There are two fuel docks with pump-out facilities.

Embarcadero Moorings. Twenty-four mooring buoys lie off the Embarcadero just upstream from Harbor Island, in a bight E of the large U.S. Coast Guard station. You can use these moorings for up to a month, but the berth is not quiet due to traffic and jet noise. Apply to the Marine Operations Department at 619-686-6227. I have never spent the night here and would avoid it if there are other berths available. It's just too noisy.

Marriott Marina. *Marriott Marina (619-230-8955).* This marina has the advantage of being very close to downtown; also nearby is Seaport Village.

The entrance lies opposite channel buoy 23, on the N side of the dredged fairway. There is 10 feet in the narrow defile between the breakwaters. Visitors are

Marriott marina.

Bob Greiser

welcome if there is space available, especially off-season, but reservations are required if possible. Apply to the dockmaster at the pump-out station or call ahead.

This is the berth for sybarites, with all the services of a top-quality hotel. There are few marine facilities, but downtown—with all its shops—is across the street.

Facilities above Coronado Bay Bridge

The bridge clearance of 195 feet allows small craft of any size to navigate freely to the upper reaches of San Diego Bay, the deep channel lying on the N side, and shallow water (4 to 12 feet) along the S shore. A large-scale chart is available. The sailing is glorious and a pleasant contrast to the more crowded waters downstream.

Glorietta Bay. Glorietta Bay lies S of the main fairway on the SE end of Coronado Island. It is approached down a 500-foot-wide dredged channel with 16 feet leading off channel buoy "G1" (Fl. G. 4 sec.), which marks the port side. Follow the markers into the Bay (15 to 17 feet). Buoy "G1" is at Lat. 32°41.2′ N, Long. 124° 32.1′ W. The tower of the Hotel Coronado is a useful landmark ashore at the head of the channel.

Glorietta Bay Marina (619-435-5203) is in the NW corner of the Bay. Reservations are required and length of stay is vacancy-dependent. The marina sometimes

Coronado Bay Bridge. Like all major harbors, San Diego has its share of abandoned boats awash in the shallows.

Bob Greiser

Bob Greiser

Glorietta Bay entrance channel.

Bob Greiser

Entrance channel to Loew's Coronado Bay Resort (see next page).

has four-hour temporary slips available, for which you pay a reduced fee—a nice idea if you want to land and explore. The Coronado Yacht Club is hospitable. I have been unable to obtain fuel at this marina.

South San Diego Bay
Chart 18773; Chart-Kit, p. 37

The deep-water channel narrows past Sweetwater Channel on the N shore, with the effective limit of navigation being opposite the channel into Chula Vista. There is between 2 and 7 feet in the head of the bay, so watch your depth gauge outside the main channel.

Loew's Coronado Bay Resort (see previous page). Loew's Coronado Bay Resort (619-424-4000) is a popular destination in the SW portion of the South Bay, accessible by a 10-foot dredged channel marked by a pair of red and white buoys opposite Sweetwater Channel. The white buildings and red-tiled roofs of the resort are prominent from a considerable distance.

Once the outer channel markers are identified (Fl. R. and G. 5 sec.), steer SSW out of the deep water across the shallows (10 to 11 feet) to enter the channel between them. Stay well N of the outermost markers until you have opened up the entrance because the water shallows rapidly inshore. The dredged channel between the buoys passes close to Crown Island. The marina entrance opens up to starboard; follow the dredged channel with care. There is a reported 10 feet in the marina. Loew's is a major resort and allows visitors to dock free for four hours while dining. Reservations for guest slips are required and may

be made during office hours. Call ahead before making the passage with an overnight stay in mind.

Do not attempt to enter the dredged channel at night until you have visited the marina by day.

Chula Vista Yacht Harbor
Chart 18773; Chart-Kit, p. 37

Chula Vista Yacht Harbor is a modern facility close to the Mexican border, a quiet destination that is highly recommended. If you want to visit Tijuana, this is the base for it.

The entrance channel can be confusing to newcomers; you will need Chart 18773 in hand. I always check off the channel markers here to ensure that I correctly identify the outermost green channel marker buoy "7" (Fl. G. 2.5 sec.), which marks the port side of the dredged approach. Turn hard to port and follow the pairs of markers toward the red triangle marker to starboard with the buff-colored industrial building behind it. You have a least depth of 15 feet but effectively no water outside the buoys, so be careful. At the mark, turn hard to starboard and follow the channel to the breakwater entrance, leaving the boatyard on the port side as you continue to the marina entrance. The marina entrance is clearly marked, with a large concrete breakwater to port and a stone jetty to starboard. There is a 5-knot speed limit inside the harbor.

Chula Vista Marina (619-691-1860). Reservations are recommended, but this marina is unusual in that it offers special rates for weekly and longer stays for cruis-

Chula Vista approach channel. Note the buff-colored industrial building. Turn hard to starboard at the marker shown in the middle ground.

Bob Greiser

ing boats. Contact the marina during office hours. There are pump-out facilities but no fuel dock. The large launching ramp is excellent, and great shore facilities are within easy reach. The marina's web address is www.chulavistamarina.com.

Anchoring Areas in San Diego Harbor. Although the situation changes from year to year due to the need for the authorities to control all activities in the harbor, there are some designated anchoring areas. *Before you anchor, however, contact the harbor police (619-686-6511 or www.sdhp.com) for the latest information.* This way, you can learn where free anchoring is permitted and avoid getting a ticket.

Wherever you anchor, be careful to display an anchor light at night and a black ball by day, as required by International Regulations. I recommend leaving someone aboard at all times and locking your boat carefully.

The current designated anchoring areas are described in the following subsections.

A1: La Playa Cove. La Playa Cove is a 72-hour weekend-only anchorage located between San Diego and Southwestern Yacht Clubs in the Shelter Island yacht basin. The hours of anchoring are from 0900 on Friday through 0900 on Monday. On holiday weekends, anchoring is permitted for 96 hours. If the holiday falls on a

Friday, anchoring is permitted from 0900 on Thursday through 0900 on Monday. If the holiday falls on a Monday, anchoring is permitted from 0900 on Friday through 0900 on Tuesday. A maximum of twenty-five boats is allowed each weekend. If there is a raft-up, forty boats are allowed in the cove. All boats must have holding tanks or portable toilets.

Anchoring permits for La Playa Cove may be obtained in person at 1401 Shelter Island Drive or by calling 619-686-6272. Requests for anchoring permits may be obtained up to ninety days in advance.

A5: Glorietta Bay. The A5 anchorage is located in Glorietta Bay, south of the Coronado Golf Course. The A5 anchorage is a 72-hour-only anchorage in any seven-day period. No permit is required for this anchorage.

A8: South Bay Anchorage. The A8 anchorage is located west of the main shipping channel, near the 24th Street Marine Terminal in National City. There are no time restrictions for vessels anchoring in the A8 anchorage and a permit is not required.

A9: Cruiser Anchorage. The A9 anchorage is located just off the U.S. Coast Guard Station. This anchorage is only available to nonresidents of San Diego County. Permits for this anchorage must be obtained in person at 1401 Shelter Island Drive and nonresidency must be proved. Permits are available to nonresidents for thirty days at a time, up to ninety days in any one-year period.

Permits are required for anchoring outside designated areas in Carrier Basin, Crown Cove, and on the N side of Shelter Island, and must be obtained in person. Each vessel is limited to one permit in any thirty-day period.

SAN DIEGO TO ENSENADA, MEXICO

From the San Diego entrance, the coast forms a large low-lying sandy bight as far as the border. The buildings of Imperial Beach are prominent, as is the city fishing pier located 1.5 miles N of the Mexican border. If you follow the coast closely, stay outside the 10-fathom line as far S as Punta Salsipuedes. The U.S.–Mexican border is marked by a white marble obelisk 41 feet above the water near a low bluff, 200 yards from the beach. The obelisk is 10 miles, 127 degrees M, from Point Loma, and is aligned with a stone mound 1 mile E to form a useful line bearing. The circular concrete bullring just S of the border is also prominent; bullfights are held every Sunday from May to September.

Coronado Islands, Mexico

It is worth mentioning the Coronado Islands because they are a popular day excursion from San Diego. The Mexican-owned Coronados lie 15 miles S of Point Loma and 7 miles off the coast. The four islands make a fine landmark when approaching San Diego from the south. The celebrated British sailor Peter Pye was there in the mid-1950s and described them as "round dry humps sticking steeply out of the water," an apt description. The Coronados extend NW for 4.5 miles and

Bob Greiser

Racing off downtown San Diego.

are surrounded by dense kelp beds. You have a choice of several fairly exposed anchorages.

Coronado del Norte

This is a deep-water island, but anchorage is possible off a lobster shack on the NE shore. Be prepared to move out in a hurry if the wind gets up.

Coronado del Sur

Puerto Cueva is on the E shore, where there is 25 feet (sand) but considerable surge. The cove is identified by the northern light [Gp. Fl. W. (3) 15 sec., 19 miles] on its S shore.

Old Hotel anchorage on the E shore of Coronado del Sur offers shelter from NW

winds off an abandoned hotel-casino, a squat building at the water's edge. Anchor in 35 to 50 feet (rock and sand) and lay plenty of scope.

All Coronado anchorages are dangerous in Santa Ana conditions. You must have fishing permits or official papers to land in the Coronados. Another word of caution: avoid approaching the islands at night. The only lights (which can be unreliable) are on the southern island, the S tip being marked by Gp. Fl. 5 sec., 22 miles.

A visit to these fascinating islands is best timed for quiet, NW weather in the summer when conditions are predictable. The seas can be quite rough off the Coronados in post-frontal winds, especially around the southern light.

The mainland coast between the U.S. border and Punta San Miguel at the entrance to Bahia Todos Santos consists of barren hills and bluffs, with cliffs as high as 80 feet. Behind are low foothills and dry mountains rising to more than 3,000 feet above sea level. This stretch of coast is becoming more developed. Following are some useful landmarks:

- *Table Mountain* is a conspicuous, flat-topped hill, 25 miles SE of Point Loma and 6 miles inland.
- *El Rosarito* is a small resort community some 12 miles S of the border. A refinery with thirteen storage tanks and a power plant with four smokestacks are prominent just N of the town. The Rosarito Beach Hotel is also conspicuous.
- *Punta Descanso* is the seaward end of a 392-foot-high bluff with an off-lying 13-foot rock, Pilon de Azucar, 4 miles SE—sometimes referred to as Sugarloaf Rock. Although fishing boats anchor S of the rock in deep water, there is no reason to closely approach this stretch of coast.
- *Punta Salsipuedes* is lower lying and is best identified by the large and well-lit mobile-home park situated at the point. This is the approximate southern limit of coastal development.

Between Punta Salsipuedes and Punta San Miguel, the coast is barren and unlit, with higher rocky bluffs crowding on the shore. You can stay well inshore by day if you wish and anchor in 35 to 50 feet (sand)

behind El Pescadero, with some shelter from the NW, if you are waiting for calm winds when northbound.

Punta San Miguel is bold and 150 feet high (Fl. W. 4.5 sec., 17 miles). The N shore of Bahia Todos Santos is backed by 50- to 100-foot cliffs and high hills. El Sauzel is a small fishing harbor ESE of Puntas San Miguel, with an enclosed inner harbor behind a breakwater. The port is often crowded and I prefer Ensenada. Stay at least 1.5 miles offshore between El Pescadero and Punta del Morro to clear kelp beds, breakers, and off-lying dangers. A course of 118 degrees M from a position that distance off El Pescadero will take you clear of dangers. Do not try to pass inshore of the kelp off Punta Morro, and give the shore a wide berth. By this time, you will see Ensenada harbor ahead.

Punta Ensenada is 370 feet high with a hexagonal house and mast on its slopes. The harbor breakwater extends SE from the point. A 150-foot smokestack and a tank are conspicuous behind the town.

Ensenada Harbor
Chart 18740
Entrance: Lat. 31°50.75′ N, Long. 116°36.00′ W

Ensenada is changing rapidly from a sleepy resort town into a sizeable commercial and tourist city. Many yachts bound for Mexico clear customs and immigration here before setting out for Cabo San Lucas.

Approach. Southbound: The port is easy to approach from NW, once you have identified the major landmarks summarized previously. Steer for a point about a mile off the end of the breakwater (about 256 degrees M from a safe point off Punta Morro). Then shape your course inside the harbor, keeping a close watch for departing traffic, especially at night.

Northbound. Approach from the vicinity of the Todos Santos Islands, either passing outside San Miguel Shoal or S of this dangerous patch, well clear of the NW island. A shortcut brings you between the Todos Santos Islands and the mainland, clear of off-lying dangers off Punta Banda, where strong N currents are reported. All approaches should be taken with caution at night because the lights are sometimes expunged. Todos Santos light [Gp. Fl. W. (4) 12 sec., 18 miles] is reportedly unreliable. Punta Banda lighthouse is Gp. Fl. W. R. (2) 9 sec., 7 miles, 10 miles.

The SW shores of Bahia Todos Santos are steep and rugged, but the land S of Ensenada is low-lying and sandy. Several excellent anchorages lie on the E shore of the SE island, but are not within the scope of this book. Ensenada Harbor lies 8.4 miles E of this island.

Entrance. The entrance is straightforward, between the breakwaters. Watch for departing traffic moving at high speed.

Berthing and Anchorage. Ensenada is a port of entry and a commercial port that has only recently developed facilities for pleasure craft. The Captain of the Port's office is on the NW side of the harbor; immigration and customs are just to the N, in the town.

The twenty-two slips run by the Baja naval yard are recommended (call on VHF channel 77). There are also somewhat dilapidated visitors' slips along the waterfront, which are often full. If you rent one, be sure to rig spring lines and plenty of fenders because the surge can make this an uncomfortable berth. There are moorings in the harbor that can be rented, but they cannot necessarily be relied upon in strong winds.

Fuel and water can be obtained at the port, provisions in the town, and engine and other marine repairs can be arranged at the harbor. Land your dinghy at the waterfront, tying it to one of the docks. If possible, tip someone to watch it and avoid unlit areas at night.

Anchorage. I prefer anchoring off in the shelter of the breakwater located between the city waterfront and halfway to the breakwater in 15 to 30 feet (sand and mud). This berth can be crowded, especially during the Ensenada Race in early May. Lay plenty of scope, buoy your anchor, and watch for submerged objects.

If the harbor is too full, you can anchor in Granada Bay just E of Punta Morro in 15 to 18 feet (sand and kelp). Sound your way carefully into the cove, and expect some surge in prevailing summer conditions.

Anchorage also may be obtained on the S side of Bahia Todos Santos in SE weather or in Bahia Papalote on the SW side of Punta Banda in NW winds.

Entering Mexico. Anyone visiting Mexico for more than 72 hours must complete a tourist card, obtainable from a consulate or at Mexican immigration in Ensenada or at the border. You must show a passport or birth certificate, which is validated on entry.

Yachts on a Baja cruise must take these documents to the Captain of the Port, immigration, and customs in Ensenada between 0900 and 1400 weekdays. Customs will issue a temporary cruising permit and stamp tourist cards. You must get the same papers stamped when you leave Ensenada, whether bound for a U.S. port or another Mexican harbor. This procedure is repeated at all Mexican ports of call, during office hours.

Of course, you should take your State Registration Certificate or Federal Documentation papers with you at all times, together with your insurance policy. Most Southern California yacht policies end in Ensenada or Punta Banda.

Ensenada gives you a tantalizing sample of the fascinating cruising grounds that lie S of our familiar California waters. A beer at Hussong's, a Mexican dinner, and mariachi bands are a delicious part of the Southern California cruising life—a life that can give you everything from ultramodern yachting harbors to unspoiled anchorages unchanged since Richard Henry Dana's day.

INDEX